Esquire's
Handbook
For
Hosts

Esquire's®

Handbook for Hosts

by Roy Andries de Groot

Illustrations by Bill Goldsmith
Introduction by Arnold Gingrich

GROSSET & DUNLAP
A National General Company
Publishers   New York

For Arnold Gingrich
Friend, critic, editor, fin bec, fisherman,
philosopher, violinist, writer,
who, in forty years of publishing, never
underestimated the taste of American readers

Acknowledgements

No book covering as wide a range of subjects—including menus and recipes, a survey of the wines and spirits of the world, an encyclopedia of mixed drinks, as well as reference guides to dining and cooking equipment, to shopping for bottles and basic ingredients, to the affinities of wines and foods—could ever have been completed without the devoted and skilled help of friends, colleagues, and expert technicians in every department of gastronomy, oenology, and publishing. To all of them, my gratitude is deep and warm.

To Bill Goldsmith, for his extraordinary sensitivity in isolating and dramatizing the essence of each chapter, with amusing, appetizing, balanced, and beautiful pictures.

To my friend Jan Flaherty, a superb amateur cook, who tested and shaped my recipes and "campaign plans" for the menus into clear and precise guides to memorable meals.

To my own group of researchers, tasters, readers, and typists, led by Lynne Spearman and including Carole Cook, Tania Ertl, Edna Gengerke, Alice Thomas, and Johanna Wright, for their devotion to the ideal of accuracy in every detail. Also my warm thanks to Barbara Joan Hansen who read the manuscript and offered valuable suggestions.

To my colleagues at *Esquire,* and especially to Sam Ferber, for constant help, sound advice, and sparkling ideas.

To the editorial and production staffs of the publisher, including my editors, Jock Bartlett and Kevin Curley, and the copy editor, Elaine Chubb, for meticulous control and admirable literary navigation.

To the research staff of the Acme Juicerator Corporation and its president, Al Leo, for technical information on the extraction of fruit and vegetable juices and oils for the dramatic flavoring of mixed drinks.

To the research and professional staffs of the Corning Glass Works, including Mary Zachary, Helen Carroll, Mary Lou Welschmeyer, and Neal O'Donnell for technical advice (during the development of my recipes) on temperature control in electric oven baking, in counter-top cooking and in the preservation of foods in sealed, refrigerator storage.

To Chef Jerry East of Cincinnati, for permission to include his recipe for garlic snail butter.

To Peter Lee of The Queng Yeun Shing Company in New York, and Sandy Cooper of the Kitchen Port in Ann Arbor, for technical advice on kitchen equipment.

To Helen O'Brien, food research director of the Taylor Wine Company, of New York, for permission to adapt and include her recipe for caviar mousse.

To the research staff of the Salton Company and its president, Lou Salton, for technical advice on temperature control in keeping cooked foods hot without drying out.

To the professional staff of the Switzerland Cheese Association, including Heinz Hofer and Helga Gruenstrass, for technical information on the cheeses and equipment described in my instructions for a Swiss *raclette* party.

To Hubert Trimbach, of Alsace, for technical information on the multitude of fruit brandies produced in his corner of France.

To the research staff of the Vita Mix Corporation, for technical information on the operation of reversible electric blenders in kitchen food preparation and mixing party drinks.

Finally, and with much love, to my noble dog, Ñusta, who lay patiently under my desk during many months of writing and was always willing at any time to taste anything, but who, to my great sorrow, did not live to see the publication of this book. Good girl, Ñusta, rest.

NEW YORK CITY   *Roy Andries de Groot*
APRIL 27, 1973

Contents

CONTENTS

Introduction

Roy Andries de Groot is that contradiction in terms, a blind gourmet. Since so much of what we taste is conditioned by what we see, Baron de Groot's eminence in his chosen field of expertise represents an extraordinary triumph of spirit over adversity. It is fully as remarkable as it would be, say, for a one-armed tennis player to achieve international calibre and ranking. I don't know of that ever having happened, but I do remember that a Major Trotter (one-time equerry of the late Duke of Windsor, when he was Prince of Wales) hung up a salmon fishing record on a Norwegian river, after he had lost an arm in World War I, that was still standing some thirty-five years later.

Roy de Groot's loss of his sight was a consequence of the London Blitz in World War II, but not an immediate one, like the sudden loss of Major Trotter's arm in the previous conflict. His sight was not blacked out overnight but rather failed over a period of several years, so that, fully aware of what was happening to him, he could set about preparing, if not to compensate for it, at least to combat it.

Having had since childhood a consuming interest in wine and food, he determined to turn this avocation into a vocation, and succeeded in the attempt. It is hard to believe that he could have accomplished it if he had not already had what amounted to a lifelong preparation for a career in the practice of gourmandise, but it is still astonishing that he was able, in the face of such an inevitable and calamitous handicap, to convert what was essentially a hobby into a successful profession.

Born of a French mother and a Dutch father, whose lingua franca was French, he had his schooling in England and his vacations on the Continent, a circumstance that only incidentally left him trilingual in the course of completing a uniquely haphazard curriculum of living that fitted him, more by accident than design, to be nothing more—or for that matter, nothing less—than the complete cosmopolite. His knowledge of music, for instance, is only slightly less thoroughly grounded than his encyclopedic knowledge of food and wines. Add the fortuitous factor that he happens also to be immensely well-read, and it seems a bit less surprising that his writings and demonstrations of his culinary learning and skill—given that he is able to place them in a sophisticated and debonair frame of reference—should have become resoundingly successful.

He is not only the author of a book, *Feasts for All Seasons,* that bears the imprimatur of the most knowing of publishers, and not only the food editor of a magazine that at least professes to be extremely knowing (how else account for the brash assurance of its annual Dubious Achievement Awards?), but he is also known to both coasts and beyond as the "Gourmet-in-Residence" of the "Today Show," a thing that has made him a more intimately familiar figure in most households than the immediate neighbors. Even his Seeing Eye Dog, Ñusta, has acquired a certain celebrity by association, in consequence of this repeated exposure. Certainly no other bitch, German Shepherd or otherwise, has ever crossed the sex barrier to membership, along with her master, in the Confrérie des Chevaliers du Tastevin. (Her little silver *Tastevin,* attached to her collar, has, perhaps because of her chronic state of animation, escaped the otherwise all-seeing eye of the television cameras, which is perhaps just as well, or Women's Lib might picket the place.)

What Ñusta can't help him with (what color is this, and what color is that?) he either gets from his wife, Katherine, or from one or another of his secretaries—usually Lynne, except for the frequency with which she returns to England.

Reading him you forget completely that he's blind, unless you stop to realize that he "sees" and makes vivid so many little details that you or I would miss entirely, because we'd simply take them for granted and, in consequence, never notice them at all.

He has, indeed, in this completely new and utterly personal version of *Esquire's Handbook for Hosts,* a book that was last revised in 1953 and first compiled in 1949, performed a feat that is only analogous to jacking up an old body and driving a brand new car under it. It appears to be an enormously improved model—running much better, smoother, faster, and with a livelier pickup. It could be that it will run even longer, which would make for quite a run.

But that's something that only time, and possibly you, can tell.

—*Arnold Gingrich*

Esquire's

Handbook For Hosts

PART I
The Art of the Memorable Host

CHAPTER 1

THE ART OF BEING A MEMORABLE HOST

It Doesn't Depend on How Much You Spend—Far More Important Are Courage, Ideas, Imagination, Sensitivity

I believe that the serving of good food and wine is the one sure way of pleasing all of the people all of the time. You can please some of the people some of the time with conversation, or by reading aloud, or telling stories. You can please some of the people by getting them drunk. You can please a few of the people at a time with sex. But the problem with conversation is that few people can agree on an interesting subject and fewer still are good listeners—or good talkers. Drunkenness almost always involves disappointment, regret, resentment on the morning after. And sex, inextricably involved as it is with the phases of the moon, is often unreliable as entertainment.

But whenever I give a successful dinner party and the thank-you calls come in next day, I know, from the warmth of the voices and the sincerity of the words, that some marvelous magic has been achieved. People have come together and found (and taken away with them) something special. Call it, if you like, friendship, hospitality, unity—something that gives the deepest pleasure—something that is created by the sharing of good food and wine, skillfully chosen and prepared. The reward to the host is that the joy of such a meal is remembered by every one of his guests for years to come. This is why, throughout my life, I have found one of my principal satisfactions in the cultivation of the art of being a memorable host.

I admit it—I am inordinately thin-skinned about my reputation as an amateur chef. Praise my food and I am your kitchen slave for life. Eat one of my best meals and drink some of my proudest wines without offering a single word of comment and you'll never be asked again. Sometimes when I am making out my Christmas card list, the vague suspicion crosses my mind that I seem to choose my best friends according to the excellence of their lunches and dinners.

It is for these friends, with an abiding interest in the arts of the table—and for all readers who are deliberately taking the road that leads toward being a knowledgeable connoisseur, toward developing the ability to choose between what is only fairly good and what is best—that I am writing this book. Therefore, even at the risk of being ambushed and shot at from every side, I propose to express frankly my personal opinions and preferences in a way that is, as the journalists say, "without fear or favor."

The Qualities of Memorable Meals

Some of the most vivid memories of my life are centered on the dining table. I remember each of my youthful girl friends, not by the ardor of her kisses, but by the best meal with which I impressed her. I can still see, in my mind, the first meal I ever had in Paris at that simple and still wonderful restaurant above Androuet's cheese shop, on the rue Amsterdam. I can still relive (and retaste) my first Provençale lunch, on a terrace overlooking the Mediterranean. And so it goes . . . a lifetime picture book of memorable meals.

The great, the classic dishes—those that are on most of the finest menus and that one tastes with renewed pleasure again and again, year after year—are, to me, like the symphonies of Mozart. Each time the waiter presents the beautifully decorated dish at table, each time the conductor raises his baton in the concert hall, it is a new performance of an intimately known work. Each time I pass in review in my mind previous performances by other chefs, other musicians. This magnificent, truffle-stuffed Saddle of Veal à la Prince Orloff, prepared for me by Chef Claude Colomb at Ernie's in San Francisco? This great performance of the Linz Symphony, under the direction of Maestro

Bruno Walter in the hushed Concertgebouw auditorium in Amsterdam? How do they compare with all the other performances of my experience? Could this be the best? Will this evening be supremely memorable? If not, then how should tonight be rated in the long sequence of my pleasures? Perhaps the veal had more flavor, perhaps the violins a fuller tone, when I was in Vienna fifteen years ago? Was the sauce more delicate, the flute player more sensitive, in London? The truffles, and the trumpets, more nearly perfect in Salzburg? The interest and pleasure of food, music, and wine continue and increase with every added year of experience. Especially with food, where one can be both performer and critic, the development of one's skill is more than a hobby. It is an art—an art of which one will never tire, because there will always be something new to learn, the art of the gourmet—the art of the memorable host.

CHAPTER 2

THE PERFECT DINNER PARTY

It Requires Perfect Guests, Perfect Food, Perfect Wine—
But Bravado and Dash Are Also Ingredients

Sometimes on a sub-zero winter's morning, when I wake to the whine of the wind whipping up the Hudson River, I stretch out warmly under my goose-feather eiderdown and half-dream about the perfect dinner party. It's a good time for concentration on thought for food. My mouth is slightly dry and thirsty. My stomach is gently rumbling its request for breakfast. My mind focuses on the various questions one by one. What would be the ideal menu for such a dinner? The ideal wine list? The ideal season of the year? The ideal place and setting? But before any of these questions can be answered I must decide on the ideal list of guests. The perfect dinner can be planned only with particular people in mind.

I have decided that the ideal number for the perfect dinner should be ten, including the host and his (permanent or temporary) hostess. In my half-dream, I assemble my guests from everywhere, past and present. I consider the possibility of bringing back Dr. Samuel Johnson from his witty dinner-table debates in the coffee and chop houses of eighteenth-century London. On second thought—no. When one guest completely dominates the dinner, no one notices the food. When one guest's wit is sharper than the carving knife, it can cut the pleasure of the others. When one of the guests lost his temper during a dinner-table debate Dr. Johnson said, "Pray, what annoys you, sir? Have I said something that you understand?"

I might decide to invite Cleopatra, not only because she was beautiful, but also because her social experience would add charm and luster to the conversation. She would be amusing if not brilliantly witty, sparkling if not supremely intelligent. And it would be fascinating to try, by subtle and tactful verbal dexterity, to find out what she had been really thinking about life and love.

The Perfect Guest List

I believe that there are certain basic rules that must be followed in assembling a compatible group of guests for the perfect dinner party. Couples too much interested in each other simply do not fit into a larger party. Two lovers so feverishly absorbed in their own relationship that they have no eyes or ears for anyone else should dine by themselves. So should couples who are feuding or fiercely competing with each other. A husband and wife whose marriage is on the point of breaking up or two politicians running against each other in a current election would put a damper on the pleasures of the evening.

I think I would invite one solidly united couple (either legally or extralegally) to give a sense of security to the party. I might ask another couple for exactly the reverse reason—that their emotional and sexual relationship, not being precisely known, would challenge the rest of the company to subtle, conversational exploration. I would invite at least one stranger, perhaps an extremely beautiful girl with a slightly mysterious background and with no obviously visible means of support, as a further challenge to the intellectual investigations of the evening. Then, to make sure that my food and wine would be noticed and intelligently discussed, I would like to have two or three gourmets in the party—perhaps representing each of the three great cuisines of the world: a Chinese, a Frenchman, and an Indian. This may be a personal conceit of mine, but it *is* always good to have some of the guests linked by a common interest, to provide at least one safe channel for the conversation. The rules for assembling a well-matched group of guests are basic and not exceptionally complicated.

The Perfect Place and Setting

As to where my perfect dinner should be given, it would be easy to decide instantly that it must be in the top-floor dining room of the great Restaurant de la Tour d'Argent on the Quai Tournelle in Paris—with one whole wall a picture window looking across the Seine to the floodlit Cathedral of Notre Dame de Paris. Or it could be in the terrace dining room of the Palazzo Gritti, overlooking the Grand Canal in Venice. But these choices are too easy and obvious.

Since my perfect dinner party is still half a dream and there are to be no limitations in terms of the logistics of reality, why not serve it in a Swiss chalet on a mountaintop with an immense view of snow-capped peaks turning pink at sunset? But mountaintops, in my experience, are for picnics, with my companion suitably impressed by the superb delicacies I bring out from my insulated shoulder basket. I remember a marvelous dinner on the terrace of the lovely, pink-walled Château Loudenne in the Médoc wine district of Bordeaux, with the evening view sweeping down the vineyard slopes to the wide waters of the Gironde estuary, where the passing green and red lights of the ships reminded us, as we dined, of the great wines of France being carried to the world.

At this point, perhaps, my half-dream begins to fade and a sharper reality takes command of my plans. I am now sure that my perfect dinner party must be around a calm and peaceful table here at home. I can at once think of a superb setting. It could be served in the dining room of Nicholas Roosevelt in his extraordinary house precariously perched at the top of a thousand-foot cliff at Big Sur, on the rocky California coast a few miles south of Carmel. As the entrée was being served, we would watch, through the picture window, the fire-red ball of the sun slowly descending into the Pacific, beyond the Bay of Whales and the Punta del Lobos del Mar, the Point of the Sea Wolves.

Or—and perhaps best, dinner could be served on the magnificent roof terrace of the house of Harry Serlis, on the peak of Russian Hill in San Francisco, with the lights of Fisherman's Wharf and the ships in the harbor, almost straight down below us and the view sweeping from the Golden Gate across the Bay to the distant misty Berkeley Hills. I would cover this terrace with a red-and-white-striped tent, open on three sides for the view, but with a roof above us, to give us a sense of privacy from the watching stars.

The time of year should be the late spring, when the San Francisco air is gently-warm, and the first fruits and vegetables of the season begin to arrive bright, luscious, sweet, from the central valleys.

The Perfect Menu

For this perfect dinner my menu would be unexpected, unusual, at some points astonishing, a dramatic tour de force. The composition of such a menu would be ruled by the basic principles that I apply to all my menu-planning. You start your guests with something they know—something safe and sound—but done with imaginative personal touches, better than they have ever had it before. If, for example, your guest of honor is a Spaniard, newly arrived in the United States, he will obviously want to try our American food, but will be enormously flattered and pleased if you start him off with a classic Spanish Entreméses Variados, prepared and presented as authentically as if he were still at home.

Next, you begin to take your guests with you on an exploratory trip. The second course may be something they immediately recognize, but prepared in a surprising way, with unexpected decorations, garnishes, and seasonings. As they taste, they think, "Wow!—this is an extraordinary combination, but very good! I must get the recipe and try it myself."

Now you have softened them for the big adventure. You give them a dish that they have never had before. You take them out with you into totally unexplored territory. I firmly believe that the secret of a truly great dinner is to have at least one magnificent, but brand-new-to-almost-everyone dish. It isn't as difficult as it sounds. Once you have discovered such a dish and worked out the techniques of its preparation, you can serve it at dinner after dinner to different groups of friends, until you have exhausted your invitation list. Meanwhile, you can be working up your second "unknown dish."

Finally, after the excitement of the exploration, you come back to a safe and sound dessert. This pattern, of course, can be infinitely varied. The big surprise might be the first or the last course. The flattery of the foreign visitor might be by a soup, a fish, a rare game meat, or the dessert. I shall try to show later that menu-planning, while being infinitely flexible, is not nearly so difficult as some people would have us believe.

Apart from the order and balance of the courses, the "secret ingredient" of a memorable dinner is preparing it with the finest of ingredients. One of the greatest of modern French chefs, Fernand Point, once said, "The secret of great cooking is butter, butter, and more butter." To this I would add the essential elements of cream, of wine, and of fruit brandies. I have never eaten a memorable meal that was produced with skimmed milk and margarine.

Sometimes I consider it good dining-table strategy to challenge directly the obstinate conservatism of a guest. We all know the man who loudly and aggressively boasts, "I don't go for this gormy stuff—I'm a steak and potatoes man!" O.K. So I'll give him what he wants. I'll poach a prime sirloin steak in Madeira, with garlic-flavored mushrooms, then flame it with Armagnac as it is set before him. If his face feels the heat of the fire, so much the better. There will be no potatoes anywhere in sight. Then, just as he thinks he is finished, his potatoes will arrive as a separate course in the form of a Gratin Dauphinois, another version of the baked casserole of the French Alps, in which the sliced potatoes are simmered in milk and heavy cream. I will then ask, nonchalantly, "How did you like your steak and potatoes?"

Before sitting down at table I would serve, for this most perfect of dinners, the one hors d'oeuvre that is universally safe, completely acceptable: large-grained, black Beluga caviar, served on small, canapé squares of black bread, with no more seasoning than a few drops of lemon juice. With this, the driest and lightest of Champagnes, Taittinger, Blanc de Blancs, Comtes de Champagne.

If caviar is not available I might begin with firmly textured, first-quality Atlantic Nova Scotia smoked salmon. The dramatic way of serving it is to have a complete "side of the fish"—a three-foot-long, boneless fillet, with the skin underneath—laid out on a cutting board, with an ultra-sharp sixteen-inch knife, on a side table, so that each guest can cut his own paper-thin slices. I often have this delicacy sent to me by Willy Krauch, a Danish fisherman who owns the last smokehouse actually operating in Nova Scotia. Most alleged Nova Scotia salmon is now smoked in large factories elsewhere.

This help-yourself method of offering it to my guests, although it creates an atmosphere of unlimited luxury, does have its pitfalls. Once, a friend called a few hours before he was due to dine with me and made the usual excuse about a friend, an attorney from a small town somewhere or other, who had unexpectedly arrived in town and could he come too? The friend, apparently, had never seen or heard of smoked salmon. We suddenly, with shocked amazement, noticed him standing in front of the cutting board, not slicing the salmon almost horizontally, but cutting straight down into it and tearing off quarter-pound chunks, which he wolfed down before making the next cut. When I rushed, horrified, to his side, he said, fatuously, "I never, in all my life, ate such delicious fish!"

The Beauty of the Table Frames the Food

Our mouths made clean by the earthy salt of the caviar or the smoked salmon, we carry our glasses with the remaining Champagne to the dining table. It is handsomely decorated, with a carefully planned balance of colors. Tonight, for the formal meal, it is covered with a white cloth, on which the china and silver sparkle with reflected light. My wineglasses are of clear, undecorated glass to dramatize the visual beauty of the wine itself. I never permit flowers as a centerpiece. At worst, their scent can interfere with the bouquet of the food and the wine. At best, unless they are very small, they are a barrier to cross-table conversation. My favorite centerpiece is a bowl of green avocados, their skins waxed so they glow and reflect the lights.

The first course at table would also be my first surprise. I would have had flown in from France, from the great three-star restaurant of the Brothers Troisgros, their Suprême de Foie Gras en Casserole—the classic, goose-liver pâté, not, in the normal commercial style, boiled, or pasteurized, or canned, or frozen, or disguised with Cognac and Madeira, but just gently, gently baked in a low, low oven until the final result is pink, pure velvet. To cut the extraordinary richness of the foie gras I would serve a lightly sweet wine, say, an Alsatian Riesling, Réserve Exceptionelle of a very sunny year.

Next, just as my guests would be beginning to feel secure about my judgment, I would give them the big shock. I would have had flown in from the Mediterranean coast of France a seaweed-stuffed barrel of the most extraordinary shellfish in the world, *les violets* (don't ask me why they are called "violets"), which are dredged up along the rocky coast between Marseille and the mouth of the Rhône. A wooden cutting board and a hefty knife would be placed in front of each guest.

Les violets are oblong, rectangular shapes, rather like light-caramel slabs of milk chocolate, surrounded by a leathery thick skin. You cut straight through one, lengthwise. Inside, you find it filled with hard, inedible white muscle, but right at the center is the animal itself, a light orange-pink, about the size of a small clam. You dig it out with a teaspoon, season it with a drop or two of lemon juice, and consume a morsel that is more refined, sweeter, more succulent than any clam or oyster you have ever had in your life. The wine is a light, refreshing dry white of the southern Alps, the Crépy from the French shores of Lake Geneva. There is to me a double pleasure in this second course—the delightfully simple balance of the food and the wine plus the informality of a finger-food—an almost picnic-style break in the middle of a formal dinner. It is a trick I use often with all kinds of foods, a trick that always seems to please and relax the diners.

Since the main course is also going to be fishy, there should now first be a touch of meat, which is supplied in the third course by a classic Italian Tortellini al Brodo—a richly strong beef consommé, garnished with tiny pasta dumplings, each filled with an aromatic mixture of ground pork, chicken, sausage, and brains—a superb balance of flavors and textures. This is the moment for the arrival of the long loaves of hot-from-the-oven sourdough bread to be snapped and cracked by the guests with a shower of flying crumbs. The wine is now a raspberry-reddish pink, light, and young Beaujolais, fresh in the bottle from the latest harvest, the Château de la Chaize of the Marquise de Roussy de Sales.

The Cook's Proudest Dish

If there is a single dish in my repertoire that I am most proud of, it is my Timbale du Roi Neptune, which I punningly translate as The Kettledrum of King Neptune. (The Arabic-derived word *timbale* means both a kettledrum and a huge earthenware cooking pot.) It is not, however, the kettledrum, but the immense brown, lidded casserole that now comes to the table as the climax of the dinner. The preparation of its contents has involved many hours of labor. It began with the cooking of several lobsters, their meat chunked and poached by the classic French method *à l'Américaine* in butter and white wine, before adding Cognac, crushed fresh tomatoes, shallots, and fresh tarragon. At the same time, in another sauté pan, several dozen crayfish were cooked *à la Bordelaise,* with white wine, more shallots, and butter. In a large copper pot a stack of oysters were simmered in Alsatian Riesling until their shells just opened. Also, from a batch of shrimp I had made a shrimp butter by sautéing them, with a blend of aromatic vegetables, adding white wine and a dash of Pernod, then pounding them into a paste and working it into a bowl of softened sweet butter.

Finally all these separate elements had been combined in the huge earthenware *timbale* and linked together by the addition of cream, mushrooms, fresh leaves of tarragon, and a garnish of black truffles. The lid had been clamped on tightly and the Timbale had been reheated in the oven to encourage the multitude of its internal flavors and savors to unite in a perfect marriage.

The final, dramatic trick is to keep the *timbale* tightly closed until it reaches the table and only then lift the lid. The first cloud of savory steam that bursts out has been known to make the diners dizzy with anticipation.

I originally developed this Timbale in a series of experiments with Mediterranean shellfish while staying in the tiny fishing village of Carry-le-Rouet on the south coast of France, west of Marseille. I would go down to the miniature harbor at five in the morning to meet the fishing boats coming in with their catch, to buy the all-alive, fishy ingredients for my various gastronomic experiments. There on the dock, at that ungodly hour, I often met the great French movie star Fernandel, who had been born in the village and still had a vacation house there, where he relaxed happily in between his movies and plays. On those early mornings, he was also in search of live fish for a Timbale recipe, which had been used by his family for generations. We exchanged notes and, after I returned to New York and was finally satisfied with my recipe, I sent Fernandel a copy. A few weeks later, I received his answer: "M'sieu, I salute you. This is it! Each mouthful of your Timbale sings on my tongue like a nightingale. I learned at school that the Greek gods, when they lived on top of Mount Olympus, used to gorge themselves on something called ambrosia! Obviously, it was another name for your Timbale. I won't even bother again with *Grandmère's recette.*"

Graceful Approach to the End

Let us get back to the menu of my perfect dinner. After the supreme climax of the Timbale, the meal descends, gradually and gracefully, to its close. There would have been, of course, a truly great wine to match the Timbale, perhaps a Montrachet of the Marquis de Laguiche, from the "Golden Slope" of southern Burgundy, or a great vintage year of the Château Laville Haut Brion, or the Domaine de Chevalier from the Graves district of Bordeaux. As soon as Timbale and wine were finished (but not before—there must be no clash between wine and vinegar), I would serve a beautifully green, well-dressed salad, to "scrape the throat clean," as a great French gourmet once put it.

Now there would be a new peak of interest at table, as we poured a great (but not too great) red wine to accompany the cheeses—perhaps a Château La Mission Haut Brion or a Château Palmer from Bordeaux, or a Chambertin, a Clos Vougeot, or a Musigny from Burgundy. There would be, perhaps, an international selection of half a dozen cheeses, each in a perfect condition of age and ripeness: probably an English farm-made Cheddar, from the Cheddar Gorge, a not too hard, not too old, crumbly and grainy Italian Parmigiana-Reggiano, a blue-green-veined French Bleu de Bresse, a richly soft and aromatic Norwegian Gammelost, a simple, earthy, peasanty Spanish Queso Manchego, from the region of Don Quixote, and, last but far from least, a well-aged and dry Oregon Tillamook. Each diner would cut his own cheese, on a wide, handsome board, from pieces of not less than a pound each, to give the feeling of luxurious plenty.

The dessert would be my own variation of a classic dish. In Bordeaux there is a much-served dessert called Saint-Emilion au Chocolat, which came originally from the small, sweet cookies handmade by bakers in the lovely hilltop village of Saint-Emilion. I make my version with the Italian Amaretti di Saronno, small, almond-vanilla macaroons, still handmade in the Lombardy town of Saronno—cookies of such superb quality that they might well lay claim to be the best in the world. I take a few dozen of these, lightly moisten each one with half a teaspoon of golden Jamaican rum, set them in neatly interlocking layers in a deep serving dish, and cover them completely with a rich, buttery, not too sweet chocolate sauce. As it sets, it seals in both the bouquet of the rum and the chewy crispness of the macaroons. These qualities form an irresistible contrast to the velvety softness of the chocolate—a balance so superb that I have instructed my doctor to offer a portion to me as the final medicine on my deathbed. Then I shall take one taste, and refuse to die.

Last, there would be sharply aromatic little cups of my favorite, "private blend" of Colombian, Brazilian, and Venezuelan coffees, suitably overshadowed by a fine selection of what the French so aptly call *les digestifs:* the Cognacs, Armagnacs, the marvelously dry fruit brandies of Alsace, and, with Green Chartreuse leading them, the sweet fruit and herb liqueurs.

The talk now flows with a smooth ease. The table is suffused with relaxation and understanding. Strangers have become friends. The woes of the world have been banished from the room. The thousands-of-years-old traditions of hospitality have been carried forward. The magic of a memorable meal has been achieved.

Naturally, the menu I have just described is a dream. It makes absolutely no compromise in terms of effort, of expense, of the difficulty of getting some of the ingredients, and of the time-consuming work of preparation. It is, however, by no means an impossible dream. My objective in describing it was to define the basic principles—and let me add, with the conviction of long experience, that provided these basic rules are followed, a memorable meal can be produced at reasonable expense and within a reasonable preparation time. Not, of course, that there is, or ever could be, an "instant memorable meal." The art of the true host demands that he make some effort and give something of himself in preparing for his guests.

There are less expensive forms of caviar than black Beluga. There is the excellent pressed caviar and the many forms of salty-tangy fish roe, including the fine *tarama,* carp roe from Greece. There are sparkling wines less expensive than Champagne, including outstanding American labels, charmingly refreshing sparklers from Seyssel, in the Alpine mountains of the French Savoy, and from Saumur and Vouvray along the Loire.

The essential point is that the opening canapés and wine should be immediately acceptable to all the guests and should express the unspoken thought that the party was carefully planned to offer the best that is possible. I would be very careful, for example, about serving snails as an opening hors d'oeuvre since some people find them intolerable and it would be destructive of the calm atmosphere at the beginning of the meal if one or two of the guests were embarrassed or troubled. The place for the unusual is later in the meal, when the guests are more secure in each other's company.

In place of the expensive pâté de foie gras, there are dozens of outstanding recipes for made-at-home pâtés and terrines, easily and quickly prepared, which I regard as among the most important guest-feeding tools of the memorable host.

It is care and imagination in planning—the skilled use of aromatic herbs in making each dish interesting and unusual, the proper balance between one course and the next—far more than the serving of expensive, imported specialties that can make, even of a simple menu, a memorable dinner. The prize earned by one's efforts is, to me, a rewarding richness of living.

CHAPTER 3

THE PERFECT ALCOHOLIC LIFT-OFF

It Isn't Only the Strength—It's Also the Prestige, the Tradition, and the Mixing Skill

The double meaning of the word *spirit* is one of the most significant facts of our life and language. On the one hand, we think of "the Spirit" as the indestructible, undying "Holy Essence" of the living human being. We speak of "a girl of spirit" and the mind instantly pictures beauty, animation, and exuberance. Much of religion is built around the concept of "the Holy Spirit."

At the same time, we use the word *spirit* for the distilled, alcoholic essence that animates every wine and every strong drink in the world. This thought—of some secret connection between the spirit of alcohol and the spirit of the human body—is reflected in virtually every language. In French, alcohol is *eau-de-vie,* "water of life." *Vodka,* in Russian, means "little living water." Even *whiskey* comes from the Gaelic word *usquebaugh,* "water of the spirit of life."

When a man says, "I need a drink!" he is expressing more than mere thirst. He is saying that he needs a shot of spirit to lift off his spirits from the dull routine of earth into what he hopes may be the upper reaches of animated strength, of uninhibited freedom, of new heights of experience in sensuous delight. This is why virtually every culture of the world has produced its own character and style of distilled spirits. What vodka is to the Russians, akvavit is to the Danes, falernian essence was to the ancient Romans, ouzo is to the Greeks, pulque was to the ancient Aztecs, tequila is to the Mexicans, arak is to the Indonesians, mao-tai is to the Chinese, pisco is to the Peruvians, and so on.

As to our modern American culture, one has to admit, whether one likes it or not (and there are occasions when I do not), that our one truly national concoction of spirits is the Dry Martini. Its power in our society is far greater than the strength of its gin, far more insinuating than the subtle balance of flavors of vermouth, lemon, olives, onions. The very sound and substance of these two juxtaposed words, *Dry* and *Martini,* at once conjure up an aura of prestige, status, success, tradition. The first lift to the flagging spirit comes long before the first sip—from the mere mention of the name. I once saw a magazine article headed: "172 Ways to Make the Perfect Martini." This reminded me of the 131 different sexual positions of the classic erotic art of India. Position 67 was the same as position 31, except that the girl had her fingers crossed.

A Personal Philosophy

I suppose I can say that I drank my first Martini when I was eleven years old. I had overeaten. I was feeling sick. My mother's standard cure for this condition was a glass of London gin with a drop or two of Angostura bitters to make the whole thing slightly more palatable and, as Robert Benchley would say years later, "to take away that ghastly watery look." Since that day I calculate that I must have drunk (sometimes even against my better judgment) at least 10,467 Martinis and have developed a strong philosophy on the subject.

I know exactly, for myself, the right number to drink, the right place, the right time, and above all the right reason. I am convinced that a Dry Martini of proper strength is not an apéritif to be consumed before a fine dinner. It does not whet the appetite. It dulls it. It refuses to play second fiddle to food. It is a meal all to its liquid self. I am willing to consume it at breakfast time, at midmorning, in place of afternoon tea, immediately (and especially) at the end of the day's work, at midnight or at four in the morning, but never within an hour of a good lunch or dinner.

At these proper times (and assuming the essentially correct techniques of preparation), I divide my Dry Martinis into four types: first, the safe and sound; second, the special occasion; third, the intensely intimate; and fourth, the downright dangerous. The first is the kind one offers to new friends at the first meeting, before one has any idea of their capacity or sophistication. I make it of three parts of London gin and one part of Italian dry vermouth, cooled by gentle stirring over ice, poured into frosted, long-stemmed glasses holding not more than two ounces, with the requisite droplet of oil of lemon sitting on the surface, the remaining lemon rind wiped around the lip of the glass, and the dropped-in green olive stuffed with red pimento. It is all quite conservative and mild, but, in interesting company, it can be excellent.

My second version is made in the same way, but with some differences in the ingredients. I use four parts of Dublin gin to one part of French dry vermouth, with the same arrangement of the lemon zest on the surface and around the lip, but with the green olive stuffed with a chewy bit of salted almond. And then, a few seconds before serving it, my secret trick is to add to the glass, from an eyedropper, a single drop of raw onion juice. This is what I would serve, on a festive weekend, to my guests at five o'clock, when dinner is planned for eight. This is what I would try to get from my favorite barman at the best bar in any city of the world, when I was meeting the loveliest lady of the region and would be taking her two hours later to the best local restaurant to dine with a group of fascinating friends.

My third, intimate Dry Martini is never served in public and never at any party larger than myself and one other person. Let us suppose that my friendship with the lovely lady has flowered and that the next time we are to dine she invites me to call for her at her apartment. The bottles, glasses, and ice are ready on the silver tray. She commands me to mix the drinks. I would mix five parts of an aromatic British gin to one part of Chambéry vermouth, with the inevitably essential routine of the lemon zest and the green olive, this time stuffed with a pearl onion. I would pour three ounces per person and my "secret trick" would be to add, from the eyedropper, two drops of juniper-flavored Holland Genever gin from its ice-cold stone crock. After this I would hope for at least two hours of intimate conversation before departing for a superb dinner.

Finally, there might come the day when the lovely lady agrees to dine *à deux* in my apartment and an entire evening of peacefully relaxed communion of two sympathetic spirits stretches before us. This would be one of the rare occasions for my fourth, my dangerous

Martini, for which I would have on hand a bottle of the finest and rarest Holland gin available. The bottle would be kept in my freezer, so that at mixing time it would have an almost glycerin thickness.

The Secret of an Extraordinary Effect

There are no parts to my recipe. I simply measure, pour over the ice, and gently stir until intensely cold, four ounces of imported Russian vodka and serve it in freezer-chilled Champagne glasses, with no more than four or five eyedropper drops of the driest Chambéry vermouth, with the lemon zest on the surface and around the lip as usual and, instead of the olive, a tiny, orange-reddish Tuscan pepper, about the shape and size of a large pearl.

Finally, a second or two before the first sip, I gently suffuse into each glass two eyedropper drops of the Genever, which is so heavily solid that it rolls down to the bottom of the glass and adds an entirely indefinable perfection. The liquid is so cold that one feels the approaching chill on the tip of one's nose. Alongside this drink of extraordinary uplifting force, I would serve a tiny dish of pearl onions, each speared on a miniature toothpick and all resting on a bed of finely crushed snowy ice. Perhaps it is the contrast between the solid ice in the dish and the liquid fire in the glass that is the ultimate drama of this extraordinary drink.

It is something very private. It cannot be taken lightly, or drawn out for too long, or, worst of all, repeated too often. I seldom find the occasion more often than, say, three or four times a year. In the right company, it can bring a brief sense of peace. It can provide a calming of the human spirit by the distilled essence of the spirit of the fruits of the earth. Soother or stimulant—it is the nearest thing I know to the perfect Dry Martini.

PART II
The Host at Home

CHAPTER 4

ARE YOU EQUIPPED FOR EVERY EMERGENCY?

A. Questions for the Host Gourmet in the Kitchen

A memorable meal can be prepared as well in a small, postage-stamp city apartment kitchenette as in a large, farmhouse-style kitchen-workroom—even, in an emergency, in a single pot on a hot plate in a hotel bed-sitting-room. Far more important than the size of the kitchen are the assembling of fine ingredients, the judgment and skill of their preparation, and the availability of the right tools for the job. They make things easy. They save time. They produce better results. So—the first question for the host with the ambition to produce memorable meals is how to organize any kitchen into an efficient hospitality workshop. The answer is to think of it, whatever its size, as being divided into four storing and working departments.

The Ice Department

The first, of course, is "the Ice Department," where foods are preserved from bacterial deterioration, where they are deliberately aged, and where they are prepared for the working routine. The modern refrigerator is now such an efficient machine that virtually nothing need be written about it, beyond the insistence that its internal temperature on the food-storage shelves should be within a degree or two of 38° F., about 42° F. in the butter-cheese compartment, and never higher in the freezer than 0° F. (I check once a week with a small refrigerator thermometer, which I consider, with meat, oven, and candy thermometers, essential kitchen equipment.)

Food scientists are now agreed that these are the essential temperatures to maintain the maximum quality of stored foods. They are also agreed that hot foods should be brought down to the storage temperature as quickly as possible, for the preservation of flavor, freshness, and texture. So I always keep an array of heatproof glass containers (both the square, stackable kind and the very modern, see-through, plastic screw-top jars, in various shapes and sizes) cold in the refrigerator, even when empty. Then I never hesitate to transfer, say, a very hot beef stew directly to the glass container (which, by its coldness, at once brings down the temperature 10° or 15°) and place it in the refrigerator, without waiting for any of the old "let it come to room temperature first" nonsense. Question two, then, for you as the ambitious host is: have you a practical range of refrigerator containers?

In reverse, I am equally against the almost universal habit of taking foods out of the refrigerator and eating them immediately, while they are still very cold. Such things as cheese, ham (and all cold cuts), fresh fruits, pâtés, terrines, tomatoes, and so on, simply have their flavors numbed almost to the vanishing point when they are ice-cold. I allow two hours for a chunk of cheese to come to room temperature right through to its center. If the process has to be speeded up (in an emergency) the food can be set in the oven for a very few minutes at a keep-warm temperature of between 150° F. and 175° F.

Steel and Wood as Essential Ingredients

The second vital division of the efficient kitchen is what I like to call "the Steel and Wood Department"—the place, preferably close to the refrigerator, where the chopping, cutting, mixing, slicing, and other advance preparation jobs are done. I enjoy nothing more than the feel of a truly sharp and perfectly balanced knife under my right hand, while my left hand rests on the warm and resiliently textured surface of a fine block of wood. I regard it as an absolute essential of the proper preparation of food to have the right shapes and sizes of chopping blocks, cutting boards, mincing and mixing bowls, boxwood spoons,

scrapers and spatulas, pestles and pushers, pastry and rolling boards. Against even the most modern materials, I still know no substitute for wood.

On the wall in front of my wooden working surface there is a pegboard with the most often used tools, and above is the herb and spice cabinet, with the store cupboard for dry goods to the right. Thus almost everything I need for fast and efficient preparation of food is in a circle around my work space.

The Work Space Checklist

As to the tools that hang from my pegboard or are filed in the subdivided drawers, here is my alphabetical checklist of some of the most essential in terms of long years of proof of their continuing efficiency and flexibility. This is not a master list for the young host setting up his kitchen from scratch. I assume that you already have the standard tools listed in every basic cookbook. To these I would add the following:

Beating Bowls, Copper Sabayon

One can truthfully say that no ambitious host can possibly afford to be without one of these handsomely decorative, shining, round-bottomed, brass-handled, professional bowls. The bottom has to be round so that there is not a single corner where a recalcitrant blob of liquid egg white can hide from the wire beater. For this reason, among others, hand-beaten egg whites are infinitely superior to eggs beaten by electric machines, or hand-turned rotary beaters. It's just that more air gets into the eggs and therefore, as an example, the soufflés rise an inch or two higher, while batters, mousses, and sabayons are all noticeably fluffier, more voluminous. The best all-around size, if you are going to have only one such bowl, is eight and a half inches in diameter, but there are also larger and smaller ones. The type with handles can also be used as a double boiler, held lightly in a pan of boiling water, in recipes that require beating while cooking.

Blender, Reversible, Slow-Speed Electric

The usual push-button blender works much too fast and hard for its own good. Let it chew up the food in its whirling teeth more than a few seconds and it delivers a pappy, soggy, tasteless baby food—tasteless because the fibers of the foods have been broken up into such minute particles that virtually all the flavor oils have been released and have evaporated. Also the food is thrown so violently upward that one has to keep stopping the machine and pushing the mash back down onto the blades. At least one manufacturer has solved this problem by providing a blender that, first, is instantly reversible so that the food, after being thrown upward, can be automatically sucked down again, and, second, has an ultraslow-speed setting for far better control of the cutting process.

Boards and Blocks, Wood

There is probably more cutting and chopping in Chinese cooking than in any other cuisine. So it is not surprising that the Chinese kitchen equipment stores generally offer the widest and most interesting range of wood boards and blocks and bowls, and at prices often half as much as those in the fancy kitchen shops. The boards are thick and heavy—immovably solid in use. There is nothing worse than a slippery-slidy cutting board. As a heavy-duty chopping block for use with a steel hatchet, I use a cross-section of a tree trunk about twelve inches across, about six inches deep, and weighing about fifteen pounds. It was imported from Hong Kong. It was only about one-tenth the price of a fancy butcher's block.

Chopper, Semiautomatic

Since onions for flavor and green parsley for appearance are an essential part of almost every party dish, anything that makes the chopping easier and quicker is a valuable addition to the kitchen. This gadget consists of a clear plastic bell that fits over the small pile of stuff to be chopped on your own cutting board. In the top of the bell there is a spring-loaded steel plunger with a handle at the top and four zigzag blades at the bottom. You jab the plunger down in a rapid series of strokes, so that the blades chop-chop onto the cutting board, and each time the spring brings them up again, they automatically rotate a quarter of a turn, thus ensuring as fine a chopping as you wish, according to how long you continue. I am so proud of my own hand-chopping skill with a chef's knife that I hate to admit that this little machine often works more efficiently and faster than my old-fashioned way.

Knife Grinder, Electric

This must be well designed, with two fast-revolving grindstone wheels, set against each other and slightly overlapping, so that a certain degree of hollow grind is given to the knife's edge as it is drawn forward over the wheels. Be careful of poorly designed "low-cost" machines. One of these, as I have found, can seriously damage the edge of a knife in a few seconds.

Knives, Chef's Kitchen

Obviously few things are more important in the host's kitchen and at his table than the ability to carve, cut, and slice with beautiful precision. So many knives shine and sparkle in the store but show themselves in prolonged use to be flabby and weak at the edge—virtually incapable of being kept in sharply athletic shape. Do not be misled by loud claims for stainless steel, or "dual-metal" blades or trickily serrated edges, or for heavily unbalanced, allegedly "automatic" electric knives. The only knives I have ever known that stay as sharp as they start are those used by all the professional chefs—the finest quality of the hardest carbon steel, made by the French specialists who, for more than five hundred years, supplied French and English noblemen with dueling swords and hunting knives. Carbon steel, of course, stains and needs a reasonable amount of regular cleaning with scouring powder or abrasive cloth. The edge has to be maintained, but this is much easier nowadays with the help of a well-designed electric dual-stone-wheel, hollow grinder. The care and feeding of each knife takes about fifteen seconds, once a week.

I keep six perfectly balanced chef's knives, with blades of two inches (mainly for mincing garlic and shallots), three inches, six inches, eight inches, ten inches, and twelve inches. Also, a specially serrated French loaf knife, which does not crush the bread. Finally, a long, narrow, fourteen-inch ham slicer, also used for cutting the best kind of slab bacon into the extra-thick slices that I prefer.

Larding Needle

It is, of course, almost essential, when preparing to roast or pot-roast very lean cuts of meat, to insert, right through the center, long lardoons of flavorful fat (often first marinated in Cognac), but this is not easy when you use a larding needle that attempts to draw them through behind it, as if each were a length of wool threaded through the eye of a darning needle. The more effective and professional instrument is not a needle at all, but a long length of grooved metal, with a handle, in which the lardoon of fat is three-quarters enclosed while being pushed, rather than pulled, with the grain of the meat, through its center. When the tip of the lardoon is showing through on the other side, it can be held firmly, while the metal blade is pulled back and out. This tool is made in France and called a *boeuf en daube* needle.

Measuring Glasses

In addition to the various standard measuring cups (one cup, one pint, one quart), I find it very useful to have various sizes of druggists' medicine measuring glasses. There is a one-ounce size, graduated in tablespoons, teaspoons, fractions of an ounce, and metric milliliters—the latter useful in conversions from French recipes. It also doubles as a more accurate measurer than the standard liquor jigger when you are experimenting with mixed drinks. There are also larger versions of this medicine glass, up to four and eight ounces, some of them so handsomely tall and tapered that they add to the general decoration.

Meat Hammer

The most efficient type is double-headed, with blunt metal teeth on one side and metal grooves on the other. Pounding a steak breaks up its fibers and tenderizes it. Escallops of veal can be spread out and thinned until they are almost like sheets of parchment. This enables you to make the most delicate and handsome folded or rolled *paupiettes,* filled with various aromatic stuffings.

Mortar and Pestle

In this case, I desert my much-loved wood, since I find that the heavy white stoneware is more solid and immovable. One can pound and grind harder without the whole thing slipping around. The best internal size is somewhere between one-cup and two-cup capacity. This is, of course, an essential tool for mashing garlic or for pulverizing juniper berries or other spices. It is also the best possible vessel for making mayonnaise and—this may surprise you—the heavy pestle is better than the proverbial wooden spoon for working (and almost grinding) the drops of oil into the mayonnaise. Never underestimate the power of a fine homemade mayonnaise in helping to create the ambience of a memorable meal!

Olive and Cherry Pitter

Admittedly one can buy pitted cherries in jars for desserts and drinks, or pitted olives for appetizers and drinks, but fresh cherries are far better, and olives with pits bought loose from large wooden barrels in Greek, Italian, or Spanish shops have much more character. Then the problem of pitting them is solved by a small metal pusher with a nest hole in which to place the fruit and a cutting rod to push out the pit through the back hole. Very simple.

Saw, Bone-or Metal-Cutting Type

I keep in my kitchen a standard plumbers' hacksaw with a twelve-inch, narrow replaceable blade set into its adjustable frame. It cuts easily and quickly through any meat bone and allows one to cut single chops from a rack of pork or veal, or large escallops from a leg of lamb.

Spoons, Boxwood

Apart from the standard wooden spoons, I keep a small collection of various lengths and sizes of the very light French boxwood spoons, to be used mainly for stirring sauces. Because they are so light, they give me the "feel" of the sauce as it thickens and help me to get exactly what I want in terms of consistency and texture.

Wire Whisks

As already discussed in connection with beating bowls, the ability to get the maximum volume of air into egg whites (so that the soufflé comes to the table in dramatic style, so that mousses are sensationally fluffy and light, so that your Zabaione al Marsala is a dream dessert) is one of the key factors in creating a memorable meal and depends on having the right kind and size of wire whisk to go with the right beating bowl. I keep three whisks neatly hanging from their ring hooks on the pegboard, all imported from London or Paris: a huge, sixteen-inch piano-wire *ballon* for the largest beating and slapping operations in preparation for the biggest of parties, a twelve-inch and ten-inch stainless-steel for smaller quantities in a smaller bowl, plus a smaller eight-inch with a light wooden handle for beating hot sauces until they have such a smoothness of creamy velvet that they bring exclamations of delight and wonder at the dining table.

Fine Control of the Fires

The third vitally important division of the ambitious host's kitchen is, of course, "the Fire Department." Here the question should be whether the controls on your cooking stove give you the maximum efficiency and flexibility. In the last couple of years there have been quite extraordinary technical developments in this department. There is at least one new design of gas stove with almost completely automated elements, for the oven, the grill, the rotisserie, and the top burners. It has, among other gadgets, spring-loaded "sensors," which come up and touch the bottom of the saucepan, measuring its preset temperature and controlling the up and down variations of the flame, so as to maintain the required heat indefinitely.

In electric units there is the new "cooking counter" in which a single sheet of fireproof glass has the thermostatically controlled heating units embedded in it, also with built-in "sensors," which raise and lower the heat, as required, automatically. The electric cooking counter, which I have been using to test my recipes for this book, has controls that are continuously variable. They do not click-click from one fixed heat setting to the next, but allow an extremely fine control of the heat, which is then automatically maintained by the built-in thermostats. There is now the all-glass oven, which actually measures the internal temperature of the meat being roasted and, as soon as the preset point has been reached, automatically turns the oven down to a keep-warm setting. Some of these units do not require special power wiring and are entirely portable, so that you can take them with you, as part of your furniture, whenever you move to a new home.

Behind my electric "cooking counter," the wall is covered by a pegboard from which hang the principal tools for all the firing operations. These include the hand tools and the lighter, smaller, most often used copper sauce, sauté, and omelette pans. Then, at arm's length to the right, is the heavier equipment (what the French call the *batterie de cuisine*) including the enameled-iron *cocottes*, the baking casseroles, and the au gratin dishes. Thermometers and other small, breakable bits and pieces are in drawers with dividers for tidy organization. Thus, my "fire department" is virtually a self-contained unit, with all the essentials immediately at hand.

The soundest advice about pots and pans that an experienced cook can give to a beginner is never to buy any equipment in what the salesmen like to call "a matched set." It is all very well, for decoration, to have a hanging line of saucepans with multicolored polka dots. It is quite another thing to find that each of these preset sizes is right for your particular job. A saucepan, an omelette pan, a *sauteuse*, or any other kitchen tool should be carefully calculated and considered as to shape, size, and above all the physical properties of the metal from which it is made.

I am devoted to two types of metal for my pots and pans: tinned copper and enameled cast-iron. I do not mean that they are interchangeable. Each has its proper function and each performs that function, in my view, more efficiently than any other material. Copper is, of course, a marvelous conductor of heat, which means that, say, a copper sauté pan heats up and cools down almost instantaneously. Also, since it allows the heat to spread around evenly, it never develops "hot spots" on the bottom immediately above the fire. So my tin-lined copper pans are ideal for all jobs to be done quickly and under my constant supervision, such as sautéing, preparing quick sauces, fast boiling, and reducing bouillons. As your skill develops, your copper pan becomes an excitingly responsive tool in your hands. This is why it is virtually the unanimous choice of professional chefs. One must always remember, though, that the tin lining melts at 425° F., so that one can never use them for searing or other operations demanding very high heat. Nothing is more disconcerting than to find, suddenly, that one's steak is covered with neat little balls of melted tin!

On the other hand, for all the slow simmering and low-temperature oven operations, I use my French cast-iron, lidded *cocottes*. (Although the word, in French, also means a bedroom companion of sexually cooperative habits, I restrict my *cocottes* to the kitchen, where the word defines a multipurpose form of lidded casserole.) To avoid the universal fault of old-fashioned cast-iron, which tended to rust, this modern cast-iron is covered on the outside with hard-baked enamel, in colors so beautiful and bright that the cooking pots can be brought to the table as serving dishes. Inside, the iron is covered with fired ironstone clay, which is entirely immune from any interaction with even the most acid of foods. Since the iron is a heavy mask, it heats up gently and gradually and then maintains an even temperature for long, slow cooking. The lids are heavy and their ground edges fit so tightly on the pot that there is hardly any evaporation of liquid and the most delicate flavors are sealed in. They help me to prepare many memorable *daubes*, pot roasts, and stews.

As to the other fire-department tools, here is my alphabetical checklist, not of the standard things, but of special gadgets that seem to me to be exceptionally useful for the ambitious host gourmet:

Asparagus Boiler

Unquestionably, perfectly cooked asparagus is one of the most luxurious of party vegetables and should always be served as a course in itself. The perfect cooking is the difficult problem. There are literally dozens of special cookers on the market that are so badly designed that they cannot ever work efficiently. It is impossible to cook asparagus properly either by completely immersing it in boiling water or by simply steaming it. The stalks should be in the boiling water, while the tips are gently steamed. I know of only one special asparagus pot, made in France, that solves this dual problem. The bunch of asparagus stands upright, just fitting into a neatly sized inner pail with holes and a handle. Water is poured in until it comes up to cover the lower tough stalks, but not the delicate top two inches below the tips. The water boils, the tight lid is put on, the top fills with a gentle steam bath. When both ends of the asparagus are perfectly done, the inner pail is lifted up by its handle and the asparagus is drained by the time it comes up.

Au Gratin Baking Dishes, Individual, Small

Serving hot hors d'oeuvres (or even simple main dishes) in brightly colored, cast-iron individual au gratin dishes, to be placed before your guest still bubbling and hissing-hot, is a dramatic and practical way of presenting one of your baked or grilled specialties. For a Sunday morning brunch there is hardly a nicer way of presenting eggs than in the form of French Oeufs sur le Plat, baked sunny-side up on an aromatic bed of chicken livers, flaked smoked fish, or minced truffles. For these occasions I keep various sizes of handsome au gratin dishes, enough of each size for a party of six to ten guests. The smallest size is usually thought of as "one-egg," the next larger, as "two-egg," and so on.

Baking Pans, Terrine, Long, Narrow

A French-style terrine—the aromatically refined version of a multi-meat loaf—is an important form of party food (of everyday food, as well, since it is one of the easiest and most flexible ways of dressing up cold cooked meats). Once you have achieved a well-balanced mixture of flavors and textures—with layers of different meat cuts to add interest and variety—the essential final technique is to bake the meats perfectly and serve them in the most attractive form. Both these requirements are met by the use of the French baked-enameled, cast-iron, long, narrow terrine pans, which go into the oven with tightly sealed lids and then come to table enclosing a terrine of exactly the right size to provide neatly square, one-portion, garnished slices. I make such constant use of these terrine pans that I keep three different sizes on hand: one twelve inches long, the second ten inches, the third eight inches.

Bells, Glass, to Fit Au Gratin Dishes

Let's face it: there is no special magic about food prepared "under glass." If, for example, Mushrooms à la Provençale or Baked Buttered Shad Roe can be baked under a fireproof glass bell, they can be prepared precisely as well in a covered casserole. The bell is simply a dramatic serving idea, and I like to keep sets of them to fit my various au gratin dishes.

Casseroles, Small, Individual, of French or Mexican Pottery

The small, lidded casseroles, so widely used for French onion soup, since they must go under a hot grill to brown the cheese and then come instantly to table, can also be used in many other ways: to present, directly from oven to guest, some specialty for breakfast, brunch, a hot hors d'oeuvre, or a main dish. Nowadays there are dozens of beautifully colored and designed small casseroles on the market and they can add something to the decorative success of your party table setting.

Coffee Pot, Turkish "Imbrik"

I should think that most people know this long-handled, brass heating pot with its unusual shape, wide at the bottom, narrowing toward the top, then opening out with a pouring flange all around. Apart from its basic function—for making Turkish coffee—I find it a thoroughly useful, all-purpose tool at the stove. Incidentally, its shape seems to prevent even milk from boiling over. I use it for making Mexican hot chocolate, frothing it up with a molinillo rotary beater (see next), before pouring it.

Molinillo, Mexican Rotary Hand Beater

This small, wooden, usually handmade tool is a most decorative addition to the wall pegboard of any kitchen and is practical and useful as well. It is twirled between the hands when foaming Mexican chocolate. The molinillo ("little mill") has paddlelike teeth and several loose wooden rings that swirl around in the hot liquid. It works best in a narrow pot and I use it in my Turkish Imbrik. Molinillos are available in various sizes in Mexican folk art shops.

Paellera, Spanish Iron Pan

Quite apart from its use in the preparation of a paella, a large *paellera* makes a wonderfully informal cooking and serving platter for a large party. The largest sizes can be three feet across and will fit across all four burners of a normal stove. Authentic versions, made of hand-hammered steel and with steel handles, are imported from Spain, and there are also American types in aluminum and stainless steel. One should never use a lid on a *paellera*. It is a frying, not a steaming pan. For this reason, because it gets very hot, it should never have plastic or wood handles. Incidentally, a *paellera*, just small enough to fit into one's oven, can be used to bake a giant pizza.

Sauté Pans, Copper, Tin-Lined

One of the basic rules of good sautéing is that the bottom of the pan must be more or less completely covered by the food being sautéed. If, for example, just two small pork chops are being sizzled in a pan of nine and a half inches diameter, they will absorb the heat from the bottom of the pan at the point where they are covering it, but the rest of the bottom is going to overheat and burn the surrounding sauce. For this reason, I keep three sauté pans—one of nine and a half inches diameter, another of eight inches and a third of six and a half inches. Be careful never to allow a sauté pan to get extremely hot, or the tin lining will melt and run into globules. Then the pan must be sent away to be professionally retinned.

Thermometers

Obviously, accurate control of heat is an absolute essential to fine cooking and, although they are somewhat more expensive to buy, I much prefer the professional, metal-rod-type, dial thermometers to the rather tinny, almost toylike, gadgety things sold as "meat thermometers," and so on, in the average kitchen shop. The professional thermometers are extremely accurate. For this reason there is no longer the slightest need to keep a so-called meat thermometer sticking in a roast in the oven and interfering with the proper basting. The thin-stemmed, sharp-pointed, professional thermometer can be stuck in for a second or two at each basting and its needle will instantly swing around on the temperature scale. Incidentally, never buy a thermometer that claims to show, for example, whether the beef is "rare" or "well-done." Rareness is not an accurate measurement but a relative condition, depending on one person's taste. It is far better to choose a set of thermometers calibrated in degrees Fahrenheit. You will need one registering from 0° F. to about 60° F. for checking the freezer and refrigerator. Another, for roasting meat, should have a range from about 100° F. to 200° F. Then, for occasionally checking the oven thermostat, the range of one should be about 125° F. to about 600° F. And, for candy boiling and deep frying, ranges of from 100° F. to 500° F.

Don't Let the Water Get into the Wine

The fourth essential division of my kitchen is what I call "the Department of Water and Wine." Need I say that the wine is the more important element? Water is fine for taking a bath or a swim, for poaching an egg, for dissolving the flavor juices of herbs, meat, and vegetables into an aromatic bouillon, but, beyond these basic uses, water can add nothing to a party dish. Any recipe that says "thin, as required, with a little water" is at once downgraded in my rating. The right wine, on the other hand, can contribute character and flavor to the food. In fact, I believe that truly fine cooking is not possible without the use of wine.

On the other hand, one must not overmagnify the role of the wine.

Wine is no instant magic that can convert a poor cook into a good one, or produce a fine dish from a poor recipe. Furthermore, the wine must be reasonably good. A cheap wine, not good enough to drink, is not good enough for cooking. Yet there are relatively inexpensive wines of strong, country character that are exceptionally good for the kitchen. Also, of course, one uses the fortified dry Sherries and vermouths, the dry fruit brandies, and the dessert liqueurs. These special kitchen bottles must be properly stored on their sides and, for this purpose, my final suggestion as to kitchen equipment is an inexpensive simple wooden eight-bottle wine rack.

The four bottles in the top row of this rack are my dry wines, red, white, and fortified, for general use in appetizers, soups, and main dishes. The four bottles in the bottom row are the dry brandies and sweet liqueurs, mainly for desserts, flaming, and marinating. The choice of bottles varies somewhat according to the season of the year. Obviously I do more flaming in winter and use more liqueurs for marinating fresh fruits in summer. Yet my master plan is fairly constant.

Basic Dry Reds

The best cooking wines are the fruity, rich, strong, "country-peasanty" types, which, fortunately, are among the least expensive in the world. I buy, for example, top-quality California jug wines, usually labeled "Mountain Red," or "California Burgundy-type." From France, a good choice would be a blended, district wine of Saint-Emilion, from the Bordeaux region, or a Côtes-du-Rhône, or a Gamay from the Savoy Alps. From Italy, I sometimes use a wine from Lombardy that lives up to its name, Inferno. From Spain, I might use a simple Rioja, or a strong Valdepeñas from the south.

Basic Dry Whites

The basic requirements of fruitiness and strength are the same as for the red wines. Since, however, white wines, once open, deteriorate faster than reds, I consider it wise to store only half bottles and to taste a drop before using to make sure the wine has not become harsh. My first choice might be a top-quality California jug wine labeled "Mountain White," or "California Chablis-type," or "California Graves-type"—never any sweet type. Once the larger jugs are opened, the wine can easily be decanted into sterilized half bottles. A good

French wine would be a Mâcon Blanc from southern Burgundy. An Italian might be a dry Frascati from the Alban Hills behind Rome, or a dry Orvieto from the province of Umbria. (Warning: Both Frascati and Orvieto also come in unsuitable sweet types, which are usually labeled "Abboccato"; the dry wines are labeled "Secco.")

Madeira—Sometimes Better than Sherry or Vermouth

Almost all good-quality, dry fortified wines are excellent for cooking because of their strongly aromatic base. Some grocery stores will sell bottles labeled "Cooking Sherry"—almost invariably something dreadful. The cooking Sherry in a professional kitchen, however, will be of far better quality, but will have enough salt added to it to make sure that it does not go down any unauthorized local throats. I often prefer to use the dry "Sercial" Madeira—avoiding any labeled "Bual" or "Malmsey," both of which would be far too sweet. Also, of course, dry white French vermouth is excellent for many cooking purposes.

Marsala and Port

Both of these fortified wines are usually slightly sweet, but in the better qualities the sweetness is delicate and is excellent for cutting the richness of venison and other game meats, including game birds. I usually buy a moderately priced "Marsala Superiore" from the town of Marsala in western Sicily, or a "Ruby Port" from Oporto in Portugal. Both of these are excellent for deglazing a frypan or sauté pan by hissing a few tablespoons into the still-hot pan after the meat, or whatever, has been removed, then scraping off the crust, boiling down the liquid until it glazes and thickens, and pouring it over the meat as a sauce.

Spirits for Flaming

Whether you flame in the kitchen, for the purpose of adding a special flavor to the dish, or at table, for flamboyantly spectacular service, you *must* use a good-quality, dry, fruity brandy, to avoid—at all costs—a bitter aftertaste in the food. Obviously one can achieve dazzling fire effects by using the superstrong, so-called 151-Overproof rums, just because they are about 75 percent pure alcohol, but for my money they have the taste of liquid tar. An alcohol proof of between 80 and 90 is entirely strong enough for adequate flaming, and the spirit may be brandy, aromatic gin, golden rum, or whiskey, with very satisfactory taste results. Among the brandies, one can get marvelous taste effects by using, as well as the more normal Armagnacs, Cognacs, and California grape brandies, some of the dry fruit brandies from Alsace, Germany, and Switzerland discussed in chapter 27.

Sweet Liqueurs for Desserts

Any remaining spaces in my kitchen wine rack are usually filled with half bottles of liqueurs for marinating fruits and dribbling over ice creams. There are two, diametrically opposite, ways of using them. If, let us say, you have fresh cherries in your dessert, you can sharpen and strengthen the flavor of the fruit by adding a few drops of cherry kirsch liqueur. Or you can be much more experimental and imaginative, by using the liqueur of an entirely different fruit, thus setting up dramatic combinations and contrasts. But don't overdo it. Only a few drops of the liqueur are usually needed. If you put in too much, everything will be completely dominated. Some excellent liqueurs, with many uses, are the Hungarian apricot called Baracklikőr, or the Alsatian raspberry Framboise, or the Alsatian Mirabelle, from small, golden plums, or Dutch Curaçao, made from the small green oranges of the island of Curaçao, in the Caribbean.

B. Equipment for the Sophisticated Service of the Memorable Meal

Even the finest food, prepared to near perfection, served piping-hot with affection and pride, cannot be fully appreciated by the guests if it is not presented at table with a touch of drama and an ambience of grace. Whether you offer your food in a mansion with tall, white double doors flung back as you invite your guests to walk through into a formal dining room, or whether you just light the candles on a table at one end of your living room and ask your guests to move over from the other end, your table must provide a handsome frame for a warmly colorful view of your memorable hospitality.

Your table setting may be completely modern, but it will still reflect the basic traditions of banquet feasting, which, for thousands of years, have surrounded the ceremonial of the entertainment of honored guests. After all, however much taste in physical things may have changed, however much our menus may be different today from those of the past, human nature has not changed and the practice of hospitality is a human and natural relationship. So your dining table will have some of the qualities of all dining tables in all countries at all times.

It will be well lighted, but without glare—like a stage set. There will be a certain glitter and shimmer about it. There may be the bright glow of the pure white tablecloth and neatly folded napkins, if it is a formal dinner, or the decoratively balanced colors of a checkered cloth or matching place mats and napkins, if it is an informal supper. The lights will be sparklingly reflected in the crystal wineglasses. On my table there will be setting plates of handsomely grained, Scandinavian teak. They will be replaced by mirror-shining white china or ceramic-glass plates, with no blatantly ornate decorations to clash with the natural colors of the foods. The forks and knives will be sparkling, handsome, but above all, practical. (The English writer George Orwell once said that the best way to make sure that everyone thinks you are a great cook is to have extremely sharp knives.) Here and there, if you are the fortunate owner, as I am, of family heirlooms, there may be the luxurious shine of an antique silver mustard pot or sauceboat.

The centerpiece of the table will be the pivot of all the decorations. It can (and should) be as simple as a few branches from some bush or tree in a loose arrangement that can be seen through. Or it might be a beautiful bowl of highly polished fruits of the season. Or something to be nibbled as part of the meal: the balanced shapes of nuts, bunches of dried muscat raisins, colorful chunks of marzipan, brightly wrapped candies . . . or (and this is one of my favorites) simply a glass bowl of green, polished, shining avocados. I always carefully avoid the possible clash between the scent of flowers on the table and the bouquet of the foods and wines. I also veto anything solidly tall, which will hide the faces of the guests across the table.

If you can achieve the ideal setting matched to memorable food, you will join the great company of hosts who deserve the classic praise once given by a great French gourmet of the past, Madame la Marquise du Deffand, who, at the end of a superb banquet at the Palace of Versailles, leaned back in her chair with a beatific smile and, taking a sip of her ancient Cognac, said, *"Souper est une des quatres fines de l'homme. J'ai oublié les trois autres."* ("Dinner is one of the four finest moments of human life. I have forgotten the other three.")

The Average, Ordinary Essentials

I have not the slightest intention of trying to compete with all those other reference "handbooks," which offer you lists, in vast detail, of all the things you must do and all the equipment you must own to be an instant success as a host. Let me simply say that you must have a dining table large enough to seat all your guests, but it must not be too large to get inside your room. If you intend to use a tablecloth, it must be big enough to fit your table. You will need one place setting, with at least one plate and one drinking glass for each guest, unless you want them to share place settings, plates, and glasses. If you intend to have candles on the table, you should have candlesticks, with suitably sized holes, in which to stick them. If you want to carve a roast of beef at table, you should have a knife with which to do so. Whether or not you decide to have background music must depend on whether or not you think your guests will enjoy it. If you have lots of money, buy expensive things for your table—if not, buy inexpensive things. You must expect, now and then, that a china plate or a glass may be broken, so you must make sure that you can get extra supplies where they came from. In case one of your guests decides to drink a toast and then throw his wineglass over his left shoulder, with all the other guests following suit, it is wise, wouldn't you think, to have two drinking glasses for each guest.

Seriously, though, I believe that, of all the things that rest on the table during dinner, the most important to the enjoyment of the meal are the wineglasses. It is essential to choose them with the greatest of care. There is no bigger mistake than to pick your glasses primarily for their decorative value. It is not the glass but the warmly lovely color, the clarity, the brightness of the wine inside it that is the best decoration. Fifty years ago it was the fashion to have rainbow-colored, engraved, ornamented glasses, and one of the reasons was to hide the cloudiness of the wine. Modern wines seldom have clouds. So today the clearer the glass the better for the wine and for the drinker.

The second essential point is the size of the wineglass. Quite apart from the practical matter of being able to swirl the wine around, to encourage the bouquet, without pouring it up one's sleeve, there is the psychological consideration. Good wine is meant to be drunk in a leisurely mood, with appreciation and judgment. To capture this mood there must be neither too little nor too much of it. Give me my wine in a glass that is too small (say, three ounces) and I will have the irresistible urge to toss it down at one gulp, as if it were a slug of gin. Give me an enormous quantity in a balloon glass and I will want to swill it as if it were foaming beer. My ideal white-wine glass holds eight ounces. My favorite red-wine glass is a bit larger and wider at the top than the white, the better for the wine to breathe, which means that it has a capacity of ten ounces. But both glasses, of course, are never filled more than one-third to halfway.

The third essential factor in choosing a wineglass is its shape. It used to be the fashion (and still is in some conservatively wealthy homes) to have a different shape and style of glass for every important wine from every principal wine region. There was an Alsatian glass with an ultralong stem, a rather similar German glass, an Anjou glass, different glasses for Bordeaux reds or whites, Burgundy reds or whites, and on and on—all very profitable for the wineglass makers. Today, I consider all that frolic and fuss out-of-date. I restrict my stock to just five types of stemmed glassware.

A Basic, All-Purpose Glass

My all-purpose eight-ounce white-wine glass is the classic tulip shape, with rounded sides, in-curving at the top lip, so as to collect inside the glass the often heavily scented fumes of the wine. This glass holds equally well every kind of white wine, including Champagne and all other sparkling wines. For an extremely festive occasion, however, I keep a set of tall, narrow Champagne *flûtes,* which hold five ounces when filled to the brim, look lovely, encourage the bubbling, and are fine for drinking important toasts. (I am happy to say that I do not own any of those so-called coupe Champagne glasses, so beloved of Edwardian dandies—glasses that are nothing more than miniature soup bowls on stems, with wide-open, impractical bowls that make the Champagne go flat as badly and as quickly as dropping in lumps of sugar.)

My all-purpose ten-ounce red-wine glass also has the essential, in-curving lip, with a top opening almost three inches across, so that plenty of air can get to the wine. In addition, I keep a set of small, three-ounce capacity, long-chimneyed, classic Sherry-tasting glasses and use them for both Sherries and Madeiras, and for any wine that should be consumed in very small quantities, such as the powerfully great honey-sweet wines and the sweet liqueurs.

Finally, there is the thorny question of the size of the French-style *ballon,* the brandy snifter. Should it be small, medium, or "giant-economy-size"? Mine is middle-of-the-road, with a capacity of ten ounces and a nice tall chimney to encourage the beautiful bouquet. My glass is large enough to swirl the brandy without spilling it, small enough to be comfortably cupped and warmed between the palms of my two hands. Even after I have drunk all the brandy, this glass remains a delight to the enquiring sensitivity of my nose. As for those super-snobs who produce a *ballon* large enough to float the liner *Queen Elizabeth* and then heat it over a flame, before pouring in a tiny tot of a brandy allegedly straight from the Saint Helena cellar of Napoleon, they apparently fail to realize that the bouquet of the brandy, upon contact with the hot glass, goes off *poof,* and is instantly gone! This sort of service of any kind of brandy is pure ceremonial nonsense!

Other Essentials for the Fine Service of Fine Wines

The preparation of the wines will generally be done before the guests arrive. The Champagne and other sparkling and still white wines will have been set to cool for about two hours in the refrigerator. The red-wine bottles will have been carefully inspected for sediment, will, if necessary, have been delicately placed in basket cradles, will have had their lead capsules neatly cut below the "drip ring" (or completely removed), and the corks will have been gently but firmly pulled with a first-class corkscrew. Then the bottle neck will have been wiped clean, inside and out, and the wine will have been decanted in front of a candle flame through a glass funnel into a clear glass decanter. Finally this decanter will have been placed near the dining table, with the bottle cork resting lightly in the opening of the decanter, so that the wine may breathe and reach the proper temperature.

There will be times, however, when some of these operations may have to be done at table, during dinner, as a ceremony in which the guests participate. So I believe that the proper tools required for these ceremonial and functional tasks should be part of the furnishings of the dining table. They are therefore checklisted at the end of this chapter.

It is generally dangerous to open a very old red wine more than a few minutes before it is to be drunk. In five or ten minutes it could fade and die. So the dramatic moment of drawing the cork, sniffing the ancient greatness, and decanting it had better be done at table. (The technique of decanting, a relatively simple matter, is described in detail elsewhere in this chapter.)

Incidentally, some foolish hosts trying to avoid the trouble of decanting use their basket cradles for serving from the old wine bottles at table. They argue that because the bottle is lying down on its side in the cradle, the sediment will not be disturbed. If only they could see inside the bottle they would be shocked at the extent to which the sediment is stirred up every time the bottle is tilted to fill a glass and then tilted back to its prone position. By the time three or four glasses have been filled there is a cloud of muddy sediment through the wine and its quality in the glass will be far below what it would have been had it been properly decanted.

Disadvantages of the Lead Capsule

When you are about to uncork a bottle, it is the normal practice, using a small, sharp knife, to cut the lead capsule neatly around the neck to expose the cork. You should make this cut, all the experts agree, not flush with the top edge of the neck, but about three-eighths of an inch down, at a point just below the drip ring, which is molded into the glass top of the neck. This drip ring serves the double purpose, during pouring, of preventing the flowing wine from coming into contact with the lead capsule and, after pouring, of preventing any drips from running down the neck. I agree that this method of cutting the seal is the easiest and simplest way of exposing the cork. I do not agree that it is the best way.

The lead capsule (sometimes, these days, it is not lead at all, but a kind of rubberized plastic, and in the case of sparkling wines it is usually golden, red, or silver tinfoil) may look very nice outside, but inside, in the mini-space between its inner surface and the cork, the atmosphere is not very pleasant. When you take off a lead capsule sometime, smell it, very close to your nose. Often it has a quite nasty smell. This is partly intentional, partly accidental.

The people who bottled the wine wanted to prevent, at all costs, any attack on the cork by malevolent bacteria or hungry insects. So they sprayed the inside of the lead capsule with a chemical sterilizer before they slipped it over the cork and the neck. Often, however, in spite of these precautions, after the capsule has been on the bottle, undisturbed, for perhaps ten or twenty years, there may be some bacterial development in that tiny space just above the cork. This (and the chemical) can be the cause of that smell. For these reasons, I have an intense dislike for any kind of bottle capsule. I insist on removing it completely—including the part around the neck. Then, before pulling the cork, I thoroughly wipe the neck of the bottle and the top of the cork with a clean damp cloth.

Destructive Qualities of a Corkscrew

There are very good and exceedingly bad corkscrews. Some seem to have been brilliantly designed for the special purpose of breaking up a cork and driving its pieces down into the wine. The positive and negative points are discussed in the checklist below. Once you have a first-class corkscrew in hand, use it carefully and efficiently. Screw it into the cork slowly, making very sure that you are going straight down the exact center. Then draw the cork steadily, without jerks, without haste or hesitation. Sometimes, in spite of your best care, an old cork will break up and fall into the wine. Then, whether it is to be decanted or not, it will have to be strained, either through a specially designed stainless-steel wine strainer or through a simple (preferably silver) tealeaf strainer.

Once an old red wine has been opened, it may, quite quickly, show signs of rapid oxidation. One can tell, by sniffing, that the bouquet is beginning to fade, while at the same time becoming slightly harsh. One should at once recork the bottle (or restopper the decanter), until the precise moment of serving. The reason why the bottle cork is usually left half-sticking into the neck of the decanter is twofold; first, the cork, with its date and vineyard printed on its side, serves to identify the wine in the decanter. Second, while there is enough intake of air to allow the wine to breathe, the opening is sufficiently closed to prevent the entry of such relatively large objects as beetles and flies. They feel, after all, that they too have the right to an occasional good drink.

There is one other task that will normally have to be done at table during dinner. The sparkling and still white wines will have to be opened just before pouring, when they are at the exactly correct temperature. A vital point, often ignored by all but expert hosts, is the extent to which the taste of a wine falls off if it is served even a few degrees above or below its correctly prescribed temperature. The red wine that is too warm becomes dull and lifeless. The white wine that is too cold loses virtually all its bouquet and flavor. There is now on the market a long-stemmed thermometer that, as soon as a bottle is opened, can be plunged down into the liquid and will show, with reasonable accuracy, the temperature. Then an adjustment can be made, either by leaving the wine to stand a little longer at room temperature, or by cooling it for a few more minutes.

Final Hot Note

Even if you have taken all this care with your wines, even if your table is a magnificent setting and your food is superbly cooked, you cannot possibly achieve a memorable dinner if the hot dishes arrive at table less than piping. Robert Benchley once summed it up, after a bad dinner: "Everything was cold—except the Champagne." Fortunately this is no longer as severe a problem as it once was. It can be solved once and for all, by one of the very modern serving carts with an electrically heated tray built into its top. I have been using one of these wagons for the past couple of years and I find that it effectively heats plates and keeps waiting dishes at a temperature low enough so that there is no more cooking and very little drying out, yet high enough so that the food, when it is served, is still hot on the tongue. Some of these heated trays even have different areas of surface at different temperatures, so that, say, a coffee pot can be kept hot in one corner.

Finally, here is the checklist of dining-table equipment for the proper service of wines:

Bottle Basket Cradle, Silver, Stainless Steel, or Wicker

Always watch for possible sediment in a red Bordeaux or Port of any age and in a red Burgundy more than ten years old. Handle a sedimented bottle most carefully as you lift it from its bin or shelf. Hold it horizontally—do not turn it—place it immediately in the basket cradle to carry to the worktable where it will be opened and decanted. The basket cradle will continue to hold the bottle securely while the lead capsule is removed and the cork pulled. Never use the basket cradle—even if yours is pure gold—for serving a bottle at table. You will only succeed in showing yourself a fool. A sedimented bottle should not be brought to table; a nonsedimented one does not need a basket cradle.

Candle and Small Candlestick for Decanting

I use a small, polished brass antique candlestick, about four inches high, to hold the candle. During the decanting the flame should be just behind the shoulder of the bottle, so that the sediment can be seen as it slides forward and the pouring can be stopped the moment the sediment shows signs of getting into the neck.

Cloth, White, for Wiping Bottle Necks

For festive use at the dining table, this can be a smallish (perhaps twelve inches by twelve inches), handsome linen towel, which shows its great cleanliness as it is used to wipe the outside and inside of the bottle neck.

Corkscrew, Excellently Effective or Devastatingly Destructive

When searching for a first-class corkscrew, do not allow your attention to be diverted by the gadgety mechanisms for lifting the cork. It doesn't matter a damn whether there are two levers, two turning knobs, or one of each. Nor does it make the slightest difference whether the upper frame is metal or wood. The vital element is the screw. Avoid as the plague a solid screw—like a large wood screw—which acts as an auger driving a large hole through the middle of the cork and breaking it up. The screw should be a hollow spiral, and the steel wire from which it is made should be stainless and should, instead of being quite round, be slightly flattened, so that it grabs into the cork firmly, but without squeezing it. Measure the length of the spiral steel. It should be at least two and a half inches, since some corks in old bottles are two inches long. Needless to say, the point must be very sharp.

Decanter, Expensively Leaded or Simply Blown

A fine wine should always look better in a decanter than it did in its own bottle. For this reason, the decanter should be of the clearest possible glass and without any carving or embellishment that might interfere with a leisurely admiration of the wine's brightness and color. There are always a thousand different designs and qualities at a thousand prices, from hundreds of dollars to less than ten. The clearest, finest, and most shimmering glass is labeled "lead crystal," and when such a decanter is also "hand-blown," it can be an exciting work of art. Much less expensive decanters are labeled either "machine-blown," or "mold-pressed," but many of these have most decorative forms and handsomely flowing lines. They help to make of wine a thing of beauty and a joy for dinner.

Glass Funnel

This is for pouring the wine into the decanter. The tube at the bottom of the funnel should be small enough so that the wine flows gently and leisurely, yet large enough so that it does not back up at the top of the funnel.

Knife, Small, Sharp

You will need this tool if you insist on cutting off the bottle capsule. I prefer to remove the entire capsule, so as to be able to wipe the neck of the bottle very clean before pouring.

Strainer, Special Wine or Silver Tea

This is necessary for the difficult occasions when the bottle cork breaks up and pieces fall into the wine, so that it must be strained whether or not it is to be decanted. There are special (usually stainless-steel) wine strainers for this purpose, but if one of these cannot be found, a standard silver tealeaf strainer will do very well.

CHAPTER 5

CAMPAIGN PLAN FOR A MEMORABLE DINNER PARTY

. . . and to hell with the expense!

To achieve a truly memorable dinner party, the prime aim must be elegance and simplicity. It is not the fashion anymore to have a vast quantity of food and drink, but quality is everything. Fifty years ago diners sat down to *eat* until they were filled and fat. Today they sit down to *taste*. The next most important factor toward memorable success is timing. Timing of the preparation—so that everything is at the precise perfection of readiness, to allow the host to greet his guests with complete confidence and relaxation. Timing of the service during the meal—always slow enough that there may be pauses for critical appreciation of the food and wine, never so fast that there is a sense of rush or strain. One of my friends, a true connoisseur of good dining, often remarks, as he goes home after a thoroughly successful dinner party, "It was good and beautifully served." Those are the basic factors in the order of their importance.

The menu that follows makes certain demands of the cook. It is not supremely difficult, but neither is it entirely easy. There is no instant road to gastronomic success. If, at first, you have some doubt about your capability of preparing this meal as well as it might be done in a fine restaurant, remember that you will have certain advantages over the restaurant chef. He works under extreme pressure. He must prepare dozens of dishes at the same time, often for hundreds of people. How much easier is your job—provided that your work is properly organized.

Whenever you study any menu or recipe, always remember that the steps in its production can be divided into two distinct parts. First, the advance preparation of its ingredients. Second, the assembling and cooking in time for the serving. The preparation can be done almost at any time at your convenience. (In a professional kitchen, it is the responsibility of the "preparation chef," who comes to work in the early morning, hours before the arrival of the main staff.) The final, supervised cooking—although, admittedly, it usually involves some problems of timing—seldom takes longer than twenty to forty minutes and often much less. As a help toward organizing this essential division of the work, the "Plan of Campaign" gives you a step-by-step sequence of jobs, from the preliminary shopping to the crucial moment of serving at table.

The recipes are also planned for maximum efficiency. The ingredients are not listed in the customary way (simply in the order of their use). In the left-hand column are the "Staples," which you might ordinarily have on hand in your refrigerator or store cupboard. In the right-hand column the "Shopping" items are assembled in such a way that foods that would normally be bought at the same store (baker, butcher, dairy, greengrocer) are listed together.

Menu for a Luxurious Dinner for Four

Tortellini al Brodo
  (Stuffed Tiny Pasta Bags in
    Beef Bouillon)   **A noble French Champagne*

Lobster à la Newburg
  with Vegetables in Season
  and Gratin Dauphinois of New
    Potatoes   **A great white Burgundy*

Salad of Belgian Endive and
  Watercress

A Selection of Cheeses
  with Sourdough Bread
  and Sweet Butter   **A top-label red Graves of*
                                 Bordeaux

Saint-Emilion au Chocolat
  (Vanilla Macaroons with Rum
    and Chocolate)

Coffee   **Cognac*

This menu demonstrates how an elegant simplicity can be attained with only three principal courses, but with dramatic accompaniments and garnishes, with subtle variations of tastes and textures, all accompanied, framed, and lifted by lovely wines. Before the guests come to the dinner table, they should be offered not more than two of the hors d'oeuvre canapés from chapter 10—perhaps the best for this occasion being the French Shrimp à la Roquefort and the Chicken-and-Spinach Mushroom Caps. (If these are chosen, they can be prepared on the morning of the day.) No drink on earth will accompany them better than one of the finest of French Champagnes—ice-cold, dry, light, supremely refreshing and appetizing in the mouth—for example, the current top vintage of Moët et Chandon, the Dom Pérignon, named after the blind monk who invented the technique of sealing the bubbles in the bottle. Or the Cuvée Royale of the ancient and honorable Reims house of Charles Heidsieck. Or the Bollinger "R.D.," which means *récemment dégorgé,* recently disgorged and recorked.

The brilliant Italian soup Tortellini al Brodo (which means "Little Tartlets in Broth" and which was included in my imaginary "perfect dinner" in chapter 2) is the famous specialty of the northern city of Bologna, where it is the prized dish of almost every restaurant and most homes. The *tortellini* are tiny little "money bags" of pasta dough filled with many different combinations of aromatically rich meat and vegetables. Once you have mastered the not too difficult art of rolling out the pasta, putting in the stuffing, and coiling the miniature bags to seal them, you will have a specialty to dazzle your friends in several different ways, since *tortellini* can be served as hors d'oeuvres, as main dishes, and in soups. Prepared *alla Bolognese,* they are sautéed in butter with sliced white truffles. Or *alla Panna,* heated in cream with Parmesan cheese. In this menu they are the garnish in a clear, strongly flavorful beef bouillon. The Champagne is continued through this soup course.

The preparation of the main course should begin with the boiling of a live lobster. One of the marvels of modern food transportation is the way in which freshly caught lobsters from Maine are now being flown, packed alive in barrels of seaweed, within a few hours to all parts of the country. The owner of a famous restaurant in Kansas City recently told me, "I can get live lobsters from Boston faster than I can get steaks from Sioux City. I call Boston early in the morning and pick up my barrel of live lobsters at the airport in midafternoon of the same day." Once you have a fine lobster, you must honor it in this dish, by flavoring it with a top-quality Spanish dry *fino* Sherry and a well-aged Cognac—probably the same as you will drink at this meal after the coffee. "Cooking Sherry" and nondescript brandy simply will not do!

The lobster deserves to be accompanied by two seasonal vegetables—lightly prepared, without, of course, any form of sauce. The casserole of baked sliced potatoes is, in my opinion, one of the world's finest ways of preparing them. The *Gratin Dauphinois* is the great regional specialty of the ancient Dauphiné province around the city of Grenoble in the high, southwestern Alps, but it is so extraordinarily good that it has spread to all parts of France and, for that matter, the world. There are dozens of different "authentic" recipes. Mine came from a famous chef in Grenoble.

Such a brilliant combination of gastronomic splendors demands one of the great white wines of the world—my choice comes from the Côte d'Or, the "Golden Slope" of southern Burgundy, below the city of Beaune, where the old Roman road passes below the glorious vineyard of Le Montrachet, the "Bald Mountain." It is said that the lands of this district once belonged to a single Montrachet vineyard. When the *seigneur* of that immense property died, however, he willed that the land be divided among his children. One part went to his eldest son, and the wine from this vineyard is known today as Le Chevalier-Montrachet, the "Knight of Montrachet." But there was another son, borne, not by the wife, but by a lovely lady in the village, and his vineyard produces the wine known today as Le Bâtard-Montrachet, the "Bastard of Montrachet." There were also two young unmarried daughters, and their part of the vineyard land produces the wine that is still optimistically called Les Pucelles, the "Young Virgins." At the center of this group of extraordinary vineyards there remains the original property, still the greatest, simply called Le Montrachet. In good vintage years, when rain and sunshine are propitious, each of these famous wines is almost equally fine and any would be a worthy accompaniment to the lobster.

It is always sound menu-planning, when the main course requires the accompaniment of a white wine, to balance the meal by a red wine with the cheeses. To follow and top the great white Burgundy, what

better than a great red Bordeaux—especially one with the elegance and subtlety of a famous château in the district of Graves. The supreme name, of course, is Château Haut-Brion, but virtually across the street from this great vineyard (now sadly surrounded by the surburban development of the city of Bordeaux) is the smaller, less expensive, less well-known Château La Mission Haut Brion. Its wines are never far behind (and sometimes ahead of) those of its prestigious neighbor. Or the red wine might be from the nearby, equally fine Domaine de Chevalier.

The name Saint-Emilion au Chocolat does not imply an attempt to embalm a holy man in a brown, sweet crust, but refers to a small vanilla macaroon, originally made in the ancient village of Saint-Emilion at the heart of the northern wine district of Bordeaux. Since these French biscuits are not available in the United States, the best alternative is the famous Italian equivalent, the Amaretti di Saronno, available at most Italian specialty groceries or the general fancy food shops. When they are combined with one of the fine, brandylike rums from Jamaica or Martinique and a rich sauce of French bitter chocolate, the result is a memorable dessert.

One more point on this menu. I regard the serving of fine bread as one of the keys to memorable entertaining. After all, the ancient biblical definition of hospitality was "to break bread together." There are two strictly native American breads that are as fine as any other in the world—including the long, narrow *baguette* of France. I discovered my favorite American loaf on my first visit to San Francisco—it must be about thirty years ago—which I at once accepted as one of the seven wonder cities of the world. Its food, of course, was part of the wonder, and of all its gastronomic delights the most indelible first impression was made by the marvelous, crispy-crackly, satisfying sharpness of the authentic sourdough bread.

I was told that it was unique to San Francisco because of a particular (and very special) strain of live yeast bacteria, which could only live in San Francisco air and San Francisco water—and would die anywhere else. I have steadfastly refused to accept this hopelessly pessimistic theory. I vowed, with my first bite of sourdough, that I would never rest until I had brought that marvelous, but elusive, yeast to the East and worked out how to bake "New York Sourdough" in my own oven. With the help of my friend Joe Flaherty, a fine amateur baker, my dream has come to reality and our New York-baked sourdough is now one of the memorable pleasures of my party table.

The baking process can hardly be called "quick and simple," but it is certainly not beyond the powers of any average, amateur cook willing to spend some time on it and assemble the relatively inexpensive baking equipment needed. I keep a supply of live sourdough yeast "starter" in my refrigerator, where, by feeding it regularly and always leaving some to go on growing and multiplying, I can have a lifetime supply. Some of this starter is worked into the dough of each new loaf, which is then baked on preheated bricks laid on the shelves of my oven. The bread is as good as any I have ever eaten in San Francisco.

Campaign Plan for the Preparation of the Meal

Two Days Ahead

Check this staple list and add the needed items to the following shopping list:

DAIRY
Cream (for the coffee)
Eggs (16 large)
Milk (1 3/4 cups)

FRUITS AND VEGETABLES
Lemon (1 whole)
Garlic (1 bulb)

OTHER ITEMS
Beef bouillon (1 quart)
Coffee
Flour, all-purpose (2 table-spoons)
Olive oil (3/4 cup)
Sugar (for the coffee)
Vanilla extract (1 teaspoon)
Vanilla sugar (1/2 cup)
Vinegar, white-wine (4 table-spoons)

NOTE: If you do not bake your own sourdough bread, buy commercial sour-dough or French-style long loaves.

HERB AND SPICE CABINET
Clove, powdered
Mustard, English dry
Nutmeg, whole
Paprika, sweet
Black peppercorns
Crystal salt

WINES AND SPIRITS
Cognac (1 tablespoon for cook-ing—more than drinking)
Rum, Jamaica golden or Martinique (3-4 ounces)
Sherry, Spanish dry *fino* (1/2 cup)

NOTE: Check the wines on the menu and if you do not have them, buy the current vintages.

The Day Before

Shopping list (plus any needed staple items from above):

DAIRY
Salt butter (1/2 pound)
Sweet butter (for cooking and
for the meal—about 1
pound)
Heavy cream (1 1/2 pints)

CHEESE
Three cheeses for the cheese
board at table—say, one
creamy, one firm, one soft
Parmesan cheese—for grating
(10 ounces)

FISH
Lobsters, live (2 at 1 1/2
pounds each—or about
1 1/2 pounds boiled meat)

GROCERIES
Chocolate, French bitter or
first-grade domestic alter-
nate (1/2-pound slab)
Pure maple syrup (1/4 cup)
Bread for toast points (1 loaf)
Flour, all-purpose (1 pound)

MEAT
Chicken or turkey breast (1/4
pound)
Ham, lean (1/4 pound)
Pork, lean (6 ounces)
Veal, lean (1/4 pound)
Veal brains (1/4 pound)

ITALIAN SPECIALTY STORE OR
FANCY FOOD SHOP
Italian mortadella sausage
(2 ounces)
Amaretti di Saronno—Italian
macaroons (1-pound,
2-ounce tin)

FRUITS AND VEGETABLES
Chives (1 small bunch)
Belgian endive (1 large spear)
Parsley (1 bunch)
Potatoes, good, waxy
(2 pounds)
Watercress (2 bunches)
Seasonal vegetables for the
meal

After the Shopping

Start making ice and continue until you have enough.
Prepare stuffing for Tortellini and fill the pasta shapes, then set out
to dry overnight (recipe steps 1-5).
Boil lobsters, then cool, remove meat from shells, cut in chunks, and
refrigerate in covered jar (recipe steps 1 and 2).
Prepare Saint-Emilion au Chocolat and store, in refrigerator,
wrapped in foil (recipe steps 1-6).
Set the table and get out all serving dishes.

Advance Preparations on the Day

Chill salad bowl and plates.

Wash endive and watercress for salad, dry and cut as in recipe—put in plastic bags and refrigerate (recipe steps 1 and 2).

Prepare vinaigrette dressing (except for chives and parsley), cover, and refrigerate.

3 Hours Before the Guests Arrive

Set out and bring to room temperature: cheeses and butter for the cheese course, Saint-Emilion au Chocolat.

Prepare Gratin Dauphinois (recipe steps 1-3).

Chill Champagne and white wines.

Set out all ingredients for lobster.

Chop parsley for lobster; set aside, covered.

Chop chives and parsley for vinaigrette dressing.

Prepare the two seasonal vegetables.

45 Minutes Before Serving

Make coffee.

Make toast points for lobster.

Warm plates.

Heat bouillon to simmering and cook Tortellini in it.

Prepare Lobster à la Newburg (steps 3-5).

Brown the Gratin Dauphinois under grill (step 4).

The Sequence of the Dinner

Light candles.

Open the red wine and decant if necessary.

Toss the salad with its dressing just before serving.

Warm bread just before cheese course.

So much for the plan of campaign for the entire menu. If, on the other hand, you want to prepare just one of the dishes, here are the separate recipes, with separate lists of ingredients, so that you can cut your dinner down to your own size, or make up your own menu in your own way.

Tortellini al Brodo

(For 4)

STAPLES

Salt butter (4 tablespoons)
Eggs (10 large)
Parmesan cheese, for grating (10 ounces)
Beef bouillon (1 quart)
Flour, all-purpose (3 1/2 cups sifted, plus more for flouring board)
Olive oil (1 tablespoon)
Nutmeg
Crystal salt
Freshly ground black pepper

SHOPPING

Chicken or turkey breast (1/4 pound)
Ham, lean (1/4 pound)
Italian mortadella sausage (2 ounces)
Pork, lean (6 ounces)
Veal, lean (1/4 pound)
Veal brains (1/4 pound)

The Day Before Serving—Preparing the Stuffing in About 45 Minutes

1. Pick over and carefully wash the 1/4 pound of veal brains and soak in cold, salted water for about 30 minutes. Meanwhile, on a wooden cutting board, dice the chicken or turkey breast, ham, mortadella, pork, and veal. Grate the 10 ounces of Parmesan cheese, dividing it into 3/4 cup for the stuffing and 1/2 cup for serving at table. Melt the 4 tablespoons of butter in a sauté pan and very gently brown the diced meats, turning now and then, and adding plenty of freshly ground nutmeg, plus crystal salt and black pepper, to taste. As soon as the brains have finished soaking, break them up into smallish bits and add to sauté pan. Cover and simmer everything gently for about 15 minutes.

2. At the end of this time, put entire contents of sauté pan through the fine cutter of a meat grinder. Work in the 3/4 cup of Parmesan and add as many eggs as may be needed to make a reasonably firm and smooth stuffing. Refrigerate until ready to use.

Kneading, Rolling Out, and Filling the Pasta Dough in About 1 Hour

3. In the middle of a fair-sized pastry board, put 3 1/2 cups of sifted flour in a heap, sprinkle on 1 heaped teaspoon of salt, make a well at the center, then gently pour in 2 lightly beaten eggs and the 1 tablespoon of olive oil. Work everything together with the fingers, adding 1 more egg and a few drops of warm water, if necessary, to produce a firmly pliant ball of dough. Continue kneading with the heel of the hand, rubbing more flour on board and hand as needed to prevent sticking, until pasta dough is thoroughly elastic, usually in about 10 minutes. Then cover ball of dough with a bowl and let stand about 30 minutes.

4. Divide ball of dough into 4 pieces and roll each out, sprinkling on more flour as needed to prevent sticking, until you have 4 sheets, each about 3/16-inch thick.

5. Using a 1 1/2-inch cookie cutter, cut rounds from the pasta sheets, and place at the center of each about 1 teaspoon of the meat stuffing. Fold each disk in half, with the upper edge a little short of the lower. Bring the two points of the half circle together, twisting them around your finger so that they make a ring, and firmly seal edges. Put filled *tortellini*, in a single layer, in a flat, floured pan, cover with a dish towel, and leave at room temperature to dry out overnight.

About 15 Minutes Before Serving

6. In a 2-quart saucepan, heat up the beef bouillon to just simmering and gently drop in the *tortellini*. They will sink to the bottom but rise to the top as soon as they are properly cooked, usually in about 5 minutes. Immediately serve bouillon and *tortellini* in hot soup bowls. Pass more Parmesan cheese to sprinkle over the top.

Lobster à la Newburg
(For 4)

STAPLES

Salt butter (1/4 pound)
Heavy cream (1 pint)
Eggs (4 large)
Parsley, chopped (1/2 cup)
Lemon (1)
Flour, all-purpose (2 table-
    spoons)
Clove, ground (1 dash)
Paprika, sweet (1/2 teaspoon)
Freshly ground black pepper
Crystal salt

SHOPPING

Lobsters, preferably bought
    live, then boiled and cut up
    (2 at 1 1/2 pounds each—or
    about 1 1/2 pounds boiled
    lobster meat)
Cognac (1 tablespoon)
Sherry, Spanish dry *fino* (1/2
    cup)

The Day Before—Humanely and Painlessly Killing, Cleaning, and Cutting Up the Lobsters in About 20 Minutes

1. Put the 2 live 1 1/2-pound lobsters into a suitably large soup kettle, then cover them with cold water and put in plenty of salt to make them feel at home. Place pot over highest possible heat, so that temperature of water rises quickly and delicate nerves of lobsters are painlessly numbed. When temperature reaches 80°F., lobsters turn red and are dead.

2. Take them out of water at once and place them on large, wooden chopping board. Now, using in turn a small, sharp cleaver and a heavy-duty fish knife, learn the right way of cleaning and cutting up lobster. Stretch out lobster on its back and open up underside of its head. Remove its stomach, or "lady"—the hard little sac where its chin would be, if it had a chin. Open up underside of tail and scrape out black intestinal vein. If lobster is a female "hen" (you can tell by the fact that she has a much wider tail fin), she will have the red "coral" inside her head. These are her eggs, a prized delicacy to be carefully removed and held in a small jar for later flavoring. Both female and male also have, in their heads, the green "tomalley," the

liver, also an important delicacy, to be carefully removed and held for later use. Now open up underside of lobsters and pull out all meat, cutting it up into bite-sized chunks. Also crack open claws and remove flesh, also tidbits from back of head. Store in refrigerator overnight in tightly covered container. Once you have mastered this simple technique and have come to realize how much better every lobster dish tastes when it starts with the live shellfish, you will never again buy preboiled, preshelled, exorbitantly expensive lobster meat.

Just Before Serving—Preparation in About 15 Minutes

3. Melt the 1/4 pound of butter in a sauté pan, taking great care that it does not brown, then gently put in the chunks of lobster meat and slowly stir them around, with a wooden spoon, for hardly more than 1 minute, to heat them up and coat them with the butter. Next, working carefully and quickly with a wire whisk, blend in, first, the juice of the lemon; second, the 2 tablespoons of flour; third, the pint of heavy cream. Keep whisking lightly and steadily as cream goes in slowly, or it may curdle. When sauce is entirely smooth, sprinkle in about 1/2 teaspoon salt, grind in black pepper to taste, a dash of powdered clove, and the 1/2 teaspoon powdered sweet paprika. Now bring everything up to gentle bubbling and let it continue, uncovered, so that sauce will boil down slightly and flavors will be concentrated, in about 5 minutes.

4. Warm up the serving dish and dinner plates until they are quite hot. Reheat the previously prepared toast points. Chop enough parsley to fill 1/2 cup.

Just Before Serving

5. Again using the small wire whisk, stir into the sauté pan the 1/2 cup Sherry. Break the 4 eggs into a small bowl and lightly beat until they are almost, but not quite, foamy, then blend into sauté pan. Keep stirring steadily until eggs thicken. Finally, blend in the tablespoon of Cognac and 1/4 cup of the parsley. Sprinkle remaining parsley over the lobster on the serving dish as decorative garnish. Rush everything instantly to table.

Gratin Dauphinois of New Potatoes
(For 4)

STAPLES
Sweet butter (4 tablespoons)
Milk (1 cup)
Garlic cloves (2 whole)
Nutmeg, freshly ground
Crystal salt
Freshly ground black pepper

SHOPPING
Potatoes, good, waxy
(2 pounds)
Heavy cream (1/2 pint)

About 2 1/2 Hours Before Serving—Active Preparation About 25 Minutes—Unsupervised Baking About 2 Hours

1. Skin potatoes and slice them in even rounds, about 1/4-inch thick. Wash thoroughly at once to get rid of starch and pat dry in towel. Put slices, loosely, into heavy iron skillet, with 2 or 3 liberal turns of the nutmeg grinder, plus salt and pepper, to taste. Pour in the 1 cup of milk, bring up to boiling. Peel and finely mince 1 clove of the garlic and sprinkle into milk. When milk boils, turn down heat and keep simmering moderately, uncovered, until all milk is absorbed into potatoes—usually in about 15 minutes—turning quite often to coat all the sides.

2. Meanwhile, prepare earthenware, ovenproof, lidded casserole in which potatoes will be baked. Thoroughly rub inside with cut second clove of garlic, then spread liberally all around with some of the butter. Turn on oven to 300° F. and set shelf so that casserole will be in center. When potato slices are ready, put them into casserole in interleaved layers, thoroughly soak them with the 1/2 pint of cream, and dot the top with remaining butter. Cover casserole and set in oven in a larger dish filled with water about 1-inch deep.

3. When potatoes are thoroughly soft—usually in 1 1/2 to 2 hours—check for seasoning and, if necessary, add more salt and pepper.

4. Then quickly brown top surface by placing casserole, for a couple of minutes, under a hot grill. All cream will, generally, have been absorbed into potatoes, making them unbelievably soft and velvety.

Salad of Belgian Endive and Watercress

(For 4)

STAPLES
  Garlic (1/2 clove)
  Crystal salt
  Freshly ground black pepper

SHOPPING
  Watercress, fresh (2 bunches)
  Belgian endive (1 large spear)

Preparation in About 10 Minutes

1. First rub inside of salad bowl with the 1/2 clove garlic. How many rubs is a matter of trial and error according to taste. Wash the watercress under running cold water and lay it on paper towels to dry. Cut off all coarse, large stems, then cut remaining leaves into bite-sized sprigs. Roll up in the paper towels and refrigerate.

2. Remove and discard the outer leaves of the endive. Cut small julienne strips about 1/4 inch by 1 inch of the inner leaves. Put into plastic bag and refrigerate.

Just Before Serving

3. Put both watercress and endive into chilled bowl, then bring to table and toss with vinaigrette dressing, plus extra salt and pepper as needed.

Basic Vinaigrette Salad Dressing

(For a salad for 4)

STAPLES
  Olive oil (1/2 cup)
  Vinegar, white-wine (4 table-
    spoons)
  Mustard, English dry (1/2 tea-
    spoon)
  Crystal salt
  Freshly ground black pepper

SHOPPING
  Chives, fresh (a few sprigs
    —enough for 1 tablespoon
    —finely chopped)
  Parsley, fresh (a few sprigs
    —enough for 1 tablespoon
    —finely chopped)

Mixing Basic Ingredients in Advance

1. Put vinegar into a 3-cup mixing bowl. With a small whisk, beat in the 1/2 teaspoon of mustard and 1/2 teaspoon of salt until both are completely incorporated. Then slowly pour the olive oil into the mixture in a thin stream, whisking continuously, until all oil is in. Add pepper to taste.

Just Before Tossing with Salad

2. Mix chopped chives and parsley into oil-vinegar mixture. Correct seasoning if necessary. Put into chilled small serving pitcher. Bring to table, pour over salad, and toss until it glistens.

Saint-Emilion au Chocolat
(Vanilla Macaroons with Rum and Chocolate)
(For 4)

STAPLES
Sweet butter (1/4 pound)
Eggs (2 large)
Milk (about 3/4 cup)
Pure vanilla extract (1 teaspoon)
Vanilla sugar (1/2 cup)

SHOPPING
Amaretti di Saronno—Italian Macaroons (1-pound, 2-ounce tin)
Chocolate, French bitter or first-grade domestic alternate (1/2-pound slab)
Pure maple syrup (1/4 cup)
Rum, Jamaica golden or Martinique (3-4 ounces)

The Day Before—Total Preparation in About 20 Minutes, Then Refrigerated Overnight

1. Soften the 1/4 pound of butter at room temperature. Separate 1 of the eggs, putting away white for some other use and holding yolk in a medium-sized mixing bowl. Scald 1/2 cup of the milk, then let cool. Cream the now softened butter with the 1/2 cup of sugar.

2. When milk has cooled to about blood heat, beat it into the yolk. Coarsely grate the 1/2 pound of chocolate and put into a 1-quart

saucepan. Add the 1/4 cup of maple syrup to chocolate, and heat gently, stirring continuously with a wooden spoon, until chocolate is melted.

3. Turn off heat, give egg-milk a final beat and gradually work into chocolate. Reheat slowly, stirring continuously. When it is hot, but still well below boiling, begin blending in, tablespoon by tablespoon, the butter-sugar. It must now be worked into a rich and thick sauce. If it becomes too thick, dribble in a little more milk; if it does not get thick enough, separate the second egg, beat yolk into remaining milk, then turn off heat and blend gradually into sauce.

4. When sauce is perfect, hold it hot, covered, over a very low keep-warm temperature or half-submerged in a bowl of hot water.

Assembling the Amaretti in About 10 Minutes

5. The amaretti must be assembled in a flat-bottomed serving dish of about 2 quarts capacity. I use a round earthenware casserole, but a china soufflé dish will also do. Cover the bottom with a single layer of amaretti, all touching each other. With the rum in a cup and using a 1/4-teaspoon measuring spoon, dribble just a drop or two of rum on top of each of the amaretti. No rum should fall in between. Too much rum on any one macaroon will sog it, and this is to be avoided.

6. Take chocolate sauce off heat and stir into it the 1 teaspoon of vanilla extract. Then, using a small ladle, dribble some of the chocolate sauce over the rum-soaked amaretti. Do not fill air spaces between. At once make a second layer of amaretti, pressing them lightly down over spaces in first layer. Again dribble with rum and ladle on chocolate. Continue this sequence, layer upon layer, until dish is full almost to its brim and there is no remaining chocolate sauce. Top with final layer of amaretti without rum or chocolate. Cover entire dish tightly with foil and refrigerate overnight.

Serving at Table

7. Serve at room temperature, using a large, flattish serving spoon, digging it straight down, so that each diner gets a balanced portion of the bottom and the top amaretti, which will have remained crisp and crunchy, imbedded in the rich chocolate.

The Fascinating Complications of
Home-Baked Sourdough Bread

Let's face it. The baking of sourdough bread is not exactly a simple matter. But it is, to me, a rewarding experience.

The basic ingredients are earthy and simple: flour, salt, water, and the wild yeast starter from which it all began. Properly combined and baked, these ingredients become the world's best bread, with a tangy taste, chewy texture, and the crispiest of crusts.

It takes over 24 hours from start to finish, as the natural yeast starter must be set to ferment the night before baking and the bread dough itself must rise slowly for hours to develop its traditional sour flavor. It is then baked on building bricks laid on the oven shelves to simulate the baker's hearth, with a pan of boiling water on the oven floor to supply the steamy atmosphere that browns and crisps the crust to perfection.

This bread requires a natural yeast starter (instead of the standard baker's yeast) to raise, or "proof," the bread. Such a starter can be purchased in dried, packaged form and once mixed, it can be kept alive in the refrigerator for years—ready for the baking of batch after batch of breads, biscuits, pancakes, and so on.

The First Step—the Natural Yeast Starter

Butter for greasing bowl (about 1 teaspoon)

Flour, hardwheat (about 6 ounces, unbleached)

Sourdough starter, mixed with warm water, according to printed instructions (1 cup)

After blending the sourdough starter into the warm water you will have 1 cup of thick liquid. Pour the liquid into a glass or ceramic mixing bowl and work in the flour, a spoonful at a time, until it forms a stiff dough. Turn dough out onto a floured board and knead with fingers and heel of hand until dough is smooth and elastic, with a satinlike surface, usually in 5 to 10 minutes. Put back into mixing bowl, now very lightly greased, then cover and set in a warm place (about 80° F.) to rise, for about 8 hours or overnight.

This basic "starter" is used to make the bread "sponge" each time a batch is to be baked. Between times it should be kept in a covered glass container (not metal) in the refrigerator. The starter must be refreshed once a week to keep it active. To refresh it, to every 6 ounces of starter, work in 6 ounces hardwheat flour and 3 ounces of water in a glass or ceramic mixing bowl. Knead as described above, cover, and let it rise for 4 hours in a warm place (it should not develop fully). Return to container and refrigerate.

The Second Step—the Starter Sponge

When you want to bake a batch of bread you must first convert the starter into a sponge, which is used as the leavening for the dough. The required ingredients:

Butter for greasing bowl (about 1 teaspoon)
Natural yeast starter, from refrigerator (3 ounces)

Water (3 tablespoons)
Flour, hardwheat, unbleached if possible (3 ounces)

The Night Before the Baking

Break the 3 ounces of starter into small pieces and place in a glass or ceramic mixing bowl, work in the 3 tablespoons of water and the 3 ounces of flour, until you have a stiff dough. Turn it out onto a lightly floured board. Knead until dough is smooth and elastic, with a satinlike surface—about 5 to 10 minutes. Put back into mixing bowl, now lightly buttered, cover and set in warm place (about 80° F.) to rise overnight.

The Final Step—Baking the Bread

Butter for greasing the bowl (1 teaspoon)
Starter sponge (previous instructions)
Flour, hardwheat, unbleached (28 ounces, about 7 level cups, unsifted)

Water (2 cups)
Salt (2 teaspoons)
Flour, rice (about 2 ounces)
Cornmeal, finely ground (about 2 ounces)

6 Hours Before Baking—Active Preparation for About 1 Hour with 5 Hours of Unsupervised Proofing

Punch down the starter sponge and break into small pieces. Place in a glass or ceramic mixing bowl and add the 2 cups water, the 2 teaspoons salt, the hardwheat flour, 1 cup at a time. Mix well with a wooden spoon until dough is too stiff to stir. Turn out onto lightly floured board and knead vigorously, until the dough is smooth and elastic, with a satinlike surface, usually 15 to 20 minutes. Put back into bowl, now lightly greased, cover, and set in a warm place (about 80° F.) to rest 1 hour. The dough will not rise much during this hour, but the rest will give the yeast a chance to spread throughout the dough.

At the end of the hour, remove dough from bowl, cut into 3 pieces. Flatten each and roll into a tight ball. Cover them with a towel and let rest on floured board 20 minutes.

One by one take each ball of dough, flatten into pancake shape, and fold into thirds by folding bottom third up over the center and then folding the top third down over the bottom third. Fold in half again the long way, pinching seams to seal them. Using the palms of both hands, roll the dough tightly, stretching it out into a long French loaf (make sure you don't roll it too long to fit your oven).

Place the loaves seam side down on a bread board covered with a rice-floured pastry cloth. Set the loaves in a warm humid place (about 80° F.) to rise, or "proof," for 4 hours. A large inverted cardboard box with a pan of tepid water inside makes a good proofing box.

While bread is rising, arrange the oven shelves so that one is near the top and the second about 8 to 10 inches below it.

2 Hours Before Baking

Cover the shelves of the oven with clean, dry building bricks and preheat to 400° F. It will take about 2 hours to heat up the bricks so that they are at the same temperature as oven.

10 Minutes Before Baking

Place a shallow baking pan on the oven floor and fill it with boiling water.

Cover a cookie sheet or a baker's peel (the flat, wooden sheet—a sort of shovel with a handle) wide enough to hold the 3 loaves, with finely ground cornmeal.

Place the board with risen loaves on the work surface near the prepared cookie sheet. Place a thin piece of Masonite or heavy cardboard the length of the loaves and 6 inches wide adjacent to the first loaf and lift edge of the pastry cloth under the loaf, rolling it carefully onto the board. Move the loaf to the prepared cookie sheet and roll it onto the cornmeal. Repeat until all 3 loaves have been moved to the cookie sheet and spaced about 3 inches apart. Using a razor blade, quickly cut 4 slightly overlapping slashes about 1/2 inch deep in the top of each loaf and slide the cookie sheet and loaves into the oven onto the lower shelf. Tilt the cookie sheet up a few inches and with a quick motion pull it out, dropping the loaves lightly onto the hot bricks. Bake for 35 minutes.

When baked, slide the cookie sheet back under the loaves and remove from the oven. Cool on a wire rack.

CHAPTER 6

THE MOST DIFFICULT RECIPE IN THE WORLD?

*But Worth Every Ounce of the Effort and
Every Minute of the Time*

I t is always a basic truth of the art of menu-planning that a single magnificent dish can, virtually on its own, make a magnificent dinner. The dish in this case is one of the most supremely great I know and has never failed to overwhelm my guests. I call my famous dish the Timbale of King Neptune, and it was described in detail as the main course of my imaginary "perfect dinner" in chapter 2. Now I propose to set down the practical plan for preparing this super-dish and constructing a fitting dinner menu around it. I admit that when I make it myself, I work partly by a sort of instinct and am never absolutely sure of how much of this and that I put in. I taste and decide—then try and taste again! So it is good discipline for me to do my Timbale once more in my own kitchen and now, for the first time, to set every detail down on paper.

A warning at the start of the adventure. This is one of the most challenging dishes in the world. First, it involves a substantial number of different operations, all of which must be ready to come together at precisely the right moment. Second, it is difficult work in terms of achieving the extremely fine blend of so many different tastes and textures, all delicately balanced, so to speak, on a tightrope of perfection. Let us face it—it involves three days of intermittent shopping and cooking. When I find I cannot spare that much time on weekdays, I start my preparations on a Friday evening, work through Saturday and Sunday, then dash home from the office as early as possible on Monday and serve the dinner to my guests that evening.

Another problem with this recipe is that it was originally given to me in a professional, summarized form by the great chef of a small country restaurant in a village on the Mediterranean coast of the south of France. Since he was working in his own professional kitchen, he naturally assumed that he did not have to tell me how to prepare the various basic stocks, sauce essences, meat glazes, and other foundations of French cooking. He had these automatically on hand in his kitchen every day, ready for any one of a couple of dozen dishes that might be ordered by his customers. It was very easy, for example, for him to tell me to "add a few tablespoons of a good fish *fumet*" (which is a bouillon made by boiling fish bones, fins, heads, and so on, with onions and parsley, plus white wine, into a strongly flavorful fish stock), since all he had to do was to stick his spoon into the gently bubbling pot on his stove. In my amateur kitchen, I have to prepare a small quantity of the fish *fumet* specially for the occasion. The same problem applies to the brown sauce, which has to be prepared separately and involves three hours of slow simmering. As to the rest of the menu, only the simplest beginning and ending are necessary, since the Timbale, with the wine that accompanies it, completely dominates the dinner.

Menu for an Olympian Shellfish Dinner for Four

Kernels of Fresh Corn Baked
   with Cream in Scallop Shells   **A Fine French champagne*

The Timbale of King Neptune   ***A Burgundy White, Chablis,*
                                            Grand Cru

Green Salad Vinaigrette

A Single Cheese: a running-
   ripe Brie or Camembert

Pineapple Marinated in Sweet
   White Wine   ***A Great Bordeaux Golden Sauternes*

Coffee   ***Armagnac*

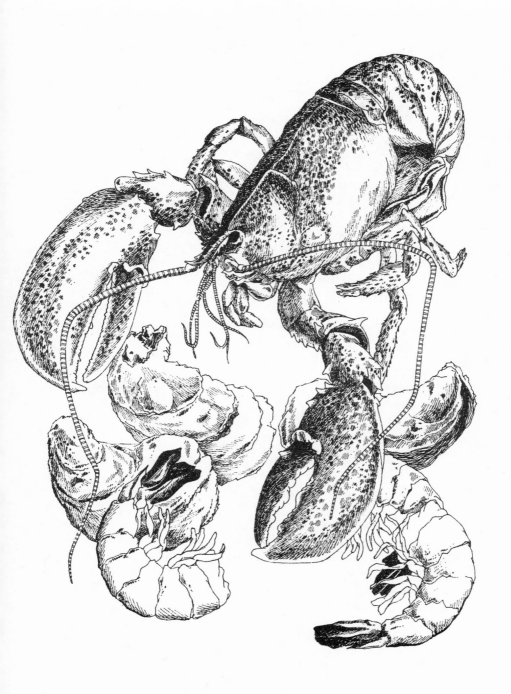

I would plan to serve the Champagne to the guests as soon as they arrived and, since the dinner will be exclusively oceanic, the preliminary canapés should be meaty—possibly very small portions of a nicely aromatic pâté or terrine. The Champagne can then be continued, at table, through the first course. From among the French labels one might choose a Krug Private Réserve Brut, a Veuve Laurent-Perrier Cuvée Grand Siècle, or a Mercier Réserve de l'Empereur, but there are also hundreds of alternative labels of sparkling white wines, from Champagne, from other wine regions of France, from the United States, and many other wine-producing countries, which seem to fit every size of pocketbook and variation of taste.

Luscious and sweet kernels of fresh corn, baked to perfection in heavy cream and handsomely served in coquille shells, are the perfectly simple yet simply perfect overture to the dramatic razzle-dazzle of the main dish. Naturally, if the corn can be picked and scraped half an hour before dinner, that is heavenly joy! But even fresh store-bought (or, out of season, first-grade canned or frozen) corn prepared in this flexible way can be very good indeed. The "secret trick" is to check the condition of the corn and then decide how much cream should be added. Add more if the corn is dry—less, if there has been heavy rain, or if the corn is very young and watery. Taste a single, raw kernel. Your tongue will tell you what to do.

I am sure that my Timbale of King Neptune deserves to be supported by an outstanding wine, and my experience has proved to me that a noble Chablis is just about the ideal. Remember, when buying Chablis, that only the finest quality may (by French law) be labeled with the words "Grand Cru" or "Grand Chablis" and, within this range, the greatest vineyard names to look for are Blanchots, Bougros, Les Clos, Grenouilles, Les Preuses, Valmur, and Vaudésir. These, because of the fame of their names, are always fairly expensive, but the next lower range of quality (which, in a good year, can be almost equally noble) often represents a better value. These wines may be labeled "Premier Cru" and the favored vineyard names I look for (from among a couple of dozen) are Fourchaume, Mont de Milieu, Montée de Tonnerre, and Montmain. Below this range of quality there are lesser wines, legally labeled simply "Chablis" without a vineyard name, or, at an even lower grade, "Petit Chablis," but these are hardly worthy of the standard of this dinner.

The dessert must be of the simplest. Fresh pineapple is usually in season at roughly the same time as corn and lobsters, so this charming and dramatic way of serving the tropical fruit is very much in order. As to the wine to drink with this dessert, it must, of course, be sweet. The word *Sauternes* seems to have become the universal term, all over the world, for a sweet wine. Primarily, of course, the name belongs to the village of Sauternes, about thirty miles south of Bordeaux, in the wine district of the same name that produces some of the greatest of all sweet wines, including those of the world-famous Château d'Yquem and, among others, Château de Rayne-Vigneau, Château Rieussec, and Château de Suduiraut. It is reasonable, therefore, to feel, as I do, that the name Sauternes should really belong to France. But then one must at once add that, besides those of Sauternes, there are many other fine sweet wines from many wine regions—from the Loire, from Alsace, from the Moselle, from the Rhine, and some outstanding examples from California. Any of these can be used as a substitute for the Sauternes. Each different wine will give its own special character and variation to this excellently simple dessert.

Campaign Plan for the Preparation of the Meal

Four Days Ahead

Check this staple list and add the needed items to the shopping list for
Three Days Ahead:

FRUITS AND VEGETABLES

Yellow onions (7 medium)
Lemons (2)
Garlic (1 bulb)

OTHER ITEMS

Olive oil (about 1 1/4 cups)
Tomato paste (2 6-ounce cans)
Tomato sauce (1 cup)
Flour, all-purpose (about 1/2 cup)
Sugar for the coffee
Superfine sugar, for pineapple
Fine bread crumbs (6 tablespoons)
White-wine vinegar for salad (4 tablespoons)
Black truffles (2 or 3)
Coffee
Beef bouillon, homemade or canned (6 cups)
Glace de viande, homemade or bottled (2 teaspoons)
Clam juice, if you do not make the fish *fumet* (1 pint)

HERB AND SPICE CABINET

Rosemary, if fresh not available
Tarragon, if fresh not available
Thyme
Bay leaves (5)
Arrowroot or cornstarch (several tablespoons)
Spices for salad
Black peppercorns
Crystal salt

WINES AND SPIRITS

Dry white vermouth (about 1 bottle)
Dry white wine (1 1/2 bottles —for cooking)
Dry Sherry (1/2 cup)
Cognac (1 cup plus a couple of teaspoons—for cooking)
Sweet Sauternes (1/2 bottle —for cooking)
NOTE: Check the wines on the menu and if you do not have them, buy the current vintages.

Three Days Ahead

Shopping list (plus any needed staple items from above):

FISH

Fish backbones, fins, heads, tails, and trimmings (2 pounds)

Lobsters, preferably live (2 at 1 1/2 pounds each)

Crayfish or large fresh shrimp, unshelled (16-24)

MEAT

Beef and veal bones, cut up for roasting (2 pounds)

Dark-smoked bacon (2 rashers)

DAIRY

Sweet butter (1 pound)

Heavy cream (1/2 pint)

GROCERIES

Italian plum tomatoes (1 pound)

FRUITS AND VEGETABLES

Tomatoes (6 medium)

Carrots (10 medium)

Green celery (1 bunch)

Parsley (1 bunch)

Mushrooms (1/2 pound)

Rosemary, a small sprig

Shallots (6)

Tarragon, a small sprig

Thyme, a small sprig

Three Days Ahead—After the Shopping

Prepare the Fish *fumet* (recipe steps 1 and 2).
Boil lobster (recipe step 3).
Chop lobster into pieces (recipe step 4).
Prepare the Lobster à l'Américaine (recipe steps 5-7).

Two Days Ahead

Prepare the Basic Brown Sauce (recipe steps 8-10).
Prepare Shrimp à la Bordelaise (recipe steps 11 and 12).

The Day Before

Shopping list:

DAIRY
Sour cream (1/2 cup)
Heavy cream (about 1 pint)
Cream (for the coffee)
Sweet butter (1 pound)
Salt butter (1/4 pound)

CHEESE
Brie de Meaux (for cheese
course)

FISH
Crayfish or medium-sized
shrimp, in their shells (1/2
pound)

FRUITS AND VEGETABLES
Button mushrooms (about
1 1/4 pounds)
Tomatoes (2 medium)
Parsley (1 bunch)
Tarragon (a few sprigs)
Whole pineapple (1)
Corn (8-10 medium ears)
Greens for salad

After the Shopping

Start making ice and continue until you have enough.
Prepare the Shrimp Butter (recipe steps 13-16).
Set the table and get out all serving dishes.
Prepare pineapple (recipe step 1).

Shopping List for the Day of the Dinner

FISH
Oysters in shell (2 dozen)
NOTE: If you do not bake your
own sourdough bread,
buy commercial sour-
dough or French-style
long loaves.

Advance Preparations on the Day

Wash and prepare the greens for salad. Put in plastic bag and
refrigerate.
Prepare vinaigrette dressing, cover, and refrigerate.
Chill salad bowl and plates.
Scrape the corn kernels from the ears. Cover and refrigerate.

4 Hours Before Guests Arrive

Remove from refrigerator various parts of the Timbale (recipe step 17).

Prepare Oysters Poached in Wine (recipe steps 18 and 19).

Set out and bring to room temperature the cheese and butter for the cheese course.

Reassemble pineapple chunks into quartered shells (recipe step 2). Refrigerate.

Chill Champagne and white wines.

1 Hour Before Serving

Preheat oven to 350° F.

Finish preparing the corn.

Prepare the final assembly of the Timbale (recipe step 20).

45 Minutes Before Serving

Put Timbale in oven.

Bake corn.

Warm plates.

Make coffee.

The Sequence of the Dinner

Light candles.

Toss the salad with its dressing just before serving.

Warm bread just before cheese course.

So much for the plan of campaign for the entire menu. If, on the other hand, you want to prepare just one of the dishes, here are the separate recipes, with separate lists of ingredients, so that you can cut your dinner down to your own size, or make up your own menu in your own way.

Kernels of Fresh Corn
Baked with Cream in Scallop Shells

(For 4)

STAPLES
    Salt butter (about 1/4 pound)
    Heavy cream (about 1/3 to 3/4 cup according to condition of corn)
    Fine bread crumbs (about 6 tablespoons)
    Crystal salt
    Freshly ground black pepper

SHOPPING
    Fresh ears of corn (8-10 medium) or out-of-season equivalent

Active Preparation About 15 Minutes—Unsupervised Baking About 45 Minutes

1. If you are using fresh corn, scrape the kernels from the ears (with one of those excellent little machines now available—with the cutter set to release the milk) and make sure to catch both milk and kernels in a mixing bowl. Now carefully check the condition of the cut corn. It should have the appearance and consistency of curdled thick cream. If it is exactly like that, stir into it 1/3 cup of the heavy cream. If it is drier (or wetter) than that, add more (or less) of the cream. Season to taste, with crystal salt and freshly ground black pepper. Preheat the oven to 350° F.

2. Liberally butter 4 large scallop shells and spoon the corn mixture into them, filling them as full as possible. Sprinkle a thin coating of bread crumbs on top and liberally dot with bits of the remaining butter. Place scallop shells on a cookie sheet or metal tray in the center of the oven and bake until corn is reasonably set, usually in about 45 minutes.

The Timbale of King Neptune
(For 4)

Fish Fumet

STAPLES

Lemon juice (1 teaspoon)
Yellow onion (1 medium)
Crystal salt
NOTE: If you are dreadfully short of time, instead of preparing your own excellent *fumet,* compromise with bottled clam juice (1 pint).

SHOPPING

Fish backbones, fins, heads, tails, and trimmings— usually given free by your regular fishmonger—or, in a pinch, use good-quality fish fillets (about 2 pounds, or 2 quarts)
Fresh mushrooms (1/2 pound)
Parsley (1 bunch)
Dry white vermouth (3/4 cup)

Lobster à l'Américaine

STAPLES

Sweet butter (11 tablespoons)
Fish *fumet* (1 cup)
Glace de viande (2 teaspoons) (This is the French name for concentrated meat glaze, which, if you do not have your own, can be bought bottled or canned at fancy food stores.)
Garlic (2 cloves)
Olive oil (4 tablespoons)
Ground arrowroot or cornstarch (about 1 teaspoon)
Bay leaf (1)
Rosemary, tarragon, and thyme (either dried, about 1/4 teaspoon each, or fresh leaves)
Crystal salt
Freshly ground black pepper

SHOPPING

Lobsters, preferably live (2 at 1 1/2 pounds each)
Carrots (4 medium)
Parsley, fresh (1 small bunch —enough for 1/4 cup, chopped)
Shallots (2)
Tomatoes (3 medium)
Tomato paste (1 6-ounce can)
Dry white wine (1 cup)
Cognac (1/2 cup)

Brown Sauce

STAPLES
- Sweet butter (1/2 pound)
- Beef bouillon (6 cups)
- Garlic (2 cloves)
- Yellow onions (2 medium)
- Olive oil (about 1/2 cup)
- Flour, all-purpose (about 1/2 cup)
- Bay leaves (2)
- Thyme
- Crystal salt
- Whole black peppercorns

SHOPPING
- Beef and veal bones, cut up by your butcher for roasting (2 pounds)
- Carrots (2 medium)
- Green celery (3 stalks)
- Parsley (3 or 4 sprigs)
- Tomatoes (3 medium)
- Tomato sauce (1 cup)
- Good dry Sherry (1/2 cup)

Shrimp à la Bordelaise

STAPLES
- Sweet butter (7 tablespoons)
- Brown sauce (2 cups)
- Ground arrowroot or cornstarch (a few tablespoons)
- Olive oil (7 tablespoons)
- Garlic (1 clove)
- Bay leaf (1)
- Tarragon
- Thyme
- Crystal salt
- Freshly ground black pepper

SHOPPING
- Fresh crayfish, if available, or large shrimp, in their shells (16)
- Heavy cream (a few tablespoons)
- Carrots (3 medium)
- Green celery (1 small stalk, with leaves)
- Yellow onions (3 medium)
- Parsley, fresh (2 sprigs)
- Shallots (4)
- Italian plum tomatoes (1 pound)
- Tomato paste (1 to 2 tablespoons)
- Dry white wine (2 cups)
- Cognac (1/4 cup plus 1 to 2 teaspoons)

Shrimp Butter

STAPLES
- Sweet butter (7 tablespoons)
- Bacon, dark-smoked (2 rashers)
- Fish *fumet* (1/2 cup)
- Lemon juice (1 teaspoon)
- Yellow onion (1 medium)
- Bay leaf (1)
- Crystal salt
- Freshly ground black pepper

SHOPPING
- Fresh crayfish, if available, or shrimp, in their shells (1/2 pound, medium-sized)
- Carrot (1 medium)
- Green celery (1 stalk)
- Mushrooms, fresh (1/2 pound, or use the caps reserved from fish *fumet)*
- Parsley, fresh (a few sprigs, enough for 1 tablespoon, chopped)
- Tomatoes (2 small)
- Tomato paste (2 teaspoons)
- Cognac (1/4 cup)
- Dry white vermouth (1/2 cup)

Oysters Poached in Wine

SHOPPING
- Fresh oysters (2 dozen)
- Dry white wine (about 2 cups)

Final Assembly

STAPLES
- Sweet butter (2 tablespoons)

SHOPPING
- Sour cream (4 ounces)
- Button mushrooms (1/2 pound)
- Parsley (several sprigs)
- Fresh tarragon, if available (several sprigs)
- Black truffles (2 or 3)
- Dry white vermouth (about 1/3 cup)

Three Days Ahead—Prepare a Finely Flavored Fish Fumet Active Preparation About 10 Minutes—Unsupervised Simmering About 30 Minutes

1. Wash fish bits and pieces under running cold water and place in 6-quart enameled or stainless-steel soup pot. Do not use aluminum or iron, which will cause discoloring of *fumet*. Peel and slice the onion and add to pot. Cut off stalks from the bunch of parsley, wash them, and add to pot. Do not use parsley leaves, which will turn *fumet* green. Chop mushroom stems and add, reserving the caps for the Shrimp Butter. Also add to pot the 1 teaspoon lemon juice, the 3/4 cup vermouth, 1/2 teaspoon of crystal salt, and enough cold water just to cover everything. Bring up to simmering, skim off any gunk that floats to surface, then continue gentle simmering, uncovered, for 30 minutes.

2. Strain off liquid through a fine sieve, then taste and add more salt, if needed. You will be so impressed by the fine taste of this fish stock that you will never want to be without it for fish aspics, fish sauces, fish soups, and so on. A very convenient way of keeping it is to freeze it into cubes. For our present needs, however, it should be simply refrigerated in a screw-top jar.

Three Days Ahead—Humanely and Painlessly Killing, Cleaning, and Cutting Up the Lobsters in About 20 Minutes

3. Boil lobsters as described in recipe for Lobster à la Newburg. After you have cleaned them and removed the coral and tomalley, they are now going to be cut up in a special way.

4. Without removing the shell, chop off the claws and legs, then chop again into manageable pieces. Chop off front part of head, also tail fin, and throw both away. Chop off remainder of head and then chop in half lengthwise. Now, starting along the underside, chop and cut along the center of the body until there are two long, separate halves. Chop each crosswise into manageable pieces.

Still Three Days Ahead—Classic Preparation of Lobster à l'Américaine in About 45 Minutes

5. Heat up a deep frypan over medium frying heat, putting in the 4 tablespoons of olive oil, 3 tablespoons of the butter, and all

the pieces of lobster, lightly salted and peppered. Stir them around and turn them over, to coat them well on all sides, for hardly more than 2 minutes. Meanwhile, on another burner, heat up a lidded casserole or saucepan. Remove lobster pieces with slotted spoon or kitchen pincers and place in second pan. Warm the 1/2 cup Cognac, pour on, and light it. Let it burn out, shaking the pan, then keep the liquid simmering, while still stirring the pieces around to continue coating them, for about 2 more minutes. Take 1/4 pound butter out of refrigerator to soften.

6. Finely chop the 2 shallots, 4 carrots, and 1/4 cup parsley. Peel and finely mince the 2 cloves garlic. Peel, seed, and dice the 3 tomatoes. Now begin adding to the lobster the shallots and carrots, a pinch or two each of dried rosemary, tarragon, and thyme (or a few fresh leaves of each), the bay leaf, crumbled, and the garlic and tomatoes. Stir everything around and continue gently simmering, uncovered. In a mixing bowl, work together the tomato paste, and 2 teaspoons of *glace de viande,* the cup of dry white wine, and the cup of fish *fumet,* then gently stir into lobster. Turn up heat slightly, so that everything now bubbles merrily and sauce begins to reduce and concentrate flavors. Add the parsley and keep merry bubbling going until sauce shows definite signs of reducing, usually in about 20 minutes. Meanwhile, in a small mixing bowl, work together into a smooth paste the red coral, the green tomalley, the softened butter, and about 1 teaspoon of ground arrowroot or cornstarch.

7. When sauce is reduced and is beginning to have a fine flavor, fish out lobster pieces and put aside. Now boil sauce hard, to concentrate flavors even more, mashing down vegetables with a wooden spoon to provide a solid body. When everything is smooth and the flavor is coming up to brilliance, turn off heat and quickly work in the coral-tomalley mixture, until sauce is slightly thickened. Turn off heat, put back lobster pieces, stir them around to cover with sauce, then store everything until the evening of the dinner in a tightly-lidded container in the coldest part of the refrigerator. This completes the first day's work. The two days of waiting will mature and improve the flavor.

*Two Days Ahead—Classic Preparation of Basic Brown Sauce
—Active Preparation About 30 Minutes—Unsupervised Simmering About 3 Hours*

8. This is another of the basic techniques of fine cooking—the essential and primary ingredient of almost all the aromatic dark sauces for grilled and roasted meats, for game animals and birds, and for certain highly-flavored dishes with fish and poultry. Once you have mastered the method of making it, you will always want to have some of it in cubes in your freezer. Preheat the oven to 450° F. Prepare the 2 pounds of beef and veal bones, by rubbing olive oil into each piece, then dipping in flour to coat on all sides. Place in open, lightly greased roasting pan in oven until bones are browned to a good dark color—usually in about 30 minutes.

9. Meanwhile, chop the 2 carrots and 2 onions and hold. Peel, seed, and dice the 3 tomatoes, coarsely chop 3 stalks green celery and 3 or 4 good sprigs parsley, peel and finely mince the 2 garlic cloves. In a 3-quart saucepan, melt the 1/2 pound of butter, and add the carrots and onions, sautéing them until lightly browned. At the same time in another saucepan, heat up the 6 cups beef bouillon, and when it boils pour it into the vegetables, making sure, with a wire whisk, that it is perfectly amalgamated. Then whisk in the cup of tomato sauce, the tomatoes, celery, parsley, the 2 bay leaves, crumbled, 1/2 teaspoon dried thyme, the garlic, 1 teaspoon crystal salt, and 10 whole black peppercorns. Let it all simmer, uncovered, until bones are ready.

10. Put the browned bones into the sauce and keep everything simmering, now covered, for about 3 hours. The bones will give a deep, rich, brown color to the sauce. Before using it in the Bordelaise sauce, check seasoning, strain, and add 1/2 cup good dry Sherry. Any part of the sauce left over may be refrigerated, tightly covered, for a few days, or frozen into cubes and kept more or less indefinitely.

*Two Days Ahead—Classic Preparation of Shrimp
à la Bordelaise—About 1 Hour*

11. This should be made, for absolute perfection, with fresh crayfish, but since they are so seldom available, a very fair compromise is achieved with 16 large, fresh shrimp. Wash, remove heads, but do not shell the shrimp, then set them aside. Finely dice

the 3 carrots and 3 onions and set them aside. In a heavy frypan over quite high heat, warm up the 7 tablespoons of olive oil and quickly sauté the shellfish, after adding salt and pepper, until they have turned a good red color. Take them out at once and reserve them, keeping them warm. In a sauté pan over medium heat, melt 4 tablespoons of the butter, add the carrots and onions, and the 4 shallots and the clove of garlic, all finely minced, then put in the shellfish, stir them around, and flame with 1/4 cup of the Cognac. Remove from heat.

12. In a second saucepan, over medium heat, combine the 2 cups white wine with the 2 cups brown sauce, then work in 1 or 2 tablespoons of tomato paste, the 1 pound Italian plum tomatoes, peeled, seeded, and diced, the small stalk of celery with its leaves, 2 sprigs parsley, 1 whole bay leaf, 1/2 teaspoon each of dried tarragon and thyme, with salt and pepper, to taste. Pour over the contents of the sauté pan and let simmer, covered, for not more than 10 minutes. Then fish out the bay leaf, the celery stalk, and the parsley, and discard them. Now, finally, thicken the sauce by working in, tablespoon by tablespoon, the arrowroot or cornstarch diluted with a little of the heavy cream, until it is thick enough to just coat the spoon. Check the seasonings once more, melting in the final 3 tablespoons of butter and adding a last teaspoon or two of Cognac, to your taste. Transfer the shellfish and sauce from the cooking pan to a tightly lidded container and store in coldest part of the refrigerator until the evening of the dinner. This ends the second day's work.

The Day Before—Classic Preparation of a Shrimp Butter in About 1 1/2 Hours

13. Again, classically, this could be made with crayfish tails, but it is just about as good with medium-sized fresh shrimp. Wash about 1/2 pound of them, leaving them in their shells, then set them aside. Prepare a basic French *mirepoix*—another basic high cuisine technique, usefully repeatable in many different dishes. Finely chop and mix together in a bowl the carrot, the onion, 1 stalk of green celery, and the 2 rashers bacon, and also add 1 crumbled bay leaf. Heat up 1 tablespoon of the butter in a small sauté pan and just soften this bacon-vegetable mixture, adding crystal salt and freshly ground black pepper, to taste. Now add the 1/2 cup of dry white vermouth and simmer, uncovered, for about 5 more minutes.

14. Finely dice the mushroom caps reserved from the fish *fumet;* peel, seed, and dice the 2 tomatoes, and chop 1 tablespoon parsley. In another sauté pan, heat up 2 more tablespoons butter, and as soon as it has reached gentle frying temperature, put in the mushroom caps and let them soak up the butter for hardly more than 2 minutes. Add the tomatoes to the mushrooms, also the shrimp, still in their shells, plus the 1/4 cup of Cognac. Flame it and, when the fire dies down, add the lemon juice and chopped parsley, then blend the entire contents of this sauté pan into the bacon-vegetable mixture. Turn up heat slightly, so that liquid bubbles merrily to reduce sauce and concentrate flavors. Help the evaporation by frequent and gentle stirring. When liquid has almost disappeared, stir in 1/2 cup of your earlier fish *fumet,* plus 2 teaspoons of tomato paste and, according to your taste, more crystal salt and freshly ground black pepper. When everything is again merrily bubbling, fish out all the shrimp and put them in readiness, on a wooden cutting board. While you work on them, the sauté pan should continue bubbling.

15. Shell the shrimp and put shells and tails into a mortar. Pound the shells very hard with the pestle, until every last drop of juice is extracted from them. Put this juice, plus the broken-up shells, back into the sauté pan. Forget the shrimps for the moment. Turn up heat under sauté pan and boil hard, stirring continuously, for a couple more minutes, then strain entire contents through a fine sieve, pressing firmly down with a wooden spoon, to extract all the aromatic juices, leaving the solids worn out and almost dry. Even so, you may not get more than 1/4 to 1/3 cup of the highly concentrated, brilliantly flavored juice essence. This is the pure gold for which you have been so laboriously planning.

16. Now back to the shrimp. Chop their flesh coarsely and put them, load by load, into the mortar, pounding them with the pestle to a smooth paste, at the same time working in, bit by bit, the remaining butter. Finally, blend into this smoothest of pastes the liquid essence from the sauté pan. You should now have an utterly superb Shrimp Butter. Resist the temptation to spread it on rounds of thin toast and consume it immediately! It must be spooned into a tightly lidded screw-top jar and refrigerated overnight, so that it can develop and ripen its flavors. Here Endeth the Labors of the Day Before.

On the Day—About 4 Hours Before the Guests Arrive—Active Preparation About 30 Minutes—Unsupervised Holding About 3 1/2 Hours

17. Take out from the refrigerator all the various parts of the great dish and let them come to room temperature: the Lobster à l'Américaine, the Shrimp à la Bordelaise, and the Shrimp Butter.

18. Now these three must be increased to four by the preparation of the Oysters Poached in Wine. Wash the 2 dozen oysters under running cold water and, with a stiff wire brush, scrub off any barnacles, impacted sand, or seaweed. Prepare to poach them in a largish soup pot with a tightly fitting lid. Pour into it 2 cups of dry white wine, or a bit more—just enough to cover the bottom of the pot about 1/2 to 3/4 of an inch deep. Now carefully stack the oysters in the pot, each with its curved shell downward, then place over high heat and rapidly bring wine to a rolling boil. As soon as pot is filled with steam, clamp on lid tightly, leaving heat full on, to build up internal steam pressure. After about 3 minutes, give pot a shake or two, to encourage oysters to open. After 5 minutes, lift lid and, using kitchen tongs, lift out each oyster that has opened and place it to cool on work counter. Replace lid, shake pot again, then reopen every few minutes and lift out more oysters, until every last one has opened. Then turn off heat.

19. As soon as oysters are cool enough to handle, force off flat top shell and throw away. Leave each oyster, now plump from absorbing wine, resting comfortably in its curved, lower shell. Let them stand at room temperature with the other parts for about 3 1/2 hours, waiting for the final assembly.

1 Hour Before Serving—Final Assembly in About 15 Minutes—Unsupervised Reheating in Oven About 45 Minutes

20. Preheat oven to 350° F. The dish is finally to be assembled in a handsome large ceramic or earthenware *timbale,* or casserole—fairly shallow (say, not more than 4 to 6 inches deep), reasonably wide (so that the orderly beauty of the various colorful ingredients will be perfectly displayed to the guests at table), and most important of all, with a very tightly fitting lid. The *timbale,* of course, must not be so large that it will not fit, for the final

reheating, into the oven. In your mind's eye, divide the bottom circle of the *timbale* into halves. Across one place the pieces of lobster, still in their shells, then spread their Sauce à l'Américaine evenly around and between them. Across the other half place the whole shrimp also still in their shells, enclosed and surrounded by their Sauce à la Bordelaise. Here already is a brilliant contrast of colorings. As the next full layer, carefully put in the oysters, still in their lower shells, then sprinkle them with a few drops of their poaching wine. Quickly sauté the 1/2 pound of button mushroom caps in the 2 tablespoons butter and spread them around in the odd spaces of the *timbale*. Next dot everything, here and there, with the Shrimp Butter. In a small mixing bowl, lightly beat together 1/2 cup (4 ounces) of sour cream with just enough dry white vermouth to make the cream thickly runny. Dribble it over the oysters and in odd corners. Finally, decorate everything with, first, a dozen or so thin slices of black truffles; second, several handsome sprigs of bright-green parsley and, if possible, some sprigs of fresh tarragon. Now clamp on the lid very tightly. It must not, under any circumstances, be opened again until the *timbale* is before the guests at table. Place it in the center of the oven and leave everything to get hot, so that the various delicate flavors can be marvelously amalgamated, for about 45 minutes.

Serving At Table

21. Bring in the *timbale,* still unopened, placing it, if at all possible, right in the center of the dining table, where the lid can be lifted with maximum ceremony. When the moment of truth arrives and you do finally lift the lid, I predict that the bouquet will be so extraordinary that your guests will virtually swoon with anticipation and delight. This is not, of course, a very conservative and formal dish. It is a meal *par excellence* for adventurous eaters, prepared to use their fingers on the shells and to pile up the debris on large, extra soup plates. Give them plenty of chunks of freshly baked sourdough or French bread to mop up the irresistible sauces. Let them have small nutcrackers with which to attack the lobster claws. Then let everyone fall to!

Pineapple Marinated in Sweet White Wine
(For 4)

STAPLES
White sugar, fine grind (a few tablespoons, if necessary)

SHOPPING
Fresh pineapple (1 whole)
Sweet white wine, either inexpensive French Sauternes or California-type, say a Château La Salle (1/2 bottle)

The Day Before—Active Preparation in About 15 Minutes—Marination Overnight

1. Using a large, sharp, heavy-duty knife, cut the pineapple downward through the leaves into 4 quarters, so that each has a section of leaves as, so to speak, its handle (see illustration). Now, using a small, pointed knife, perform the necessary neat surgery on each separate quarter. Lay it on its skinny back, holding the leafy handle in your left hand. First cut off the woody core all along the peak of the flesh. Next make a series of downward cuts, each about 1/2-inch apart, to divide the flesh into bite-sized sections, but do not cut right down through the skin. Now carefully cut underneath each triangular section, so as to release it completely from its skinny base. Remember that the base is to remain whole as the serving dish on which the triangular fruit sections will be brought to table. When you have operated on all 4 quarters, put all the triangular chunks into a storage bowl, cover them with the sweet wine and refrigerate overnight. If you have a sweet tooth, you may add some of the sugar.

1 Hour Before Serving

2. Reassemble the triangular chunks onto their respective skinny bases. If you have cut them all to the same size, they will reassemble easily in any position. Dribble a little of the marinating wine on top of each and, if you wish, sprinkle on a bit more sugar. Each diner gets one of the quarters and picks off his chunks with a small fruit fork. There is an extraordinary balance between the tart freshness of the pineapple flesh and the sweetness of the marinating wine. Each seems to magnify the best qualities of the other. Serve a sweet wine—preferably of a slightly different type, with a contrasting character—as the accompaniment.

CHAPTER 7

BUT YOU DON'T HAVE TO SPEND ALL THAT MUCH MONEY AND TIME

*Ideas and Imagination Instead of
Imported Ingredients*

The conspicuous consumption of luxuriously expensive foods is not at all essential for a memorable dinner party. Nor is it necessary to wow one's guests with exotic and rare ingredients. The most basic and truest skills of the amateur chef are proved when he takes quite ordinary raw materials and balances them so brilliantly—both within each dish and from course to course—that the memorable qualities of the whole dinner rise far above the sum of its individual parts. I believe that the following menu firmly proves this point. It is based on a dinner I once tried to serve to Ernest Hemingway.

It was to me a memorable occasion because I lost my temper. My friend Deems Taylor had launched me into a whirlwind of anticipatory preparations by announcing that Ernest Hemingway was briefly visiting New York and that the great man would be willing to come to dinner at my home on the following Friday. There was, however, one proviso. Hemingway was, under doctor's orders, on a strict diet and must be served only lean meat, green vegetables, and fresh fruit. I couldn't possibly offer *that* to the other guests I would invite to what I hoped would be a scintillating party. How could any party scintillate without decently rich food? It was springtime and I found a baby suckling pig. I stuffed its little belly with chestnuts, pistachios, raisins, apples, nectarines, and pears and filled the spaces in between with a delicate mixture of lightly aromatic meats, enriched with butter, cream, and eggs. It was baked to a brown-gold and the rind was as crisp as a cracker. The piglet came to table with a bright red apple in his mouth, green marbles for eyes, a watercress chain around his neck, and a crisp curl to his little tail.

I also did my very best for the guest of honor. In fact, I invented a dish for him. I had my butcher cut an extra thick round *tournedos* of prime beef filet mignon and gently poached it in an individual casserole, of beautifully glazed earthenware, with Armagnac, vermouth, and dry Madeira, baby mushrooms, young green beans, and tiny white onions. Hemingway was charming, although slightly condescending. His casserole was placed before him, he lifted the lid, and the aromatic bouquet made me quite sure that he was well served. He cut the first piece of beef, tasted it, and smacked his lips. Then he looked across the table at the roast piglet and, announcing that he was a bit tired of lean beef, asked if he might have some of the pork, together with all the creamed vegetables and pan-fried potatoes that went with it. He wasn't on a doctor's diet. He was just slimming. I could not suppress an audible snort. I virtually snatched his wine-poached beef from under his nose and slapped it on the floor at my feet. It was the best dinner that my German Shepherd bitch, Ñusta, had ever had. She licked the casserole clean.

The dish I invented for Ernest Hemingway is the main dish of the following section.

Menu for a Much Less Expensive Dinner for Four

Ratatouille à la Niçoise	**A fine Alsace Rosé de Pinot Noir*
Ernest Hemingway's Beef en Casserole with Puree of Chestnuts or Fluffy Mashed Potatoes or Steamed Saffron Rice	**Beaujolais Red, Côte de Brouilly*
Green Salad Vinaigrette	
A Selection of Cheeses	
Lemon-Nut Tart	
Coffee	**Armagnac*

The ratatouille of southern France now seems to have caught on in the United States to such an extent that it may soon be equal in popularity to gazpacho and paella. But most people still know it as a sort of ragout of hot vegetables served as an accompaniment to the main dish. It can also be an attractively refreshing opening to a meal, when it is prepared the day before and its various tastes and textures are blended and matured overnight.

People who can never spare a single good word for rosé wine—who claim that it is not "good with everything" but is "good for nothing"—should realize that there are a few rosés of truly remarkable character in their own right. They are neither hotted-up whites nor toned-down reds. They stand firmly on their own special quality. Among this small company, one of the best is the unique wine made in the virtually all-white vineyards of Alsace from a small planting of the Black Pinot grape of Burgundy. It is called simply Rosé de Pinot Noir and is made by only one firm, the ancient house of Lorentz in the lovely village of Bergheim. It is one of a number of noble or fine rosés (others might be the Château de Tigné from the Loire or a first-class Tavel from the Rhône or a top-label Gamay, Grenache, or Grignolino rosé from California) robust enough to balance the strong personality of the ratatouille.

Once you have mastered the technique of gently poaching a good piece of beef in a blend of wines and spirits held prisoner in a tightly lidded casserole—so that the fruitiness of the drinks works its way into the meat while the protein and vegetable juices combine into a superb sauce—you can apply this flexible technique to all kinds of foods. Not only the best cuts of the four main meats but also game animals and birds, as well as fish and poultry, can be substituted for the beef. Whenever, for example, a hunting friend brings me a wild duck of somewhat questionable age, I never take the risk of roasting it, but always poach it in this way, so that I can keep it simmering for as long as it takes to tenderize its possibly tough meat. One can also, of course, use cuts of different beef and vary the blends of the alcoholic liquids and of the combinations of the accompanying vegetables.

With such a nicely winy dish, one need not—in fact, one should not—choose a big and heavy wine. A truly fine Beaujolais is the ideal partner. But a truly fine Beaujolais is often hard to find among the bewildering array of nondescript, noncharacterful, nonsatisfactory, nonentity wines that flow from that bottomless well of mass vinification. More "Beaujolais" is sold in the restaurants and shops of Paris alone than is ever produced in the Beaujolais district. One basic rule, worth learning by heart, is that some of the best of Beaujolais—some of its most elegant and subtle wines—are produced in and labeled with the name of the village commune of Brouilly. Among these special wines, my favorites for this menu would include the Château Thivin, the Château de la Chaize, or the Côte de Brouilly of Jean de Besse. The production of these wines is small. They are always hard to find. They are worth the search.

The pouring of the new Beaujolais will, of course, be suspended during the salad (since the vinegar dressing would clash with the wine). Then the bottles can be brought back and finished, with the added dimension that always comes from tasting wine with cheese.

Finally, the dessert is one of the special favorites of my own household and, because lemons and nuts are almost always available, this tartly fruity pie can be equally at home on the coldest or hottest of days.

Campaign Plan for the Preparation of the Meal

Two Days Ahead

Check this staple list and add the needed items to the following shopping list:

HERB AND SPICE CABINET
Basil, if fresh not available
Coriander seeds, whole
Mustard, English dry
Crystal salt
Black peppercorns

OTHER ITEMS
Olive oil (about 1 1/4 cups)
White-wine vinegar (4 table-spoons)
Flour, all-purpose (3/4 cup)
Dark-brown sugar (1 cup)
Fine-grind white sugar (several tablespoons)
Sugar (for the coffee)
Coffee

FRUITS AND VEGETABLES
Garlic (4 cloves)
Yellow onions (3 medium)

DAIRY
Sweet butter (at least 1/2 pound)
Eggs (2 large)
Cream (for the coffee)

WINES AND SPIRITS
Dry Madeira (1 cup)
Dry white vermouth (1 cup)
Armagnac (1 cup—more for after dinner)

NOTE: Check the wines on the menu and if you do not have them, buy the current vintages.

The Day Before

Shopping list (plus any needed staple items from above)

DAIRY
Heavy cream (1 cup)

GROCERIES
Almonds, blanched (4 ounces)
Italian plum tomatoes
(1-pound, 1-ounce can)

BAKERY
French bread (2 loaves)

MEAT
Thick individual rounds of
prime beef, not too soft, best
cut from filet or sirloin strip
(4), or a single Chateau-
briand for 4 (2-4 pounds,
according to greed)

CHEESE
A selection for the dinner

FRUITS AND VEGETABLES
Apple, tart, preferably
greening, Rome Beauty
(1 medium)
Lemons (3)
Green beans (1/2 pound)
Carrots, baby (8)
Eggplants (2 medium)
Mushrooms, white button
(1/2 pound)
Onions, small white (12)
Shallots (2)
Green peppers (3 medium)
Zucchini (3 medium)
Greens for salad
Basil, fresh if available
(1 bunch)
Fresh chives (1 small bunch)
Parsley (1 bunch)
Watercress (1 small bunch)

After the Shopping

Start making ice and continue until you have enough.
Prepare the Ratatouille (recipe steps 1-5). Refrigerate in covered
serving dish until dinnertime next day.
Set the table and set out all serving dishes.

Advance Preparation in the Morning of the Day

Prepare Lemon-Nut Tart (recipe steps 1-3).
Prepare and wash greens for salad. When completely dry, put in
plastic bag in refrigerator.

Advance Preparation in the Afternoon of the Day

Prepare the vinaigrette dressing (except for chives and parsley);
cover, and refrigerate (see recipe, page 67).
Prepare the starch accompaniment to the meal (the pureed chestnuts, the mashed potatoes, or the saffron rice).

Three Hours Before the Guests Arrive

Set out and bring to room temperature cheeses and butter for the cheese course.

Chill the rosé wine, set out red wine and Armagnac.

Chop enough chives and parsley for Ernest Hemingway's Beef en Casserole and the vinaigrette dressing; cover, and set aside.

Prepare the Beef en Casserole (recipe steps 1-3).

Warm plates.

Make coffee.

The Sequence of the Dinner

Light candles.

Take out rosé wine and put into ice bucket to chill.

Open the red wine.

Warm Armagnac and complete Beef en Casserole (recipe step 4).

Warm Lemon-Nut Tart.

Toss the salad with its dressing just before serving.

Warm bread just before the cheese course.

So much for the plan of campaign for the entire menu. If, on the other hand, you want to prepare just one of the dishes, here are the separate recipes with separate lists of ingredients, so that you can cut your dinner down to your own size, or make up your own menu in your own way.

Ratatouille à la Niçoise

(For 4)

STAPLES
Olive oil (1/2 cup)
Yellow onions (3 medium)
Garlic (2 cloves)
Dried basil (only if fresh not available)
Whole coriander seeds
Crystal salt
Freshly ground black pepper

SHOPPING
Eggplants (2 medium)
Green peppers (3 medium)
Zucchini (3 medium)
Fresh basil (1 bunch)
Parsley (1 bunch)
Italian peeled plum tomatoes (1-pound, 1-ounce can)

The Day Before—Active Preparation About
20 Minutes—Cooking 50 Minutes

1. Put into a casserole or stewpot with a tightly fitting lid the 1/2 cup of olive oil, but do not heat it up until the vegetables have been prepared.

2. Peel the 3 onions, coarsely chop, and hold separately. Finely mince the 2 cloves garlic and hold in a small covered jar. Remove the central seed pods from the 3 green peppers and cut into bite-sized chunks. Cut off stem ends of the 2 eggplants and also chunk without peeling. Chunk the 3 zucchini without peeling.

3. Now heat up the oil in the pot and quickly sauté the chopped onions until just transparent. Now add the chunked vegetables and the garlic. Stir around to coat with oil, turn heat down to simmering, cover, and gently bubble them in their own juices for 40 minutes. Almost no attention is required, except occasional stirring and checking to make sure that the juices keep bubbling to maintain steam inside the pot. Measure 1 1/2 teaspoons of whole coriander into a mortar, coarsely grind, and hold. Chop a small handful each of parsley and fresh basil, if available.

After 40 Minutes of Bubbling

4. Vegetables in pot will now be swimming in a good deal of juice. Gently stir them around once more, then add the canned tomatoes with their juice, the coriander, and salt and pepper to taste. Blend everything well together. The next objective is gently to boil away all excess water so that the flavors are concentrated. Leave lid off from this point onward. Turn up heat slightly so that the bubbling continues. Gently move vegetables around to give moisture a chance to escape for about 10 minutes. Now gently blend in chopped parsley and fresh basil (or 1 teaspoon dried basil).

5. When ratatouille is done put it into a covered icebox container and refrigerate overnight. Next day serve slightly chilled but not ice-cold.

Ernest Hemingway's Beef en Casserole
(For 4)

STAPLES
  Sweet butter (about 10 table-
    spoons)
  Olive oil (about 4 tablespoons)
  Garlic (1 clove)
  Crystal salt
  Freshly ground black pepper

SHOPPING
  Individual rounds of prime
    beef, 1-1 1/2 inches thick,
    not too soft, cut from filet or
    sirloin strip (4) or a single
    Chateaubriand for 4 (2-4
    pounds, according to greed)
  Green beans (1/2 pound)
  Onions, small white (about 1
    dozen)
  Carrots, baby (8)
  Mushrooms, white button (1/2
    pound)
  Shallots (2)
  Chives (1 small bunch)
  Watercress (1 small bunch)
  Madeira, dry Sercial (1 cup)
  Vermouth, dry white (1 cup)
  Armagnac brandy (1 cup)

About 3 Hours Before Serving—Active Preparation of Mushrooms About 10 Minutes—Unsupervised Cooking About 10 Minutes

This is the method of preparing mushrooms known in the French cuisine as *à la Provençale*. It is one of the best of all ways and can be used, quite apart from its incorporation into this dish, for plain mushrooms on toast, or in dozens of different variations. You can use more or less garlic, according to your taste.

1. In a suitably sized saucepan over low heat begin melting 1/4 pound of the butter while you finely mince the clove of garlic. Then stir garlic into butter, cover saucepan, turn down heat to gentle simmering, and let garlic be absorbed for about 2 minutes. Meanwhile, wipe clean the 1/2 pound of mushrooms (never wash them), trimming ends of stems as required, but leaving each mushroom whole. Put them into the hot garlic butter and stir around gently with a wooden spoon until all are well coated.

Sprinkle on salt and pepper to taste. Continue the gentle stirring for about 2 or 3 minutes. The object is to encourage the mushrooms to expel their internal water and to absorb the aromatic butter. Now put on lid and let mushrooms steam in their own juices for about 10 minutes. The time is not critical—they may be left a few minutes longer.

About 2 1/2 Hours Before Serving—Active Preparation of Main Dish About 30 Minutes—Entirely Unsupervised Cooking About 2 Hours

2. While mushrooms are still steaming, prepare remaining aromatic herbs and vegetables. Finely chop enough of the chives and watercress leaves to make 1/2 cup and set aside. Other vegetables may be assembled together in a single bowl: the 1/2 pound of green beans, topped and tailed; the 8 whole baby carrots, lightly scraped if necessary; the dozen whole white onions, peeled. Finely mince the 2 shallots and hold separately. Preheat oven to 200° F. Into a fairly large sauté pan, over medium frying heat, melt 2 tablespoons of the butter with 2 tablespoons of the olive oil, then very lightly sauté the beans, carrots, and onions. Remove them with a slotted spoon and hold them. (From this point onward, it is assumed that you will use 4 individual casseroles with 4 separate rounds of beef, but the dish is equally effective with a single piece of meat in a large casserole, and for this the changes in instructions are obvious.) Choose 4 casseroles (or French *cocottes*) with tightly fitting lids. The modern, handsomely colored enameled cast-iron types are ideal. Set them to heat up gently on top burners of stove. Pour into each 1 ounce of the Armagnac, 2 ounces of the Madeira, and 2 ounces of the vermouth, then let them come up slowly to gentlest simmering. With the heel of the hand, press crystal salt and black pepper, to taste, into both sides of each of the 4 rounds of beef. Add more butter and olive oil, as needed, to the sauté pan, turning up heat slightly, quickly brown each beef round on all sides. By this time, wines in casseroles should be gently bubbling. Place a round of beef in each casserole and fill spaces around and above it with equally divided portions of green beans, carrots, onions, and sautéed mushrooms. Sprinkle equal quantities of the minced shallots over the contents of each casserole. Turn off heat and tightly clamp on the 4 lids. (Incidentally, if you are using ceramic casseroles and lids are not entirely tightly fitting,

it is a good plan to make a flour and water paste and use this to seal lids completely. Paste can be easily broken and scraped off just before serving. The success of this dish depends on preventing the aromatic internal steam from escaping in the oven.)

3. Immediately place the 4 hot casseroles in the center of the oven and let them cook, in the gentlest possible and most private manner, with never even a thought of lifting the lid to see what is happening, for all of 2 hours.

Serving at Table

4. Just before serving, heat up in a small copper pan 4 more ounces of the Armagnac until it is just hot to the tip of the finger. Do not open the lids until the casseroles are safely before your guests. When lids finally are lifted, the bouquet of the meat and vegetable juices mingled with the aroma of the wines and brandy will be magnificent. Pour equal quantities of the warmed Armagnac into each casserole and flame. When flames die down, sprinkle chopped chives and watercress onto each casserole.

FINAL NOTE: If you feel you need a starch accompaniment to this dish, serve a light puree of chestnuts, or fluffy mashed potatoes, or saffron rice.

Lemon-Nut Tart
(For 4)

STAPLES
  Sweet butter (5 tablespoons)
  Eggs (2 large)
  Lemons, whole (3)
  Flour, all-purpose (3/4 cup after sifting, plus extra for flouring board)
  Dark-brown sugar (1 cup, tightly packed)
  White sugar, fine-grind (several tablespoons to taste)
  Crystal salt

SHOPPING
  Almonds, blanched (4 ounces)
  Apple, tart, preferably greening, Rome beauty (1 medium)
  Heavy cream (1 cup)

Prepared Ahead and Slightly Reheated—Active Preparation
About 30 Minutes—Unsupervised Baking About 30 Minutes

1. Preheat oven to 425° F. Prepare piecrust dough. Put the 3/4 cup sifted flour into a mixing bowl, sprinkle over it 1/4 teaspoon salt, cut into it the 5 tablespoons butter until you have the texture of coarse cornmeal. Then work it into a dough, gradually adding, as needed, 2 to 3 tablespoons of cold water. Turn out onto floured pastry board, roll out, and line an 8-inch pie plate, or layer pan. Thoroughly prick bottom of shell to prevent it from puffing and bake, in center of oven, until firm and lightly browned—usually in 10 to 15 minutes.

2. Meanwhile, prepare filling. Carefully peel the 3 lemons, removing all the white skin, then cut flesh into neat, thin slices and set aside. Using coarse cutter of grinder, grind almonds and put into mixing bowl. Core, but do not peel, the apple, cut into chunks, and also pass through grinder, adding it to almonds. Also add the 1 cup of brown sugar and mix all three thoroughly, then hold. Put the 1 cup of heavy cream into another mixing bowl, break into it the 2 whole eggs, and hold.

3. As soon as pie shell is ready, evenly spread across its bottom the apple-nut-sugar mixture. Next, on top of this, neatly lay the lemon slices in circles. Lightly whisk the egg-cream mixture, only just enough to mix thoroughly, then gently pour over lemon slices. Sprinkle with a couple of tablespoons of the fine-grind sugar, then bake, in center of oven, until set and lightly browned—usually in 25 to 35 minutes.

4. This luscious pie tastes best when served lukewarm. If it has been made earlier in the day, it should be gently and slightly reheated. Serve with more fine-grind sugar, if guests are sweet-toothed.

CHAPTER 8

AN INEXPENSIVE
AND SIMPLE PARTY SUPPER

The Practice of True Economy

At least a dozen times a year, a telephone call forces the difficult decision. It's almost the end of the month and I am wildly overspent on my food and drink entertainment budget. I am determined to get it balanced by the last day of the month—or bust! I am seeing what I can do with the bits and pieces left in the icebox and the remaining jars and packages on the shelves of the store cupboard. For myself, I am neither underfed nor unhappy with my concoctions of eggs, spaghetti sauces, rich soups boiled down from the ham bone, slightly improper cheese fondues, wildly extravagant mixtures of oddments—good honest stuff, but hardly party fare.

Then—on Friday evening—the telephone rings. Friends whom I haven't seen for three years have just arrived in town, entirely unexpectedly, for the weekend. While my voice greets them with genuine affection, my mind flashes instantaneously back and forward. The last time I visited them their hospitality was overwhelming. At this unfortunate financial moment, if I were to try to repay them half as well I would need to take out a bank loan. Yet I haven't the heart to say, "Oh, I'm terribly sorry! I'm leaving in ten minutes on a trip." I cut through the dilemma by inviting them to Saturday night supper—with the following budget party menu.

This menu illustrates some of my basic rules for eating well and entertaining dramatically even at low cost. The Greek *tarama,* carp caviar, the Hungarian paprika chicken, and the Indian *Kachumar* Salad with *Raita* are classic dishes of three relatively nonaffluent countries, where the agricultural life is still strong and where the wives of cattlemen, farmers, and fishermen have learned, over the centuries, how to eat well, not with imported luxury foods, but by skillful preparation of the simplest of raw materials at hand. In other words, when I want to find dishes that are inexpensive yet outstandingly good, I look for the country fare of the farm regions of the world.

All the foods on this menu have the charm, richness, and simplicity of dishes not hurriedly "invented" in a white-tiled test kitchen, but gradually evolved and improved from generation to generation of loving home cooks. Every ingredient is economical. Yet the precise combination of all of them provides a meal that is rich in aromatic interest, in luxurious silkiness on the tongue, and in excellently balanced nutritional value. They involve relatively little time in the kitchen, they can be prepared in advance, and any part remaining at the end of the meal will be equally good when brought out again the next day. In short, these are dishes that delight me again and again by their harmony and variety of natural flavors.

Menu for a Simple Party Supper for Four with California Wines

Greek Taramasalata

**Sonoma Valley, Pinot Chardonnay*

Hungarian Chicken Paprikás
  with Vegetables in Season
  and Johanna's Corn Bread

**Napa Valley, Cabernet Sauvignon*

Indian Kachumar Hot Salad
  with Cold Cucumber Raita

A Selection of Cheeses

American Orange Ambrosia

**Livermore Valley, Muscat de Frontignon*

Coffee

**California Flame Tokay Brandy*

The Greek *tarama* (carp roe) caviar seems to be catching on so rapidly across the United States that it is now being prepared commercially by a number of American companies, in addition to the several versions imported from Greece. It is universally available in Greek groceries (usually scooped out of a barrel, as if it were pink ice cream) and is widely available, in jars, in fancy food shops. It is too salty to eat as is, but whips up, with oil, in an electric blender into a marvelously aromatic kind of mayonnaise, which is then served as a dip for vegetable tidbits.

If we agree that there has been a wine "explosion" in the United States during the last ten years, we must also concede that part of the boom has been caused by the "explosion" in the quality of American wines. Especially in California (which, in terms of the excellence and volume of its production, is now one of the major wine regions of the world), where the ideal soil of the rolling hillsides and the even climate and soothing Pacific mists encourage the abundant and luxurious growth of the noblest wine-grape varieties of Europe, there is now a wide choice of labels available at every price level, from the simple equivalent of the *vin de carafe* as served in every bistro in France up to the finest of vintage-year, vineyard-bottled reds and whites of truly noble character and personality. No intelligent, reasonable, and unbiased wine connoisseur, of course, expects to find in California a Château Lafite, a Château Latour, a Domaine de la Romanée-Conti, a Château d'Yquem, or a Schloss Johannisberg. These are among the dozen or so unchallenged giants of the world of wine. But the world's supremely great vineyards make up much less than 1 percent of world production, and in every other class California now competes in fair and equal measure. The anatomy of American wines in general (and California wines in particular) will be discussed in practical terms for the wine stocking of the home library in chapters 19 through 24. Now I shall simply suggest a few suitable and alternative California wines of the basic geographic and varietal types for this particular menu.

The Pinot Chardonnay grape produces, in France, the great white wines of Chablis and of the "Golden Slope" of southern Burgundy, including the Meursaults and the Montrachets. It grows beautifully in California and makes, to my mind, the most elegant, most luscious, most powerful in personality, and generally the best of American white wines. If you are lucky enough to live in California and can drive out weekends to the vineyards around San Francisco, you may be able to pick up a few bottles of Pinot Chardonnay from the small family-owned vineyards, where the demand is so great and the production so limited that the wines seldom get farther than the thirsty throats in the San

Francisco area. Among these noble American Pinot Chardonnay whites I have warm memories of tasting those of Freemark Abbey, Hanzell, Heitz, and Stony Hill. But if you live in another state, as I do, you must rely on the larger California producers able to ship their wines to most or all parts of the country. Among these I have tasted some fine Pinot Chardonnay examples from Almadén, Beaulieu, Buena Vista, the Christian Brothers, Inglenook, Martini, Mondavi, and Wente.

The recipe for my paprika chicken was discovered on a walking tour of Hungary. I was exploring the magnificently forested shores of Lake Balaton. I stayed in farmhouses, eating the peasant foods and drinking the local wines of that gastronomically rich region. At one lakeside village I found an old widow who was a superb cook. Her Chicken Paprikás was almost perfect in its simplicity—a delicate balance of herbs and sweet spices. Paying my respects to the old lady in her kitchen and battling the language barrier, I asked her if she would give me her recipe. As she described to me her method, her voice expressed pride, dedication, and devotion to the earth that provided her raw materials. She discussed what kind and age of chicken was best, what sort of herbs she picked in the fields to go into the dish, how she ground her fresh paprika by hand. Slowly, with difficulty, I translated and wrote down her recipe. I have never found a better version.

Years later, I gave the recipe to the French chef of one of the New York men's clubs. Within a few weeks, lunching with one of the members, I saw *Poulet à la Paprika* on the menu and ordered it, eager with anticipation. I was first shocked, then secretly and maliciously delighted that the professional chef's version was nowhere near as good as mine. He had dolled it up—using butter in place of the simple pork lard, adding, it seemed to me, an entirely unnecessary lashing of heavy cream, enriching and thickening the sauce with beaten egg yolks. The marvelously earthy strength of the old lady's dish was gone. The reality of the shores of Lake Balaton had faded away. We were now in a showoff Parisian tourist bistro. Suddenly I knew that the secret "something" in the preparation of a great recipe is more than technical skill—it is also devotion, loyalty, and understanding.

The homemade bread served with the chicken will always be associated with the coming into my life of Johanna, about twenty years ago. She came, first, as a "cleaning lady," but I soon discovered that she was a brilliant, natural Southern cook. Over the years she has taught me many of her specialties and has convinced me that the elegantly simple cooking of the South is one of the true pleasures of American gastronomy. I began this exploration on the day when

Johanna brought me the first pan of her corn bread. My joyous appreciation of it has not changed in twenty years. She makes it luxuriously with butter, eggs, and milk, so that it comes out of the oven golden yellow, crumbly light, chewy, earthy, nutty. Then she serves it very hot, in large chunks topped with extra pats of butter, to melt into tiny, golden pools.

The wine with the chicken and corn bread should be a light red; ideally from the noble Cabernet Sauvignon grape, the mainstay of the greatest château bottlings of Bordeaux, which grows superbly in, among other places, California's Napa Valley. It is, to my mind, the finest of American reds. Again, if you can shop at the vineyards around San Francisco, you can buy the top wines of the small producers, where noble quality goes with fierce demand and very limited circulation. Among these rare-as-a-jewel reds I remember tasting the Cabernet Sauvignons of Heitz in Napa, of Mayacamas and of Sebastiani. And as to those in cross-country distribution, my favorite list includes the Cabernet reds of Beaulieu from the Napa Valley, of Buena Vista, the Christian Brothers, Concannon, Inglenook, Krug, Martini, and Mondavi.

After the lightly sweet pepperiness of the chicken, I always feel that my mouth is prepared for the more strongly aromatic pepper of an Indian salad. With this, naturally, the wine should be withdrawn, since it cannot compete with the pepper. But with the cheeses the wine comes back in force, and the Cabernet Sauvignon is particularly good with such basic American types as Wisconsin Blue, Brick, Monterey Jack, New York Poona, or Oregon Tillamook. Truly American cheeses, they do not simply imitate foreign types.

The dessert of this menu is well matched to the peasant-style country simplicity of the other courses. There must be a hundred "authentic" recipes for a mixed-fruit ambrosia from the early days of American history, when most of the fruits were picked in the garden, when every ingredient was absolutely fresh, and when the kitchen preparations were marvelously and tastefully simple. Perhaps it was the best time for a truly American cuisine. Over the years I have tried many Ambrosia recipes and, taking the best ideas from all of them, have finally concocted my own. The fruit goes beautifully with a lightly sweet wine, and here again we need go no farther than California. The Muscat de Frontignan grapevine was transplanted from southern France to the Livermore Valley, where I have tasted a charming Muscat wine made by the Concannon Brothers. I also remember with pleasure the Angelica of Heitz, the Château La Salle of the Christian Brothers, and the Semillon of Martini. Finally, the coffee can be accompanied by an American brandy, of which there are now a number of exceptional types, including the three outstanding names: the X.O. of the Christian Brothers, the Conti Royal of East Side, and the Yettem blend of Setrakian. Other excellent products are by Almadén (Centennial), Korbel, and the Flame Tokay Royal Host.

Campaign Plan for the Preparation of the Meal

Two Days Ahead

Check this staple list and add the needed items to the following shopping list:

DAIRY
Cream (for the coffee)
Milk (2 cups)
Eggs (2 large)

FRUITS AND VEGETABLES
Lemon (1 whole)
Limes (3 whole)
Yellow onions (6 medium)
Sweet red onions (2 small)

HERB AND SPICE CABINET
Dill salt
Hungarian medium-hot red paprika
Crystal salt
Black peppercorns
Mexican chili powder
Whole caraway seeds
Whole white cardamom pods
Ground cinnamon
Ground cloves
Whole coriander seeds

OTHER ITEMS
Olive oil (1 1/3 cups)
Double-acting baking powder (2 teaspoons)
Sugar, white, fine-grind (1/2 cup)
Sugar (for the coffee)
Coarse white water-ground cornmeal (2 cups)
Granulated instantized flour (1/4 cup)
Tarragon white-wine vinegar (3 tablespoons)
Maple syrup (2 tablespoons)
Coffee
White bread (4-5 slices)
Bread for the cheese course

NOTE: If you do not bake your own sourdough bread, buy commercial sourdough or French-style long loaves.

WINES AND SPIRITS
Dry Sherry (2 tablespoons)

NOTE: Check the wines on the menu and if you do not have them, buy the current vintages.

The Day Before

Shopping list (plus any needed staple items from above):

DAIRY
  Sweet butter (3/4 pound)
  Sour cream (1 pint)
  Yogurt (1 pint)

MEAT
  Broiler-fryer chicken or young capon, cut up into pieces (3 1/2 pounds)

SPECIALTY FOOD STORE
  Greek *tarama* (carp roe) (1/4 pound)
  Greek Kalamata olives
  Mexican hot green *serrano* chilies (4 medium)

GROCERIES
  Pecans, whole, shelled (1/2 pound)

FRUITS AND VEGETABLES
  Green peppers (3)
  Cucumbers (4 medium)
  Carrots (5 medium)
  Celery (1 small bunch)
  Mint (1 or 2 sprigs)
  Ripe tomatoes (3 medium)
  Watercress (1 bunch)
  Oranges (6)
  Bananas (4)
  Sweet cherries (1 pound)
  Coconut (1 whole)
  Pineapple (1 whole)
  Seasonal vegetables

CHEESE STORE
  A selection for dinner

After the Shopping

  Start making ice and continue until you have enough.
  Prepare Indian *Kachumar* Hot Salad (recipe step 1).
  Set the table and get out all serving dishes.

Advance Preparations on the Day

  Chill salad plates.
  Prepare Taramasalata (recipe steps 1 and 2).
  Prepare American Orange Ambrosia and refrigerate (recipe steps 1-3).
  Prepare corn bread (recipe steps 1-3).

3 Hours Before Guests Arrive

  Chill white wines.
  Prepare *Raita* (Indian *Kachumar* Hot Salad, recipe step 2).

1 Hour Before Guests Arrive

Set out and bring to room temperature cheese and butter for cheese
   course.
Preheat oven to 350° F.
Prepare the seasonal vegetables and hold warm.
Prepare the Chicken Paprikás (recipe steps 1-3).
Warm plates.
Make coffee.
Finish preparing Taramasalata (recipe step 3).
Finish preparing the *Raita* (recipe step 3).

Sequence of the Dinner

Light candles.
Open red wine.
Warm corn bread.
Warm bread just before cheese course.

So much for the plan of campaign for the entire menu. If, on the
other hand, you want to prepare just one of the dishes, here are the
separate recipes, with separate lists of ingredients, so that you can cut
your dinner down to your own size, or make up your own menu in
your own way.

Greek Taramasalata

(Plenty for 4)

STAPLES
   Milk (about 1 cup)
   White bread (4 or 5 slices)
   Olive oil (about 1 cup)
   Dill salt
   Freshly ground black pepper

SHOPPING
   Greek *tarama* (carp roe) (1/4
      pound)
   Sweet red onion (1 small)
   Fresh limes (2 or 3)
   Salad scoops for the dip: green
      pepper chunks, cucumber
      strips, carrot strips, celery
      sticks, Greek Kalamata
      olives, etc.

At Any Time Beforehand—Active Preparation of the Taramasalata About 30 Minutes

1. Flexibility is the key to a perfect Taramasalata dip. I mix, taste, and adjust. Put 3 slightly heaped tablespoons of the *tarama* into a mortar, reserving the rest. Decrust the bread slices and mash them in a bowl with as much of the milk as they will absorb. Squeeze the juice from the limes. Finely grate the onion, saving the juice. Now gently mash the stiff *tarama* with a pestle, gradually working in some of the grated onion and its juice. Adding the olive oil a teaspoon at a time, soften the *tarama* to a smooth paste and switch from the pestle to a wooden spoon. Squeeze a piece of the bread mash as dry as you can and work it into the *tarama,* adding more olive oil and onion. Also begin adding spoonfuls of the lime juice. As the fish eggs absorb the oil, the *tarama* expands to the top of the mortar and should be spooned into a large round mixing bowl and beaten with a wire whisk. Continue adding, alternately, squeezed bread, oil, onion, and lime juice, balancing them until the *tarama* begins to fluff like mayonnaise. Then start beating it, with more and more olive oil, until it becomes creamy pink and completely fluffy. Beat in dill salt and freshly ground black pepper, then adjust for final flavor and texture. More oil thickens. More lime juice thins. When perfect, store in a covered bowl in the refrigerator.

About 1 Hour Before Serving—Preparation of the Vegetables About 20 Minutes

2. Cut inch-long chunks of the green peppers, thin lengthwise strips of the carrots and the cucumbers, and sticks of the white celery. Cut the stones out of the olives and stick them on toothpicks. Keep them all crisp in a covered bowl in the refrigerator. Taramasalata can, of course, be served on crackers or canapé rounds, but I prefer it with the vegetable tidbits.

About 10 Minutes Before Serving

3. Both the flavor and texture of the Taramasalata dip are improved by whipping in tiny lumps of fresh *tarama* just before serving. Put about 1 tablespoon more of the raw *tarama* into the mortar and break it into tiny lumps with a little more lime juice. This should be rapidly beaten into the dip with a wire whisk. Pile it

like mayonnaise in a pretty glass bowl and set in the center of a large serving platter. Arrange the cut vegetables around the bowl.

FINAL NOTE: Not much Taramasalata is usually left by the guests, but if any is available the following day it can be blended with mashed potatoes or used in a salad dressing.

Hungarian Chicken Paprikás
(For 4)

This dish is never worth preparing without a first-class grade of Hungarian medium-hot paprika. The stuff that comes in small cartons or cellophane bags or tins that cannot be properly resealed after opening has about as much character as brick dust. Good Hungarian paprika, properly packed, is now available from many fancy food stores, or it can be ordered by mail from Hungarian specialty shops in New York City. It gives a subtle fruitiness as well as warmth to the authentic version of this dish.

STAPLES
  Chicken fat or goose fat or, as a compromise, sweet butter (3 tablespoons)
  Yellow onions (3 medium)
  Lemon (1)
  Crystal salt

SHOPPING
  Broiler-fryer chicken or young capon, cut up (about 3 1/2 pounds)
  Sour cream (3/4 pint)
  Hungarian medium-hot red paprika

About 1 1/4 Hours Before Serving—Active Preparation About 15 Minutes—Unsupervised Cooking About 30 Minutes

1. Peel and chop the 3 onions and hold. Rub the pieces of chicken with the cut side of 1/2 the lemon. This dish should be prepared in a stewpot with a tightly fitting lid, large enough to hold all the chicken, loosely packed.

2. Set the pot over medium-high frying heat and melt the 3 tablespoons of fat, then lightly sauté the chopped onion until just gilded. Now turn off heat and blend in the paprika, the exact amount depending on its quality—1 tablespoon is enough if it is strong and fresh; otherwise the amount may have to be substantially

increased until the onions are bright red and they taste fairly strongly peppery. Now put in the pieces of chicken, one by one, making sure that each piece is well coated with aromatic fat and lightly sprinkling each with salt. When all chicken is in, turn on heat to medium boiling temperature and cover pot tightly. (It is entirely wrong either to fry chicken or to add any liquid. The basic Hungarian trick is to steam chicken in its own juices.) Do not open lid for the next 30 minutes. As pot heats up, temperature should be adjusted by listening closely and judging sound coming from inside. There must be a gentle sizzling, no more, no less.

About 30 Minutes Before Serving

3. After the first 30 minutes, check chicken and continue steaming until it is just tender, usually in about 5 or 10 minutes longer. Then remove chicken pieces to a bowl and quickly stir into sauce in pot about 3/4 pint of sour cream, at the same time turning up heat to bring cream as quickly as possible almost to boiling. Put back chicken and see that each piece is thoroughly coated with cream. Adjust heat so that cream stays just below boiling, replace lid, then leave for about 15 minutes longer. When chicken is thoroughly reheated and impregnated with sauce, finally recheck seasoning, add both salt and paprika if needed.

Johanna's Corn Bread

(For 4)

STAPLES

Sweet butter (1/4 pound)
Eggs (2 large)
Milk (about 1 cup)
Pork cracklings, optional
   (1 cup)
Double-acting baking powder
   (2 teaspoons)
Coarse white water-ground
   cornmeal (2 cups)
Granulated instantized flour
   (1/4 cup)
Crystal salt

About 45 Minutes Before Serving

1. Set the 1/4 pound butter out to soften.

About 35 Minutes Before Serving—Active Preparation About 10 Minutes—Unsupervised Baking About 25 Minutes

2. Preheat oven to 350 ° F. and put in a 9- or 10-inch cake pan to heat up. Assemble in a large mixing bowl the cup of cracklings and the 2 cups of cornmeal, then sprinkle on in turn the 1/4 cup of flour, the 2 teaspoons of baking powder, and about 1 teaspoon salt. Mix thoroughly. Lightly beat the 2 eggs and gently work into mixture, also the softened butter—but reserving about 2 teaspoons to grease the pan. Continue working together, lightly but thoroughly, adding enough of the milk to make a batter that will just pour.

3. Remove hot pan from oven, quickly butter it, using a pastry brush, then pour in the batter and bake in center of oven until top is lightly browned, usually in 20 to 30 minutes.

Indian Kachumar Hot Salad with Cold Cucumber Raita

(For 4)

STAPLES
  Yellow onions (3 medium)
  Tarragon white-wine vinegar (3 tablespoons)
  Crystal salt
  Whole caraway seeds
  Whole white cardamom pods
  Ground cinnamon
  Ground cloves
  Whole coriander seeds
  Freshly ground black pepper
  Mexican chili powder

SHOPPING
  Ripe tomatoes (3 medium)
  Mint (1 or 2 sprigs)
  Watercress (1 small bunch, enough for 1/3 cup, chopped) (an Indian cook would use fresh coriander leaves, but these are hard to find except in Indian groceries, or in Chinese markets, where fresh coriander is called Chinese parsley)
  Cucumber (1 medium)
  Sweet red onion (1 small)
  Mexican hot green *serrano* chilies (4 medium) (available in Mexican or Spanish groceries)
  Plain yogurt (1 pint)

The Day Before—Preparing the Salad in About 10 Minutes

1. This salad can be made more or less hot, according to your taste, by adding more or less of the Mexican hot chilies, of the pepper, and of the Mexican chili powder. The amounts in this recipe are for medium heat. The *raita*-cucumber-yogurt mixture is served separately, very cold from the refrigerator and beautifully cooling in the mouth. Thus, by alternating mouthfuls of the salad and of the *raita*, you can, so to speak, start a small fire in your mouth and then immediately extinguish it! Begin by preparing the salad ingredients and assembling them directly into the salad bowl: peel and finely chop the 3 onions, finely chop the 3 tomatoes, chop enough watercress leaves to fill 1/3 cup (or chop enough coriander to fill 1/4 cup) and finely chop about 4 medium-sized *serrano* chilies. After gently mixing these ingredients with a wooden spoon, sprinkle over them the 3 tablespoons of vinegar, with salt to taste, then cover bowl and refrigerate overnight.

*Several Hours Before Serving—Preparing the Raita in
About 15 Minutes*

2. Take salad bowl out of refrigerator and, again using a wooden
spoon, stir gently but thoroughly. Then re-cover and return to
refrigerator until serving time. Now choose a handsome serving
bowl (which will be brought to table) and assemble directly into it
the *raita* ingredients: the pint of yogurt, its curd broken up by being
lightly beaten with a wire whisk; then, in turn, sprinkled over the
top of the yogurt, 3/4 teaspoon whole caraway seeds, 1/8 teaspoon
each of ground cinnamon and clove, 1/2 teaspoon of the chili
powder, plus 3/4 teaspoon of salt and a very few grindings of black
pepper. Into a mortar put 5 of the whole cardamom pods and 1/2
teaspoon of whole coriander seeds. Grind to fine powder with
pepper and sprinkle on top of yogurt. Now beat again with wire
whisk to mix all the spices in evenly. Peel the cucumber, slice it
paper-thin, then stir gently into yogurt with wooden spoon. Cover
bowl and refrigerate until serving time.

10 Minutes Before Serving

3. Slice the red onion paper-thin, so that it breaks up into fine rings.
Chop enough mint leaves to fill 2 tablespoons. Using wooden spoon,
gently stir onion rings and mint into yogurt *raita*. Put back into
refrigerator, again covered, until moment of serving. Both Kachumar Salad and *raita* are served ice-cold. Each diner gets a portion
of salad on his plate, with a separate small bowl of *raita*. The trick is
to alternate between forkfuls of peppery salad and spoonfuls of
soothing cucumber-yogurt.

American Orange Ambrosia
(For 4)

STAPLES
  Sugar, white fine-grind (1/2 cup)
  Pure maple syrup (2 tablespoons)

SHOPPING
  Bananas (4)
  Sweet cherries (1 pound)
  Coconut (1)
  Lemon (1)
  Oranges (6)
  Pineapple (1)
  Pecans, whole, shelled (1/2 pound)
  Spanish Sherry, dry (2 tablespoons)

About 3 Hours Before Serving—Active Preparation About 1 Hour—Unsupervised Refrigeration About 2 Hours

1. First prepare the coconut. Preheat oven to 300° F. Make a hole in end of coconut and drain out milk. Place coconut in oven to split shell and make it easy to remove meat, usually in about 15 minutes. Meanwhile, in a medium-sized mixing bowl, coarsely grind the 1/2 pound pecans. In another bowl, measure out the 2 tablespoons maple syrup and add the 2 tablespoons Sherry.

2. When coconut is ready, crack open shell, pare meat, and coarsely grind or grate. Mix with pecans, adding the 1/2 cup sugar. Prepare the fruits and hold separately: peel and slice the 4 bananas and sprinkle with lemon juice; de-stem and pit the 1 pound cherries; peel the 6 oranges, slice 1 of them and segment the rest; peel, slice, and chunk the pineapple.

3. Use a glass dish, preferably round, about 10 inches in diameter, in which to serve the ambrosia. Holding back a few cherries and the sliced orange for decoration, arrange the fruits as follows: put a layer of orange segments in the dish and sprinkle with the nut mixture; next put a layer of pineapple chunks and sprinkle with the nut mixture; then a layer of cherries and banana slices, sprinkled again with the nut mixture. Continue in this way with a layer of oranges, sprinkled with a final layer of the nut mixture. Stir the maple syrup and Sherry and pour over fruit. Decorate with remaining cherries and orange slices. Place in refrigerator to chill for about 2 hours.

CHAPTER 9

COCKTAIL CANAPES AND BEER BUFFETS

*For the Conservative Cream of Your Friends—
or the Massed Multitude of Your Acquaintances*

Whether the party is for a dozen or a dozen dozen, whether the drink is a single, superb bottle of 1959 Château Latour or gallon jugs of sangría, the ability to produce precisely the right canapé at precisely the right moment is always the key to success. Opinions vary violently as to what is right. One of those many know-it-all guidebooks to the so-called Etiquette of Entertaining may expect you to memorize a couple of hundred recipes. If you bother to read them carefully, you find that at least half of them are simply small variations of the same concoction. The inevitable slice of pâté de foie gras on the inevitable round of toast, with a ring of green olive on top, is called "The Green Goddess on page 14." Exactly the same foie gras, with a chunk of black olive on top, is "The Black Diamond on page 41." Some "experts" advise that, if you want *really good* canapés, you should go out and buy them ready-made. As if such indefinable things as the warmth of hospitality, or the loving care of preparation for your guests, or the sensitive skill of precisely prejudging their mood were commercial commodities to be bought by the yard in the marketplace.

I believe in producing my own canapés—complicated or simple, as

125

the occasion demands. For example, I sometimes roast a standing rib of beef to a beautiful brown on the outside and a rare redness inside, then stand it, cooled to room temperature, on a handsome wooden cutting board as the centerpiece of the party. Thin, thin slices are carved off, rolled into cigars and handed to the guests on little paper napkins, without complication of fork or plate.

Ah! the purists will say. This is not a canapé. A canapé has to be on a round of toast. I admit that the classic French use of the word involved the bread. But I think this definition is as out-of-date as the sixteen-course dinner. Who wants to fill his belly before dinner with relatively tasteless fried or toasted bread? My modern definition of a canapé is any finger food—invariably without bread or biscuit—served anyhow or anywhere away from the dinner table. The same bit of food, served to you while sitting at the dinner table, immediately becomes an hors d'oeuvre. But you don't even have to call it by those French names. In other great gastronomic countries there are different names. In Italy it would be an antipasto—something "before the pasta." In Spain a few tidbits at a bar are *tapas,* or, in the living room at home, *entreméses.* In Greece, they serve a glorious infinity of *mezethakia*—rich with a dozen varieties and variations of tiny fish from the Aegean Sea. In Russia, before going into the dining room, one gathers around the *zakuski* table—a buffet-style table of maybe two dozen forms of finger and fork foods.

Over my many years of gastronomic travel, I have gradually boiled down, concentrated, and reduced my favorite finger-food recipes to the shortest possible list of the best possible concoctions. After all, I would rather be known among my friends for a few superb specialties than as the host with the most of a varied assortment of mediocre monstrosities. My personal list, then, comes down to a dozen recipes. All of them are reasonably easy to prepare, some of them are quite inexpensive. Please forgive my immodesty in calling them:

The Twelve Most Universal and Most Useful Canapés in the World

American Crab-Cucumber Wheels—Cold
(About 20 servings)

STAPLES
Sweet butter (1 1/2 table-
  spoons)
Milk (1/4 cup)
Flour, all-purpose (4 tea-
  spoons)
Crystal salt
Freshly ground pepper
Mustard, dry English

SHOPPING
King crab meat (1 cup—about
  1/2 pound)
Chives (1 small bunch, enough
  for 4 tablespoons, chopped)
Cucumbers (2 long)
Shallots (2)
Watercress (several sprigs)

*At Any Time Beforehand—Active Preparation About
30 Minutes—at Least 2 Hours of Refrigerated Chilling*

Peel the 2 cucumbers and cut off ends. Core with a narrow, sharp paring knife and discard seeded centers. Sprinkle with salt and pepper, stand upright on paper towels to drain.

Cut up into small pieces enough crab meat to fill 1 cup and set aside. Finely chop the 2 shallots. Melt the 1 1/2 tablespoons butter in a medium-sized heavy saucepan and gently sauté chopped shallots until limp. Add the 4 teaspoons flour and whisk until mixture foams, usually in about 2 minutes. Add salt and pepper to taste. Add the 1/4 cup milk and continue whisking until sauce thickens. Remove from heat. Mix 1/8 teaspoon mustard with 1/4 teaspoon water and gently mix into the sauce. Then add the chopped crab meat. Set aside to cool.

Meanwhile, finely chop 4 tablespoons chives, and when crab mixture is cool, stir in the chives. Then stuff each cucumber, as solidly as possible, with the mixture, working from each end and standing cucumber vertically on a board. Refrigerate till serving time.

Serving to Guests

Cut each cucumber crosswise into 1/2-inch segments and place them, like stuffed rings, on a serving dish, prettily garnished with watercress.

Belgian Chicken-and-Spinach Mushroom Caps—Hot

(About 20 servings)

STAPLES
  Sweet butter (10 tablespoons)
  Dried bread crumbs (about 3 tablespoons)
  Crystal salt
  Freshly ground black pepper
  Freshly ground nutmeg

SHOPPING
  White breast meat from small chicken, previously baked or boiled (enough when minced to fill 1 cup)
  Heavy cream (1/2 cup)
  Mushrooms with fair-sized open caps, about 1-1 1/2 inches across (20)
  Shallots (4)
  Spinach, fresh (8-10 ounces, enough after cooking and chopping to fill 1/2 cup)

At Any Time Beforehand—Active Preparation About 30 Minutes—Heating in Oven About 15 Minutes

Measure the 1 cup of minced cooked chicken breast and hold. Puree the 1/2 cup of spinach at slow speed in an electric blender for only a few seconds. Finely chop the 4 shallots. Heat 2 tablespoons of the butter in a 2-quart saucepan and gently sauté the chopped shallots until golden. Add the 1/2 cup heavy cream and heat gently. Add 2 tablespoons of the bread crumbs and 1/4 teaspoon nutmeg. Whisk until mixture thickens. Remove saucepan from heat, add minced chicken and pureed spinach. Mix thoroughly, season to taste with salt and pepper. Cover and let cool while preparing mushrooms.

Wipe (never wash) the 20 mushrooms. Remove stems and reserve for some other use. Carefully melt the remaining 8 tablespoons butter in a sauté pan, then remove from heat. With tongs, roll each mushroom cap in this butter, being sure to coat the inside as well as the outside surface liberally. Set caps in shallow metal or glass fireproof dish or platter. Stuff spinach mixture into each cap, piling it up in the center. The mushrooms may now be covered and set aside until you are ready to heat them.

About 20 Minutes Before Serving

Preheat oven to 350° F. Uncover dish of mushrooms. Sprinkle each top lightly with the remaining bread crumbs and set in center of oven. When they are nicely hot—usually in 10 to 15 minutes—transfer them to a heated serving platter.

British Angels on Horseback—Hot
(12 servings)

STAPLES	SHOPPING
Bacon, dark-smoked, thinly sliced (12 rashers)	Fresh oysters, shucked at home or by your fishmonger (1 dozen)
Lemon (1)	Anchovy paste (about 1 tablespoon)

At Any Time Beforehand—Advance Preparation About 15 Minutes

Squeeze the juice of the lemon and hold. Spread each rasher of bacon with about 1/4 teaspoon of the anchovy paste. Dip each oyster lightly in the lemon juice. Then wrap each oyster in a bacon rasher, anchovy side inward, and stick on skewer. Each "angel" should be about 1 inch from the next. When first skewer is loaded, start on second, until all "angels" are skewered. Then hold.

About 10 Minutes Before Serving—Grilling in 5 Minutes

Preheat grill and rest skewers on a roasting pan about 2 inches under the grill so that "angels" are suspended. Cook and turn until bacon is pale straw color and crisp on all sides—usually in 4 to 5 minutes. Serve "angels" sizzling hot, sliding them off skewers onto a very hot platter and impaling each on a toothpick.

Chinese Hin Kow Clam Balls—Hot

(About 20 balls)

STAPLES
Egg (1 large)
Cornstarch (2 tablespoons)
Crystal salt
Oil for deep-frying the balls

SHOPPING
Cherrystone clams, either
shucked at home or by your
fishmonger (1 dozen)
Water chestnuts (6)
Shallots (4)
Dry Sherry (2 teaspoons)

At Any Time Beforehand—Advance Preparation About 20 Minutes

Finely chop the 12 clams, the 4 shallots, and the 6 water chestnuts. Assemble in a medium-sized bowl and mix thoroughly. Lightly beat the egg and add. Also add the 2 tablespoons cornstarch, the 2 teaspoons Sherry and 1/2 teaspoon salt. When thoroughly mixed, shape into balls about an inch in diameter. Hold until ready to fry.

About 7 Minutes Before Serving—Deep-Frying About 2 Minutes per Load

In a deep fat fryer, heat the oil to 375° F. Fry the clam balls (putting in as many as will fit without overcrowding) until golden, usually in about 2 minutes. Serve immediately.

Dutch Edam Cheese Basket—Cold

(For 12)

STAPLES
Whole caraway seeds
Ground cloves
Ground cinnamon
Cumin
Freshly grated nutmeg

SHOPPING
Whole Edam cheese (4 pounds)
Cream cheese (24 ounces)
Heavy cream (2/3 cup)
Scallions (1 large bunch,
enough for 1 cup tops,
chopped)
Watermelon rind (2-pound
jar)
Dry Sherry (1/2 cup)

Best When Made About an Hour Before the Guests
Arrive—Active Preparation About 30 Minutes

Take a knife and make 2 marks, each about 1/2 inch from the center of the Edam cheese. Cut down on both these marks to a depth of about 2 inches. This will form the handle of the basket. Cut off the segments on either side of the handle and carefully scoop out the cheese, leaving a 1/2-inch shell lining the basket. Finely chop 1 cup green scallion tops and 2 cups drained watermelon rind and hold. In a mortar and pestle pound 1/2 teaspoon of caraway seeds. Add 1/2 teaspoon each of ground cinnamon, cloves, and cumin.

Grate the cheese pieces and put in a heavy 2-quart saucepan over very low heat. Add the cream cheese and slowly soften, blending thoroughly. Remove from heat, gradually mix in the 2/3 cup cream and 1/2 cup Sherry. Now add the ground spices and freshly grated nutmeg to taste. Blend until the mixture is of a smooth spreading consistency, adding a little more cream if necessary. Mix in the chopped scallion tops and watermelon rind. Spoon the mixture back into the cheese basket and leave at room temperature until serving time. Reserve the remaining cheese mixture to refill the basket as needed.

French Shrimp à La Roquefort—Cold

(About 30 servings)

STAPLES	SHOPPING
Crystal salt	Medium shrimp (1 pound)
Freshly ground black pepper	Cream cheese (3 ounces)
Bay leaves	Roquefort cheese (5 table-
Cayenne pepper	spoons—about 2 1/2
Mustard, dry English	ounces)
Garlic (2 cloves)	Green celery (2 stalks)
Tarragon white-wine vinegar	Parsley (1 bunch)
(1 to 2 cups)	Shallots (2)
	Dry white wine (1 to 2 cups)

The Day Before—Boiling the Shrimp in About 45 Minutes

First prepare the boiling liquor, remembering that it must be very strong to the taste if it is to inject its flavor into the shrimp.

In a 2 1/2-quart saucepan put 1 cup each of vinegar, wine, and cold water. Add the 2 cloves garlic (slivered), the 2 bay leaves, the 2 stalks of celery with their leaves, all finely chopped; at least 1 tablespoon of crystal salt, 6 or more grinds of pepper, and enough cayenne (gradually added) to make the liquid peppery to the tongue. Bring to a boil and simmer, covered, for roughly 30 minutes to bring out and mingle the flavors.

Meanwhile, wash the shrimp under cold running water, remove the legs, but do not shell. When boiling liquor is ready, drop in shrimp all at once, adding more vinegar and wine in equal parts, if needed, to cover. Return to a boil as quickly as possible, then time for 3 or 4 minutes. Turn off heat and let shrimp cool to room temperature in the liquid. Turn entire contents of saucepan into a storage bowl and refrigerate for at least 24 hours. This is when the shrimp absorb the flavor, and the process cannot be speeded up.

At Any Time on the Day—One Hour Before Preparing Stuffing

Let the Roquefort and the cream cheese soften at room temperature. Drain the shrimp. Shell and devein them. Using a small, sharp knife, slit the shrimp down the back about halfway, but do not let the halves come apart. Cover and refrigerate. Peel and mince the 2 shallots and hold in a covered jar. Finely chop the parsley and hold.

Stuffing the Shrimp in About 30 Minutes

Mash the 5 tablespoons Roquefort with the 3 ounces cream cheese. When thoroughly blended, add the minced shallots. In a small bowl or cup combine 1/2 teaspoon dry mustard with 1/2 teaspoon water. Add to the cheese mixture and blend thoroughly.

Now stuff this mixture into the slit of each shrimp, using a small knife, making a smooth outer surface of the cheese. When all the shrimp are stuffed, roll them in the parsley to coat the outer cheese surface. Arrange on a serving platter, cover, and refrigerate until ready to serve.

Greek Mezethakia—Dolmadakia Hirino
Pigs in a Blanket of Vine Leaves—Hot or Warm

(35 servings)

STAPLES
Olive oil (2 tablespoons)
Long-grain rice, previously
  cooked (1/4 cup)
Crystal salt
Freshly ground black pepper
Ground cardamom seed
Thyme

SHOPPING
Pickled grape leaves (35)
Pork, lean (1 pound)
Mushrooms (about 1/4 pound)
Parsley (1 small bunch, enough
  for 1/2 cup, chopped)
Almonds, shelled, blanched
  and slivered (2 ounces)
Scallions (1 bunch, enough for
  1/2 cup, chopped)

At Any Time Beforehand—Advance Preparation
About 45 Minutes

Prepare the ingredients and hold separately; finely chop 1/2 cup mushrooms, coarsely grind the pork, and finely chop 1/2 cup parsley and 1/2 cup scallions.

In a heavy frying pan over medium heat put the 2 tablespoons olive oil and sauté the chopped mushrooms until tender. Remove and set aside. Put the ground pork in the pan and sauté over medium-high heat until no trace of pink remains. Reduce the heat, add the sautéed mushrooms, the slivered almonds, the 1/4 cup cooked rice, the chopped scallions and parsley, 1/4 teaspoon cardamom, 1/2 teaspoon thyme, 1 teaspoon salt, and pepper to taste. Stir until well blended and cook 3 minutes. Set aside to cool.

Meanwhile, prepare the pickled grape leaves. Plunge the leaves into hot water for a moment or two to loosen one from another. Transfer them to a bowl of cold water and carefully separate them. Place them one by one on paper towels. Place paper towels on top and gently pat dry.

Stuffing the Grape Leaves in About 15 Minutes

Arrange the leaves on a work surface with the stem side facing you. Place 1 or 2 tablespoons of the filling on the center of each leaf, and carefully fold the 2 sides over the middle to make each packet 2 inches wide. Overlap the edges if necessary to obtain uniform width. Rolling away from you, roll the leaf into a tight cylindrical packet. Hold, covered and refrigerated, until ready to cook.

About 1 Hour Before Serving with Unsupervised Simmering About 45 Minutes

Bring stuffed grape leaves to room temperature. In a shallow pan with a tightly fitting lid, place the grape leaves in a single closely packed layer. Add enough water to cover grape leaves by 1/2 inch. Bring quickly to a boil, reduce heat, cover, and simmer gently for 45 minutes. Remove to a serving platter and serve hot or warm.

Indian Sikh Kebabs
Meatballs Grilled on Skewers—Hot
(12 kebabs)

STAPLES
Lemon juice (2 tablespoons)
Yellow onions (2 medium)
Indian Besan chick-pea flour, or all-purpose flour (2 tablespoons)
Crystal salt
Freshly ground black pepper
Whole caraway seeds
White cardamom pods
Chili powder
Ground cinnamon
Ground cloves
Whole coriander seeds
Fresh or ground ginger

SHOPPING
Ground beef, top round, all-lean (1 pound)
White beef fat, also ground, and evenly mixed into the above (3 ounces)
Plain yogurt (4 tablespoons)
Watercress (1 small bunch, enough for 1/3 cup of finely chopped leaves)

About 20 Minutes Before Serving—or Can Be Made in Advance and Reheated

For the preparation of these kebabs, you will need about 6 small skewers, either metal or wood, on which the kebabs are spiked while being grilled. Into a mortar put 6 of the cardamom pods and 1 teaspoon of the coriander seeds, then grind and pound with the pestle into a powder and hold. Put the ground meat and 3 ounces fat into a large mixing bowl and sprinkle over it, in turn, the cardamom and coriander from the mortar; the 2 tablespoons of flour; 1/2 teaspoon caraway seeds; 1/4 teaspoon cinnamon; 1/4 teaspoon cloves; a few grinds of pepper; 3 teaspoons salt; the 2 onions, finely chopped; 1/3 cup of the watercress leaves, finely chopped; the 2 tablespoons lemon juice; about 1 tablespoon of fresh ginger, finely minced (or 1 teaspoon ground ginger), and 1 teaspoon of the chili powder. Using clean fingers, knead all this thoroughly until all the ingredients are completely blended with the meat. It should end up as a firm, smooth paste. If it needs to be stiffened slightly, work in more flour. If it gets too stiff, add more lemon juice.

About 10 Minutes Before Serving

Now detach a small handful of the mixture and work it around one of the skewers, until it is the shape and size of a 1-portion sausage. If the skewer is long enough, you may put on 2 or 3 kebabs, or you may grill and serve each kebab on its own miniature skewer. Preheat your grill and set the rack about 2 inches below the heat. Using a pastry brush, thoroughly wet each kebab on all sides with the yogurt. Then grill kebabs, turning the skewers every minute or two, until meat is just cooked through—usually in 4 or 5 minutes. As they begin browning, baste them with more yogurt. Finally, either in the kitchen beforehand, or on the plates of your guests, slide the kebabs off the skewers. They may be munched as is, or dipped into Indian mango or mint chutney.

Mexican Guacamole Dip
with Fried Tortilla Triangles—Cold
(For 12)

STAPLES
Crystal salt
Freshly ground black pepper
Whole coriander seed, if fresh
sprigs not available

SHOPPING
Avocados (2 large)
Fresh coriander, if available (2
sprigs, enough for 2 table-
spoons, chopped)
Lime (1)
Pimentos, optional (2 small)
Tomato (1 medium)
Green Spanish tomatoes (2
small)
Mexican hot green *serrano*
chilies (4 small, or
according to taste)

*At Any Time Beforehand—Advance Preparation About
30 Minutes—Refrigeration at Least One Hour Before Serving*

Halve the 2 avocados, remove pits, and scoop out flesh. Press
through a food mill, using a fairly coarse cutter, and hold. Chop about
1 tablespoon fresh coriander, if available, or pound about 1/4 teaspoon
whole coriander seed in a mortar and pestle.

Prepare and put in a medium-sized mixing bowl the 3 tomatoes,
peeled, seeded and chopped, and the 4 chilies, seeded and chopped, and
the pimento, chopped. Season with the juice of the lime, the coriander,
and salt and pepper to taste. Add the avocado and blend thoroughly,
but gently.

Put mixture in a glass bowl and refrigerate, covered until ready to
use. Serve with fried tortilla triangles.

Russian Zakuski—Eggs with Anchovies—Cold
(12 servings)

STAPLES
Sweet butter (6 tablespoons)
Eggs (6 large)
Crystal salt
Freshly ground black pepper

SHOPPING
Anchovies, flat fillets (12)

At Any Time Beforehand—Advance Preparation About 10 Minutes

Hard-boil the 6 eggs. Soften the 6 tablespoons of butter. Cut each anchovy fillet in half and hold. Cut the hard-boiled eggs lengthwise, dig out yolks, and put into a mixing bowl. Hold the halved whites in the refrigerator for the "little boats" into which the stuffing will be piled.

Mix the butter with the egg yolks, adding a little of the oil from the anchovies drop by drop, until you have a smooth, soft paste. Add salt and pepper to taste. Fill the halved whites with this mixture, leveling the top. Then, on top, put two neat curls of anchovy. Refrigerate everything until eggs are to be served.

Scandinavian Caviar Mousse—Cold
(For 12)

STAPLES
Sweet butter (14 tablespoons)
Sugar, white fine-grind (1 teaspoon)
Garlic (1 clove)

SHOPPING
Tuna fish, water-packed (2 7-ounce cans)
Herring tidbits (6-ounce jar)
Danish black Limfjord caviar (4-ounce jar)
Red caviar (4-ounce jar)
Scallion tops (small bunch, enough for 1 teaspoon, chopped)
Dry white wine (3 tablespoons)

*At Any Time Beforehand—Advance Preparation About
25 Minutes—Refrigeration at Least 1 Hour*

Using 2 tablespoons of the butter, liberally grease the inside of a
1-pint mold. Then line the mold with strips of wax paper, also
buttered, for easier removal of the mousse. Chop enough of the scallion
tops to fill 1 teaspoon and hold. Peel and finely mince 1 clove of garlic
and hold, covered, in a small glass jar.

Melt the remaining 12 tablespoons of butter and pour into jug of
electric blender. Switch on to medium speed and add the drained tuna
fish and the herring tidbits a little at a time, stopping machine and
pushing everything down with a wooden spoon between each addition.
Add the chopped scallion tops and minced garlic, together with the
teaspoon sugar and 2 teaspoons of the black caviar. Continue blending
until smooth and fluffy. Pack in the prepared mold and refrigerate to
harden.

10 Minutes Before Serving

On a pretty platter, unmold the caviar mousse as you would a
gelatin salad. Spread sides of mousse carefully with the remaining
black caviar. Spread red caviar over top. Serve with small rounds of
pumpernickel or rye.

Spanish Entreméses—Empanadillas de Chorizo
Spicy Sausage Turnover—Hot
(About 40 bite-sized turnovers)

STAPLES
Eggs (2 large)
Milk (2 tablespoons)
Double-acting baking powder
(1 teaspoon)
Flour, all-purpose (1 1/2 cups
after sifting)
Olive oil (2 tablespoons)
Crystal salt

SHOPPING
Spanish chorizo sausage—or
thin Italian pepperoni sausage—enough for 40 slices,
each about 3/8 inch thick
(about 3/4 pound)
Anchovy flat fillets (about 10)

The Day Before—Active Preparation of the Pastry Dough About 15 Minutes

After sifting the 1 1/2 cups flour, make a mound of it in the center of a pastry board and sprinkle on 1 teaspoon each of the baking powder and the salt. Then dig a well in the middle of the mound and put into it 1 whole egg, lightly beaten, the 2 tablespoons of olive oil, and about 2 teaspoons of the milk. Now, using the tips of the fingers, thoroughly work all these ingredients into the flour, gradually adding the rest of the milk, until you have a firm and flexible dough. Knead it thoroughly for about 5 minutes, using the heels of your hands, then roll it into a ball, cover it lightly with wax paper, and refrigerate overnight.

On the Morning of the Day—Active Preparation of the Empanadillas About 15 Minutes—Unsupervised Baking About 20 Minutes

Cut sausage into about 40 thick slices. Preheat oven to 400° F. Divide ball of dough into two halves and roll out first half on lightly floured board until it is a rectangle of dough about 1/4 inch thick. Put the spicy sausage on it in neat rows, each slice about 1 inch away from the next and lightly pressed down into the dough. On top of each slice, put 1/4 of an anchovy fillet. Roll out second half of the dough until it is the same size and shape as first, then lay it on top of sausage slices and lightly press it down. Using a cookie cutter, or an inverted, fairly thin water- or wineglass, cut out each sausage slice, with about 1/2 inch of dough around the outside. Using a pastry brush, wet the edges of each turnover with a bit of water and press firmly together all around. Separate the second egg, reserving white for some other use. Put yolk into small bowl and lightly beat. Beat about 2 teaspoons of water into egg yolk and lightly brush this mixture on top of each turnover. Prick each turnover with fork and slide onto slightly greased cookie sheet, then place in center of oven and bake until lightly browned—usually in 15 to 20 minutes.

Serving to the Guests

The Empanadillas may be served cold, but to my mind are better slightly warmed for a few minutes in an oven at 180° F. Obviously, other aromatic meats may be used as the filling—even things remaining from previous meals—and the dough may be any kind of unsweetened pastry left from previous project. Empanadillas are nothing if not flexible.

After you have dutifully read these recipes, I can hear you say, "Yes. They're fine. But next Thursday evening I won't be back from the office until 5:30 and my first guests will arrive for drinks at six. I simply *can't* prepare anything. . . ." So you want me to tell you what I would do. I would still not buy commercial, ready-made canapés. There are solutions to your problem that are much simpler to arrange, less expensive, more personal to you, and therefore more effective in pleasing your guests. A tray of bought canapés always looks exactly that—a last-moment compromise, something set up in a hurry, with a minimum of thought and effort on the host's part. Instead, let us offer something that, however simple it is, radiates quality, care, and imagination in selection, with the spark of the unusual that lights up the faces of your guests and consolidates your reputation as the always memorable host.

Let your guests cut their own thin slices from a whole ham—but no ordinary ham! Get one of those Parma-style prosciutto hams, now being superbly smoked and dried by small Italian, family-owned firms in various parts of the United States. No need to boil or roast such a ham. It can be served in the French style of *jambon cru,* the dark-smoked, lean meat, almost as translucent as the finest smoked salmon. Give your guests a long, narrow-bladed supersharp ham knife and teach the beginners how to slice the flesh paper-thin. The challenge of the ham adds to the fun of the party.

Or get a whole, medium-sized Roquefort or Stilton cheese. Cut off the top crust, exposing the whole circle of the beautiful blue-green mottled pasta. Stick into it, at a rakish angle, a shining, strong red-handled cheese scoop, and let your guests go digging for the aromatic and sensuously soft curls.

Perhaps not too far away there is a fancy grocery, or a specialist butcher, or a high-cuisine delicatessen where the owner makes his own *terrine de campagne* or *pâté du chef.* Splurge. Buy a fairly small whole one—preferably in the shape of a loaf pan. (In New York I can get them as small as two or three pounds.) Turn it out onto a handsome platter and decorate it colorfully with green watercress, red tomato wedges, and so on. Supply your guests with a spatula and let them cut off or dig out what they want. Or perhaps one of these stores could provide a whole boned and stuffed capon, duck, or tur-key—reconstructed around the stuffing so that it looks perfectly normal. It is always a dramatic moment when, to everyone's surprise, the host makes the first cut, straight down, right through the bird—the magic rabbit from the magic hat!

These examples should suffice to establish my basic principle. When you cannot, for one valid reason or another, offer your guests something of your own, then offer them instead a do-it-yourself game—but with the fun always supported on a foundation of sparkling imagination and impeccable quality.

From Cocktails to Buffet Is a Small Step

Any one of these do-it-yourself centerpieces from your cocktail party would do equally well as the central show dish of a buffet table of any shape or size. Whether you serve beer or wine or sangría from huge jugs or punch from a great silver bowl or (shame on you!) strong spirits in lethal doses or natural fruit juices or hot Mexican chocolate or iced tea or (perish the thought!) you-know-what cola, the general configuration of the finger and fork foods on the table is usually (and rightly) so much a matter of the classic tradition that it hardly requires discussion.

Whether it is a stand-up lunch for a thousand in a *palazzo* on the Grand Canal in Venice, or whether the invitation reads *"un petit buffet intime pour une centaine"* at the town houses of the Rothschilds or the Rubensteins in Paris, or the same for perhaps 20 in your home or mine, the basic menu pattern will be the same. There will likely be a beginning, at one end of the table, with handsome, double-handled cups of hot or cold light, clear soup. Then, at the center of the table, *les grosses pièces de buffet froid,* the big, cold, showpieces—a beautifully decorated, whole, cold salmon surrounded by silver sauce-boats of green, red, and yellow mayonnaise, a galantine of chicken in pink aspic, a fruited and glazed ham, cold sliced filet of beef *à la Strasbourgeoise* garnished with foie gras, plus pâtés and terrines with every conceivable kind of birdy, gamy, or meaty fillings and every degree of delightfully designed decoration. Finally, at the other end of the table, there will be the large cakes and tarts, wildly curvaceous with whipped cream, irresistibly tempting with the aromas of fruit spirits. Around and in between these big dishes will be platter after platter of the *petites pièces,* the "little bits," which might be any of the canapés described in this chapter (usually calculated to allow three per person), the same number of bite-sized cakes and pastries, tiny fruit gartlets, petits fours from the nearest French bakery, and, alongside the buckets of ice for the Champagne, larger pails of ice surrounding the decorated half-gallon containers of mixed fruit sherbets and multicolored ice creams.

Since almost all of these items involve only the simplest planning (plus a modicum of critical judgment as to quality and determined control as to service), I prefer to concentrate on my creative part of the proceedings. I always insist on arranging (and preparing myself) the centerpiece dish, which will be, so to speak, my personal signature on the occasion and will set the tone for the rest of the buffet. Here are a few of my favorites, which may sometimes be hot, sometimes cold, sometimes conservatively formal, sometimes wildly informal and do-it-yourself, but invariably trying to achieve that imaginative flair that engraves the memory of the party on the minds of the guests.

The Terrine of Mixed Meats Comes First

It hardly needs to be said that this is one of the most universal of all the gastronomic tools of your entertaining. It is the perfect centerpiece for a buffet, a cocktail party, a wine tasting, after-theater supper, Sunday brunch, or midafternoon snack, for a picnic, or a birthday gift to a food-loving friend. The terrine can be presented with absolute simplicity in the oval ceramic terrine (yes, the dish took its name originally from the crock in which it was baked) and simply topped with a covering of diced red-wine aspic. Or it can be covered, according to your skill as a pastry chef, with a magnificently curlicued, flaky-pastry crust. Or it can be shaped in the fanciest of copper molds, then covered with a skin of multicolored aspic and unmolded on the stand in solitary significance on a handsomely decorated and garnished platter. But the outer show is always less important than the gastronomic qualities of the inside filling. It may be, as in this recipe, a mixture of domesticated meats, or it can be a memorably aromatic concoction of feathered or furred wild game.

Whenever a hunting friend brings a gift of wild game there is always the problem of those little lead pellets from the shotgun. I remember, when one of my books was about to be published, giving a most important dinner party in honor of the senior editor (or, should I say, "editress," since it was a charming lady, distinctly dignified, even slightly haughty) of the great publishing company. A hunting friend had brought me a large hare and I converted it into a magnificent terrine. It was a sensational start to the dinner. The lady editor was beaming at the subtle hint of Cognac as she bit into the first mouthful. Suddenly, there was a noise from her mouth as if gears were being ground in a stick-shift racing car. The face of the lady editor was pale. She removed the piece of terrine from her mouth and poked at it with her fork. Two small lead pellets clinked on her plate. If only it had been one, I would have tactfully hinted that she should pay a visit to her dentist. But *two?* I said, brightly and loudly, "Let's have some more of the Chambertin," and asked the lady editor whether she thought there was any truth to the rumor that Howard Hughes was going to write his memoirs.

It is because of this danger of broken teeth that my favorite recipe no longer contains game meat.

Here is the best of my personal recipes. But each time you prepare a concoction such as this, you should try to improve it. Each time you taste it you should say to yourself, "Yes. Fine. But what can I do better next time?" Ultimately you will develop a concoction so particularly personal to you, so memorably subtle in every detail and taste and texture, that you will be famous for it among all your friends.

There is a story about the great French writer and gastronome Alexandre Dumas that his terrine was so magnificent that when friends could not accept his invitation to supper they asked if they might, nevertheless, send around one of their servants to bring back their portions of the terrine. Your friends, too, will ask you for your recipe, and then you will be faced with a difficult decision. To give, or not to give? Or—to cheat a little? To hold back that "secret ingredient" and make sure that no one else prepares it quite as well as you do! So now, let me start you off on the royal road to *your* own great terrine.

My Own Simple and Flexible Terrine of Mixed Meats
(For about 20)

STAPLES
Sweet butter (4 tablespoons)
Eggs (4 large)
Beef stock (about 1/2 cup)
Garlic (2 cloves)
Crystal salt
Freshly ground black pepper
Bay leaf
Ground cinnamon
Juniper berries (10 whole)
Mace
Thyme
Freshly ground nutmeg

SHOPPING
Chicken livers (1 pound)
Ham, cooked (1/2 pound)
Pork, lean (1 pound)
Veal, lean (1 pound)
Fresh pork fat, to line and cover terrine, fairly thinly sliced (about 1/2 pound)
Shallots (6)
Cognac (1/2 cup)
Dry white vermouth (about 1 cup)

2 Days Before—Marinating the Ham

Chop up the 1/2 pound ham into cubes, put in a dish, and pour on enough vermouth to cover the ham. Refrigerate, tightly covered, overnight.

The Day Before—Active Preparation About
50 Minutes—Unsupervised Baking About 3 Hours

In a heavy skillet over medium-high heat, sauté the pound of chicken livers in the 4 tablespoons butter until just firm, no more. Warm the 1/2 cup Cognac, pour over the livers, and ignite. When flames have died down, remove livers from pan and hold. Add the 1/2 cup beef stock to the sauté pan, cover, and simmer very gently for about 30 minutes.

Meanwhile, using the fine cutter, grind the pound each of pork and veal. Hold both in a large mixing bowl. In a mortar and pestle put the 6 shallots and 2 cloves garlic, both peeled, and pound together with the 10 juniper berries, then add 1/2 teaspoon each of mace and thyme, 1/4 teaspoon nutmeg, the bay leaf, crumbled, a pinch or two of cinnamon, 1 teaspoon salt, and pepper to taste. Preheat oven to 300° F.

Using a food mill, grind the chicken livers and add to the meats in the bowl. Drain the ham cubes, reserving the vermouth, and also add.

Mix thoroughly. Lightly beat the 4 eggs and add, together with the pounded spices. When thoroughly mixed, add the now reduced beef stock and vermouth until the consistency is like that of mud.

Line inside of terrine, or loaf pan, with fresh pork fat and heap in the mixture. Cover completely with remaining fat. Stand terrine in tray with 1 inch of water, then slide tray into oven and bake 3 hours.

When cooked, remove from oven and leave in tray. Place aluminum foil to cover terrine and weight top. When cool, remove weight and refrigerate overnight.

FINAL NOTE: This terrine will keep for 2 to 3 weeks in the refrigerator. Never freeze it.

My Delicately Smoky Version of a Direct-from-Maine Fish Chowder
(For 12)

On a frosty winter evening nothing could be better as the centerpiece of a hearty buffet. I would serve it, slightly steaming, its aroma filling the room, in a huge copper tureen, or a brightly enameled soup pot, resting on an electric hot plate set at 180° F. to keep it all hot enough so that the first spoonful just burns the tongue, but not so hot that it continues cooking.

This recipe was taught me by a fisherman friend who lives on an island in Casco Bay. My variation of his original is pure, creamy white, uncorrupted by any green, red, or yellow vegetables. The mixture of fish must always be the freshest I can find. Everything must be enriched with butter. The "secret trick" is to let the salt pork brown so that the whole chowder will have a delicately smoky flavor.

The guests can never quite recognize the different fish, for everything is blended to a delicate subtlety of taste and texture. I always try to serve, with this chowder, the Alsatian white wine, the Clos Sainte Hune, made by my friends the brothers Bernard and Hubert Trimbach from the Riesling grapes of their famous vineyard near the village of Hunawihr—a wine so light, so fruity, so refreshingly aromatic that it lifts the chowder to a stratosphere of delight. One guest, after tasting the chowder with the wine, said, "I feel faint—but I am not sure whether it's from ecstasy—or indigestion!" The precise recipe follows.

STAPLES
  Salt butter (about 1/2 pound)
  Milk (about 3 pints)
  Yellow onions (15 medium)
  Crystal salt
  Freshly ground black pepper

SHOPPING
  Boneless fillets of 1 fish or a mixed assortment—possibly bass, bluefish, cod, or other fish in season—all cut into 2-inch squares (about 6 pounds)
  Lean salt pork, in 1 piece (about 1 pound)
  Light cream (3 pints)
  Starchy boiling potatoes (18 medium)
  Hungarian medium-hot red paprika

About 1 1/2 Hours Before Serving—Active Preparation About 45 Minutes—Cooking About 30 Minutes

Coarsely dice the pound of salt pork and spread across bottom of cold soup pot with a tightly fitting lid. Peel the 15 onions, slice them about 1/4 inch thick, and hold. Peel the 18 potatoes, slice 1/4 inch thick, and hold. Wash and dry the fish and pull off any stray bones or unwanted bits of skin. Set soup pot over medium frying heat and sauté salt pork dice only until they have released enough liquid fat to coat bottom of soup pot, then turn off heat.

While sautéing is in progress, bring about 3 quarts freshly drawn cold water to a boil. When heat is off under soup pot, put a layer of fish on top of the salt pork cubes and lightly season with salt and pepper. Then put in a layer of onion slices, followed by a layer of potatoes, with more seasoning as needed. Repeat this procedure with fish, onions, and potatoes until all are used up. Now pour into soup pot only enough boiling water to come up to 1/2 inch *below* the top layer of the solid ingredients. (The critical decision is the exact amount of water, and this is slightly adjusted as one gains experience in preparing the dish.) Turn on heat under soup pot and adjust so that water is gently bubbling, to produce a small amount of steam; cover and leave bubbling, without opening lid, for at least 20 minutes. Then check whether fish is just flaky, potatoes are tender, and water is all absorbed. If not, replace the lid and continue bubbling for 5 or 10 minutes longer.

About 40 Minutes Before Serving

In a 4-quart saucepan mix the 3 pints each milk and light cream and heat mixture to just below the boiling point.

When fish and potatoes are finally done, turn up heat under soup pot for 2 or 3 minutes, to boil off remaining water, until sizzling noise signals that bottom layer is beginning to fry and brown. Let this continue for about 1 minute. Then turn off heat under chowder and pour in hot milk-cream. Turn on heat under soup pot and, being careful not to let milk-cream boil, bring everything up to just below simmering and let flavors blend for about 5 minutes, uncovered, before serving. The chowder bowls should be very hot and each portion should be dotted with bits of yellow butter and sprinkled with bright red paprika.

Clam and Oyster Roast with Butter-Pecan Sauce
(For 12)

STAPLES
  Salt butter (1 1/2 pounds)
  Tarragon white-wine vinegar
    (2 tablespoons)

SHOPPING
  Oysters and clams, unopened, bought in sacking (about 6 dozen of each)
  Pecans, shelled (about 12 ounces)

One Hour Before Serving—Active Preparation About 45 Minutes—Roasting of Oysters and Making Sauce About 10 Minutes

Place a large, flat, open iron pan, balanced over the fire. (I use a Spanish *paellera,* 18 inches across.) Since "roasting" is very quick, next prepare all ingredients.

Scrub and wash the oysters and clams. Also rinse out the sacking as this will be used later for cooking. In a smallish iron pot melt the 1 1/2 pounds butter and keep lukewarm. Coarsely grind the 12 ounces shelled pecans.

About 15 Minutes Before Serving

Thoroughly soak the sacking, and when the large open pan is spitting hot, quickly lay on as many oysters and clams as pan will hold, curved shell downwards. Cover at once with the wet sacking. This involves much hissing and steam.

Now heat up the butter until it starts sizzling, add the ground pecans, and stir until darkish brown, being careful not to let them burn. Then add, all at once, the 2 tablespoons vinegar. Sauce will froth violently. Stir once and remove from fire.

Oysters and clams should now begin to be ready. Lift edge of sacking and, with tongs, remove each oyster and/or clam that has opened sufficiently for a knife to be inserted. Replace each with another oyster and/or clam waiting to be cooked. Discard flat top shell. Spoon butter-pecan sauce over each and serve.

Do-It-Yourself Swiss Cheese Raclette
(For 12)

This party version of a traditional Swiss "cheese roast" seems to be sweeping the country and may soon outdistance in popularity the ubiquitous Swiss cheese fondue. Good cheese shops in almost every city nowadays are prepared to rent an electric *raclette* grill for a ridiculously small sum—on the commercial understanding, of course, that you will buy your *raclette* cheese from the shop in question. Naturally, though, if you own your own fireplace in which you can develop a roaring fire you don't need any machine. There are also ways (although they involve a slight compromise in terms of the toasty flavor) of melting the cheese under a grill, or in a hot oven. The word *raclette* is both the generic name of a number of Swiss semihard mountain cheeses, the name of the dish, and the name of the method of preparation. So it would probably be correct to say, "Come for a *raclette* party at which six kinds of *raclette* cheese will be properly *racletted* into various *raclettes.*" Obviously, the word comes from the French *racler,* "to scrape." The first essential for a super-*raclette* party is to get hold of exactly the right types of cheese, which will melt easily but not too easily, will become, under the strong heat, softly chewy but not rubbery chewy, and will burn ever so slightly so that the room will be filled with the irresistible aroma of a fireside picnic in a mountaintop log cabin. Dominate your cheese merchant by letting him know that you know exactly what you want and will not be fobbed off by any old cheese called *raclette.* Insist on getting Bagnes or Belalp, or Belsano, or Bratkase, or Gomset, or Mutschli. These are all slightly rubbery and will melt evenly and smoothly under the heat.

The second essential is that the melted cheese *must* be eaten instantly. So the meal becomes a continuous round of different people melting a portion and at once going off to eat it themselves, or, if they are charmingly chivalrous, handing it to some other beautiful member of the party to eat first. With *raclette,* there is no such thing as all starting together. The third absolute essential is that the plates be almost as hot as the cheese. They should be continuously reheated in an oven set at about 150° F. In fact, one of the latest models of electric grills has a built-in feature for keeping a pile of plates hot right alongside the cheese. My favorite solution, however, to this problem is to use wooden plates, which are good heat insulators and therefore require no special heating in order to keep the melted cheese warmer longer. The traditional accompaniments to the melted cheese are boiled potatoes and tiny cucumber pickles, the kind that are called in France *cornichons.*

I agree with my Swiss friends that it is bad for the digestion to consume, with any kind of hot melted cheese, any kind of ice-cold drink. So I usually serve one of the several excellent imported labels of Dôle, the charming light red wine of the Swiss canton of Valais. So now, having assembled at least two ceramic, or china, plates (or one wooden plate) for each guest, some form of fire or grill with which to melt the cheese, a blunt-edged spatula (or the straight back of a chef's kitchen knife) with which to scrape off the surface of melted cheese (or, if you are going to use the grill or oven method, heat-proof plates from which your guests will eat and some form of wooden board or stand in which to place them so that they will not burn the tablecloth), let us begin.

STAPLES
Crystal salt
Freshly ground black pepper
First-quality sweet red paprika

SHOPPING
One of the Swiss *raclette*-type cheeses—essential to have half a wheel, with a large, flat surface, to be grilled (about 7 1/2 pounds)
Boiling potatoes, small, to be cooked in their jackets (about 3-4 pounds)
White pickled onions, small (about 6 per person)
French imported *cornichons,* tiny pickles, or domestic alternative (about 6 per person)

About 30 Minutes Before the Party Begins

Thoroughly clean the skins of the potatoes, as they are to be eaten. Boil or steam the potatoes and hold them warm. Preheat oven to 150° F.

When Guests Are Assembled and Raclette Party Is Ready to Begin

Set all the plates to get hot in the oven. Place the 1/2 wheel of cheese in front of the heat source, about an inch or two away from it. Watch it carefully. As soon as the surface begins to be tipped with brown and starts bubbling, put whole potato on the side of the plate and, using the blunt straight edge of back-of-knife or spatula, scrape melted cheese downward onto the center of the plate. Put pickled cucumbers and onions all around and eat instantly. Cheese is at once returned to heat for next serving of next guest. In between each serving, plates should be washed in hot water, dried, and returned to warming oven. After the first few minutes, the whole routine will revolve smoothly and, as guests learn quickly how to handle and watch cheese, there will be less and less work for the host.

The Variation from the Canton of the Bernese Oberland

In the German-speaking parts of Switzerland, *raclette* is also called *bratkase,* or baked cheese, and is prepared under a grill or in an oven. The plates for the guests have to be ovenproof and must have wooden stands into which they fit, so that they can be safely carried to and set down on the table. A portion of sliced potatoes is placed on one of these plates, the cold cheese is sliced about 1/8 inch thick, and 2 or 3 slices, each about 3 inches square (say about 3 ounces per person) are placed on top of the potatoes, then briefly baked in the oven at 425° F., or placed about 2 inches under a grill. Again, as soon as the cheese is tipped with brown and is bubbling (usually in about 10 minutes) it is garnished with the onions and pickles and eaten instantly.

Other variations, from other cantons of Switzerland, involve melting the slices of cheese in a non-greased frypan, or cutting largish cubes of cheese, sticking them onto skewers and half melting them over glowing-hot coals. (I suspect this last method is p-r-e-t-t-y dangerous and the loss of lumps of cheese into the fire is fairly high!)

Incidentally, if you absolutely cannot get any of the proper Swiss cheeses, you can extemporize a modified (and somewhat compromised) form of *raclette* with domestic or imported Muenster, or Tilsit, or California Monterey Jack. Perhaps I should add a final warning. You will be astonished at the number of servings of *raclette* that your guests will consume and the amount of liquid refreshment they will soak down with it. Incidentally, if you run out of wine, not-too-cold beer is also an excellent accompaniment.

CHAPTER 10

A LAZY LUPPER INSTEAD OF A BREEZY BRUNCH

But Why Only on Sundays?

I am horrified whenever I open one of those "entertainment etiquette" guidebooks and find myself being told how to "set a sumptuous brunch table" by noon on any and every Sunday. Holy Sunday smoke! What do they expect? Any one of their proposed menus would involve at least five hours' work. Am I supposed to get up at seven and spend my Sunday mornings slaving over a hot stove, just to make an impressive show at noon?

I consider my first duty on any "day of rest" is to rest, to revive my body and soul by lazing in bed with newspapers and music—not for any particularly planned or prescribed time, but just as long as my mood (and my old backbone) demands on that particular day. So—my requirement number one is that there shall be no noon deadline. Instead of brunch, I have invented a form of gastronomic entertainment that involves invitations to an "almost open house" party in the mid- or late afternoon. My menu may include some relaxing reminiscences of breakfast, but it is mainly a combination of a lazy lunch and a savory supper. Hence, "lupper," which to me has a much more pleasantly liquid and smooth sound than "brrrunch," which sounds more like a growl or a shudder.

I demand, for my lupper menu, something different from the foods of working days, something unique to a day of relaxation. The most important ingredients of the meal should be a leisurely perfection of

153

preparation and a lovely appearance on the table—whether side buffet or sit-down spread. Then I try to add my personal garnish: a feeling of easy, timeless relaxation. It is this rare combination of ambience, atmosphere, and refreshment that, once again, makes the meal memorable.

The final advantage of my late, lupper hour of entertainment is that there can be no question about serving spiritous apéritifs before the meal, lovely wines with the lovely foods, and fruit brandies with and after the coffee. And why must this delightful combination be restricted to Sundays? How about Saturdays? And all the other holidays? I am AGAINST "a fast early walk through the park to work up an appetite," or "a sunrise swim to loosen the limbs," or "a brisk bicycle ride to fill your lungs with the cool morning zephyrs." I am FOR more mornings in bed and more late-afternoon luppers.

Menu of a Conveniently Late Lupper for Four

Alpine Mountain Seyssel Sparkler with Exotic Fruits
and/or
Champagne-Guava-Strawberry Punch
and/or
Coup de Vache—French New Orleans Milkshot

Brandied and Fruited   **More Ice-Cold Champagne,*
French Toast   *or Sparkling Seyssel*

Homemade Brioche "Head" Loaf—Grosse Brioche à Tête
with a Selection of English Marmalades,
Jams, and Jellies and Sweet Butter

Coffee   **A Selection of Alsatian Dry Fruit Brandies*

The opening trio of drinks is planned to meet the tastes both of those guests who prefer a fruity, sparkling lightness and of those who feel they need a sharp, spiritous uplift. The first "sparkler" switches from the normal, breakfast-style grapefruit and orange sections to a balanced array of supermarket exotica. White-fleshed, pitted and skinned lichee fruit now comes in cans from Taiwan. Mandarin orange sections come canned from Japan. Glacéed golden kum-quats—like miniature dollhouse oranges—are bottled in Florida. And

deep red *cascos de guavas,* the "hooves" or narrow ends of the guava fruit, arrive canned from Spain. For the second drink the Champagne is fruited with unsweetened guava nectar, now widely available in bottles and cans. This drink is best, of course, when it can be garnished with fresh strawberries, but the quick-frozen kind will do in a crunch, or a pinch. Go easy with the milkshot. Behind its almost bland, deceptively nutritive smoothness, it has a kick that is a cross between a bullshot, a muleshot, and a gunshot.

If you have never tasted the lovely, sparkling white Seyssel Blanc de Blancs from the little town of Seyssel in the High Alps of Savoy in southeastern France, you have missed a sizable piece of the joy of living. The wine is as dry and light as the mountain air, as bubbly and refreshing as a stream tumbling over rocks, and, not the least of its virtues, it is now being imported at prices roughly half those of many other famous-name "bubblies." In fact, for my money, the Seyssel has better qualities of character in the medium-to-low price range than some equivalent Champagnes. So I am always happy to serve the Seyssel, not only in the opening fruit Sparkler but also as the accompanying wine through the rest of the meal.

Do not be deceived by the simple "French Toast" label on the main dish. This one is like no other and never fails to provoke demands for the recipe. It is refreshingly tart with pureed fresh fruits, velvety-smooth with an egg custard, and forcefully surprising with the hidden inner power of the marvelous Calvados apple brandy of Normandy.

In this menu the bread is virtually a main course in its own right. Instead of serving small brioches, bought from the local French bakery, here is how to make your own dough and then shape it into the classic *Grosse Brioche à Tête,* the loaf with a head on it. Served still warm from the oven, carved into thin slices, and eaten with English bitter Seville orange marmalade, or fresh fruit preserves, it can be the climax of the meal. To offer a separate dessert would be an insult to the bread and to everyone else concerned with its consumption.

Finally, as the room is filled with the warm glow of friendship and unity, while the conversation flows easily and smoothly, why not offer your guests a selection of two or three of the great dry fruit brandies that are brilliantly concocted by the distillers of Alsace from the wild fruits that grow on the slopes of the Vosges Mountains? The names are as evocative of the purity of the forested slopes as the bouquet and taste of these extraordinary *eaux de vie: framboise sauvage,* distilled from the wild raspberry; *baies de houx,* from holly berries; *kirsch,* wild cherry; *marc de prunes,* red plum brandy; *mirabelle,* golden plum; *mure des bois,* wild blackberry; *myrtille,* wild huckleberry; *poire Williams,* Williams pear; *quetsch,* from the small purple plum; or *sureau,* elderberry. A magnificent ending to any meal.

Alpine Mountain Seyssel Sparkler with Exotic Fruits

Shopping

(For 4)

White, pitted lichees in syrup, (4-ounce can)

Mandarin orange sections in syrup (4-ounce can)

Glacéed golden kumquats, in syrup (4-ounce bottle)

Cascos de guavas, in syrup (4-ounce can)

Pineapple juice, unsweetened (1 cup)

Fresh mint (several sprigs)

Seyssel Blanc de Blancs sparkling wine (1 bottle)

The Night Before—Preparation of Fruits in About 10 Minutes

To prepare and serve this, you will need a handsome bowl of about 1-quart capacity which is fairly deep, a nice-looking ladle, and a stemmed white-wine glass of, say, 8- to 10-ounce capacity for each guest. Set ladle, glasses, and unopened bottle of Seyssel to chill in refrigerator overnight. Drain each of the exotic fruits, reserving each juice separately, and if necessary cut them up into conveniently smallish bite-sized pieces. Put them all together into the serving bowl and pour over them the cup of pineapple juice. Now, stirring with a wooden spoon, add, dash by dash, some of the lichee syrup, the mandarin orange juice, and the kumquat syrup, but go very carefully with the guava syrup, which, while adding its beautiful red color, is almost sickly sweet. Add some, but not too much. When the liquid in the bowl is exactly to your taste, add a couple of dozen mint leaves, fairly finely chopped, then set the bowl, covered, to chill overnight in the refrigerator.

Serving on the Day

Into each chilled glass, ladle a total of about 4 ounces of the fruits and their liquid, then fill up each glass with the ice-cold sparkling Seyssel and float a sprig of mint on top.

Champagne-Guava-Strawberry Punch
(For 4)

STAPLES
Lemons (2)
Sugar, white fine-grind (1/4 cup)

SHOPPING
Guava nectar (12-ounce can)
Strawberries (small basket, 1/2 cup after slicing)
Champagne (1 bottle)

The Night Before—Advance Preparation About 15 Minutes

Use tulip-shaped Champagne glasses and set in the freezer overnight. Put the unopened bottle of Champagne in the refrigerator overnight. In a 1 1/2-quart glass pitcher, put the 12 ounces of guava nectar, the juice of the 2 lemons, and the 1/4 cup sugar. Stir well until sugar dissolves. Slice the 1/2 cup strawberries and add to pitcher, cover, and also place in refrigerator overnight.

Serving on the Day

Into each glass put 1 or 2 ice cubes. Half-fill each glass with the fruit mixture and top up with the Champagne.

Coup de Vache—French New Orleans Milkshot
(For 4)

STAPLES
Milk (1 quart)
Freshly ground nutmeg

SHOPPING
Banana liqueur (2 ounces)
Orange Curaçao liqueur (2 ounces)
Cognac, fine-quality (8 ounces)

The Night Before

Make sure that all ingredients (except nutmeg, of course) are chilled overnight in refrigerator. You will need a handsome, tall 12- to 14-ounce tumbler for each guest and these should also be chilled overnight. And there should be a supply of brightly colored straws.

Mixing and Serving

Pour 1 cup of the cold milk into each chilled tumbler. Add 1/2 ounce banana liqueur, 1/2 ounce orange Curaçao, and 2 ounces Cognac. Plop in 1 or 2 ice cubes, or none, as you please. Stir well. Float 1 or 2 grinds of nutmeg on top—mainly for the nice bouquet—but don't overdo it. Serve with a straw.

Brandied and Fruited French Toast
(For 4)

STAPLES
  Sweet butter (1/4 pound)
  Eggs (3 large)
  Milk (1 1/2 cups)
  Confectioners' sugar (2 to 3 tablespoons)
  Granulated white sugar (1/4 cup)
  Table salt
  Whole vanilla bean
  Pure vanilla extract

SHOPPING
  Fruits, according to season: strawberries, raspberries, peaches, plums, etc., or frozen equivalents (enough to make 1 cup mashed)
  Light cream (1 1/2 cups)
  French bread (1 long loaf)
  French Calvados apple brandy (about 1/3 cup)

The Night Before—Advance Preparation of Fruits
About 15 Minutes

Remove skins, stones, pits, stalks, and so forth from the fruits and mash the flesh into a coarse puree with a fork, or run the fruits in the electric blender for just a second or two. Hold puree, covered, in refrigerator.

About 50 Minutes Before Serving—Active Preparation About 35 Minutes—Unsupervised Baking About 15 Minutes

Prepare a vanilla egg custard. Put the 1 1/2 cups of milk into a 1- to 1 1/2-quart saucepan, preferably copper, for instant response to adjustments of temperature, then stir in 3 tablespoons of the granulated sugar. Cut a 3-inch length of the vanilla bean in half lengthwise, then, using the point of a small, sharp knife, scrape out the central seeds from each half and drop them into the milk. Cut the 2 halves into 1/2-inch lengths and also drop into milk. Place pan over fairly gentle heat and bring up slowly, stirring fairly regularly, almost to boiling, but do not let it actually boil. Then turn off heat and let it cool. Meanwhile, over second burner, arrange a double boiler and adjust heat so that water in lower half is only just simmering. Break 2 of the eggs into a medium-sized bowl and beat very hard with a wire whisk, at the same time incorporating 1/4 teaspoon salt. While still beating, incorporate 2 tablespoons of the hot vanilla milk. Next, still beating, slowly pour in remainder of hot milk. Strain mixture into top of double boiler, getting rid of bits of vanilla bean, which have now completed their job. While mixture is heating up in double boiler, stir continuously, until it thickens and coats a metal spoon, usually in about 5 minutes. At once remove top from double boiler and dip it into a pan of cold water, to cool custard. Taste, and if necessary add a little more sugar and a few drops of pure vanilla extract. Cut a circle of wax paper and press it very lightly onto surface of custard to prevent skin from forming. Hold at room temperature until needed.

When custard is thick and cool, blend in the fruit puree. Cut the French bread on a slant into thick slices. In a mixing bowl beat the remaining egg with: the 1 1/2 cups of light cream, 1 tablespoon of the confectioners' sugar, the 1/3 cup of Calvados, and 1/4 teaspoon salt. Set a sauté pan on medium frying heat and melt just enough butter to lubricate the bottom. Each slice of bread is now dipped into the egg-cream batter and fried on both sides until brown. Melt in more butter as needed. Turn on oven to 400° F. Butter an open heatproof dish, which can be brought to the table, and arrange the browned pieces of bread on it. Pour over them the custard and sprinkle on confectioners' sugar. Then bake in oven until the top is lightly browned, usually in about 15 minutes.

Homemade Brioche "Head" Loaf—
Grosse Brioche à Tête

(A feast for 4, with maybe, some remaining for next day)

STAPLES

Sweet butter (13 tablespoons, plus more for greasing bowl and molds)

Eggs (5 large)

Milk (1 tablespoon)

Flour, all-purpose (about 2 cups, plus more for flouring board)

Sugar, white fine-grind (1 1/2 tablespoons)

Salt (1 teaspoon)

Vegetable oil (about 1 teaspoon)

SHOPPING

Dry active yeast (1 packet)

The Day Before—Active Preparation About 40 Minutes—Unsupervised Proofing of Dough About 5 Hours

Lightly butter a 3-quart mixing bowl. Cut up 12 tablespoons of the butter into small pieces and allow to come to room temperature. The butter should be soft but not melted. Also, allow about 1 tablespoon to soften to be used for brushing dough. Dissolve the yeast in 1/4 cup fairly warm water, but not hot to the tip of the finger—about 100° F. Then let yeast mixture rest for 5 minutes.

Into a 2-quart mixing bowl, break 3 whole eggs and 1 more egg yolk, add the 1 1/2 tablespoons sugar and 1 teaspoon salt. Preferably using an electric beater, blend at low speed and slowly add 1 cup of the flour. Increase the beating speed to medium, or continue by hand, and gradually add another cup of flour and the 12 tablespoons softened butter, 1 tablespoon at a time. Beat until well blended.

Reduce speed and, using a dough hook on the mixer if available, continue beating until dough retracts and pulls away cleanly from the bowl—usually in about 10 to 15 minutes.

(Beating brioche dough is very important because it is too soft and rich to knead by hand. If you have to beat by hand, do so by lifting pieces of the dough out of the bowl and slapping it back until it begins to hold its shape and pulls clean away from the bowl. This is a messy job because the dough is extremely sticky, so if at all possible use an electric beater.)

Turn dough out onto a floured board, shape into a ball, and place in the buttered mixing bowl. Brush top with the softened butter, cover, and set in a warm place, 70° to 75° F., where dough will rise and triple in bulk—usually in 4 to 5 hours. This rising must not be hurried by allowing the temperature to exceed 75° F. or the dough will take on a yeasty flavor.

4-5 Hours Later—Punching and Proofing About 12 Hours

When dough has risen, punch down, turn out onto a floured board, and shape again into a ball. Return to bowl, cover, and refrigerate at least 12 hours. The dough will rise again and may double in bulk.

The Next Day—Shaping and Proofing Brioche About 2 1/2 Hours—Baking About 50 Minutes

Butter the inside of a 3-cup fluted brioche mold. From this point on, work quickly on a cool, lightly floured surface (if possible, on a pastry marble). If the temperature is too warm and the butter softens, the dough will become a sticky mess and will have to be refrigerated again before continuing.

Take dough from refrigerator and punch down. Cut off four-fifths of the dough for the base of the Brioche à Tête and use the remaining piece for the head. Flatten each piece of dough and fold in half and in half again. Fold the corners into the center, turn over, and roll into a tight ball, keeping the top smooth.

Place the large ball into the buttered mold, pressing it down firmly to fill the mold about two-thirds full. Mark its exact center and press a conical-shaped hole into the dough. Shape the smaller ball into a teardrop shape and seat it firmly in the hole. This forms the head which must be right in the middle of the base dough, otherwise it will rise and bake crooked.

Using aluminum foil, make a collar the height of the head, lightly oil the inside surface and wrap around brioche head. Fold and pinch a seam in the foil to fasten the ends. This will help hold the shape of the brioche head. Set in a warm place, 70° to 75° F., until dough has risen to fill mold—usually in about 2 to 2 1/2 hours.

About 15 Minutes Before Baking

Preheat oven to 450° F. Beat an egg yolk with the 1 tablespoon milk. Carefully remove aluminum collar and brush brioche with egg-milk, but avoid getting this glaze on the mold or in the crack between the base and head. Set in oven and bake 10 minutes, then lower heat to 350° F. and bake 20 minutes more. Then check, and if top is browning too quickly, cover with aluminum foil for the final 20 minutes.

CHAPTER 11

WHEN LUCULLUS DINES ALONE

The Art of Boiling Water for Nourishment Against Time

Whaen modern gourmets describe a magnificent meal as being "a Lucullan feast," they are paying tribute, after more than two thousand years, to the man who has often been called the greatest of all gastronomes of ancient Rome, Lucius Lucullus. He gave some of the largest, most lavish and expensive dinners in history. He also enjoyed dining alone. On one such day he felt that the menu and the preparation of the dishes by his cook were not quite up to scratch. The little roasted birds with which the meal began were not quite crisp enough. The sauce on the fish did not quite have the perfection for which the cook was famous. Lucullus clapped his hands and ordered the cook to the dining room. He bowed deeply and expressed abject apologies when he heard his master's complaint. "But, my lord," he excused himself with a trembling voice, "I did not think it necessary to prepare a supreme banquet when you were dining alone." The voice of Lucullus was as cold as ice: "That is precisely when you must be most careful, for then I have my most critical of all guests—Lucullus is entertaining Lucullus."

Two thousand years later, for precisely the same reason, I find interest and pleasure in dining with myself. I would feel that I was being rude to myself if I turned on the phonograph or the television. On the contrary, now is the moment for special concentration on the fine details of the food, however simple it may be. Now is the moment to experiment with that new and revolutionary recipe that I would not dare to try on my friends until I had tried it on myself. Now is the time to taste new and highly unorthodox marriages of foods and wines in the hope of discovering some marvelous new combination that no one has ever thought of before.

Yet, of course, there are inevitably many occasions when one must eat, not only interestingly and nourishingly, but also quickly. Then I usually turn to the simple art of boiling water, which can cover a multitude of my Lucullan needs. It boils and poaches eggs. It cooks the most complicated shapes of pasta. It preserves, by its steam, the subtlest flavors of fish and meats. Bubbling water makes the bouillon for rice pilaf, the aromatic risotto, or the *cassoulet* of goose-flavored baked beans. Above all, bubbling water is the essential start of a great soup.

I like to believe that soup is the second oldest of all cooked foods, preceded only by the meat that the hunter brought back to his cave and grilled over the open fire. It is still one of the most essential of gastronomic commodities—especially when Lucullus dines with Lucullus. Soup, made in advance, can be hidden in the refrigerator as insurance against a sudden attack of the hungers. Hundreds of famous soups are highly satisfying one-dish meals. Every important farming region of the world has its own special richly hearty soup, brought to table in a huge earthenware pot, or casserole, or *marmite,* or *olla,* or *toupin,* according to the language of its homeland. All these soups are simple to prepare; they improve with keeping and reheating. I find them much more timesaving, economical, and delicious than the so-called short-cut foods.

Here, then, are a few of my favorite Lucullan soups. I prepare them in a large, old, and handsomely browned earthenware *marmite*; they simmer slowly in a very low oven for hours without the slightest attention, then are stored in the refrigerator as a basic supply from which an instant good meal can be reheated at any hour of the day or night. All of them, of course, are good enough for an informal party.

But dining alone does not have to be tied to even the most succulent of soups. Some of my other favorite recipes follow. The "secret trick" of my Garlic Snail Butter was given me by the brilliant young American chef Jerry East. His recipe, of course, begins, "Take 10 pounds of the best butter . . ." but I have cut it down to my size and

usually keep a pound or two on hand, not only for snails, but also to spread on hot country-ham biscuits, to use with anchovies as an appetizer dip, or to be added in small quantities for the enrichment of many other dishes or sauces. Once you have mixed your basic butter, you can store it in the refrigerator for days, or in the freezer for weeks, removing only as much as you need at any one time.

The Southern Wine Hash is my variation of a classic American regional dish, in my opinion the finest way of "reglorifying-with-wine" almost any cooked meats and vegetables remaining in the refrigerator from previous meals. But this hash is so good that I often buy fresh ingredients and make it from scratch! I accompany it with country-ham biscuits spread with the snail butter.

When one dines alone, the great standby, naturally, for combined nutrition, pleasure, satisfaction, and "instant preparation" is Steak Tartare. It often appears on my solo table, but I like to vary it with my version of Armenian Aromatic Lamb Tartare, which involves no more time and trouble than grinding up a portion of completely lean, first-quality loin of young lamb and quickly blending into it some of the spices of the Middle East.

Finally, instead of gooey, oversweet, calorie-charged desserts, I prefer fresh fruits and one or another of my most-loved combinations of cheese and wine. It is certainly not true that "any cheese goes perfectly with any wine." There are some very special affinities, and a few of those that I have adopted as my own are listed at the end of this chapter.

Three Great One-Dish-Meal Soups

French Potage Chasseur—Hunter's Soup

(Several solo meals)

I learned this recipe in the kitchen of a Spanish Catalan family living in one of the more remote Alpine valleys of the High Savoy in southeastern France. The dish takes its name, obviously, from the fact that it can be made with almost any cut of almost any animal brought home by one of the mountain hunters. If you live, as I do, rather far from any mountains, you can use a piece of ham, or smoked pork, or virtually any other meat to add its variety of flavor to this highly flexible stew. It should traditionally be prepared in a lidded earthenware pot, but you can also use an enameled cast-iron *cocotte*, or any kind of soup kettle that will fit into the oven.

STAPLES
   Garlic (3 cloves)
   Olive oil (about 4 tablespoons)
   Crystal salt
   Freshly ground black pepper
   Bay leaves
   Whole cloves
   Thyme

SHOPPING
   Large ham bone, with plenty of
      meat on it (about 3 pounds),
      or a smoked pork butt of the
      same size
   Green cabbage (1 small)
   Leeks (2 medium)
   Bermuda or Spanish onions (2
      large)
   Green pepper (1 fairly large)
   Italian peeled and seeded plum
      tomatoes (1-pound can)
   Beef bouillon (2 cups)
   Dry white wine (2 cups)

Active Preparation About 45 Minutes—Unsupervised Oven Simmering About 2 Hours

Preheat oven to 300° F. and put in, to heat up, the large, empty soup pot. Make ready all the ingredients and hold each separately: peel and finely mince the 3 cloves garlic; peel and slice the 2 onions; thoroughly clean and chunk the white parts of the 2 leeks; peel off the tough outer leaves of the cabbage and cut its heart into 8 segments; wash, seed, and coarsely chop the green pepper. Put 4 tablespoons of olive oil into a fairly large sauté pan, heat it up to low frying heat, and put in the garlic, the sliced onions, and the leeks. Let them gently simmer for about 10 minutes, stirring them often, so that they melt but do not brown. Then add the can of tomatoes, with all their juice, and the chopped pepper. Keep them simmering, stirring occasionally, for about 15 minutes.

Meanwhile, in 2-quart saucepan, heat up the 2 cups each of beef bouillon and wine, with 2 cups of freshly drawn cold water, almost to boiling, then keep hot. Take the main pot out of the oven and put into it the piece of ham or pork, surrounded by the segments of cabbage. Put back into the oven, covered, to let them sweat.

When vegetables in sauté pan have simmered about 15 minutes, again take the pot out of the oven and pour in the entire contents of the sauté pan. Add 2 crumbled bay leaves, 3 whole cloves, 2 teaspoons dried thyme, plus salt and pepper to taste. Pour in the 3 pints of liquid, cover, then put pot back in oven, tightly lidded, to simmer for at least 2 hours. Add more water, if necessary, to keep everything well covered.

Serving at Table

Lift meat out of pot and carve off as many slices as your hunger demands, placing them in your hot soup bowl and sprinkling them with 2 teaspoons of fresh olive oil. Ladle soup and vegetables over meat and finally adjust seasonings to your taste.

Athenian Fish Soup Avgolemono
(Several solo meals)

This is a modified, fishy version of the classic Greek egg-lemon soup. It is best when you can get a whole, firm-fleshed fish, with its head on, such as, for example, a red snapper, a sea or striped bass, or a small cod or haddock.

STAPLES
Eggs (1 large for each serving)
Lemons (1 for each serving)
Yellow onions (2 medium)
Olive oil (1/2 cup)
Crystal salt
Freshly ground black pepper
Oregano
Thyme

SHOPPING
Whole fish, cleaned and scaled, but with backbone in and head on; red snapper is ideal (about 3 pounds)
Green celery (1 bunch)
Green peppers (2 medium)
Italian peeled and seeded plum tomatoes (1-pound 1-ounce can)
Elbow macaroni (1 1/4 cups, before cooking)
Dry white vermouth (1/3 cup)

Active Preparation About 30 Minutes—Simmering About 20 Minutes

Prepare this soup in a 3- to 4-quart soup kettle, or stewpot, on top of the stove. Put into it the 1/2 cup olive oil and heat up to gentle frying temperature. Add the 2 onions, peeled and sliced, the 2 green peppers, seeded and chunked, the heart only of the celery, chunked (including some of the leaves, finely chopped), and the can of tomatoes. Let them all simmer gently, stirring from time to time, until quite soft—usually in 15 to 20 minutes. Meanwhile, see that fish is cleaned and properly scaled, then cut it across into large chunks, keeping the head as one of these chunks. In a large saucepan, bring up to boiling 2 quarts of freshly drawn cold water. As soon as vegetables are soft, add fish (including head) to main pot, plus 1 teaspoon oregano, 1 teaspoon thyme, with salt and pepper to taste and the 1/3 cup vermouth. Then pour in only enough boiling water to cover everything and simmer until fish is just firm and flaky—usually in about 10 minutes. Meanwhile, separate 1 egg, putting yolk into small bowl and reserving white for some other use. Beat yolk lightly and hold. Squeeze juice of 1 lemon into another bowl and hold. Set your oven to keep-warm temperature, about 150° to 175° F.

The moment the fish is done, remove chunks from soup, discard head, and keep chunks warm in covered dish in oven. Sprinkle the 1 1/4 cups macaroni into soup in main pot and stir around to mix. Keep soup bubbling merrily, covered, until macaroni is just done, but *al dente*, still nicely chewy—usually in 10 to 15 minutes. Meanwhile, take out as many chunks of fish as your hunger demands, remove and discard skin and bones, then flake flesh into bite-sized pieces and continue to keep warm. Remaining chunks of fish can now be refrigerated, covered, for future use.

Serving at Table

Warm your soup bowl, but do not make it too hot, or egg yolk will set. Pour egg yolk into soup bowl and at once strongly beat into it with a wire whisk the lemon juice. Now, continuing to beat strongly all the time, dribble in hot liquid (avoiding solids as much as possible) from main soup pot. Egg will begin to thicken. At once beat in more hot liquid, until you have as much liquid as you want for 1 serving. It should be creamy, smooth, handsomely pinkish yellow in color, and nicely lemony in flavor. Now fill up your bowl with as much macaroni and vegetables as you need, plus the flaked fish. Remaining soup will, of course, be refrigerated and, the next time you want to serve it, you can reheat just as much as you need, with more of the fish, plus the egg and lemon thickening beaten into each bowl. If you want to serve it to several people, you should have 1 egg yolk and the juice of 1 lemon for each person, and then it is best to do the beating all together in a warm tureen.

My Modified Version of Spanish Fabada Asturiana
(Several solo meals)

This is the famous specialty of the mountainous region of Asturias in northwestern Spain. The name *fabada* comes from the white *fabe* bean, which grows there and is the main ingredient of a magnificent stew with the aromatic local smoked meats and sausages, all surrounded and washed down by Asturian tart hard cider. In place of these purely local ingredients, I use large white haricot beans, with Spanish-style *chorizo* sausage (when I can find it in Spanish, Puerto Rican, or Latin American stores), or the Italian *pepperoni,* long, narrow sausage.

STAPLES
    Garlic (3 cloves)
    Yellow onion (1 medium)
    Crystal salt
    Freshly ground black pepper
    Bay leaves
    Cloves, whole
    Dill, dried, if fresh not available
    Oregano
    Saffron in strands (1 teaspoon)
    Savory

SHOPPING
    Ham hock, with bone and plenty of meat (about 2 pounds)
    Spanish *chorizo* sausage, or Italian *pepperoni* (about 1 pound)
    Pigs' feet, fresh, cut in half lengthwise by butcher (2)
    White haricot, Great Northern, or marrowfat dried beans (1 pound)
    Spanish onions (4 large)
    Green pepper (1 medium)
    Potatoes (4 medium)
    Green cabbage (1 small head)
    Hard cider (1 bottle)
    Dry white vermouth (1/3 cup)

The Day Before—Soaking the Beans—Working Time 5 Minutes

In a 3-quart saucepan, heat 2 quarts of water to a rolling boil, then dribble in the pound of white beans slowly enough so that water never stops boiling. Continue bubbling hard for 2 minutes, then turn off heat, cover, and leave to soak overnight.

*The Next Day—Active Preparation About 30
Minutes—Unsupervised Simmering About 2 Hours*

Drain the soaked beans, saving the soaking water and straining it through a fine-mesh sieve. Wash beans under running cold water and pick them over, discarding any that are broken. Put ham hock on bottom of your large soup pot, surround it with soaked beans, pour in bottle of hard cider, and add just enough of the soaking water to cover everything about 1 inch deep. Peel the yellow onion, leaving it whole, stick 4 whole cloves into it on 4 sides, and add it to the pot. Also add 1 teaspoon each of dill, oregano, and savory. Place pot over high heat and bring rapidly to the boil, then turn down heat and simmer very gently, covered. This dish will be mushed and ruined by any hard boiling. Meanwhile, prepare more vegetables and assemble them together in a mixing bowl: peel and chunk the 4 Spanish onions, peel and finely mince the 3 cloves garlic, core and chunk the green pepper. Into a very small, butter-melting saucepan, put the 1/3 cup dry white vermouth and heat up gently to just above blood heat—so that it stings the tip of the finger. Into this hot liquid put the 1 teaspoon of saffron, stir it around with a small wooden spoon, and leave it to soak and exude its bright-yellow oils until it will be added to soup.

20 Minutes After Simmering Begins

Add the onions, garlic, and green pepper to soup, with 2 crumbled bay leaves, and stir in. Then add vermouth and saffron to soup pot, carefully rinsing out all yellow oils from small pan with a spoonful or two of the hot soup. Cut up *chorizo* or *pepperoni* sausages into 1 1/2-inch lengths and add to main pot. Into a separate pan put the 4 halves of the pigs' feet, cover with cold water, and bring rapidly to boiling, skimming off any rising dirt or scum; simmer them until they are just soft—usually in about 30 minutes. Drain them and add feet to the main soup pot. Peel and coarsely chunk the 4 potatoes and add to pot. While gentle simmering continues, remove tough outer leaves from cabbage, coarsely shred its heart, and hold. Occasionally check level of liquid in main pot. All ingredients should remain well covered. If not, add more of the soaking water from the beans.

After 1 1/2 Hours of Simmering

Taste 2 or 3 beans for doneness. They should be quite soft. If not, continue simmering another 15 minutes and taste again. As soon as beans are soft, add shredded cabbage to pot. Continue simmering 5 to 8 more minutes, according to whether you like your cabbage crisp or soft. Finally, check soup for seasoning and add salt and pepper to taste. This is always done at the last moment with this dish, since one can never tell in advance how much salt and pepper will be exuded by the meats.

Serving at Table

Make sure, of course, that you get a balanced mixture in your soup bowl of chunks of ham and pig meat, of pieces of sausage, of beans, and everything else in this rich conglomeration. When the main pot has cooled—and before putting it away in the refrigerator—remove and discard all bones, cutting the meat into large chunks. After a few hours of refrigeration, you can also lift off the thin layer of fat that will have solidified on the surface. For the next meal, just heat up as much as you need.

Jerry East's All-Purpose Garlic Snail Butter

(About 1/4 pound to keep on hand)

Although the preparation of this aromatic butter is as simple as the square root of four, the superb balance of its flavors requires accurate measurement. Chef East, being a professional, insists on weighing all his ingredients—even his pepper. Since most of us do not have such accurate scales, I include the closest possible approximation of measurements by cups and spoons. Remember, though, that you will get the best results by weighing.

STAPLES

Sweet butter (1 pound)

Garlic, already peeled (1 ounce—about 8 medium cloves)

Crystal salt (1/2 ounce—about 1 tablespoon)

Freshly ground white pepper (0.15 ounce—about 1 teaspoon)

SHOPPING

Parsley, leaves only (1 1/4 ounces—about 1 1/2 cups, fairly tightly packed)

Shallots, already peeled (1 ounce—about 10 medium cloves)

California not-too-sweet dessert wine (1 1/4 ounces)

Preparation and Mixing in About 20 Minutes

The "secret" of this magnificently aromatic butter is the use of the slightly sweet (but not too sweet) wine. You simply mix everything in a large bowl. Put in the butter and let it soften. Finely mince the garlic. Do the same with the shallots. Finely chop the parsley leaves. Add all these and the salt, white pepper, and the wine. Working firmly and indefatigably with a wooden spoon, completely blend everything. Make sure that there are no unmixed pockets anywhere. With spatula and spoon, mold the butter into a tightly lidded crock and refrigerate for later use.

Just Before Serving—Cooking in About 5 Minutes

Measure the precise amount you need and put it into a small sauté pan. Heat up quite gently until butter starts to bubble. Watch bits of garlic and shallot very carefully. They must just be clarified and not, under any circumstances, browned. As soon as the garlic or shallot starts to color, the butter will take on a bitter taste. This must be avoided at all costs. Better to undercook than to brown, but best of all to learn to recognize the precise moment when garlic and shallots have become clear and butter should be removed immediately from heat and served. At this point it is marvelously aromatic and nutty—I am such an addict that I soak it up with soft bits of sourdough bread.

My Modified Southern Wine Hash

(Several solo meals)

STAPLES
Sweet butter (3 1/2 table-
    spoons)
Beef bouillon (1 1/2 cups)
Yellow onion (1 medium)
Flour, all-purpose (1 1/2 ta-
    blespoons)
Crystal salt
Freshly ground black pepper
Thyme

SHOPPING
Beef, top-round (1/2 pound)
Carrots (2 medium)
Green pepper (1 small)
Potatoes (2 medium)
Dry red wine (1 cup)

*Total Preparation Time 1 Hour—Active Work About
25 Minutes—Cooking About 35 Minutes*

Cut up the 1/2 pound beef into 1/2-inch cubes. Peel and cube the 2 potatoes. Scrape and dice the 2 carrots. Finely chop the onion and green pepper. In a medium-sized, lidded sauté pan, over high heat, melt 2 tablespoons of the butter and brown the beef with the chopped onion and pepper. Add the chopped potatoes and carrot, the 1 1/2 cups beef bouillon, 1 cup red wine, 1/2 teaspoon thyme, and salt and pepper to taste. Cover, reduce heat, and simmer.

Meanwhile, prepare a *beurre manié*. Soften the remaining 1 1/2 tablespoons butter. Now smoothly work it, a teaspoon at a time, into the 1 1/2 tablespoons flour, until you have a smooth, thick paste, then hold.

When hash is cooked, thicken it slightly by adding the *beurre manié*, teaspoon by teaspoon. You may not need to use it all. Continue simmering, stirring the while, until sauce is well blended, usually in 8 to 10 minutes.

Serve hash with freshly made country-ham biscuits, lavishly spread with the garlic snail butter.

Hot or Cold Country-Ham Biscuits

(About 20 biscuits)

Whenever I expect to be dining alone, one of my most regular and reliable standby meats is a fine-quality ham, which, if properly wrapped, seems to keep almost indefinitely. By "fine-quality" I do not, of course, mean the mass-produced ham of the average market, which is bland to the point of boredom and over-weighted with fat, gristle, and deliberately injected water. Instead, I insist on getting (ordering by mail direct from the producers, if I can find no local source) one of the fine, American farm-made hams, still being produced in limited quantities in all parts of the country. The king of American hams is the true Smithfield, which must legally be made in or around the town of that name in Virginia. Its meat is dark, nutty-dry, slightly crumbly, almost winy in flavor—the result of the all-peanut diet of the cosseted and pampered porkers of that district. Less dominant in personality and lighter, but still superb in fineness of flavor, are the "country hams"—from porkers fed on a mixed diet of peanuts and grain. Often, when I have some of this type of ham left over, I grind it up and blend it into these irresistible Country-Ham Biscuits. . .

STAPLES

    Country ham, coarsely
       ground (3/4 cup)
    Bacon or ham drippings
       (2 tablespoons)
    Milk (3/4 cup)
    Flour, all-purpose
       (2 cups) after sifting
    Double-acting baking powder
       (2 teaspoons)
    Salt

Total Preparation About 30 Minutes

Having sifted the flour once before measuring it, put it back in the sifter, sprinkling on the 2 teaspoons of baking powder and resifting together into a fair-sized mixing bowl. Blend into the flour, with light strokes, the 3/4 cup of ham and, according to its saltiness, a very little extra salt, to taste. Next, using a pastry cutter, work in the 2 tablespoons of softened drippings, until the emerging dough has the look and texture of coarse cornmeal. Add the milk, dash by dash, using as little as possible to achieve a soft dough.

Preheat your oven to 450° F. Using a gentle touch with your fingers, gather the dough into a ball and set it on a lightly floured pastry board. Knead gently for about 30 seconds. With a lightly floured rolling pin, roll out the dough to about 3/8-inch thick and, with a 1 1/2-inch diameter round biscuit cutter, press out the biscuits.

If Serving the Biscuits Hot—Final Baking in About 15 Minutes

Set the biscuits on a baking sheet and slide into the center of the oven. Bake until golden brown—usually in 12 to 15 minutes. They are also fine served cold.

Armenian Aromatic Lamb Tartare
(For 1)

STAPLES
Crystal salt
Freshly ground black pepper
Chili powder

SHOPPING
Lamb, top-quality, lean
  (1/2 pound)
Cracked wheat, ready to eat
  (1/4 pound)
Green pepper (1 small, enough
  for 2 teaspoons chopped)
Parsley (1 small bunch, enough
  for 4 tablespoons chopped)
Scallions (1 small bunch,
  enough for 4 tablespoons
  chopped)
Italian plum tomatoes (1/4
  cup)

Total Preparation About 20 Minutes

Using the finest cutter, grind the 1/2 pound lamb 3 times. Finely chop 4 tablespoons each of parsley and scallions, and 2 teaspoons green pepper. Into a medium-sized mixing bowl put the meat with the 1/4 pound cracked wheat. Knead mixture, gradually adding about 1/3 cup water, until meat develops into heavy "paste." It should not be mushy and all the water should be absorbed. Add half the chopped parsley and scallions, all the chopped green pepper, and salt and pepper to taste. Mix well, then gently add 1/4 cup tomatoes, without juice. Shape into a patty and chill in refrigerator until you are ready to dine.

When You Are Ready to Dine

Take lamb tartare out of refrigerator and place on a bed of the remaining parsley and scallions. This is best when eaten with Middle Eastern *lavash* bread or *pita*.

Perfect Marriages of Cheeses and Wines

1. *In the winter:* a platter of French Beaufort from the Savoy and domestic or imported Muenster and Roquefort,

 WITH a strong Rhône red from Châteauneuf-du-Pape, Côte Rôtie, or Hermitage; or a red California Pinot Noir; or an aromatic strong white, such as an Alsatian Gewürtztraminer.

2. *In the spring:* a platter of French Brie and imported Swiss Appenzeller and Gruyère,

 WITH a light red from the Pomerol or Saint-Emilion districts of Bordeaux; or a light Volnay from Burgundy; or a red California Cabernet Sauvignon.

3. *In high summer:* a platter of French Coulommiers from Champagne, Pont l'Evêque from Normandy, and one of the several cheeses covered with roasted grape pits,

 WITH an ice-cold Alsatian rosé de Pinot Noir; or a Château de Tigné from the Loire; or a Gamay rosé from California.

4. *In the autumn:* a platter of French Boursault or Délice de St.-Cyr from the Ile-de-France or Camembert from Normandy and Reblochon from the Savoy,

 WITH a white Muscadet of Sèvre-et-Maine from the Loire; or a light French Champagne, or a light sparkling wine from California or Seyssel; or white Crépy from the Savoy; or French Beaujolais or light red California Gamay.

CHAPTER 12

MIDNIGHT MACHINATIONS WITH FIRE AND SPIRIT

Will She? Won't She? Old Questions, New Answers

The more the world changes, the more the old questions come back full circle. When Hospitable Male invites Liberated Female to an early theater (or a concert, or the opera) and includes a midnight supper for two at his home afterward, there is no longer much of a social question as to whether she will or will not accept. Ogden Nash is gone and has taken with him his Dandy Candy. Most of the girls, it seems to me, can now absorb liquor quicker than most of the boys. And yet? Will she? Won't she? The key questions overhanging your midnight party remain the same.

Of course, you have planned for candlelight and *very* soft music. And the food and drink are as ready as the most careful planning can make them. All you have to do is to sit her down with her first drink and perform a few semimiraculous strokes with a few deliberately mysterious incantations. But, will she be truly impressed by what she observes of your gastronomic skill, as you move with the calm relaxation of the professional between the final preparations in your kitchen and on the dining table? Won't she perhaps withhold the complete "suspension of her disbelief" if the food you place before her lacks the final perfection of absolute rightness for the occasion? Will she after the last bite and the last sip, be completely won over to the acceptance of your brilliant gifts as a memorable host? Will the atmosphere of your room be warm with admiration? Will time be moving slowly? Will you have achieved the poet's dream of an ambience soft with "balance and beauty, luxury, relaxation and pleasure"? I submit, with cold calculation, that it all depends on your menu.

Let me not fall into the trap of boastful exaggeration. Yet I must tell you that the menu presented here is the result of long years of experience and is sharpened to the cutting edge of dazzling performance. We begin with an extraordinary little do-it-yourself appetizer ceremony, in which aromatic and potent gin is amusingly combined with a touch of sugar and, believe it or not, an avocado! You and she work together at it, in close communion, across a small table. She will, assuredly, never before have experienced (or even dreamed of) this mysterious way of beginning a meal. You are her teacher. She is your pupil. At last, when the moment comes for tasting—her eyes looking into yours, bright with confidence—the alchemy of the mixture of spirit, sweetness, and velvety fruit casts its spell.

Next, you pop the Champagne while she watches you prepare the main course at table in your chafing dish or electric frypan. How proper that this method of preparing two small filet mignon steaks should be officially named after the fieriest of lovers, Giovanni Casanova. As you complete your task, the flames from the pan rage around you and the luxury of the foie gras melts and penetrates into the fibers of the rare beef.

Finally, you bring out your disarmingly simple bowl of mixed cut fruits, but carrying at its center a hidden, magic potion of irresistible power. Seven alcoholic liqueurs went into it—in a sequence of amounts and proportions balanced on a knife-edge. You must absolutely resist making the slightest change in the list or the measurements. At once, the magic would be lost. Nor can any single one be left out. The number must always be seven. They are symbolic, after all, of the seven veils of Salomé, when she danced before Herod.

Bon appétit! Bonne chance!

Menu for a Midnight Supper for Two

Avocado with English Aromatic
   Gin à la Mary Francis
Filet Mignon with Foie Gras
   Flamed with Cognac à la
   Casanova   **Rose-pink Champagne*

Macedoine of Mixed Fruits
   with the Seven Liqueurs
   of the Seven Veils

Coffee

Campaign Plan for the Preparation of the Meal

One Day Ahead

Check this staple list and add the needed items to the following shopping list:

DAIRY
   Cream (for the coffee)

HERB AND SPICE CABINET
   Crystal salt
   Black peppercorns

OTHER ITEMS
   Olive oil (2 tablespoons)
   Sugar (for the coffee)
   Sugar, white superfine
      (2 tablespoons)
   Coffee

WINES AND SPIRITS
   English aromatic gin
      (2 ounces)
   Marsala (2 ounces)
   Cognac (5 ounces for cook-
      ing—more for drinking)
   Dry cherry kirsch (1 1/2
      ounces)
   Orange Cointreau (1 ounce)
   Benedictine (1 ounce)
   Sweet maraschino cherry
      liqueur (1 1/2 ounces)
   Sweet kümmel (1 ounce)
   Brut Champagne (6-ounce
      split)

NOTE: Check the Champagne on the menu and if you do not have it, buy the current vintage.

The Day Before

Shopping list (plus any needed staple items from above):

DAIRY
Sweet butter (3 tablespoons)

FRUITS AND VEGETABLES
Avocados (1 ripe for eating; 4-5 for show)
A selection of fresh mixed fruits (enough for about 3 cups)

BAKERY
French bread (1 long loaf)

MEAT
Beef filet mignon, perfectly shaped, round, fatless, about 1 1/2 inches thick (2)

SPECIALTY STORE OR FANCY FOOD SHOP
French foie gras (3 ounces)
Champagne wafers

After the Shopping

Start making ice and continue until you have enough.
Set the table and get out all serving dishes.

Advance Preparations on the Day

Prepare Macedoine of Mixed Fruits (recipe step 1).

3 Hours Before Leaving to Meet the Lady

Marinate steaks (recipe step 1).
Set out avocados, sugar, and gin.
Measure Cognac and Marsala. Put in covered containers.
Measure butter and foie gras, cover, and refrigerate.
Chill Champagnes.
Chill coupe glasses.

1 Hour Before Leaving

Sear steaks (recipe step 2).

Immediately on Return

Warm plates for steaks.
Make coffee.
Set out ingredients for flaming the steaks.
Decorate bowl of fruit (first part of recipe step 2).
Warm bread.

The Sequence of the Dinner

Light candles.
Prepare at table Avocado with English Aromatic Gin à la Mary
    Francis (recipe steps 1-3)
Prepare at table Filet Mignon with Foie Gras Flamed with Cognac
    à la Casanova (recipe step 3)
Decorate and serve Macedoine of Mixed Fruits with the Seven
    Liqueurs of the Seven Veils (last part of recipe step 2).

So much for the plan of campaign. If, on the other hand, you want to
prepare just one of the dishes, here are the separate recipes, with
separate lists of ingredients.

Avocado with English Aromatic Gin
à la Mary Francis
(For 2 alone)

STAPLES
    White sugar, superfine grind (1
      or 2 tablespoons)

SHOPPING
    Avocado, ripe to perfection (1,
      plus 4 or 5 for show)
    English aromatic gin (about 2
      ounces)

All Done at Table in Less Than 5 Minutes

1. You need only one avocado, but it makes a good show to have
several on the dish and to pick up each one in turn, to sniff it carefully
and to press it gently with the thumb, as if making sure to pick the very
best for this most important of occasions. Now wipe its skin with a
snow-white napkin until there is a mirror shine. Cut it exactly in half

with a small silver knife and remove the stone. From the hollow left in each half, lightly scrape away the inner skin of dark coloring from the stone. Place the better half on the plate in front of your lovely guest and begin her indoctrination into the mysterious rites of this mystical ceremony. Each of you will be armed with a small silver fork and spoon. There will also be, on the table, a tiny silver dish with a small mound of superfine white sugar and a bottle of English aromatic gin.

2. Sprinkle about half a teaspoon of the sugar into the hollow of the avocado. Then, using the back of the teaspoon, lightly spread the sugar evenly all over the inside surface. Gently press the sugar into the flesh of the avocado. Quarter teaspoon by quarter teaspoon, add more sugar and spread it around, until the entire inside surface is evenly and tightly covered with a thin white layer. Now switch to the small silver fork. Begin pushing its points through the sugar coating into the avocado, so that both begin to be riddled with dozens of tiny holes. Now sprinkle in a teaspoon of the gin and, with the fork, begin lightly mashing the sugar and gin into the avocado. Gradually work deeper and deeper, adding more gin, drop by drop, until all visible sugar has disappeared and the center of the avocado is a fluffy, light, smooth mash. The trick is to let it become neither too sweet, nor too mushy with gin. For a fair-sized half avocado, one never uses more (and often less) than 1 ounce of the gin.

3. When you are satisfied with your work—or when your wrist begins to tire—start eating, in a mood of mystical fervor.

Filet Mignon with Foie Gras
Flamed with Cognac à la Casanova
(For 2 alone)

STAPLES
  Sweet butter (about 3 table-
    spoons)
  Olive oil (about 2 tablespoons)
  Crystal salt
  Whole black pepper, coarsely
    cracked in a mortar

SHOPPING
  Beef filet mignon, perfectly
    shaped, round, entirely fat-
    less, about 1 1/2 inches
    thick (2)
  French foie gras (3 ounces)
  Cognac (3 ounces)
  Marsala (2 ounces)

Earlier in the Day—Preparing Steaks in About 5 Minutes—Unsupervised Marination 2 Hours

1. Place steaks on a wooden board and press into both sides of them, using the heel of the hand, a fair coating of crystal salt and coarse black pepper. Pour the olive oil into a flat plate and slosh the steaks around in it, thoroughly covering them on all sides. Let them rest in the oil, turning them occasionally, for about 2 hours.

2 Hours Later—Searing the Steaks in About 5 Minutes

2. Heat up your heaviest iron frypan to very-high sizzling temperature. The steaks must brown so fast on the outside that the inside is hardly warmed. They should certainly not be in contact with the pan for a second longer than 1 minute on each side—perhaps even less. Now leave them at room temperature until the midnight hour. Have all the other ingredients measured and ready, but, of course, the butter and foie gras must remain in the refrigerator.

Preparation and Flaming at the Table in About 6 Minutes

3. Heat up your chafing dish or electric frypan to medium frying heat (if there is a variable control, set it to 325° F.) and melt the 3 tablespoons of butter. Slice the foie gras and add it, bit by bit, to the hot butter, working it in with a wooden spoon, so that it all blends into a thickish puree. Gradually thin this by working in, dash by dash, the 2 ounces of Marsala. As soon as it is all bubbling, put in the steaks and spoon the hot sauce over them. Turn the heat up to high frying temperature (375° F.), pour in the 3 ounces of Cognac, and instantly set it on fire. Tilt and shake the pan so that the flames spread and keep on roaring as long as possible. Do not singe your beard. As soon as the flames have died out, the steaks are done. Serve them on very hot plates with the luxurious sauce poured over them. There should be lots of French bread with which to mop up the remaining sauce.

Macedoine of Mixed Fruits with
Seven Liqueurs of the Seven Veils
(For 2 Alone)

Let me repeat here the warning already given. The seven liqueurs are very finely balanced as to affinities and combinations of flavors. Do not leave any out; do not, under any circumstances, vary the measurements. There is a secret magic to this formula. You would do better to forget the whole thing than to try to compromise with the liquid ingredients. The fruits, of course, can be slightly varied, according to the season.

SHOPPING

> A selection of mixed fresh fruits, say, bananas, pitted cherries, peeled and diced plums, chunked peaches, ripe pears, seeded grapes, oranges, tangerines, etc. (about 1 1/2 cups of cut-up fruit per person)
> Cognac (2 ounces)
> Dry cherry kirsch (1 1/2 ounces)
> Orange Cointreau (1 ounce)
> Bénédictine (1 ounce)
> Sweet maraschino cherry liqueur (1 1/2 ounces)
> Sweet kümmel (1 ounce)
> Brut Champagne (6-ounce split)

Earlier in the Day—Preparation in About
30 Minutes—Refrigerated Marination at Least 3 Hours

1. In your handsomest glass or silver bowl, assemble the fruits as you peel, seed, and chunk them, holding out, for the moment, the orange and tangerine. Thoroughly mix the first 6 spiritous liquids (not the Champagne, yet) in a jug, pour them over the fruits, and mix

everything gently but thoroughly with a large wooden spoon. Cover the bowl and set it in the refrigerator to chill and ripen for at least 3 hours. Set the split of Champagne in the coldest part of the refrigerator until serving time. Peel the oranges and tangerines, then divide them into sections, removing pits, and holding them in a tightly covered jar in the refrigerator for last-minute decoration just before serving. At least once or twice, the fruit in the bowl should be gently turned over.

Just Before Serving

2. Turn over the fruits once more and shake them into a nicely rounded mound. Decorate the bowl with the orange and tangerine segments, perhaps placing them on their backs in circles around the bowl, or in any other imaginative formation. At the table, open the split of ice-cold Champagne and gently dribble it over everything in the bowl. Serve at once in chilled coupe glasses. Accompany the fruits with Champagne wafers.

PART III
The Host at a Restaurant

CHAPTER 13

HOW TO GET A GREAT MEAL AT A GREAT RESTAURANT

The Art of Being a Tiger

Again, let us come back to the basic principle of the old British recipe for rabbit pie which begins: *"First catch your rabbit. . . ."* The problem is the same in getting a great meal. First find your great restaurant. The search is not easy. For every truly great restaurant dedicated to the perfect service of superb food, there are a hundred where the chief concern is the dramatic manipulation of luxurious show. What is the use of a Honduras-mahogany pepper mill the size of a young cannon if the filet mignon being peppered is cold? How justifiable is it to flame the Faisan au Foie Gras à la Souvaroff with specially doctored brandy to produce a fireball of H-bomb dimensions, if the meat of the bird then tastes as if it had been soaked in nitroglycerin? What good is a side-table performance with a giant coffee machine as complex as the atom smasher at the Argonne Laboratories if the resultant potion is the kind used by the Borgias to get rid of their enemies?

For many years I have used a simple yardstick, a kind of instant measure of the sincerity or fraudulence of a restaurant. I call it my "fire and ice test."

I dined not too long ago in a Chicago restaurant much publicized for its luxury. So deep was the crimson carpet that it would have been a help to have had snowshoes to reach one's table. Sweet music came from an orchestra dressed, it seemed, in the uniform of the Czarist Cossack Guard. The menu came on yellowing sheets of parchment, hand-written in gold ink, about the size of one of Mao Tse-tung's wall posters. The prices were liable to be mistaken for the annual report of General Motors.

The names of the dishes seemed to be flickering in a golden light because my table was entirely surrounded by massive flames. At the left, a dish of Crabs Casanova was blazing mightily. To the right, a roast guinea hen was afire from stem to stern. In front, a burnt offering of Crêpes Suzette. Behind, bacon-wrapped oysters glowing on a sword. And in all directions, flaming cups of Café Diable.

The captain now approached, bowing as if he were trying to kiss my feet. In his tailcoat of midnight blue, I mistook him, at first glance, for Prince Philip. He was flanked, in military formation, by six waiters. Almost kneeling, they begged me to begin with the *grande spécialité de la maison:* a salad of hearts of palm, Chinese water chestnuts, capers, and bananas, with an Oriental spice dressing.

My order taken, the captain and his escort backed off, bowing at each retreating step. As they neared a table engulfed in sheets of flame, I feared that they would all be incinerated.

A long time passed. Then the silver-plated kitchen doors opened, and a line of gleaming wagons moved slowly to my table. Busboys stood at attention. The first wagon carried such a load of ice, it looked like a model of the North Pole. Resting on it was a boat-shaped silver dish, carved and fluted as if it had come from the workshop of Benvenuto Cellini. And there was my salad, arranged as a tropical garden. As the captain placed it before me, the orchestra was stilled. Surely, as I lifted the first taste to my mouth, they would break into the "Triumphal March" from *Aida.* It felt like an epic moment in the annals of gastronomy.

There was only one flaw. The salad was, if not exactly hot enough to burn my tongue, considerably above the overheated temperature of the room. The principal ingredients had obviously just been taken out of cans stored on shelves in the hottest part of the kitchen. Clearly they had not had any serious contact with the ice. At this warm temperature, the four ingredients exactly canceled each other out, while the peppery red dressing gave the whole thing the ambience of a Texas barbecue.

For one of the later courses, I had ordered a bottle of Champagne. It, too, was rolled in on a gleaming wagon, the bottle resting

Restaurant de la Pyramide

FERNAND POINT

VIENNE (ISERE,

Brioche de Foie gras
Pâté de gibier en gelée
Turbot au Champagne
ou Quenelle de Brochet Nantua

Pintadeau poêlé aux Chanterelles
Gratin Dauphinois
d'estragon

Sorbet
aux Succes
dises
lées de fruits
sans vin

horizontally on top of—not immersed in—a crushed iceberg. Half a dozen waiters then went through a performance worthy of the Bolshoi Ballet. The glasses were sluiced with ice and twirled with napkins. The bottle was picked up by one waiter, ceremoniously wiped by a second, the seal removed by a third, the cork drawn by a fourth. . . . When the Champagne was poured, it was just below boiling.

Finally the proprietor joined me over the Borgia-type coffee. I asked him whether he didn't agree that a great restaurant could hardly merit that adjective if it placed all the emphasis on show at the expense of the food? Surely elegance symbolized by fire and ice was fake elegance?

The proprietor was in a candid mood. He admitted the melancholy truth, but neatly flicked the blame onto the shoulders of his customers. He described the new generation of expense-account patrons:

"They spend lavishly on food and drink as a status symbol. They know almost nothing about gastronomy, but they are uniformly delighted and impressed by ostentatious service. They don't understand a word of the menu, so they ignore it. They look around the dining room and if they see a table in flames, or an attention-getting bottle the size of the Eiffel Tower, they say, 'Give me what that guy's having.' They think Boeuf à la Mode is something with ice cream on top. They wouldn't lower themselves to order the *plat du jour,* even if it were the best thing in the house. We have to serve our customers what they demand. A restaurant, after all, is a profit-making business. If they want to buy a show for a customer or a girl friend, we'll sell them that. It isn't an idea that the restaurants have dreamed up. It's a crazy by-product of our crazy times."

All this is bunk. There have always been (and always will be) restaurants fraudulently catering to fools.

The truly great restaurant—where the total concentration is on perfect quality and impeccable service—is one of the unifying factors of the world. One can dine in one of these establishments anywhere on earth with the assurance that the food and the service will be entirely consistent. Once you have learned to find your way through the menu and to get your way with the staff while ordering, say, Le Suprême de Sole en Goujons at La Caravelle in New York, or the Feuilletée de Ris de Veau, Sauce Périgourdine at the Mirabelle in London, or a Filet de Turbot Dugléré at Prunier's in Paris, or the Faisan Brabanconne at La Couronne in Brussels, or the Coeur de Filet Empereur in the Borgia Room of the Hostaria dell'Orso in Rome, you will feel at home in any great restaurant from Madrid to Madras, from Beirut to Bangkok. The menu (apart from a few local specialties) will be in

French and punctuated with *les plats classiques.* The wine list will be as invariable as the rising of the sun. The chefs, busboys, waiters, captains, maîtres d'hôtel (even if they are charming and attentive Orientals) will most likely have been trained in Paris or Geneva and will most certainly speak fluent French and English. The rules of the great eating game are the same everywhere. And this is the essence of the matter. There are rules. They must be learned.

To begin, there are some hard facts to be faced. A great and successful restaurant is a high-pressure supermarket of cooked foods where every member of the service staff is a skilled salesman. The attack on the customer's sales resistance begins with the maître d'hôtel at the door of the dining room. This gentleman is no longer (as the romantic writers are so fond of describing him) a dodderingly dignified figure with the face of a scholarly marquis who expresses his degree of respect for the regular customers by the depth of his bow. The twentieth-century maître d'hôtel is a calculating technician, a cross between Sherlock Holmes and a professional mind reader. He has developed a special skill, which the Germans call *Fingerspitzgefühl,* a virtually untranslatable word that means, in effect, that he has radar beams radiating from his fingertips. During the five seconds or so that you are walking toward him, he is assessing you in microscopic detail, from the assurance of your step to the authority of your voice. Immediately he places you in one of four categories of customers. You become either a "Skunk," a "Monkey," a "Lion," or a "Tiger."

This rating system of the clientele is a fact of life in all the great and fashionable restaurants of the major cities (above all, in New York and Paris). The restaurant is benefited by certain types of guests and injured by others. Beautiful women and handsome men, superbly well-dressed, lift the gaiety and pleasure of the entire dining room. Others are neutral and nondescript and will profitably pad out the far corners. Yet others will depress the room and must be rigorously excluded. These are the Skunks.

During the great days of Le Pavillon, when it was owned by the late Henri Soulé, he had as a regular customer one of those international wealthy widows who move from resort to resort and everywhere make a fetish of unreasonable demands, of complaints in a rasping tone, and of unbearably aggressive behavior. She was ancient, formidable, and grim.

One day she telephoned in advance to order for her dinner a Contrefilet à la Clamart, which took the chef two hours to prepare.

When it was served to her, she sent it back. Soulé decided that she was a Skunk.

Next day she came in through the front door with the face of an angry mandrill and the voice of Lionel Stander. Soulé bowed very slightly and said that he was terribly sorry, madame, but there was no table available, all were reserved.

Her eyes snapped as she hissed, "Listen. I'm not in the habit . . ."

That was as far as she got. Like a flash storm, a cloud of rage darkened Soulé's face: "Madame! This street is crowded with restaurants, most of them empty and eager for your patronage. Good night, madame."

In the heyday of Jack & Charlie's "21" in the 1930s, there was a more subtle system for excluding unwanted patrons. As soon as you stepped through the polished street doors, you came face to face with a shark-eyed little man behind a desk. This was Jimmy, the concierge (the word was borrowed from the palatial old hotels of Europe, where the concierge was the man-for-all-problems who controlled the entry and exit of the guests). If Jimmy recognized you as an approved and regular customer, he looked up with a smile and said, "How do you do, sir." Instantly, six brilliantly uniformed bellboys rushed forward to disengage you from your hat and coat. If Jimmy did not look up or speak, not a muscle stirred in your direction. Some people were so overawed at this point that they turned on their heels and left without a word. But if you insistently demanded attention and service, Jimmy would look up and say, with an infinity of regret in his voice, "Sorry, sir, we have no table for you this evening. All reserved." However, if you appeared well enough dressed, well enough behaved, and had a wallet pocket that bulged suitably, or if Jimmy simply decided that you were an unknown quantity worth the risk, you became a Monkey.

The name originated in the thirties at El Morocco, where the less desirable guests were seated in the crimson-curtained back room, which was known to the staff as the "Monkey House." There was a similar room at "21," known among the waiters as the "Dog House," with a separately printed menu offering only a few of the less exotic dishes and each of these at exactly double the price charged in the main dining room.

This matter of seating is of supreme importance in getting a great meal. Charles Masson, the owner of La Grenouille, likes to say that every table in his restaurant is desirable, but some are a good deal more desirable than others. The seating arrangements at any great restaurant are as arbitrary as the pew list for a royal coronation at Westminster Abbey.

The curious fact is that all social lions want to see and be seen as they dine. They do not want to eat in comfortable privacy in an inner room. The most sought-after tables are those virtually in the entrance lobby where there is continuous traffic. The small corner table nearest the front door of the Colony was always reserved for the Vanderbilts whenever they wanted it. Marlene Dietrich preferred to sit at a tiny and uncomfortable table in the center of the floor of the entrance room, where she could greet and be greeted as people passed in and out. The favorite table of the Duke and Duchess of Windsor at Le Pavillon was so close to the front door that their Royal Highnesses received a blast of cold air every time it revolved.

You will never achieve one of these desirable tables if you are classified as a Monkey. The maître d'hôtel will lead you to a back-of-the room table "in Siberia." There he will convey his opinion of you to the captain by a lifted eyebrow signal, and as a result you will receive less than the best service, and though you may get a good meal, it will not be a great one and you will pay more than the people sitting at the best tables.

Some Monkeys panic when they see the menu prices and try to extricate themselves with some such remark as "I'm not very hungry. I'll take an omelet, but make it a little on the rare side." Or "Could I get a hamburger? But I prefer it *bien cuit.*"

In judging Monkeys, restaurateurs are not infallible. Henri Soulé once admitted a bad mistake. Two ladies came in for lunch. They did not impress him particularly. He led them to a faraway table deep in Siberia where they sat down without protest. He was faintly surprised when they did not consult him about the menu but immediately ordered *Quenelles de Brochet à la Nantua.* When they left, the taller of the two said to Soulé, "You have a nice restaurant. It's a pity that you don't know your New York." A few minutes after they had gone, he learned that it was the first Mrs. Nelson Rockefeller.

The best tables are filled by the Lions and Lionesses. These star guests are on the most-wanted list of any great restaurant anywhere. They bring with them prestige and publicity because of their newsworthy names, the influence of their business, political, or social positions, or simply because of the revolting size of their bank accounts. I am told that one visit by Jackie Kennedy Onassis to any top New York restaurant, duly reported the next day in the gossip columns, is worth $10,000 in new business. If she comes back two or three times, the place is permanently jammed. So it's hardly surprising that Lions get the best tables, the most efficient waiters, and the best food at what amounts to discount prices.

One of the most ruthless and terrifying of restaurant Lions was Nubar Gulbenkian, often called "the richest man in the world." He always chose the table he wanted regardless of reservations made for other customers. While his food was being prepared, he would walk into the kitchen to check that the ingredients were fresh and that they were being cooked exactly to his taste. He is typical of a long line of Lions that has dominated the great restaurants of New York and Paris for almost a hundred years. The history of dining is full of fantastic characters and fabulous episodes. In the Gay Nineties the ultimate measure of status was to spend money on conspicuous consumption. The size of the check was the test of the diner's social position.

Diamond Jim Brady, when dining at the Old Waldorf, Bustanoby's, Jack Dunstan's, the Café Martin, or Rector's would start his dinner with a gallon of chilled orange juice; continue with six dozen oysters, a saddle of mutton, half a dozen venison chops, a whole roasted chicken, a brace of mallard ducks, a whole pheasant, and a twelve-egg soufflé; and eventually finish with the entire contents of a five-pound box of Page & Shaw chocolate creams. It was a spectacle that unnerved the diners at nearby tables and put them off their food. They gathered around the Brady table and cheered him on, while making side bets among themselves as to whether or not he would drop dead before he reached the dessert.

At Rector's one night Brady was told by a friend from Paris that the chef of the famous Café Marguery had invented a wonderful new way of garnishing sole with mussels and shrimp, called Sole Marguery. Brady at once informed Charles Rector that if he wished to keep Brady as a customer he had better make arrangements to serve Sole Marguery in New York in the very near future. Old man Rector was desperate. He withdrew his son, George, from the senior class at Cornell and sent him to Paris. There he managed to land a job as a dishwasher in the kitchen of the Marguery. After loitering for fifteen hours a day for two months near the fish chef, George had a blueprint of the recipe, cabled his father, and caught the next boat for New York. As the liner docked, George saw that the man standing beside his father at the foot of the gangway was Jim Brady. That night Brady took over the entire restaurant for his private dinner party. Finally, after midnight, George was called out of the kitchen and Brady said,

"Marvelous! I had nine helpings, and right now, if you could pour another half gallon of the sauce over a Turkish towel, I could eat the lot."

Many people thought that James Gordon Bennett, the spendthrift, temperamental, and undisciplined young owner of the New York *Morning Herald* newspaper, was a raving lunatic, but there was no doubt of his status as a Lion when it came to restaurants. He was virtually exiled from New York society after being involved in a "horrible incident" at his engagement party to Caroline May. In the presence of the ladies, he half-filled the drawing room with steam by pissing onto the burning logs in the fireplace. The next day he was horsewhipped by Caroline's brother on the sidewalk outside the Union Club. Bennett then transferred his home to Paris and founded the Paris *Herald*.

He was unrepentant, especially in his dining habits.

> *Like many of the upper class*
> *He liked the sound of smashing glass.*

One night, in a glass-smashing mood, when he appeared at Maxim's and was told that the place was full, Bennett pushed past the maître d'hôtel, marched down the full length of the center aisle of the dining room and, as he passed between the tables, grabbed all the tablecloths on either side and dragged them off, so that the crockery and food, all the flowers and glasses, the green turtle soup and the Château Lafite flooded into the laps of the diners. At the end of the room, Bennett turned around and announced that everything would be repaired, that new food would be served at his expense, that spilled wine would be replaced by bottles of at least double the price, and that cleaning bills for personal clothing should be sent to him at the Paris *Herald*. The amazing thing was that no one jumped up and punched Bennett in the nose. In fact, most of the diners seemed vaguely amused, as if the act of being doused with hot soup by a crazy American publisher were some sort of *haut monde* status symbol.

During winters in Monte Carlo, Bennett patronized a small restaurant on the hill, with a terrace looking down on the repulsive wealth of that pleasure town. One night he arrived to find his favorite terrace table occupied. The maître d'hôtel was desolate. Bennett marched in to see the proprietor, who was cowering behind the bar. "Is this restaurant for sale, right this minute?" The proprietor named a fantastic price. Bennett accepted instantly and, armed with the authority of ownership, threw out the people at the table he wanted.

His dinner was particularly good. Bennett felt benevolent. In lieu of tip, he gave the restaurant to his waiter, then, as an afterthought, asked his name. It was Jacques Ciro, who was later to learn a great deal more about restaurant Lions in the brilliant establishments he founded in Biarritz, Paris, London, New York, and even in Hollywood.

So much for Lions, Monkeys, and Skunks. The fourth—and most important—category of restaurant diner is the "Tiger." The best definition of who and what he is was given me one night when dining in New Orleans on a Coeur de Filet de Boeuf Marchand de Vin with Roy Alciatore, the owner of Antoine's, the greatest regional restaurant in the United States.

He was talking about the Louisiana Lions (a temperamental and demanding cross-section of the old Southern families at the turn of the century) who had made the restaurant famous under his grandfather, Antoine, and his father, Jules. "Today," he said, "our clientele has changed. Our name is so well known nationally that we are largely filled by gastronomically innocent tourists."

Although some two hundred superb dishes are listed on the still-magnificent menu, nine out of ten guests order the Oysters à la Rockefeller, the Pompano en Papillote, or one of the other over-publicized and somewhat overrated specialties. "But," continued Alciatore, "the people we most enjoy serving are the knowledgeable gourmets with finely developed tastes and a sharp judgment of our cuisine. They make demands on us. They pick up the captains and waiters on the slightest laxity of service. They send dishes back to the kitchen with critical messages to the chef. They keep a restaurant great. We only wish there were more of them."

This is the perfect definition of a restaurant Tiger: a patron without public name or influential position, but with the knowledge and assurance to dominate any restaurant and to bring out the best that is in it. And the beauty of it is that the art of Tigermanship can be learned by almost anyone. It takes reasonable intelligence, an average degree of social grace, some well-cut clothes, a few spare dollars, a period of steady practice, and the right information. What follows in the next chapter is a short basic course.

CHAPTER 14

THE RULES OF TIGERMANSHIP

*You Can Dominate a Great Restaurant
if You Understand Its Mechanics*

One night in Chicago, about twenty years ago, I was dining in the notorious Pump Room (which Lucius Beebe once called "a platinum pavilion of pish-posh") and was joined over the flaming Café Diable by the proprietor, the late Ernie Byfield. We discussed the administration of a large restaurant, and he stressed the fact that it is an extremely complex and highly traditional organization. Even when its equipment is as modern as a computer, its human structure is based on rules that go back almost five hundred years. Chefs are trained in techniques developed before the French Revolution. Waiters use serving procedures from the sixteenth century. Our system of tipping is based on habits formed under the Hapsburgs. Phrases printed on even the simplest menu may date from the year 1571. History has molded the mentality of the men who run restaurants, and their basic attitudes toward their customers.

I asked Byfield what he thought were the qualifications required of a great restaurateur. He replied, "Only men of low moral character can succeed in the business!" He was obviously exaggerating, but there was perhaps a hidden grain of truth based on his sound knowledge of restaurant history.

Before the middle of the fifteenth century, there was no such thing anywhere as a public eating house run for profit. Travelers looked for refreshment and rest in monasteries and temples, or simply in homes along the way. The dangers and discomforts of travel were the basis of the strict laws of hospitality. Commercial inns were first set up in Germany, and Charles Reade described one of them in *The Cloister and the Hearth*. The hero, Gerard, caught in a storm at night in the Black Forest, sees a light shining between the trees and finds the inn, The Star of the Forest. A single large room is heated by a ceiling-high clay oven in the center and all around it are clothes hanging up to dry, while half-naked men, women, and children sit on the floor, giving off terrible smells of sweat and dirt. They have just supped on meat puddings heated in the oven and handed around on tin plates. Garlic fills the interstices of the air. When Gerard asks the landlady for food, her reply might be the voice of almost any restaurateur in any out-of-the-way place, addressing a late-arriving guest: "Supper is over this hour and more. . . . All the world knows 'The Star of the Forest' sups from six till eight. Come before six, you sup well. Come before eight, you sup as pleases Heaven. Come after eight and you get a clean bed and a horn of kine's milk at the dawning. . . . Inns are not built for one."

The inns of sixteenth-century England were called "public houses," an apt name because the fixed cost of the meal was, in effect, the purchase price of an invitation to dinner with the owner and his wife. All meals were at set times. There was no menu or choice of dishes. There were no separate tables. Everyone sat around the "table of the host," a phrase still commemorated in today's menus as "table d'hôte." The meals were simple. Eating out was not yet regarded as a form of luxurious pleasure, but a matter of convenience and necessity. An Englishman referred to such a meal as "an ordinary." The word *restaurant* did not come into use until about the middle of the eighteenth century, when a Parisian doctor, Jean André, developed a recipe for a restorative soup (a simple beef broth with vegetables) and called it *le potage restaurant*. It became the rage of Paris, and taverns that served it put out a sign saying "RESTAURANT." The word became a part of almost every language in the world.

The conversion in dining out from an "ordinary" to a luxurious form of entertainment was an accidental by-product of the French Revolution. When the noble châteaux all over France were sacked and their noble owners carted off to the guillotine, hundreds of great chefs, terrified of the people's wrath, went into hiding. They must have worried desperately about the future possibilities of earning a living. Then, as the emotions of the revolution subsided, one of these chefs, Paul Beauvilliers, had a brilliant idea. He would prove that he was a

true democrat by opening a restaurant, where he would offer the general public the chance to taste the great dishes once available only to kings and princes. He opened La Grande Taverne on the hill of Montmartre, the first restaurant in the world with a large and luxurious menu and a choice of many dishes for each course. Other chefs hastened to follow Beauvillier's example in every city in France. Thus, *la haute cuisine* was brought down to the man in the street and France became the leading nation of gastronomy.

It remained for two of the greatest names in French cuisine to appear, to merge their brilliant talents, and to carry the art of restaurant dining to its highest peak. At Voisin's in Paris, there was an ambitious young waiter named César Ritz. At Le Petit Moulin Rouge there was a rising young chef named Auguste Escoffier. They became partners, with Ritz as the business organizer and Escoffier the genius of the kitchen. For twenty-five years, from 1890 to 1915, they created the greatest era of public dining in history. In the Escoffier restaurants of the Ritz in Paris, the Savoy and the Carlton in London, the Ritz-Carlton in New York, and in every other place touched by their magic, the guiding principle was individual and personal service. Menus listed hundreds of dishes and it was assumed that the diner knew the French names and had the skill to assemble and order a great meal. He was free to ask for variations in the ingredients of any dish, or even order entirely different dishes not on the menu. New dishes were invented by Escoffier in honor of his famous patrons and are still served as classics of the French cuisine: Pêches Melba, Poulet Tetrazzini, Tournedos à la Rossini, and so on. The customer was king and it was inconceivable that the restaurant should try to dominate him, or fool him with phony show-off.

This great era ended with a bang at the start of World War I, when the lamps went out all over Europe. Since then, gourmets have watched restaurant history recede into a steady decline. Fewer and fewer truly great chefs. (Escoffier retired and died between the two world wars.) Shorter and shorter menus. Less and less flexibility in the kitchen. More and more automation. Less and less individual service. And most damaging of all, a flood of new and unskilled customers lacking the knowledge to make demands and keep the restaurant up to its own mark of excellence.

When Roger Chauveron was still running his Café Chauveron in New York (before he moved it to Bay Harbor Island, near Palm Beach), he once told me, "We serve an average of 800 portions a night on a sort of production-line basis. The marvel is not that we are not

better than we are, but that we are not far, far worse." Yet his Café
Chauveron wherever it is remains a restaurant still devoted, in my
view, to the ideal of Escoffier, as are other restaurants in cities around
the world, country inns and small bistros, offering classic splendor or
relaxed simplicity, but all capable, if properly pressed, of providing a
great meal.

First Find Your Great Restaurant

The surest way to find a great restaurant is through the personal
advice of a first-class gourmet who dined there the night before. This
time element is crucial. Beware of the man who sends you to a
"marvelous little place" he knew two years ago. A truly great
restaurant is always delicately balanced on a peak of perfection. It can
lose its chef (or be sold to a crass new owner) and a few months will
find it in the wide valley of mediocrity. If you can find a local member
of one of the great international wine and food societies, you are on safe
ground. The French-oriented Confrérie des Chevaliers du Tastevin
has chapters in many major cities. In London, there is the Wine and
Food society; in Paris, Le Club des Cent. Members of such organizations, if they can be reached, can give advice.

Failing this, one turns to the more trustworthy gastronomic guides
to the major eating areas of the world. The best, not surprisingly, are
written in French, by Frenchmen, for French tourists. They can be
specially ordered from any bookshop that deals in foreign editions.
Once you have found an interesting and readable gastronomic guide,
take it to bed with you and study it as if your life depended on it.

New York and several other major U.S. cities are covered with
brilliant wit and uproarious satire in the *Guide Juilliard*. The French
provinces and other parts of Europe are listed in the *Guide Kléber*.
The good old *Michelin* is always safe, but it tends to be ultraconservative, and it takes an unreasonably long time for a good new
restaurant to be included. However, the *Michelins* for Spain and for
Belgium, Holland, and Luxembourg are excellent. No guidebook
seems to be able to unravel the subtle complications of the restaurants
of Italy. For non-French-reading gourmets, there is Waverley Root's
wonderful guide to Paris and Kate Simon's scintillating general guides
to New York, Paris, Mexico City, and London. Meanwhile, Great
Britain is adequately covered by *Egon Ronay's Guide*. The trouble
with all such books is that they become rapidly out-of-date. Be

especially wary of guides published by governments, which tend to list all restaurants indiscriminately and without critical judgment. Always remember that there are very few truly great restaurants anywhere.

If all advance planning is impossible—if you suddenly land in a strange city, without friends and without guides—say a prayer and ask around. I once landed in Amsterdam at nine in the evening, at the peak of the tourist season, hungry, and with no hotel reservation. In the airport terminal building, I walked to the car rental desk. An intelligent and charming young man began writing out my contract for an Opel sports model. On a sudden hunch I said to him, "If, in the next few minutes, you met the most beautiful and desirable girl in the world and she said yes, yes, yes, to everything you asked, where would you take her to dinner this evening and where would you stay the night?" He laughed, thought for a couple of minutes, then wrote on a slip of paper the names of three restaurants and two hotels. I went to the nearest telephone booth. The first of the hotels gave me a room overlooking the Prinzengraacht Canal on the top floor of a converted sixteenth-century house. I have been back there a dozen times and would never dream of staying anywhere else in Amsterdam. A telephone call to the second restaurant on the list, an Indonesian bistro, established that it would be open until 2 A.M. and that a table would gladly be reserved. The bistro turned out to be a small place on a short and narrow back street near the docks, frequented by Indonesian seamen. It served me an unquestionably great forty-dish Rijsttafel. Three days later, I had another Rijsttafel at the most expensive and glamorous Indonesian restaurant in midtown Amsterdam. The bistro's was better!

Zeroing in on the Target

It is suicidal to make the first visit to a great restaurant without a reservation. It is almost equally fatal simply to call and make a reservation for "Mr. John Smith." The result will be a table in the darkest far corner, probably behind massed potted palms, next to the kitchen service door, attended by an apprentice waiter who may spill hot consommé down your neck.

Before you lift the phone to make a reservation, work out your personal ploy. Never call as yourself. Either change your voice slightly, or have someone call for you, saying that he or she is the executive assistant of Mr. John Smith, who is . . . Now you must work out not more than five words to establish the importance of your business and/or social position. You could, for example, be the president of the International Resting House Corporation. (There is always a lot of noise at the restaurant end of the telephone and misunderstandings are conveniently frequent.) Or it might be said that you are the brother of the ambassador from the Republic of Roaringtania. Pick your own titles.

The most outrageous ploy in restaurant history was used by A. J. Liebling during the time of U.S. Prohibition when he was doing a gastronomic tour of Burgundy. Through a friend he started the rumor that he, Liebling, was an American millionaire bootlegger, who had come to Burgundy to buy wines in order to stock a transatlantic liner as a fabulous *bateau cave* that would eventually be sailed to New York, then hoisted like a lifeboat out of the water and moved at dead of night into a specially built skyscraper with a false hinged front. On that basis, Liebling got to eat more free great meals and drink more free great wines in a month than most people are able to command in their entire lifetimes.

When speaking to the maître d'hôtel, be sure to gabble all the names and titles at high speed and in a lofty tone of such a degree of assurance as to imply that it is simply inconceivable that the maître d'hôtel does not already know all about Mr. Smith. If he asks for any of the names to be repeated, disregard him and proceed at once to the second part of the message: "Mr. Smith is considering dining with you, but before he decides, he would like to see your menu. We will send a messenger within the next thirty minutes. Please give him copies of both your luncheon and dinner menus. Then perhaps we'll call you back and make a reservation." Sometimes the maître d'hôtel is so impressed that he offers to send his own messenger. Do not accept, unless you are living in the most luxurious apartment building in the city, or are staying at the most expensive hotel. Send your messenger. Sharpen your red pencil.

You have now achieved your first two objectives. You have established John Smith's name at the restaurant. You will be able to analyze the menu in your own relaxed time.

The Language of a Great Menu

The menu tells you a great deal about the restaurant and its owner. First, its physical appearance. It should be a simple card, or single folder, quite light to hold and it should not be enclosed in any sort of fancy cover. If it is oversized or overheavy—if it looks like a leather-bound book, embossed, or encrusted with gold, or if it has any tricky gimmicks about it—begin sniffing the air for a tourist trap. Next, the general appearance of the text. Is it clearly printed in an orderly arrangement? Are the *spécialités de la maison* made to stand out, either in different-colored ink, or written in by hand, or in a box, or under a special heading? Above all (and this is crucial), there must be no explanatory paragraphs describing the dishes in salesman's terms. A notorious Chicago restaurant used to describe its Porterhouse steak:

> Ah, the Porterhouse! Aristocrat of Steaks! Most delectable of Steaks! Carved from vintaged cornfed beef . . . , your Porterhouse is broiled under a high heat which seals in the glorious juices and sears the fat to a crispy succulence! Specify to your captain the precise degree of doneness and tell him, too, whether you wish it to be basted with garlic's subtle flavor!

Another Chicago menu begins:

> The entree has been carefully chosen and especially prepared for the discriminating palate of the connoisseur.
> The dishes featured express the Chef's individuality and imagination with the instinctive feeling of an artist in preparing each dish.
> The testing of seasoning is carried out through the entire process of cooking, requiring time, skill and patience.
> The result is the difference between merely eating and the satisfaction derived from the well-flavored and carefully prepared entree.

If any such nonsense appears on your menu, cancel your plans at once. A great restaurant must assume that its customers know the elements of high cuisine.

Faced by a new menu, in leisurely relaxation, I take my red pencil and begin to mark it. First, I cross out all the dishes that I never eat in a restaurant. When I place myself under the gastronomic care of a great kitchen, I want to taste dishes that are the product of the brilliant skill of its staff. I do not want things that come out of a can or that I could prepare for myself in two minutes at home. Among the hors d'oeuvres, I am not interested in Le Demi Pamplemousse, half a grapefruit. Or Les Sardines à l'Huile, a couple of sardines. For the same reason, I never order caviar or Pâté de Foie Gras in a restaurant.

Nor am I much interested in a plain Biftek, such as Le Sirloin, or Le T-Bone, since these are my more or less regular fare at home. I apply the same considerations to every dish on the menu, down to the last dessert.

I have now usually eliminated about one-third of the menu, and the dishes that remain are of two types: the *spécialités de la maison* and the universal preparations of *la haute cuisine*. On my first visit to a great restaurant, I try to balance my dinner between the two. The chef and his staff are on trial. I am willing to let them give me some new experiences, but the measure of their skill lies in their approach to perfection in the classic dishes. One of the best tests is a Petite Marmite Henri IV, the marvelous clear bouillon with a taste precisely balanced between beef, oxtail, chicken, and aromatic vegetables, all entwined with the delicacy of fresh herbs. Other classic tests are a simple Poulet Rôti à l'Anglaise, a Sauce Béarnaise, or a Boeuf au Chambertin (with exactly the right grade of Chambertin).

I have now narrowed down my choice to three or four alternatives for each course. Next to be considered is the question of the best day and hour for the dinner. If you reserve a table at the restaurant's busiest time, when it is filled by its regular Lions, you will almost certainly get a poor table and second-string service.

The pattern of great restaurants in all major cities is roughly the same. The busiest months are from mid-September to mid-December. November is almost always the peak. From mid-December to mid-January is a slack time. Then the Lions return and keep the place busy until June. Many great restaurants close during July and August. During the season, Tuesdays and Wednesdays are the busiest evenings. Lions disappear from Fridays to Mondays, but their places are taken by crowds of weekend tourists. The busiest hours of the day are obviously between 1 and 2:30 for lunch and 7 and 9 for dinner. Reservations outside these hours can make all the difference in service.

Now you are ready to lift the telephone and call back the maître d'hôtel. Again, the "executive assistant" speaks for John Smith, saying that the big man is pleased by the menu and wishes to reserve. . . . How to handle the restaurant when you arrive—how to make sure that you get a truly great meal—is the subject of the next chapter.

CHAPTER 15

THE HUNGRY TIGER AT THE RESTAURANT

Composing the Great Meal

Punctuality in arriving at a great restaurant is more important than at a private dinner party. The hostess is sure of her guests, even when they are a few minutes late. Restaurants get dozens of reservations every week from punks who neither show up nor have the decency to call and cancel. No restaurant can be expected to hold a table (especially for a new and unknown customer) for longer than thirty minutes. I avoid arriving five minutes early. That gives the maître d'hôtel the excuse to ask me to wait at the bar. Many inferior restaurants use this trick to increase bar profits. I absolutely refuse to play their game. If the maître d'hôtel insists that my table is not ready, I demand that my party be seated on chairs in the lobby away from the bar, and I stick out my long legs to make sure that as many people as possible trip over them. This almost always ensures a table within a couple of minutes.

The next point to be settled is the degree of priority given to your reservation. When it was called in, your name was entered in the large reservations book, but with no table yet assigned. This morning, about an hour before the restaurant opened, the maître d'hôtel (or the proprietor) reviewed all the names and allocated the tables, in light pencil, with many erasures and changes of mind. This is a tightly controlled social game, which Roger Topolinski, the owner of the great Lapérouse in Paris, calls *Le Jeu de Dames.*

I can begin to judge my own priority as I walk behind the maître d'hôtel toward the table assigned to me. I note the general arrangement of the tables, and if I sense that I am being led too deeply "into Siberia," I steel myself to do battle for a better table. Sometimes, of course, there is no better table available, and then one has to accept the inevitable with charm and tact.

I remember taking a beautiful and diplomatic English girl to dine at the great (but very small) Restaurant Adrian in Amsterdam. I had not been able to make my reservation until an hour or two beforehand. With apologies, the owner, Adrian de Haas, led us to a table much less desirable than the one usually given to me. I was about to explode when the girl said, "Don't worry. Wherever we sit, we make it a good table." De Haas gave her an admiring and adoring smile.

Once I have decided that I will return regularly to a restaurant, I note down the various numbers of my favorite tables. One will be in a quiet corner suitable for a serious discussion or a flirtatious tête-à-tête, another may be in the most public position for a magnificent and beautiful extrovert who wants to see and be seen. I keep a "little black book" with all these numbers for my favorite restaurants around the world.

As soon as you are seated, you can begin to judge how you are being rated by what happens next. If the maître d'hôtel bows and departs, leaving matters in the hands of the captain, you are rated at about C. If the maître d'hôtel stays and offers to discuss the menu, you are around B. If, however, the proprietor appears suddenly, is introduced by the maître d'hôtel, and offers to help, you have achieved A.

As soon as the menus are in hand, I always say, "Give us a few minutes to consider." The captain withdraws—but never forget for a moment that he and his staff are watching and listening. This is not a matter of idle prying. It is the professional job of every member of the staff—every waiter, even every busboy—to cooperate (by instant and silent communication) in sizing you up, so as to give you the kind of meal and service that will satisfy you. If you happen to remark to the lady next to you that you don't like flowers on the table when dining, someone, within a few seconds, will remove the flowers. Above all, the captain wants to know whether you are a high gourmet, or whether the dinner you have in mind will begin with Le Shrimp Cocktail,

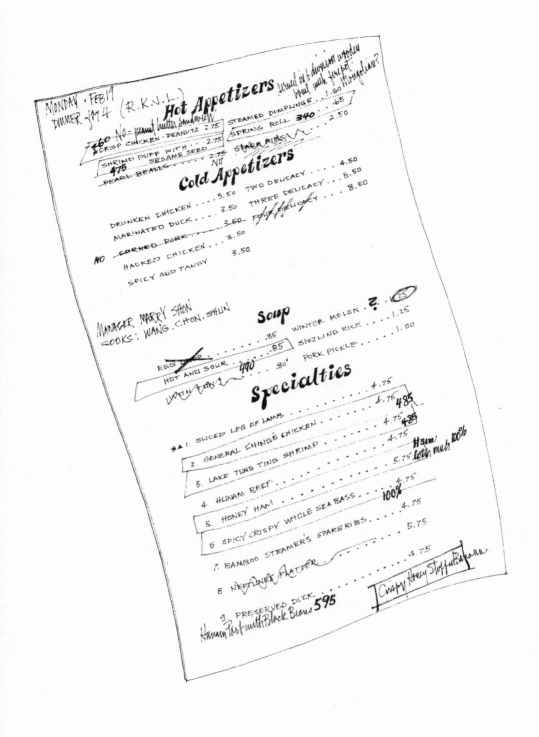

MONDAY · FEB 19
DINNER for 4 (R.K.N.L.)

Hot Appetizers

served w/ diagram wooden *serval with frypot* · 1.60 Mongolian?

~~1.60~~ No - peanut butter sandwich
✗CRISP CHICKEN · PEANUTZ 2.75   STEAMED DUMPLINGS .... .65
SHRIMP PUFF WITH ... 2.75   SPRING ROLL **340** 2.50
     475   SESAME SEED   STARR RIBS
~~PEARL BALLS~~   2.75 NO

Cold Appetizers

DRUNKEN CHICKEN .... 3.50   TWO DELICACY 4.50
MARINATED DUCK .... 3.50   THREE DELICACY .. 6.50
NO ~~CORNED PORK~~ .... 3.50 FOUR DELICACY 8.50
HACKED CHICKEN ... 3.50
SPICY AND TANGY   3.50

MANAGER MARRY SHON
COOKS; WANG. CHON. SHUN

Soup

                                 WINTER MELON 2. · (25)
                                 .85   SIZZLING RICE 1.25
EGG .... .85   PORK PICKLE 1.00
HOT AND SOUR **990** .... .80
WON TON

Specialties

                                            4.75
▲ 1. SLICED LEG OF LAMB 4.75 **485
   2. GENERAL CHING'S CHICKEN 4.75 **485**
   3. LAKE TUNG TING SHRIMP ....   4.75   Have
   4. HUNAM BEEF ....   5.75 lots. mut. 100%
   5. HONEY HAM 100%   4.75
   6. SPICY CRISPY WHOLE SEA BASS 4.75
   7. BAMBOO STEAMER'S SPARE RIBS 5.75
   8. NEPTUNES PLATTER 4.75

   9. PRESERVED DUCK
Hunam Port with Black Beans **595**

Crispy Honey Stuffed Banana.

proceed to Le Biftek, and finish with Le Ice Cream. Do you have an intimate knowledge of menu French, or will the menu have to be translated for you? Can you afford the most expensive *spécialités de la maison* and the finest wines? Do you lean toward *la haute cuisine*, or *la cuisine bourgeoise*? Do you have a stomach ulcer that forces you to eat only bland foods? What is your relationship to the lady beside you? Are you anxious to show off to her your magnificent knowledge of gastronomy? Or is she your wife, taking you out to a surprise dinner on your birthday? Will she make the final decisions? Or will you? During these few moments before you start ordering, you are very much "on stage" and your relationship with this restaurant (which may continue for the next thirty years) is being subtly shaped by your every word and action.

Although I have already analyzed the menu earlier in the day, I now check it again carefully for any last-minute changes. Perhaps a new *plat du jour* or a *plat bourgeois* has been written in by hand. I make firm proposals to my guests. I have nothing but disrespect for the host who simply sits back and says to each guest, "What would you like?" He is evading his responsibility as a gourmet and will never compose a great meal. How can he possibly plan the wines if one person is eating chicken and another, venison? When guests come to dinner in my home, they don't expect a choice of dishes. Why should it be different when they are my guests in a restaurant?

Yet an important part of the special ambience of a great restaurant is the luxurious multiplicity of superlative choices, and I try to keep them all dangling as I nod to the captain to indicate that I am ready to order. I never do so at once. First, I start a discussion with him and invite his suggestions. If this is our first meeting, the conversation is crucial and potentially high-pressure. To gain the true cooperation and respect of this man, one must understand the conflicting psychological forces that drive him.

His job compels him, first, to be a salesman. Early this morning, the owner (or manager) of the restaurant started his working day by going to the kitchen to inspect the cold storage larders and confer with the chef. They reviewed what foods were left over, how they would be served up and presented to the customers, and how urgently they had to be sold. Obviously the stewed Boeuf à la Mode Française will hold (and even improve) for several days; the Salade de Crab à la Mayonnaise will not. Together, owner and chef plan the "hard-sell" dishes of the day. The owner then moves to the dining room, where the service staff is assembled, captains in front, waiters behind. The owner instructs them precisely on which dishes are to be pushed.

The late Arnaud Cazenave, owner of Arnaud's in the French Quarter of New Orleans, used to make a slightly sinister boast as to how he could sell every last fading portion before the end of the evening. He would get a message from the kitchen saying how many portions of the unwanted dish (let us call it *plat X*) remained unsold. While discussing the menu, he pretended to hang on every wish of the customer, but would scrupulously avoid any mention of *plat X*. He suggested several other dishes in rapid succession, giving the customer mouth-watering thumbnail sketches of each and no time for consideration. The customer became confused. At that precise moment, Arnaud casually hinted that *plat X* was particularly delicious tonight, although so many people had ordered it that he was not sure whether there was any left. The customer was at once eager. Arnaud called over a waiter and dispatched him to the kitchen to find out. Invariably, the message came back that exactly the right number of portions remained.

Another of Arnaud's ploys was casually to intervene while the customer was discussing the menu with a captain. Taking part for a moment or two in the discussion, Arnaud would say in a tone of considerable surprise, "Didn't Jules suggest *plat X*? It's marvelous tonight!" A reproachful stare was directed at the captain, who instantly put on an abashed look. Before the last diner left at the end of the evening, every portion of *plat X* was sold.

This form of pressure is practiced by many great restaurants. To counter it, the Tiger must never allow himself to be confused. Instead, he must appeal to the other, more idealistic side of the captain's nature. Certainly, if he thinks that the customer is a sucker, he will never give him an even break! But the moment the captain realizes that he is facing a Tiger gourmet, determined to compose a truly great meal, he rises at once to his own pride in his skill and his own devotion to the traditions of fine service. He feels a sense of participation in a rare adventure. He begins ministering to a pleasure he thoroughly understands. He is won over.

There have been dozens of occasions when an enthusiastic captain has advised me, even against the interests of his employer, as to the state of the kitchen and the larder. He has been in and out of the kitchen all day. He has overheard the chef swearing at the rump of veal. He is aware of the traps behind some of the fancy names on the menu.

I remember once asking about the Côte de Veau Grand'mère à la Mode Périgourdine. *"Oh, non, m'sieur,"* whispered the captain, "the veal was tough this morning." I asked about the Canard Bigarade au Grand Marnier. *"Non, m'sieur,"* he said, "there were no fresh ducks this morning, so we are using frozen." I remember being fascinated by the fabulous title of one dish that I had never seen before, "Coeur de Filet Mignon au Feu de Bois du Roi Albert." It seemed obvious that the reference was to the late King Albert of the Belgians, who loved hunting and used to smoke his meats, while grilling them over a campfire in the forest, by throwing on fresh woodland herbs. I couldn't imagine how this could be done in a New York restaurant. I didn't smell any woodland smoke around. I gave one critical look to the captain and he grinned from ear to ear. *"Oh, non, non, m'sieur! Ce n'est pas vrai. C'est grillé sous le gaz."*

A truly great meal is almost impossible without this happy cooperation. How to achieve it? The first essential is to establish your authority. There are some ploys that may help.

You suggest that the meal might very well be started with some *ikra*. If the captain admits that he does not know what that is, you draw yourself up and, in your most austere and superior voice, point out that the word *caviar* does not exist in the Russian language. While he is momentarily off balance you plunge in with a question about what kind of caviar they have in stock. You let him know that you understand precisely the differences between Beluga, the name for the very large eggs from a huge sturgeon—often more than twelve feet long, Osetrova, the medium-sized eggs from a fish about six feet long, and Sevruga, the small eggs from a fish about four feet long. Finally, you slam down your advantage by asking point-blank how many ounces of caviar the restaurant serves per portion (it should be about two ounces). At this point, not intending to order caviar anyway, I say the caviar is obviously unsatisfactory and order something else.

I confess that I have learned many of my ploys from Ludwig Bemelmans, who was one of the greatest restaurant Tigers of all time. He used to say that ploys (both those used by restaurants and those used by customers) could sometimes be carried so far that they backfired. Bemelmans told the story of a Viennese dentist who was looking for a good investment for the profits from his drilling. Deciding on a restaurant, he hired a chef and they discussed what kind of restaurant it should be. The chef was against any kind of national cuisine. Vienna already had too many of those. Why not give the new restaurant the unique title "Chops from Every Animal in the World"? The dentist was scared, but finally agreed and had the name put up over the doorway of the new place in huge and well-lighted red letters. On opening day, the dentist acted as his own maître d'hôtel. He broke into a slight nervous sweat when he saw that there, among the first few customers that had walked in, was one of Vienna's leading restaurant Tigresses. She was alone. He led her to one of the best tables. Without waiting to see a menu, she gave her order in a low and calm voice: "An elephant chop, please."

To cover his instant confusion, the dentist asked, "How would madame like it prepared?"

Without batting an eyelid, or raising her voice even one decibel: "Medium-rare. *A la Milanais.* Sautéed in butter. A little *al dente* spaghetti over it. Sprinkled with grated Parmesan. Garnished with an anchovy fillet. A black olive on top."

The dentist tried to hide the mounting terror in his face: "That sounds very good, madame." And he almost ran into the kitchen and screeched hysterically to the chef, "God! What do we do now?"

Without a word, the chef put on a clean apron, straightened his *haut chapeau,* walked with a calm step to the Tigress's table, and bowed. Speaking with silky politeness: "Madame will eat her elephant chop alone?"

There was an immediate sense of annoyance in the sharpness of her nod. He persisted: "Madame expects no one else?"

An almost explosive: "No."

"And Madame herself wants only one chop?"

"Yes, yes. Why all these stupid questions?"

The chef drew himself up to his full height: "Because—I am terribly sorry, madame—for one single chop we cannot kill our elephant."

Yet, although ploys may be useful tools, there is no "instant method," no quick, slick, or trick way to gain the cooperation and respect of the staff of a great restaurant. You must simply have done your homework. You must be able to prove that you know as much (or more) about food and wine as the captain. Like a jigsaw puzzle, piece by piece (usually starting with the main entrée and balancing the earlier and later courses against it), the parts of the great meal are fitted together. The pressure relaxes. But if the greatness is to be consummated, continuous vigilance is essential at each succeeding step.

How to Fight Without Actually Drawing Blood

When the food begins to come to the table, and the blade of one's judgment is removed from its sheath. Again, the rules for serving are classic and there is every sound and practical reason for seeing to it that they are maintained. The food is brought to a side table for "finishing" and serving, not for the purpose of putting on a huge and flaming dramatic show, but to allow the diner to control the final arrangements. The captain presents the dish and waits for the host to nod his approval and give his instructions. There may be a choice of rare or medium, light or dark, and so on. The vegetables, garnishes, and sauces are served individually, only after the plate has been placed before the diner, so that he can control the exact amounts. When everyone is properly served, the maître d'hôtel should appear, look over the entire table, and bow to the host, signifying that the service is up to the standard of the restaurant. Then, the moment of truth. Is it up to *my* standard?

Nothing will more quickly build your prestige with this restaurant—nothing will more solidly ensure that you get better and better service each time you come—than the proof that you can recognize within the first two mouthfuls any mistake or fault of slapdash preparation. If you have ordered the Terrine de Canard Sauvage et de Faisan Truffé, and it comes padded out with veal and ham and mushrooms, you call over the captain and send the offending dish back to the kitchen. If you order Tournedos à la Rossini, and find that the slices of pâté de foie gras and black truffle on top of the filet mignon have been replaced by a tired piece of liver sausage and a mushroom, you refuse it.

If there is one thing that American restaurants lack, it is customers with courage enough to send back mediocre food. Yet one must be secure in one's judgment. The brash young man who, to show off to his girl friend, sends everything back, will be (and should be) put on the Skunk list of that particular restaurant the following day. Equally unacceptable is the man who eats half the dish—and then sends it back. He makes himself ridiculous.

Sending a dish back, of course, also disorganizes the tight kitchen timing of the meal. If you return a soup or an omelet, you must expect to wait about fifteen minutes for a replacement. To replace fried or grilled meats, or grilled fish, or roasted chicken, or a cheese soufflé, you will have to wait about thirty minutes. For a complicated *plat composé*, often as much as fifty minutes.

I remember giving a farewell dinner for a friend who was leaving for several years of work in Europe. The hors d'oeuvre, the soup, and the fish were perfect. The entrée was to be Le Carré d'Agneau aux Primeurs, with the lamb lean and pink. When it was served, it was running in fat, grossly overcooked, and instead of being prepared *aux primeurs* (with fresh garden vegetables), it was *à la Languedocienne* (slathered in garlic butter). I sent it back. It could not be replaced in less than forty-five minutes, so we changed to a cold Caneton Rôti en Tranches en Gelée de Son Jus.

I did not "never go there again." It was obviously an unlucky night. My good relations with the owner and the chef (who came out to apologize the next time I was in for lunch) were cemented by this adversity. It is still a great restaurant.

How to Check the Check Without Giving the Appearance of Being Unable to Afford the Price

There is much less opportunity for a restaurant to overcharge for a great meal than there is for a plumber to overcharge for the repair of a toilet. The precise price of every dish chosen (plus any cover or service charge) is clearly printed on the menu. The main problem, when the check comes, is psychological. By the time the second Cognac has been finished and the diners have all relaxed into a rosy state of euphoria, there is an atmosphere of such pampered luxury that any cold question of accounting is an insulting sour note. The late Fernand Point, owner of the famous Restaurant de la Pyramide, once told me at the end of a supreme meal, "For such a dinner one does not ask the price." This is restaurant propaganda. One *does* ask the price. And one makes sure that no improper charges have been included and that the addition is sincere. Yet despite my care, I admit that I have been fooled at least once.

This happened in Venice, where I went to lunch at a small *taverna* on the Bacino di San Marco with my dog, Ñusta. (Venice is nice to dogs; they are allowed in everywhere.) I took a table on the covered terrace overlooking the canal. The maître d'hôtel took my order, then said, "And your dog, signore, what would she like?" I avoid feeding Ñusta in public places. I don't want her to get into the habit of looking for food. So I brushed him off by saying, "Oh, she doesn't care about eating." A few minutes later, I was surprised to see all the fuss made over the dog. First, a napkin was placed on the floor in front of her. Then she was served, in a silver bowl, consommé containing slivers of prosciutto. Then spaghetti with bits of fish on a silver platter. Finally, cubes of steak covered with melted butter. Ñusta loved it all. When she had finished, the waiter wiped her mouth with the napkin.

I drank up my coffee and asked for the check. The total was staggering. I called over the maître d'hôtel and said, "Is this *my* check?"

"Yes, signore, that is your correct bill."

I pointed out that I had had the Zuppa di Verdura at 200 lire and the Fegato alla Veneziana at 650.

He agreed.

Then what was this Prosciutto in Brodo at 450? And this Spaghetti alle Vongole at 450? And this Filletti San Pietro al Burro at 900? And why were there two cover charges?

"For the dog, signore."

"For the dog?"

"*Si*, signore."

My lunch had cost 1,000 lire, Ñusta's, almost 2,000. He insisted that I had ordered it. I had to pay.

It has been my experience that the richer the diner, the more careful he is about checking the check. When the multimillionaire Nubar Gulbenkian called for his check, he asked for the menu at the same time and put on his monocle to cross-check the price of each item. His meticulous care was admired and respected by the proprietors and their staffs wherever he dined. Yet there is nothing that is more deeply resented by restaurant owners than the customer who tries, unfairly, to niggle over the price of some item which was clearly marked on the menu.

I was once dining at Le Grand Véfour in the days when the owner of that famous Paris "three-star," Raymond Oliver, was a good deal less mellow than he is today. At the next table, a lone woman of extraordinary beauty and supreme elegance had just finished dining. Glancing at her check, she called Oliver over and said angrily, "I am not going to pay this *couvert*. The bill is high enough."

Oliver nodded and smiled broadly (whatever happens, Oliver always smiles). "I don't blame you, madame la Comtesse. But does madame ever go to market in the morning?"

The woman shrugged. "Of course not. I have servants."

"I thought not, madame. So you are not familiar with the prices in Les Halles these days?"

The woman flared up: "I don't care a damn. At your prices, an added *couvert* is an outrage and I will not pay it."

Oliver's face remained smiling, but his stare was glacial. He turned to the captain and said loudly enough for everyone in the dining room to hear, *"Pas d'addition pour madame la Comtesse."* And walked away. Everyone was staring. La Comtesse was so embarrassed and unnerved that she immediately paid the entire bill and left. I doubt that she ever came back.

Checking the check can sometimes be a delicate social problem. The owner of Ernie's in San Francisco, Victor Gotti, once told me of a respected customer who regularly lunched with his dark-haired wife, but (almost equally) regularly dined with a slim-slam blonde. At the close of one lunch, the man questioned the price of the wine, a Château Pichon-Longueville. Victor, who was talking to a customer at a nearby table, felt as if the earth was opening up beneath his feet as he heard the captain say, "It is much less expensive, m'sieur, than the Château Lafite that you enjoyed so much last night."

How to Tip Like a Tiger and Leave Like a Lion

When the great dinner comes to its rosy end and one is troubled by the high cost of the tips, there is a consoling thought in remembering how many people were involved in the magnificent occasion. You were ushered in by the doorman—your coats taken by the hatcheck girl—led to the table by the maître d'hôtel—order taken by the captain—apéritifs poured by the barman—service by two waiters and probably three busboys—the wine bottles found by the cellar steward and served by the sommelier—your food ordered from the market by the kitchen steward, its storage controlled by the garde-manger, its preparation supervised by the chef de cuisine and various parts cooked by five sous-chefs and perhaps three apprentice assistants—your dishes washed and pans cleaned out by five plongeurs—your check prepared by a cashier—the whole place run by a manager and/or a proprietor. Thus your dinner required the services of thirty people. The average in a great restaurant is about one employee for every three diners.

The tradition of restaurant tipping was developed in Vienna during the long sweep of the Hapsburg Empire. The diner would leave three piles of money on the table. The biggest, in the center, was for the *Zahlkellner,* or captain. The one on the right was for the *Speisenträger,* or waiter. The third was for the sommelier. The piles had to be as widely spaced as possible, for the restaurant law was that the waiter could have all the money that he could pick up within the reach of his outstretched thumb and index finger. That old tradition, somewhat adapted, still remains.

The first principle of tipping, I am convinced, should be that the tip reflects the degree of the diner's satisfaction with the service. I do not agree that the tip should be a fixed 15 percent added to the bill without a moment's thought. If the service has been less than perfect, the tip might be 12 1/2 percent or even 10 percent. Restaurant proprietors, when they speak frankly, agree that a variable tip makes for better all-around service. If you add the tip to your bill, remember that the waiter gets it all, even though the captain did a large part of the work.

If you want the captain to receive a part of your general tip, you write the amount on the check and indicate "P.P." (*pour partager,* "to be divided") against it. On this basis, if the service was good, add a tip of 20 percent. On the other hand, if the captain has performed special services, I may leave off the "P.P.," so that the waiter gets the whole of the write-in tip. Then I tip the captain separately, usually one dollar for each person served. The sommelier gets one dollar for each bottle. I think it unnecessary to tip the maître d'hôtel at each visit since he shares the captain's tip, but if I am a regular customer, I give him something special at holidays and at the start of his vacation.

I am strongly opposed to overtipping. All of us have seen an overrich and overfoolish man leaving a great restaurant in a green snowstorm of dollar bills. Waiters are glad, of course, to make an extra-fast buck, but they hardly respect the overtipper. The next time he comes in, he gets exactly what he deserves: extradeep bows and a lot of showy servility, but less, rather than more, gastronomic service.

The chair is drawn back. I stand up from the table. Swaying slightly, I correct my balance and concentrate on laying the groundwork for the next great meal. Deep down in the heart of every captain and waiter there remains the touch of an artist. He longs to know what I really feel about the evening's performance. This is the moment when every well-deserved thank you is not only due, but is worth its weight in gold for the future. A squeeze of the arm to the busboy. A press of the shoulder to the waiter. A touch of the hand to the captain. Congratulations on the meal to the maître d'hôtel. If the proprietor appears in the lobby, it is not enough to say that everything was fine.

Mention some extraspecial detail for praise, so that he realizes how observant you are. The most fundamental of all principles is that in a great restaurant a great meal comes only to the diner who can build and maintain a great reputation.

Afterthought

In this discussion there has been almost no mention of the high cost of great meals in great restaurants. All that can be said might have been put into twelve words by J. P. Morgan, had he paraphrased his famous remark about the expense of his ocean yacht: "If you have to worry about the cost, you shouldn't be there."

CHAPTER 16

OUTWITTING
THE WINE STEWARD

Antisnobbery Saves Money and Tempers

Although this may sound like heresy, I do not believe that a great meal demands the accompaniment of very great wines. Some superb restaurants with outstanding cellars list wines of such rare and extraordinary vintages, of such complexity and subtlety of flavors—sometimes of such dominance and power—that they can completely overshadow the food. A superbly great wine does not accompany the food: the food has to be chosen to accompany great wine. For example, nothing brings out the qualities of a rare vintage red Bordeaux or Burgundy more than a piece of Swiss Bagnes cheese. Nothing does more for a great white Graves, or a Montrachet, or a Corton-Charlemagne than the simplest of poached white fish, with the gentlest of Sauce Mousseline. An exceptional red Rhône is best brought out with goat cheese. Great vintage Port is never better than with freshly shelled walnuts. And as to the rich Moselle and Rhine wines of the greatest years, they are best sipped slowly by themselves, after a carefully planned light and small dinner. Hardly the ingredients of a great restaurant meal! Another point is that the true appreciation of such very rare wines requires a quiet and contemplative atmosphere, not the gay and noisy hubbub of public dining.

Finally, since a restaurant has to add to the price of a bottle a share of the storage and service costs, great wines can be extremely expensive on restaurant wine lists. In New York, the price is often five times the retail tag of the same bottle in a wine store. A noble wine at twenty dollars in the store may be one hundred dollars in the restaurant. In Paris, the markup is about four times. In London and other major European cities, about three times.

But whatever the wines chosen, one must maintain absolute discipline over the sommelier, or wine steward, as to the classic rules for the service at table. They are founded on the practical experience of a thousand years, yet it is surprising how often they are broken by even the best of restaurants.

When it is time to serve the first wine, the sommelier brings the unopened bottle, so that the label (and especially the vintage year) can be verified and the seal checked for leakage. The bottle is opened in your presence and you are immediately handed the cork for inspection as to security and for smelling as to moldiness or mustiness. If you have any doubts, voice them at once. The sommelier then pours a small quantity (usually about 1 1/2 ounces) into the host's glass and stands, bottle in hand, awaiting approval. Note whether the glass is the right shape and size for this wine. Swirl it around in the glass, inhale the bouquet; taste, judge, and check the temperature. Take your time. If the sommelier shows the slightest sign of impatience, or puts on an I-dare-you-to-complain look, or makes some such remark as "Isn't it magnificent, m'sieur?" I immediately use a ploy taught me many years ago by my father.

He had taken me to Brussels and we were dining at the oldest restaurant in the city, L'Epaule de Mouton. The chef, old "Oncle René" Chantraine, was preparing his great specialty, La Truite de Mon Village and my father had chosen a Corton-Charlemagne.

His wine-tasting arrogance was perfected to the last detail. He kept the sommelier hanging. The tasting was interminable. At last the glass was returned to the table without the slightest sign of pleasure, recognition, or appreciation. Not even a nod of thanks or a grunt of assent. My father considered it enough of a signal if he did not refuse the bottle.

In normal circumstances, I spend about five seconds on the tasting, before either nodding my approval or refusing the wine. If it is acceptable, but too warm, I send it back to the cooler. If it is too cold, I suggest to my guests that they warm their glasses with the palms of their hands.

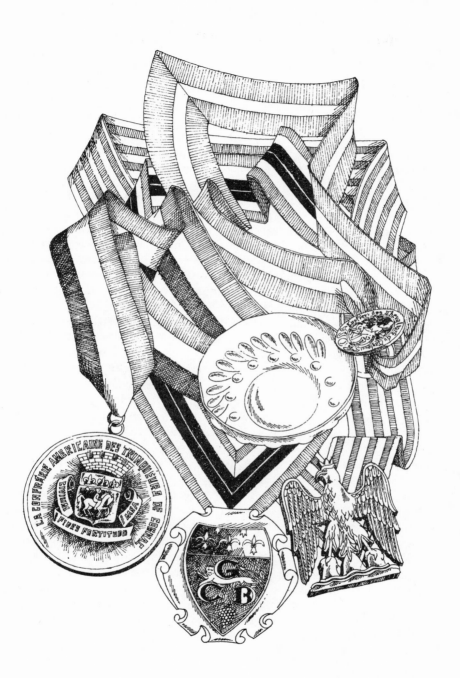

When the second wine is to be served, the waiter must remove the first glass, but if there is still wine left in it, he must ask, "Do you wish to finish your wine?" The empty bottle is left at the table, in case there is any later query. I never hesitate to ask for the label to be soaked off for my files.

Some wine stewards who, correctly or incorrectly, regard themselves as professionals of high prestige are extremely temperamental and must be handled with tact, but always with absolute firmness. Not long ago, at one of the most famous restaurants in Paris, the dessert was to be a Soufflé Flambé aux Marrons, accompanied by a flower-decorated bottle of Champagne Perrier-Jouet Cuvée Belle Epoch. As soon as the soufflé was presented, we saw that it was severely overcooked. We mentioned this to the captain, who agreed at once, but asked us to taste it. The crust was thick and hard. The inside was almost as firm as a cake. I sent it back. We were so disgusted that we refused to wait for any replacement, but ordered fruits and cheese. The wine steward came to open the Champagne. I told him that we no longer wanted it, but would change to a Port with the cheese.

Quickly he took off the seal from the Champagne bottle and said, "You see, m'sieur, it is already opened."

I simulated a voice of cold fury: "You may open it if you wish, Pierre, but I have not the slightest intention of paying for it."

He half-threw the bottle back into the ice bucket in such a way that my lady companion was slightly splashed. I turned the restaurant inside out and had the proprietor at my table in one minute flat. He offered abject apologies and canceled all charges for the entire dinner.

At the end of any great meal, when the coffee has been served, the assumption, in a great restaurant, is that the conversation among the diners is now mellow and philosophical and that it should not be interrupted. So the waiters do not normally clear the last of the wine glasses or the empty brandy snifters, but stand aloof, unless called, until the host signals the end by asking for the check.

The final and absolute rule is that you should drink exactly what you like and should not allow yourself to be influenced by any considerations of prestige or status, even in the greatest of restaurants. When John F. Kennedy was a senator and sometimes dined in Manhattan at Henri Soulé's Le Pavillon, he occasionally ordered a glass of milk. A pint bottle was brought to the table neatly hidden in a small silver bucket of ice.

PART IV

The Host in His Wine Library

CHAPTER 17

WHY SHOULDN'T I BUY ONE BOTTLE AT A TIME?

And "Shake It Up Good" on the Way Home to Dinner

My friends Celia and Henry are charming and sophisticated hosts. Both are excellent cooks. They would not dream of inviting me to dinner without serving at least one bottle of wine. But they refuse to make the effort, or take the time, to learn something about wine. In the early afternoon of the day when they are going to serve, say, a fillet of sole baked in a cream sauce with mushrooms, followed by a grilled rack of lamb with fresh vegetables, Celia goes to her local wine merchant, tells him her menu for the evening, and asks him to suggest a bottle. The condition of that wine by the time it is poured at table was best described one day by Celia's fourteen-year-old son, who, holding a bubbly glass of cola in one hand and a glass of wine in the other, said, "I like wine best when you shake it up good."

I am always telling Celia and Henry that buying wine one bottle at a time is the worst possible way. It is overexpensive and inefficient in terms of matching the wine to the food, and above all boring, dull, and uninteresting in terms of the fascinating game of exploring the extraordinary range and variety of the pleasures of wine.

To save money, to be able to open better bottles more often, to serve exactly the right wine with the right food—in short, to gain the reputation among your friends as a memorable host in terms of wine also—I believe it is essential to set up some kind of storage arrangement at home, even if you live in a one-room studio apartment and open only a couple of bottles a week. Let us not become involved in nonsensical cliché talk about "building a wine cellar." The ridiculous word *cellar* ought to be eliminated from the modern vocabulary of wine. Obviously it is an anachronistic impossibility in a city apartment, in a single-level ranch house, or a beach cottage on stilts. If there is a below-ground-level space in the modern home, it probably houses the furnace, the brightly lit, often smoke-filled playroom, or the buzzing vibrations of the power-driven home workshop—hardly right for the slow aging of wine, which requires coolness, darkness, the absence of any smell or smoke, and a silent, vibration-free stillness.

Recently, when I visited the great Château Latour in Bordeaux, I found that its enormous, classic "cellars" were not really below ground at all, but were a series of block-long granite sheds. After walking, it seemed, for miles along the lines of barrels and among the racks of bottles, my guide, the cellar master, opened a side door and there we were, at grass level on the sloping hillside looking out across the waters of the Gironde. If Château Latour doesn't need an underground cellar, I certainly don't!

What every good home drinker of wine needs is what I like to call a "wine library." The parallel is precise. You buy your favorite books according to your taste. There are so many possibilities in the shops that you must learn to pick and choose. You develop loyalties to certain kinds of books, to certain authors, certain subjects. Sometimes you buy an extremely expensive book because it is so magnificent that you feel you must have the experience of owning it. At other times, by diligent searching, you find a little book at a giveaway price that brings you a pleasure far beyond its value. As you gain experience in collecting books, you learn the two most fundamental rules. First, never let yourself become a victim of high-pressure promotion—never buy a show-off book simply because it is the fashionable thing to do, simply because you think its ownership will give you prestige among your friends. Second, never choose a book by its price tag—if it is a bad book, it is a bad book at any price. The principles are exactly the same for the wine library.

Every sound rule of wine-buying points to the advantages of the home wine library. At the simplest level, there is that automatic 10 percent discount on a case of twelve bottles—even, at most stores, on a mixed case of your own choice. You can take immediate advantage of

the "special offers," which many stores advertise as an enticement to bring in new customers. If you study the sales catalogs and search diligently from store to store in your neighborhood, you can often find unusual and remarkable buys, sometimes for as little as half the normal price, which, if you have reasonable storage space, can give you enough inexpensive bottles to last for several months.

Then there is the problem of "shaking it up good" on the way home for dinner. No good wine—and especially not a fine old red wine—should be moved around or violently jogged shortly before it is opened. There is often a slight, sometimes almost invisible, powdery sediment in the wine, which should be left at the bottom of the bottle and not consumed as floating dust in the wineglass. So I keep every important bottle lying on its side, with the label facing upward, in my wine library for at least a month. By always remembering to keep the label up when removing the bottle, carrying it to the table, and gently removing the cork, one avoids rolling around any sediment that might have quietly settled. I would never dream of consuming today the bottle I bring home today. I choose from the small backlog in my wine library.

There remains the question of "the perfect marriage" between the wine and the food. Your local merchant—even assuming the excellence of his goodwill and knowledge, and discounting his natural desire to increase his profit by selling you a more complicated and more expensive bottle—can never, without an intimate knowledge of your cooking style, give you more than the standard clichés about white wine with white meat and red with red. But how rich is the sauce that accompanies your white fish? Will your red steak be served with its natural juices, or with a Béarnaise or other luxurious sauce? It makes a big difference to the wine. The creamier and richer the dish, the richer and softer should be the wine. It isn't the color that counts—it is the aromatic dominance of the food against the power of the personality of the wine (see Chapter 22). You will never learn about "the marriage that makes the meal" if you buy only one bottle at a time, here and there, haphazardly, and probably a different bottle every time. Your wine library should provide you with an immediate range of choices of wines you already know, from the most delicate, light, and subtle, up to the most dominant and powerful—so that you can choose, with the assurance of previous experience with these particular wines, the precise companion to the particular dish of tonight. This kind of service should be built into your wine library.

Finally, there is the much-debated question of aging wines at home.

I am not suggesting for a moment that any of us can or should hold noble wines for twenty, thirty, or forty years, as rich connoisseurs did years ago. Comparatively few wines are now made with such lengthy "home cellaring" in mind and yet it is still possible to buy a fine young wine, at a relatively reasonable price, with the near certainty that it will improve enormously in both quality and value with up to four or five years of careful keeping. Thus, at a time when wine prices have nowhere to go but up, if you can keep such an aging program going, on a rotating basis, setting aside some wines every year, you will always be able to offer your friends currently expensive wines with the knowledge that you did not pay expensively for them. Let us take a specific example.

In January, 1960, the 1959 Château Latour, only three months old and still, of course, in the barrel, was offered for sale at $3.50 a bottle for U.S. delivery in 1962. By 1961 the price had risen to $5 a bottle. In 1962, upon U.S. delivery, the price was $7 a bottle. By 1964 the price was $10 a bottle. In 1973, approaching its peak, it sells, if you can find it, for between $60 and $85 a bottle. Such treasures are simply unavailable anywhere in the commercial market. (And what more perfect gift to honor, say, the birthday of a friend, than one of your irreplaceable bottles.)

My own wine library is divided into three parts. Close to my dining area, in a spot I can reach with hardly more effort than stretching out my hand, I keep a metal rack that holds up to two dozen bottles of what my French friends call *"vins de consommation courante du jour,"* wines of current, day-by-day consumption. But don't be fooled by the French definition. Usually at least half of my everyday, inexpensive wines—wines instantly ready to slake a sudden thirst, bottles to be opened to pour a glass to accompany my luncheon tray at my desk—at least half of these simple wines in my rack nowadays are American: from California, Maryland, New York, Ohio, or Wisconsin. Many of them still work out at less than two dollars a bottle. Very few are above the three-dollar mark. I say "work out," because, of course, I sometimes buy them in gallon or half-gallon jugs, although as soon as the jug is opened I pour the remaining wine into standard bottles, tightly recorked for better keeping. Such wines—in fact, any bottle, once opened, whether it contains red, white, or any other color—will, in my opinion, hold their character for a day or two if refrigerated. A red bottle from the refrigerator, of course, should be given two hours to come back to room temperature before being reopened and repoured.

The second division of my wine library is a honeycombed "wine wall," facing away from the light in an air-conditioned room, where the temperature is never allowed to rise much above 70° F. I deliberately store these "here-and-now party wines" at from 10 to 15 degrees above the normally accepted temperature in order to age them slightly more quickly for use within the current year. This wine wall of mine can hold up to twenty cases of wines of the middle range of price and quality, with enough varietal sweep of character, personality, and power that, for any dinner-party menu, I can pick exactly the right wine for that "perfect marriage" for which one is always trying.

How many wines do you need for this pursuit of perfection? You certainly do *not* need as many as my 240 bottles. I am sure that, with careful and regular choosing, you could provide yourself with a sufficient variety within the scope of a minimum of four cases, 48 bottles. Here again my favorite California wines are given status equal to those of France, Germany, Italy, Spain, and Switzerland, while the best wines of Australia, Chile, Greece, Hungary, and Portugal are never far behind. Let me say that my devotion to our American wines has nothing to do with national pride. I choose and buy my wines entirely on the basis of "blind comparison" in terms of quality and value. In this vast middle range of the wines of the world, our California varieties are now generally the equals of their imported counterparts, while some Californians have special qualities of freshness and fruit that are unduplicated in foreign wines.

Perhaps for this reason, I usually find (without especially thinking about it) that my "party wine wall" is usually one-third to one-half full of California bottles. In this middle-range category, one has to say California, because when the noble wine grapes of Europe (the varieties from which all the finest wines of the world are made) were brought to the United States, they thrived only in the temperate, mist-soaked, richly earthed, rolling valleys of the West Coast. In other parts of the country—among the Finger Lakes of New York, along the Ohio shores of Lake Erie, in Maryland and other grape-growing areas—the winters are just too fierce for the delicate European vines, so the wines of those regions (often attractive, country-style wines for simple meals) are made from our native grapes, which were growing wild here long before the coming of the Colonists.

The third division of my wine library is a locked "secret closet," with a miniature air conditioner keeping it always at 55° F., where my great wines can rest comfortably and age gracefully, year after year, as the magical and mysterious development of supreme wines demands. There are never very many of these bottles at any one time. The great wines have now become as sought-after and valuable as rare jewels. Unless one rides on mountains of money, one has to wait for the exceptional opportunity, the chance to buy a young wine of great promise, or a suddenly supreme vintage of a relatively unknown producer. My secret closet is never opened, no bottle is ever gently lifted from the racks, without serious consideration. The occasion must be important. The menu must be special. The guest of honor must be a worthy connoisseur. The qualities of the greatest wines are so complex, so subtle, so much a matter of fine shades of personal opinion and taste, that I can see no point in offering them to unskilled amateurs. I am absolutely opposed to the host who offers a Château Lafite, a Château Latour, a Schloss Johannisberger, or a Château d'Yquem of a truly great vintage simply for the prestigious show of these famous labels. The old proverb may have put it harshly, but "pearls before swine" is still a philosophical truth. Great wines should always be wedded to great occasions.

This is the wine library that best suits my needs. Many connoisseurs keep much larger stocks—sometimes up to 3,000 bottles, or even more. I am often asked my opinion as to the minimum practical wine library, when there are sharp limitations of money and space. I would still keep to my three divisions. I would begin by spending, say, fifteen dollars on six inexpensive bottles for immediate daily use—three reds, three whites. For the medium-priced "party selection" wine wall, I would spend, let us say, two hundred and fifty dollars on forty-eight bottles—perhaps twenty reds, eight first-class rosés, and twenty whites. As to great (or potentially great) wines, it is almost impossible to give detailed advice. The opportunities are so varied and the range of prices so wide. I do know, for example, that at this time of writing, I could buy a bottle of noble to great wine in New York, already reasonably aged for current drinking, for a price somewhere between twenty and thirty dollars a bottle. I could pay as much as one hundred dollars a bottle. A less well known label, but with good prospects for future greatness if properly stored for a few years, might cost as little as eight or ten dollars. This is how it works. These are the pleasures of the exploration, the investigation, the gamble. The tracking down of leads. The sifting of the evidence. The pitting of one's present judgment against future prospects. All the endlessly fascinating rules of the great game of setting up and maintaining one's own wine library.

CHAPTER 18

THE HOW AND WHERE OF THE WINE LIBRARY

A Useful First Step Is to Learn to Read

The three sections of my wine library, or any other bottle-filing system you may choose, must provide, in simplest terms, a means of storing the bottles on their sides without rolling around and of extracting any one of them, from the highest or lowest positions, without all the others collapsing. If you are the wood-working type, you can construct notched shelves, or diamond-shaped bins (each designed to hold twelve bottles of the same label), or even walls of eight- to ten-inch-deep pigeonholes. But if you feel that fingers were made for holding wineglasses, not twist drills, you can go out and buy standard, metal, plastic, or wood wine racks designed to hold any number of bottles from six to six hundred, at prices that start at around fifty cents per bottle—that is, about $6 for a twelve-bottle rack. When shopping around, always calculate the price on a per-bottle basis, for purposes of comparison. I believe strongly in purely functional wine racks. Naturally, if you allow yourself to become hypnotized by decorative stunts, you can pay almost any price. The other day, in one fancy store, I saw a twenty-five-bottle rack of sensuously curvaceous Plexiglas for $125—or $5 per bottle. There was also a fifty-bottle refrigerated closet for $1,000—or $20 per bottle. Another type of refrigerated storage held twenty-five bottles at

$350—$14 per bottle. Just think how much good wine you could buy for all that extra money!

For myself, I insist on a much simpler setup. For the bottles and half bottles for use in the kitchen, there is an eight- to twelve-bottle wooden rack standing in the far corner of the work counter, at the farthest possible point from the hot stove and the bright light of the window. The everyday instantly-ready-to-drink bottles are kept in a free-standing, simply but nicely designed, strongly riveted twenty-four-bottle metal rack, which is normally kept in the dining area, but, for a party, can be moved around. For my main supply, my wide range of lunch and dinner wines, of sweet wines and liqueurs, of apéritifs and spirits, I use honeycomb units, of aluminum or plastic, grooved so that they can be fitted together with complete flexibility as to the shape and size of the wall space to be filled. My wine wall could, at any moment, be taken apart and, unit by unit, bottle by bottle, fitted together again against some other wall, or divided up into several smaller units.

Finally, for my long-term, aging library I use—because there is comparatively much less coming and going, putting in and taking out—the cheapest form of storage rack I know. I bought, from a construction supply company, ten-inch lengths of standard, four-inch-diameter, fired-clay drainpipe and with it lined three walls of my locked closet from floor to ceiling. The pipes are fairly heavy and thus remain very solid when neatly stacked, row upon row. Also, the clay itself is a reasonably good insulator, that resists sudden changes of temperature—all to the good for the sake of the bottles. And the cost, even at today's prices, works out at between twenty-five cents and thirty-five cents per bottle. You can hardly do better than that.

As to the problems of the temperatures of the various departments, I make no special effort to cool down my kitchen rack but make sure that each bottle is used up by the end of each month. (Incidentally, one need take no special care of the "fortified" wines—the Madeiras, Ports, and Sherries, for example, fortified by the addition of brandy or distilled spirits, are virtually indestructible.) Nor do I worry much about my everyday wines, other than keeping their movable rack away from hot radiators and sunlit windows, except that, of course, rosé and dry white bottles are cooled in the refrigerator for a couple of hours before being poured. Sweet wines, which should be drunk a good deal colder, are refrigerated for about four hours.

As to my 240-bottle wine wall, the ideal temperature for relatively short-term storage (in my case, usually not more than a year) is around

55° to 60° F., but these temperatures can fluctuate up to, say, 68° F., or down to about 45° F. without serious damage to the wine, provided that the fluctuations are gradual. You should avoid, for example, a room that in winter is powerfully heated during the daytime and allowed to get cold at night, or in summer is strongly air-conditioned during the day and allowed to heat up at night. This sort of treatment month after month, perhaps year after year, will eventually harm the wine.

In my library of great wines, being held for long, slow aging, I try to maintain a constant temperature of about 50° F., but variations of not more than 5 degrees, up or down, are permissible. Again the main concern is to avoid abrupt or constant changes.

Everyone, of course, knows that each bottle is stored on its side to keep the liquid in contact with the cork, so that it does not shrink and allow the entry of too much air, with the danger of the wine turning sour. Fewer people, however, are aware that the wine does "breathe" through the cork and thus remains alive. This is why the natural wine—unlike distilled spirits—continues to develop in the bottle. There is no need, of course, to lay down bottles sealed with screwcaps, a form of closure that does not allow any "breathing." Screwcap bottles, obviously, are for immediate consumption. Screwcaps are also quite satisfactory for distilled spirits, where no further bottle development is expected.

Stocking the Shelves of the Library

Now, having set up the "bookshelves" of our library—each at its proper temperature—we must start the business of buying the bottles, and this is where it helps to learn to read the language of wine labels. My own most basic rule is never to allow myself to become exclusively "hooked" on one particular wine. I resist saying to myself, "I like this wine so much, I'll stay with it and not bother to try any others." It's fine, of course, to return to a wine one knows well and deeply enjoys, but I always find the major part of my interest and pleasure in expanding the range of my experience. Even among the most inexpensive labels, as at every other level of price and quality, there is a virtually inexhaustible variety from which to choose—provided you know how to read.

There are also, if you are concerned about keeping down expense, good and bad times of the year in terms of finding wine bargains. A good time, for example, is the first week or two of January, when wine merchants usually reduce their prices to clear the stocks left over from the Christmas rush. Then between Memorial Day and the Fourth of July they again clear their stocks before their customers disappear for summer vacations. Again, immediately after Labor Day there is usually a sale to induce returning vacationers to begin restocking and to clear the store shelves for the new shipments building up toward Christmas.

But whether you buy the least-expensive bottle in a cut-rate store in Manhattan, or the wine of the most lordly château in the fanciest "marchand de vin" in Paris or Lyon, or a single bottle or two "at the winery" in the Napa Valley of California, the problem of reading and judging the label is the same anywhere in the world. The words printed on that label can be roughly divided into two, usually intermixed, groups. Let us call the first group the sales message, the arguments designed to persuade you to buy. With these, provided there is no direct breach of the "truth in advertising" code, the bottler has a pretty free hand. He may print his label in the most brilliant shades of green and red. The lettering may look as if it had been painted by hand. There may be a frame of gold medals won at various exhibitions. The wine may be given a copyrighted, fancy "proprietary" or "trade" name. It may be called "Black King," or "Red Queen," or "White Knight," or "Little Flower of the Moslle," or "Little Drops of Gold" (all these actually exist, in one language or another), but the names tell virtually nothing about the character, personality, or quality of the wine.

It is the second group of words on the label that are all-important and that one must learn to read and interpret confidently. These are the words required and enforced by the laws of each wine-producing country to define the wine in the bottle, with legal accuracy, coldly, clearly, without exaggeration, and exactly according to the official regulations. (In the United States, for example, any label on any bottle must first have been approved for accuracy by the Federal Government.) These definitions are of three types:

1. The geographic definition of where the wine was made. This generally gives an immediate clue to its character. A red from Bordeaux has certain family traits that are different from those of a red from Burgundy—differences that one can learn to expect and recog-

nize. Every wine region of the world has these family traits, born fundamentally from the climate and the soil. With practice, one can relate each wine to one's personal tastes.

2. The label also defines who made the wine, how it was made, and how many times it changed hands before it was bottled and shipped to the retail store. This tells us, at once, whether it was made and bottled in relatively small quantities by the vintner who himself owns the vineyard and grows the grapes, or whether it was made in huge quantities in assembly-line style, from many different wines, from many different vineyards, and finally blended in an automated, computerized, "wine factory." There is nothing cheapjack or slipshod about this type of production. The mass-vintner controls his buying and works out his blending with infinite care, trying to satisfy and serve the widest possible range of public taste at the lowest possible price. He is, however, up against the inexorable fact that the greatest and noblest wines of the world—those with magnificent character and personality—all come from precise vineyards, from small plots of earth, and that those precise qualities are progressively blurred when many different wines from many different places are mixed together. One of the most brilliant of all wine technicians, Jean Paul Gardère, wine master of one of the greatest of all vineyards, Château Latour, once said to me, "Monsieur, when you look at a rainbow, you see that it has many brilliant and lovely colors, each capable of standing out on its own. But if you mix all those colors together, what do you get? A monotonous shade of gray!" This is the most basic of all facts of the world of wine. The more precise the source of the wine, the better (and more expensive) it is likely to be.

3. Finally, the legal definition may, in some regions, state the variety of the grape used to make the wine. This name, as one enlarges one's tasting experience, is another clue to the character of the wine. Quite soon one learns the names of the principal grapes (Cabernet Sauvignon, Chenin Blanc, Gamay, Gewürztraminer, Pinot Chardonnay, Pinot Noir, Riesling, Sylvaner, Syrah, Zinfandel, and so on) and develops opinions as to which provides the most consistent pleasure. In some districts, of course, there is no need to print the grape name on the label, since all wines from that source are legally required to be made from certain listed grapes. A French Chablis, for example, must be made from the Pinot Chardonnay. A red Bordeaux from the Médoc is always produced mainly from the Cabernet Sauvignon, with small additions, generally, of the Malbec and Merlot grapes. Thus you can

learn to know what to expect from the wine by knowing its grape or blend of grapes.

The world of wine, however, is very large and it is difficult to learn one's way around it unless one begins at once to draw up one's own personal road map. On the day that you install your wine library, set up also a system for keeping notes and records on the wines you have been drinking, are drinking now, and propose to drink in the future. Also have some form of what is called "inventory control." In other words, you must have a warning system against running out of any particular type of wine, so that you can reorder either the same label or some other wine of similar character and in the same price range. Let us deal with this second, simpler problem first.

Let us say that I buy twelve bottles of Château X and slip them, in a neatly solid block, into my wine wall. Of course, I note the details of the label, with the date of arrival, onto a file card and I also tie a small tag (red for red, pink for rosé, white for white) onto the neck of each bottle, so that it can be identified without being disturbed. When I use the first bottle, I soak off the label and paste it up above the block of the remaining bottles, for instant identification. As each succeeding bottle is emptied, I remove the neck tag and throw it into a file box. Once a month, I check all neck tags in the box and, as soon as I find nine used tags of Château X, I am warned that it is time to reorder that wine.

But even more important is the routine for recording my opinion of the wine. Let us face it, our taste buds have very poor memories. It is virtually impossible to compare the wine one is drinking tonight with another that one drank a year ago, or even a month or a week ago. The only way to form solidly based opinions is to keep a file card for every wine one drinks. Some people put this sort of information down in a "cellar book." I find a file card system much more flexible, since it can be juggled so that comparable wines can be filed close together.

Each of my cards—in the same colors as the tags—is divided into three columns. At the left I indicate the category to which the wine belongs: the country of origin, the region, the district and commune, the vineyard and grape type. Thus all cards of Beaujolais, of California Cabernet Sauvignon, of German Rhine, of Italian Chianti, or of Spanish Sherry, come together in the file and can be continually compared. Down the center column of the card, I copy the label details, including the names of producers, shippers, importers, and retail merchants. At the right there are the numbers: the vintage year, price, date of purchase, plus my own ratings for quality and value. On the back of the card, I note the occasion on which I served it, my personal judgment of the wine, and the comments of friends who shared it. Thus at any time, if I begin to think about ordering some Beaujolais, I can within a few seconds check the various Beaujolais villages, one against the other, then check the various vineyards within each village and come up with all sorts of facts and figures as to which are, most consistently, the best-rated and best-value wines.

I began my card file at sixteen and have continued to keep it for almost forty years. I calculate that I taste about a thousand bottles a year (and please note that I did not say "drink"—I may only taste a single sip of some wines!), so that I now have a file of almost forty thousand cards. They are my most valuable reference guide. In a few seconds I can check on a wine I have had before, or relate a new wine to the others in its class.

These colored cards are also my indispensable guide to the selection of wine with food. The cards provide the answer to almost any question. What was the wine that was such a success with the orange-flamed duck at that dinner party last fall? What would be a good-value, reasonably inexpensive Champagne to serve at next Sunday night's buffet supper? My card file—the tangible record of a lifetime of experience—is the source of almost all of the information in the following wine chapters.

I am not, of course, suggesting that everyone must have a card file as detailed and as large as mine. But even a small, desk-top box of cards, with your notes on the wines as you taste them and your impressions of how well each went with the food, can quickly become an instant arbiter in solving the constant question of what goes with what.

As you build up a file of your own opinions, you will find it the most dependable of all guides for your future selections—far more in tune with your own tastes than the commercial judgments of your wine merchant, the enthusiastically fuzzy advice of your wine-loving friends, or your own hopeless struggles to remember, unaided by any notes, the name of that glorious little château-bottled red you so enjoyed in that Paris bistro on the Left Bank five years ago!

THE GREAT WINES
OF THE WORLD

The Cost Need Not Be As High As the Sky

E verybody talks about "great wines," but few people understand precisely what is meant by "greatness" in a wine. It is not a vague sales slogan. Among the technical experts, it is a precise score on a rating chart—the achievement (after years of patient, slow development) of a degree of color, of clarity, of aroma, of taste, of acid-sugar balance, of body texture, of alcoholic strength, and of mature smoothness of 80 points, or more, out of a possible 100—of at least 80 percent of an imaginary perfection. I have never tasted a faultless wine. The highest score, in my almost forty years of experience, was 96 percent. That was a rare and memorable occasion.

Such a wine is the product, first of all, of a piece of what the French call "privileged soil"—almost always a relatively small vineyard, with exactly the right blend of minerals in its earth, with the ideal slope for the proper runoff of the rain, the correct angle to the sun and prevailing winds, the proper proximity to water for the evening and morning mists, and a reasonable security from killing frosts during the growing season. In this superb vineyard, according to its geographic position, there must then be the right varieties of grapes, with the proper proportion of old vines for aromatic flavor and new for youthful vigor. These plantings must be properly pruned and tended throughout the year.

I am prepared to name, in all the wine regions of the world, only seventy-nine such "great vineyards." Each is mysteriously delimited by its fairly narrow boundaries. One of the most famous of these vineyards is in the village of Gevrey, in the ancient French province of Burgundy. From its beginning, it was called The Field of Farmer Bertin. He discovered, by patient trial and error, that grapes grown in one of his fields would produce a superb red wine. In the next field, five yards over the gray stone wall, the wine was noticeably less than superb. The magic vineyard became known as Le Champ de Bertin. For a thousand years, no one has found the secret of expanding it by even a few square yards. Its wine is still acknowledged to be the greatest of the district—Le Chambertin. The same mysterious limitation applies to every other great vineyard.

But even if everything is perfect with the vines, the chance for a "great" wine, every year, still remains a gamble with the weather. Each May and June the rain and sun must encourage the perfect flowering of the vines, which will determine the perfect size of the future bunches of grapes—neither so large that the juice will be watery, nor so small that it will be an overconcentrated essence. The weather in July will develop the oils in the sap, which will decide the bouquet and finesse of the future wine. The weather in August will control the heaviness or lightness of the wine. Then there must be steady sunshine through September and into the October harvest. Small wonder that, on the average, a "great" wine comes only once every five years.

Finally, the perfectly ripe grapes must be picked on the perfectly right day. The technicians of wine chemistry must make all the right human decisions as to the degree of crushing of the grapes, the control of the seething and bubbling fermentation in the vats, the encouragement of the invisible yeast spores that convert the sugar into alcohol and of the benevolent bacteria that eliminate the acids, the slow aging in the wooden barrels, and the precise moment, years later, for the bottling. Small wonder that, of all the production of all the vineyards of the world, the great wines are much less than one-tenth of 1 percent and that their prices are as high as their prestige.

In the face of currently skyrocketing costs, my own system for acquiring great wines at less than the top prices depends on a keen understanding of the two factors that the vintners take into account when deciding, after each harvest, how much to charge for their top bottles. First, the public prestige of the vineyard name. Second, the precise, technical meaning of that much-misused phrase "the vintage year." The top vineyards—from Château Ausone to Château d'Yquem—are supreme because they produce great wines more

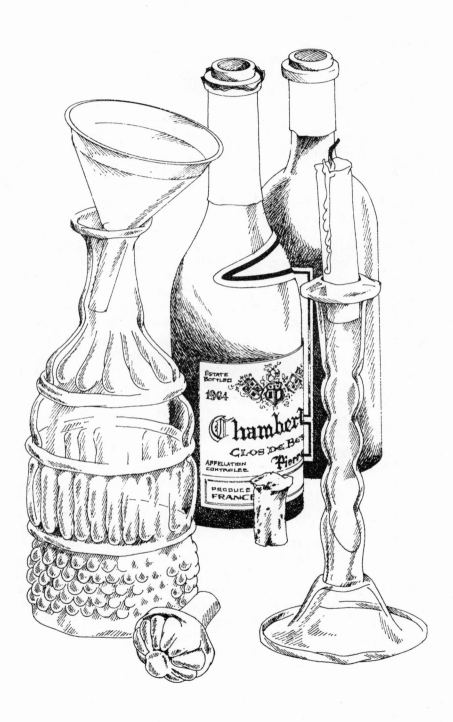

consistently than the others. Yet hardly a year passes without some much less well-known vineyard producing, partly by the accident of its position or by the good luck of some special circumstances, a wine of supreme pleasure at a fraction of the highest price for the year. One must always be watching for these opportunities.

There are also the cost-saving opportunities presented by the widespread misunderstanding in regard to the so-called bad vintage years. Some people are enslaved by their vintage charts. The traditional idea that such-and-such a year was "bad" and that all its wines are unacceptable, while such-and-such a year was "good" and that all its wines are to be unquestionably trusted, is as dead as the dodo! In the last fifteen years, modern vintners have learned so much about the chemistry of making wine that today there is no such thing as an irretrievably wasted year. Naturally, if there is snow in June and rain every day in September, one can hardly expect vinous master-pieces. But, in those halfway "off years," when there is a certain degree of public panic and sales are slow, I have again and again found wines with which the vintner has succeeded in largely overcoming the disadvantages of a poor harvest. Modern technology is bringing the smart buyer more and more opportunities for unheralded bargains.

Finally, even when the experts declare that a certain vintage year is "great" and give it a potential rating of, say, 90 percent, it is essential to understand what they mean. They do *not* mean that the wine was great from the day it was born. They are saying that the wine has the potential to become great after a certain, still-undefinable number of years of development. They are judging the wine against the future. But it is hardly very practical to look up to its "peak" and say, "Look how high it's going to go!" One must also judge how far up the slope it has risen thus far and how fast its rate of climb is.

It is all very well, for example, to be asked to pay an enormous price for the unquestionably great but slow-maturing 1961 vintage, in the hope that it may be at its peak by 1990. But at the present time there are a number of less great wines destined to rise to much lower peaks, which have, so far, climbed much faster than the giant and will provide relatively better drinking over the next five years. Some of these smaller wines, because of their lower potential, command only half the price of the still-sleeping giant. I refuse to be a slave to my vintage charts. It is a waste of money—and a form of infanticide—to drink a supreme wine a decade before its maturity, just because one is dazzled by the vintage year on the label.

How best to set about finding the great wines? The search is easiest in Bordeaux. It is one of the richest wine-producing areas in the world, with more than four thousand clearly and legally defined vineyards, of which, of course, only a handful produce great wines. Finding them is simply a matter of knowing the names and being able to read the labels. The most important phrase in Bordeaux (and anywhere else in France) is *appellation d'origine contrôlée,* often shortened to *appellation contrôlée,* or *A.O.C.,* or *A.C.* It means that the basic information on the label conforms to the regulations of the National Institute in Paris, the controlling authority for all the major wines of France. On such a "controlled" label, any false statement would involve the owner of the vineyard in criminal proceedings. If, for example, the label states that the wine is from the village of Margaux, every grape that went into that wine must have been grown within the regulated limits of the community. If the label says Château Lafite, then every grape must have been grown on the delimited Lafite property. No vineyard owner, however irresponsible at heart, can buy even a single gallon of wine from an outside source and add it to his barrels with the object of expanding his production. Other regulations control the types of grapes that may be used in various districts and the alcoholic strength of the wine. (Incidentally, other European wine-producing countries are now adopting the French system of controls, and the words on new Italian labels are *denominazione di origine controllata,* and in Spanish the phrase is *garantía de la denominación de origen.* Germany, too, is setting up controls under its new wine law.)

The word *château* on a Bordeaux label does not necessarily mean that the wine was made in a magnificent old stone castle with crenellated turrets. There may be an historic mansion, in which the owner may, or may not, live, but the "château" may be just a country cottage. I know of one "château" that is an abandoned railroad station converted into a modern winery. *Château,* means, basically a legally delimited vineyard property.

The next most important label phrase is *mis en bouteille au château,* which means that the wine was made and bottled at the vineyard where the grapes were grown and that the owner therefore takes full responsibility for the quality. Be careful to watch for tricky variations of this wording. For example, *mis en bouteille par le propriétaire* does not guarantee that the wine was bottled at the vineyard, but may mean that the wine was carried by the owner to some other place, where, probably, he had a large, mass-production winery where he could do an automated job more cheaply and quickly. This may be all right with a responsible proprietor but it does involve a certain risk to the buyer. Another version of the phrase is *mis en bouteille dans nos caves.* In this case, "our cellars" could be right on the vineyard, but could also possibly be in Reykjavik or Rio de Janeiro.

As to the greatest vineyard names in Bordeaux, there has been no debate for more than a hundred years. The top five of the districts of the Médoc, Graves, and Sauternes remain unchallenged—the red wines of Château Haut Brion, Château Lafite, Château Latour, Château Margaux, and the golden-sweet wines of Château d'Yquem are each rated as *premier grand cru classé,* or "first-classed growth." Other châteaux, rated in groups as "second," "third," "fourth," or "fifth," always use the somewhat vague phrase *grand cru classé,* or "great-classed growth," without stating their numerical position in the pecking order. No château, apparently, wants to appear to be less than first. (In fact, Château Mouton-Rothschild while it was a second growth before it was recently elevated to first, said as much in its slogan, "First am not permitted to be, second do not choose to be, am myself, Mouton.") Many of these "less than first" vineyards have, in the past years, been so assiduously improved by their wealthy owners that in some years (but with increasing regularity), they now produce wines equal to those of the top names. I would certainly include in my own list of the consistently great Bordeaux vineyards: among the reds, Château Ausone, Château Cheval Blanc, Domaine de Chevalier, Château La Mission Haut Brion, Château Mouton-Rothschild, Château Palmer, Château Petrus; among the whites, again Domaine de Chevalier, Château Laville Haut Brion; and, among the golden sweet wines, Château Climens, Château Coutet, Château Filhot, Château Rieussec, and Château Suduiraut. But great wines, in my experience, have also come from other substantially less well-known names, and the "discoveries" of these bottles have been among the memorable moments of my life with wine. They have included the third-classed Château Calon-Ségur, the second-classed Château Cos d'Estournel, the brilliant vineyard of Saint-Emilion, Château La Gaffelière, the numerically unrated Château Gloria, the fifth-class Château Grand-Puy-Lacoste, the second-class Château Gruaud-La-rose, the numerically unclassed Château Guadet-St-Julien, the third-class Château Langoa-Barton, the two magnificent vineyards of Pomerol Château Gazin and Château Petit-Village, also the fourth-class Château Prieuré of Margaux in the Médoc.

Finding the great wines of Burgundy is slightly more complicated.

The names of the villages and vineyards are less clearly defined and, because the always adroit Burgundians have done some pretty fancy juggling with their real estate over the centuries, you have to be a good deal more careful about reading the fine print on the labels. Let us deal, first, with the tricky question of the hyphenated Burgundian names.

Each of the wine villages, which includes within its borders one of the world-famous vineyards, has hyphenated its own name with that of the great vineyard. Thus the village of Gevrey, which includes the great Le Chambertin vineyard, now calls itself Gevrey-Chambertin. This means that even the least distinguished vineyard of Gevrey can now use the magic Chambertin name on its label. If you want a great Chambertin, you must read the label carefully enough to make sure that the wine was actually produced and bottled in the one and only Le Chambertin and not just in any little Gevrey-Chambertin vineyard. The same considerations apply to the other principal villages (Morey-Saint-Denis, Chambolle-Musigny, Flagey-Echézeaux, Vosne-Romanée, Nuits-Saint-Georges, Aloxe-Corton, Puligny-Montrachet, and so on), where, in each case, if you want a great wine, you make sure that it comes from the famous vineyard that is the second half of each hyphenated name.

After you have learned the village and vineyard names, you also have to know about the great proprietors and shippers. This is because of the multiple ownership of the greatest vineyards. One of the most celebrated, for example—a prestigious name on any bottle of Burgundy—is the immense and magnificent enclosure within the gray stone walls of the historic Cistercian Abbey, the Clos Vougeot, which covers 125 acres. It is divided among about sixty-seven owners. Not all of them, frankly, are equally determined to make the greatest possible wine or are equally skilled in the work of producing it. Also, not every parcel or plot within the vineyard is as good as the best. Those on the higher ranges of the slope are substantially better than the ones down near the river and the road. So a bottle of Vougeot with the name of Bouchard as the owner-producer may be worth its weight in gold, while another Vougeot, with a less prestigious proprietor's name, may be only silver. This basic Burgundian rule about looking for the owner's name applies in every district and village. You must, with experience, get to know the names of the owners as well as you know the names of their vineyards.

It is even more important in Burgundy than in Bordeaux to look for the legally protected phrase about the wine having been *mis au domaine* (which has the same meaning as *mis en bouteille au château* in Bordeaux) and be doubly suspicious of any vague phrase allowing a loophole for the wine to have been carried off and bottled somewhere else. All the great Burgundy vineyards are also classified, and it is easy to find out, from standard reference books, which, in each famous community, are the *Têtes de Cuvée*, which means, so to speak, "top of the class." (But, remember, again, that some owners of each vineyard are more "top" than others.) Those that have delighted me with their truly great wines over the years are: among the reds, the Château de Beaune, Les Bonnes Mares, Le Chambertin, Le Corton, Les Grands Echézeaux, Le Musigny, Les Richebourg, La Romanée Conti, La Tâche, the Clos Vougeot; and among the whites, the Chablis "Vaulorent," Corton-Charlemagne, and Le Montrachet with its adjoining Chevalier Montrachet.

Great white wines also come, with impressive regularity, from Germany, from grapes grown on the towering hillsides above the valleys of the Rhine and the Moselle, with some equally great vineyards on the gentler slopes along the smaller rivers.

German wine labels are as accurate, precise, and thorough as the German character. (Even before you read the label, the color of the glass and the shape of the bottle instantly tell you where the wine comes from—a brownish red "steeple" from the Rhine Valley, a blue green "steeple" from the Moselle Valley, a potbellied flagon from the province of Franconia.) The first bit of information on the label—at least, on a great bottle—is the vintage year and the place where the wine was made: "1959'er Niersteiner." The "er" means "from," as in "New Yorker." So you read the label as *From* 1959 *from* the village of Nierstein." If you have experienced the family character of Niersteiner wines, you at once expect something flowery, fruity, lovely, soft. Then comes the name of the vineyard: "1959'er Niersteiner Rehbach." O.K. One of the best vineyards in town. But, as in Burgundy, it has multiple ownership. You look below for the family name: "Franz Karl Schmitt." O.K. again. This leading family has been in business in Nierstein for more than four hundred years, during which time they have managed to acquire most of the best plots of the best vineyards. You can reasonably hope for this wine to be among the greatest of this particular year. Then come the special German complications.

Almost every German vineyard, in almost every year, makes from three to five different grades of wine from the same vines on the same plot of earth. Since the German vineyard country is the most northerly wine-producing area on earth, the weather is always extremely uncertain. When the owner first begins picking his grapes, as many as half of the bunches may still be unripe. If there is hope of more sunshine, he leaves them on the vines. He makes the wine from his first grapes and labels it as his basic, standard wine of the year. After a few more days of sunshine, he picks more grapes, but still leaves some of them to ripen further. On the labels of this second wine, he puts the word *Spätlese*, "late picking." The wine is slightly richer, softer, more luscious than the first and commands a higher price. Now he picks his third harvest, still, if the weather looks good, leaving some grapes for further ripening. The third wine, richer, higher in price, is labeled *Auslese*, "selected picking." Now, if warm weather continues into November—something that happens about once in every five years—some of the grapes are allowed to become overripe; these are picked by hand, single berry by single berry. From these comes a marvelous wine, acid-sweet, golden-rich, very expensive, which is labeled *Beerenauslese*, "berry-selected picking." Finally, perhaps once every ten years, if the hot sun continues into early December, the final grapes have dried and shriveled almost into raisins and are covered with "noble mold," (which also makes the great sweet wines of Sauternes). There is so little juice left in them that it takes one picker one whole day to collect enough to make one bottle of wine. This glorious drink is labeled *Trockenbeerenauslese*, "dry-berry-selected picking." I have seen one of these bottles sold for $150—for a single bottle! These words are the essential vocabulary of German labels. They warn you in advance as to the general character of the wine and as to its price.

Apart from the names of the owner of the vineyard (often long-drawn-out with noble phrases and titles) there are other, legally controlled words and phrases on the labels. If the owner has bottled the wine himself, he puts *original Abfüllung*, or *orig. Abf.*, "bottle filled on the original estate." The same information may be worded as *original Abzug*, or *orig. Abz.*, wine drawn from the barrel on the original estate. So far, fine. But watch out for *Kellerabzug*, wine drawn and bottled in the cellar. It may be the cellar of the original owner, but it could just as well be someone else's cellar, indicating that the wine was sold in barrel. This is much less secure. The word *Kabinett* on a label dates from the historic time when Germany was still divided into small, independent states, each ruled by a minor prince. The best local barrels were set aside for members of the prince's cabinet. Today the word means that the wine is a special selection, slightly better and more expensive than the normal product of the year. Some of the very great vineyards indicate other gradings of their wines by using different colors for the lead caps that cover their corks. Since each range of colors has different meanings for each vineyard, you simply have to learn them by heart. I told you the German wine producers are thorough.

But no amount of label complication can possibly dim the glory of the richest of the German white wines from the ancient and dramatic vineyards. The great wines that I remember include, of course, the four supreme vineyards Schloss Johannisberg, the Scharzhofberg, the Steinberg, and Schloss Vollrads; with memorable tastings, also, of Ayler Herrenberg, Bernkasteler Doktor, Eitelsbacher Karthäuserhofberg, Eltviller Kalbspflicht, Forster Jesuitengarten, Graacher Himmelreich, the three supreme Niersteiners—Brudersberg, Orbel, and Rehbach; also Uerziger Würzgarten, Wehlener Sonnenuhr, and Winkler Hasensprung.

Beyond the immense and prolific regions of Bordeaux, Burgundy, the Moselle, and the Rhine, one occasionally finds great bottles in other parts of France and in other wine-producing countries. Sometimes, when there is an extraordinary year of hot sunshine in Alsace, a few of the best wines develop so much sugar and alcohol that they last for years and develop qualities of near perfection. I remember great white bottles of Hugel Gewürztraminer, Schlumberger Riesling and a Trimbach Gewürztraminer.

Among Champagnes, the great cuvées come more regularly: the Heidsieck Cuvée Royale, the Moët et Chandon Dom Perignon, the Mumm Cordon Rouge, the Roederer Crystal, the Taittinger Comtes de Champagne, and the Veuve Cliquot La Grande Dame.

Also, along the valley of the Loire in magnificently sunny years, some of the wines develop keeping qualities that lead to greatness, and I remember, especially, the Vouvray Domaine du Haut-Lieu and some of the bottles of Coteaux du Layon in the Barrier cellars.

From the valley of the Rhône, I have tasted great bottles made in Châteauneuf-du-Pape from the Domaine du Beaurenard, from La Bernardine, from Château Fortia and from the Domaine du Mont-Redon.

And from Spain, from the red Rioja district, south of Bilbao, I remember great bottles of red *clarete riserva* from the superb vineyards of the Marqués de Riscal in Alava.

One evening, about a year ago, I was dining at a superb French restaurant in New York with a brilliant young French wine-maker visiting the United States for the first time. The talk was of wine and, consulting the restaurant's immense list, the Frenchman ordered bottle after bottle to help him prove his various debating points. Finally, over the dessert, our discussion turned to American wines and I explained how and why it was that the noble French varieties of grape had been transplanted only to California. Suddenly my friend asked, "Are there any truly great wines in California?" I resented the slight snigger in his voice. He had been trying to ride me with his French chauvinism all evening. Now it was my turn to take over the driver's seat. I called for our check, hailed a taxi, and took the Frenchman to my home.

Fortunately my wine library held several of the best bottles he had made, under his famous label, over the past few years. I lined them up and, against them, I poured a matching series of California types from my own collection. As he lifted the first glass to his nose, the Frenchman was cocky. An instant later he was deadly serious —completely concentrated on his tasting judgment. It was not that all the Californian wines were better than his, but certainly almost all of them were in the same league. With every comparative pair of glasses, he was never quite sure whether he was winning or losing. In the end, he had to admit that one or two of the Californian wines were better than anything he had ever made, while several others were only a point or two below his best. We agreed that, on rating points scored, the final result of the contest was virtually a dead heat.

The rules for reading great California labels are, again, almost exactly the same as for European wines. As always, the greatest Californians come from relatively small vineyards and are bottled by the owners. The words on the labels are also controlled by federal and state regulations. There are such phrases as "Estate Bottled," "Private Reserve," "Special Selection" or "Produced by . . ."—the latter phrase being legally permitted only when the owner has himself grown 75 percent of the grapes from which the wine was made. Also, with California wines that are in the so-called varietal category, the name of the predominating grape type is printed on the label. Among the wines of California I have found quite a number that I rate—by the cold calculation of scoring points on a tasting chart—as being among the great wines of the world. The greatest California wine I have ever tasted was an ancient Inglenook Charbono, but among other reds I remember great tastings of Beaulieu Cabernet Sauvignon and the fortified Ficklin Tinta Madeira, while among the whites there have been the Freemark Abbey and Heitz Pinot Chardonnays, the Martini Muscatel, and two whites from Stony Hill, the Gewürztraminer and the Pinot Chardonnay.

A few months ago I was trying to give a lesson in wine to a friend who was a rank beginner. I offered to line up for him and let him taste and compare three great vintages, from three different years, of the same great vineyard. He said, "But why would I want to taste all three? Surely each vintage, from the same place, would be the same?" He did not, of course, realize the abysmal nonsense of his questions. Two different vintage years from a single vineyard would never be the same in a thousand years. How could they be? In order to be even remotely similar, the vines would have to develop in exactly the same way, with exactly the same amount of moisture and sunshine each day, day by day, throughout the entire seven months' growing season. Every factor of the soil would have to be the same, of the development of the grapes, of the chemistry of the fermentation and making of the wine.... The odds on two different vintage years being exactly the same must be a million to one against. I am happy about those long odds. One of the best of the many joys of drinking great wine is its eternal variety.

CHAPTER 20

THE MIDDLE RANGE OF
THE WINES OF THE WORLD

So Much Variety—How Much Value?

The range is enormously wide. It stretches all the way from a vineyard that is only a point or two below the greatest down to an honest "community" or "district" wine named, not for a single vineyard, but for the village, town, or legally delimited local area where it is blended from the grapes of many small vineyards by a wholesale wine-maker, who guards his reputation as jealously as he guards the secrets of his cellars. Many of these basic "secrets" are, of course, well and widely known among professional experts, and this knowledge is the key to the practical problems of finding good value in the bins of your local wine merchant during this difficult time of uncontrollably-rising wine prices. Let us begin with a clear understanding of how wine in the middle range of cost and quality is produced, distributed, and sold.

In every wine region there are tens of thousands of medium-sized or small vineyards where good grapes are grown and harvested at the point of perfect ripeness. Let us define these owners as "growers." Most of them—but by no means all—also have their own wine-making and bottling machinery and their own aging cellars, so that they can eventually sell their wines under their own labels. Let us define these owners as "grower-vintners." They are the main source of the middle-range wines. Some of their names are almost as famous as the greatest vineyards and their prices are almost as high. But always remember that as you move down to the less well known names, the price of the wine falls much more rapidly than the quality.

Let us say, for example, that you may have to pay sixty-five to one-hundred dollars for a current bottle of Château Lafite, which has a quality rating of, say, 90 percent. Against this, a bottle of the excellent, nearby Château Loudenne, which rates at about 60 percent (two-thirds of the quality of the Lafite) does not sell for two-thirds of the Lafite price but for less than one-tenth of the lowest Lafite cost—around six dollars per bottle. On the basis of this kind of calculation, I have worked out my own "value-rating" system, which measures the quality of the wine against its cost. In the above example, the Lafite would have an "average cost factor" of ninety-two cents per rating point, while the Loudenne would be ten cents per point. This means, in my book, that the Loudenne offers about nine times better value than the Lafite!

This is the sure way of finding good-value wines. Continually explore new labels. Rate each wine against its current cost. Choose the wines you like best, at the prices you are prepared to pay, and keep a record of their names.

Let us now take a further step in our practical exploration of the wine business. There are many "growers" of grapes who do not want to invest their capital in wine-making machinery, but who simply want to sell their grapes each year as a cash crop. Other "grower-vintners" are prepared to ferment their wine and put it into barrels, but do not want to age it and bottle it. They want to sell their barrels of wine as soon as possible after the harvest, for immediate cash. These grapes and barrels are sold to a middleman, who is not a farmer but who concentrates on making and blending wine. Let us call him a "maker and bottler." Let us be even more specific. Let us take, as an example, the ancient and honorable Bordeaux firm of Nathaniel Johnston & Sons, which has been a family business since the time of Napoleon. As the present Mr. Nathaniel Johnston drives around Bordeaux, visiting dozens of growers and vintners, tasting their wines and deciding which he will buy, he has various choices open to him within the *appellation contrôlée* laws and regulations. He may, in one case, buy barrels of wine only from various vintners within the delimited area of the village of, say, Pauillac. He may then blend, age, and bottle those wines and will be legally allowed to label the result as "*appellation contrôlée* Pauillac" (which, in fact, he does). This wine,

because it all comes from the special soil of this very small area, has a strong, local, Pauillac character—a character well worth preserving, since Pauillac is also the home of Château Lafite, Château Latour, and Château Mouton-Rothschild. But Mr. Johnston's Pauillac, because it does not have the prestigious name of a great vineyard, sells for about one-tenth of the price.

But there are other choices open to Mr. Johnston. If he wants to make a less expensive wine in much larger quantities, he can buy his barrel wines from growers and vintners in a much wider area—let us say, all over the district of the Médoc—and then he can blend, age, and bottle a wine that he is not allowed to label with the name of any particular village, but which he *may* label as *"appellation contrôlée* Médoc" (which again, in fact, he does). This wine, obviously, will have a less sharply defined character, but it will still be recognizable as a general Médoc wine and it will be made in fairly substantial quantities, so that it can be sold at a competitive price.

These are just two of the many choices open to Mr. Johnston every year. The more definite and precise the area from which he buys his barrel wines, the more precise will be the character of his blended wine. The more precise the character, the greater the pleasure of the wine and the higher its price. Mr. Johnston is required by law to tell you on his label precisely what he has done. You can choose exactly the wine you want.

Let me now apply these basic buying rules to the labels of specific wine regions. I propose to begin with California, for two good reasons. First, California labels, having no foreign technical terms, are easier to understand. Second, since out of every four bottles of wine (domestic and imported) opened and drunk every day in the United States, three are Californian, it seems proper to begin with the largest and most universal product. In California, as everywhere else, at the top of the heap of prestige and quality there are the single vineyards where the owner grows his own grapes, then makes, ages, bottles, labels, and sells his own wine. It may legally be labeled "Estate Bottled" and the label will usually also specify a vintage year, the name of the owner, and the geographic location.

Other growers do not bottle any wines of their own, but sell their grapes or barrels to larger firms of makers and bottlers. Some vineyard owners crush and ferment some of the grapes in making their wines, but expand their production by buying extra barrel wines from their neighbors. Since this practice may involve some risk of a slight reduction in the quality of the wine, there is, at once, a legal requirement for the wording of the label. If the vineyard owner crushes and ferments a minimum of 75 percent of the grapes himself and buys a maximum of 25 percent of barrel wine from someone else's vineyard, he must, in front of his own name on the label, insert the phrase "Produced by ..." If, however, he enlarges his production to such an extent that he crushes and ferments only a minimum of 10 percent himself, while "importing" 90 percent of barrel wine from other vineyards, he is legally required to preface his own name on the label with "Made by ..." I have found, in my long experience, that these phrases on California labels have a direct and strong relationship with the quality of the wine inside the bottles.

California also has its large-scale makers and bottlers (some of them the largest-scale in the world!) and they may label their wines—exactly as did Nathaniel Johnston in Bordeaux—either according to precise and small geographic areas, or on a much larger scale, by whole counties or huge regions. There may, for example, be a "Napa Valley Red," or a "Monterey Chardonnay," or simply an all-encompassing "California Mountain White." In each case, it is generally true that the wine that is restricted to a smaller area has a more recognizable character. It comes, of course, largely from the climate and soil in which the grapes are grown and, in these terms, the important growing areas are the northern coastal valleys around San Francisco: Alameda, Livermore, Mendocino, Monterey, Napa, San Benito, Santa Clara, and Sonoma—important names on a wine label.

As well as telling you who made the wine, roughly or precisely how he made it, and roughly or precisely where the grapes were grown, a California label also either approximately defines the principal variety of grape in the bottle or gives a rough idea of the type of wine that the maker intended to produce. I am forced to use the word *approximately* because of an unfortunate loophole in American wine law. If a white wine is labeled as being made from, say, the famous, noble Pinot Chardonnay grape of Burgundy, the clear implication is that the wine will have the fruity, luxurious, strong family character of the Pinot Chardonnay grape. According to American labeling law, however, the wine labeled "Pinot Chardonnay" (or with the name of any other grape) is only required to contain a minimum of 51 percent of the named grape. The well-known wine writer John Storm, in his book *An Invitation to Wines,* comments on this surprising legal loophole as follows: "This poses a question of some delicacy. Can milk which has been diluted with 49 per cent water honestly be called 'milk'? Why then should a wine be allowed to be labeled Pinot Noir, or Riesling or

some such other aristocratic name when it has been diluted with 49%
...?" I have discussed this question with several California producers,
who now believe that the legal requirement should be raised to at least
75 percent, and some already make their varietal wines at this figure.
A few producers make 100 percent varietals, and these wines, when
you find them, are almost always substantially the best. I have many
times tasted and have always been much impressed by, the 100 percent
varietals of Beaulieu, Beringer, Chappellet, the Christian Brothers,
Heitz, Inglenook, Krug, Mondavi, Schramsberg, Souverain, and
Stony Hill.

Since more and more of these top-quality varietal wines are now
being made in California, it may be useful to compare the family
resemblances of these noble grapes with their counterparts in Europe.
Naturally a Pinot Chardonnay vine transplanted from Burgundy to
California does not grow in the same way in its new conditions of
climate and soil, but the family character remains. Among the
California reds, for example, a Cabernet Sauvignon can be offered
with almost any meal where one might otherwise have served a fruity,
light young Bordeaux. A California Barbera or Grignolino can
reasonably replace the Italian wines with those grape names. The
California Gamay or Gamay-Beaujolais is a fair substitute for the
young and fruity French Beaujolais. The California Petite-Sirah is a
possible substitute for a firm, solid young red of the same grape, from
the Rhône. The California Pinot Noir is, to my mind, less a substitute
for a big Burgundy, and more the equivalent of the fruitier, lighter,
younger reds from Mercurey. The California Zinfandel, which has no
equivalent in Europe, serves, in my opinion, as a wine halfway
balanced between a Beaujolais and a Rhône Côte Rôtie, so that it goes
excellently with not too rich, light red meats.

Among the whites, the Pinot Chardonnay (California's best wine),
in its finest bottlings, is unquestionably the equal of some of the top
whites of Burgundy. The California Chenin Blanc, sometimes called
by its French name, *Pineau de la Loire,* is interchangeable with many
of the Loire whites. The California Pinot Blanc, which came originally
from Burgundy, is a very fair substitute for the Burgundian Mâcon
Blanc. The California Gewürztraminer or Sylvaner are reasonable
substitutes for the wines made from the same grapes in Alsace. The
California White Riesling (often still labeled "Johannisberg") is
reasonably interchangeable with the fruity, light young wines of the
German district of Hessen—the home of Liebfraumilch. The Cali-

fornia Sauvignon Blanc is often a fair substitute for the dry, fruity whites of the Bordeaux district of Entre-Deux-Mers.

Among the California rosés, I find the Grenache to be reasonably interchangeable with the light rosés of Anjou or Touraine along the Loire, or the sunny rosés of Provence.

The California sweet wines, largely made from the various types of the Muscats, the Malvasia, or the Sémillon grape, are fair substitutes for the sweet *abboccato* Italian whites of Orvieto, or for similar wines from southern France or Spain.

Among the names of the vintners and wine-makers on the labels, some are large firms with distribution of their wines all over the country, and these include Almadén, Beaulieu, the Christian Brothers, Gallo, Krug, Inglenook, Martini, Masson, and Wente. Others are much smaller and sell most of their wines in California, but have some distribution through selected wine merchants in major cities. The names on the labels include Buena Vista, Concannon, Cornell, Ficklin, Freemark Abbey, Hanzell, Heitz, Korbel, Mayacamas, Mirassou, Mondavi, Schramsberg, Sebastiani, Souverain, Windsor, and Weibel.

Returning to France in search of medium-range wines, I am continually delighted and impressed by the quality and value of the white wines of Alsace. The general pattern of the labeling is in the same varietal style as in California, with the principal grapes (at least, of the majority of bottles reaching the United States) being the spicy Gewürztraminer, the lusciously rich Riesling, and the dryly light Sylvaner. Most of these wines are blended from the grapes of various vineyards, but there are a few individual properties where the grapes are kept separate after the harvest and the wine is, in effect, "estate bottled." These are the cream of the crop, and those that I most regularly enjoy are Les Murailles, the Clos Sainte Hune, Les Sorcières, and the Clos de Zisser.

There are no red wines of any importance in Alsace, but there is one rosé, which I consider to be among the best, the Pinot Rosé d'Alsace, made in the fairy-story village of Bergheim.

In Alsace especially, because of the large scale of the blending, the names of the makers and bottlers are often the most important words on the label. (Incidentally, on a French label, the man who "puts together" the wines, then ages and bottles it, is shown as the *éleveur,* which means, literally, the "bringer-up" of the wine. But if you see the word *négociant* next to the name, you know that this man—or, generally, a substantial firm—was the "negotiator" or, as we say, "the shipper," who probably had nothing to do with making the wine, but merely bought and sold the filled bottles, perhaps adding his own label during the transaction.) The Alsatian firms that I have found to be the most reliable (and almost all, in the Alsatian tradition, growing their own grapes as well as being *éleveurs-négociants*) are Dopff au Moulin, Dopff & Irion, Hugel, Jux, Klipfel, Lorentz, Trimbach, and Willm.

In Bordeaux there are literally hundreds (if not thousands) of lesser and smaller château vineyards producing red, white, and golden-sweet wines in every price range, from near-top to downright reasonable.

It is just a question of continually exploring new labels, of tasting diligently and of remembering the vineyard names. Then there are the blended "village wines," including those of Listrac, Margaux, Pauillac, Saint-Estèphe, Saint-Julien, and the "district wines" of the Médoc, of Graves, of Saint-Emilion, and of Sauternes, all "put together" by the ancient and reliable firms, which, in my experience, include Barton & Guestier, Calvet, Cruse, Eschenhauer, Ginestet, Johnston, Kressman, and Sichel.

From Burgundy, also, there are dozens of less well known villages and vineyards producing acceptable wines in the medium range, and the only problem is to find them by searching and tasting.

Again, since there is a good deal of blending of community and district wines, the names of the famous *éleveurs* and *négociants* on the labels are often the all-important words. Among the medium-priced red wines with a good, strong Burgundian character there are some excellent examples made in and around the city of Beaune and sold with the legally defined label of *"appellation contrôlée* Côte de Beaune," or *"appellation contrôlée* Côte de Beaune-Villages"—the word *villages* indicating that the wine was made only from the grapes of certain named villages near Beaune, where it is considered that the soil is above average and the wine will thus be of better than average quality. All the big firms, willing to accept this quality control, use this general label, each adding his own name.

I also search for good buys among the blended "community" whites of the villages of Meursault, Chassagne-Montrachet and Puligny-Montrachet. As to the Pouilly-Fuissé from further south, it has now become so popular and overexpensive that I have switched my allegiance to the nearby wines of Saint-Véran, which are almost as refreshing at nothing like the price.

As to the Beaujolais of southern Burgundy, one must never forget the warning that any Beaujolais with a general label, unconnected with the geographic location of a particular village, can (and usually does) contain a goodly proportion of wine that came a long way before it got into a Beaujolais bottle! I stick firmly with the Beaujolais labels that have the *appellation contrôlée* of the famous legally delimited villages, where all the wine in each bottle must be locally grown. I especially admire the Château de la Chaize and Château Thivin of the village of Brouilly, with the other villages of Fleurie, Juliénas, Morgon, and the tight district of Moulin-à-Vent never far behind. In Beaujolais, as in all parts of Burgundy, I rely on the names of the long-established firms, including Bouchard, Chanson, Chauvenet, de Besse, Drouhin, Jadot, Latour, and Patriarch.

I am virtually addicted to the whites from the Loire Valley—the light, flinty-dry Pouilly-Fumé from the village of Pouilly-sur-Loire (not to be confused with the Pouilly-Fuissé of southern Burgundy), with the delightful refreshers from the hilltop village of Sancerre and its neighbor Quincy, and with the softly luxurious wines of Montlouis and Vouvray—the latter unquestionably the all-round best of the Loire. But Vouvray has its problems. Its hills, almost across the river from the city of Tours, are so much exposed to the weather, so much subject to storms and lack of sunshine, that Vouvray wines can be anything, from year to year, between almost sharply acid and honeyed sweet. Fortunately for all of us, the more acid wines are ideal for being made sparkling by the "Champagne method," and sparkling Vouvray is one of life's abiding pleasures. So be careful to look beyond the word Vouvray on the label for the definition of the type of wine. *Sec* means "dry." *Demi-sec* means "half-dry." *Moelleux* means "sweet." *Mousseux,* coupled with a Champagne-styled cork, means a sparkling Vouvray. Finally there are some lovely golden-sweet wines from the small side valleys of the tributary rivers of the Coteaux du Layon.

From the valley of the Rhône there is memorable enjoyment in the middle-range red, white, and pink wines. There is an attractive "spiciness" to the better reds, which, in these days of modern wine-making methods, are not nearly as heavy or strong as they used to be. The light reds of the district of the Côte Rôtie, the "Roasted Slope," have an irresistible charm and gaiety. There are two sides to the slopes—one labeled Côte Blonde, the other Côte Brune—and you must decide by tasting which you prefer. If you can't make up your mind, there is one wine that is a blend of the two and is labeled Brune et Blonde. Then there are the red and white Hermitage wines, as spectacular in their drinking qualities as is the single steep, terraced hill from which their grapes are harvested. On days when you feel you cannot afford the magnificence of a red from the vineyard of the Mure de la Sizeranne, or the luxury of the bouquet of mountain flowers of the white Chante-Alouette, the thing to do is to look for labels marked Crozes-Hermitage or Saint-Joseph. Both these nearby villages have roughly the same soil and produce wines that might be called "the thrifty man's Hermitage."

There are less than well-known vineyards in Châteauneuf-du-Pape, eminently worthy of exploration by tasting, and then, across the river and a little to the south, is the famous district of Tavel, which, to my taste, produces the finest of all the rosés. The best Tavel labels carry the names of individual vineyards. Others are community blends of the local village of Tavel. There are considerable variations of price and quality.

From Germany there is an enormous range of white wines, from sharply dry and light-as-a-zephyr, to magnificent, aromatic sweet wines. If one wants to find exceptional values, one must avoid the almost too famous villages, where the name on the label immediately assures the inflated price of too much popularity. Yet there are dozens, if not hundreds, of less famous villages with vineyard estates known mainly to connoisseurs and experts. Another trick is to watch for the names on the labels of the great wine-making families, which have owned many of the vineyards for centuries and are so jealous of their reputations that even the wines from their lesser estates are cared for and cosseted with such concern for quality that each bottle comes to represent above-average value. I watch, for example, for any wine from around the village of Deidesheim labeled as having been made by the Bürklin-Wolf family; or, from Forst, by the Basserman-Jordans; or, around Wehlen or Zeltingen, by the Prüms; or, around Bernkastel, by the Lauerburgs.

With increasingly strict government controls of quality, Italian wines in the middle price range are offering better and better values. Again, the historic family names on the labels are often a sound guide, at least until you have formed your own opinions on the basis of tasting and rating. Among the deep-red Barolos, often old and powerful, made from the famous Nebbiolo grape grown on the mountain slopes above Lake Garda, there is always the family name of the Marchese di Barolo. Among the hundreds of Chiantis, good and bad, from Tuscany, one must avoid the straw-covered *fiaschi* bottles (the contents of which are usually a fiasco) and expect the finer wines to be in straight-sided, Bordeaux-type bottles labeled with the *Marca di Gallo,* "the Little Black Rooster," which is the mark of quality control of the producers in the delimited Chianti Classico district. Among the centuries-old production families, one watches for the names of the Marchese Antinori, the Conti Machiavelli, the Barone Ricasole. Among the lighter reds, my favorites are the Barbaresco, the Barbera, the Bardolino, the Gattinara, the Grignolino, the Valpolicella, and the white, dry, sometimes almost steely Soave from the Alpine slopes just west of Verona.

There are excellent, middle-range reds and whites from Switzerland, and the most elegant among them, in my opinion, is the Dézaley from the village of that name in the canton of Vaud, just north of the Lake of Geneva. Other Vaud wine district names on Swiss labels well worth exploring are those of the Chablais, with its vinous village of Aigle. The canton of Neuchâtel sends us its own wine, usually bottled so young that it crackles on the tongue. The village to watch for on these labels is Auvergnais. Then, from the canton of the Valais, comes the dry, light white Fendant and the charming red Dole, both among the best middle-range wines of Europe.

I have been steadily tasting and rating the middle-range wines for many years. The factor of quality is, of course, always independent of the price, but, after first judging each wine on its merits, I always relate the price to the overall drinking pleasure. I prefer to do this by cold mathematics—by relating rating points to dollars on a chart and coming up with a "value factor." On this unemotional basis, I have found, year after year, that the middle-range wines represent the best values. When one buys a great wine, with a world-renowned label, one is paying, more or less heavily, for the prestige, the showoff, the status symbol. When one buys extremely inexpensive wines, mass-blended and mass-produced almost solely on the basis of price, the quality falls to a mass-average, which, often, is at a low value level. Quite apart from the dramatic excitement of an extremely rare great wine, it is in the middle range that I have found my most consistent pleasures, from wines "produced with love" by dedicated and skilled vintners, asking for no more than a fair return for their labors in the vineyards of the world. For thousands of years the making of fine wine has been the business of the small, individualistic farmer. It cannot be industrialized into the production of automated, mechanized big business. The finest wine is not just the work of Man. It is the creation of Nature.

CHAPTER 21

THE INEXPENSIVE AND SIMPLE WINES FOR MORNING, NOON, AND NIGHT

But NOW You Must Read BETWEEN the Lines

I often call them my "everyday staple wines," because I buy them with the same regularity as bread, butter, coffee, cream, or eggs. This is not to say that I buy any of these things without continuous awareness, serious consideration, and sharp judgment. It is no less important to battle for the freshness of one's butter and eggs, or to experiment with the roasts of one's coffee, than it is to measure the quality and value of every bottle of even the most inexpensive wine.

It is, of course, hardly possible to discuss cost in these pages. As I write, we are in a time of rapid inflation of all wine prices. It is the historic operation of the law of supply and demand. Production simply cannot keep up with the demand of "the wine explosion." Yet I can still find some very fair everyday wines at around $1.50 or $1.95 and there is an immense choice of good (with a few superior) wines at somewhere between $2.50 and $3.95. Let us agree, then, that the word *inexpensive* as used in this chapter means (provided that inflation does not make a liar of me) a wine selling in the store at between $1.50 and $3.95 for a single standard-sized bottle. The price should be proportionately lower by the case, or in half-gallon or gallon jugs.

But to judge wine—and especially low-cost wine—by price alone is a good deal more risky than betting on horses. Of all the cheap, universally distributed commodities, wine is perhaps the most subject to the possibilities of what Winston Churchill once called "terminological inexactitude." Perhaps that is why Julius Caesar, a wine drinker, coined the phrase *caveat emptor,* let the buyer be doubly aware! With the inexpensive wines, you must learn to read the labels even between the lines.

I explained, in a previous chapter, how the French *appellation d'origine contrôlée* regulations are a guarantee of the truth of any statements on a label as to the origin and the maker of the wine. There is also, in the smaller, less famous wine regions, a secondary form of legal control. This is signified on the label by the letters *V.D.Q.S.,* which means, in exact translation from the French, "Wine Delimited Quality Superior." This is the legally enforced guarantee, by the National Institute in Paris, that all the grapes were grown and the wine made in the place named on the label, that the grape types were from the list approved for that region, and that the legally defined standards for quality production were met. An inexpensive, small French wine without these guarantees could be (and generally is) a mixture of many liquids from many places.

This is how the vast mass of wine is sold, simply as *vin blanc,* or *vin rouge,* and since there is nothing on the label to show where it came from, no legal regulations apply. Large firms of makers and bottlers buy huge quantities of such wines in bulk and then put them out under labels with copyrighted, proprietary trade names. Under this arrangement a wine labeled "Château La Rose Blanche," with no indication as to where the "château" is, need offer no guarantee of either origin or quality.

There has been a great deal of publicity recently in Europe about "deceptions and exaggerations" of some wine labels. There was an official report by the Common Market Executive Commission. There have been "exposés" in some of the most conservative British newspapers. British labeling laws are not as strict as those of France or the United States, and some irresponsible shippers had carried bulk wines to England for blending and bottling there. One of these bulk wines, an extremely low-cost plain, simple "Vin Rouge Blend 1" was said to be a mixture of wines from Provence and Algeria. Another, somewhat lighter, "Vin Rouge Blend 2" was said to be a mixture of various wines from the Languedoc, the source of many of the cheapest bulk wines, generally known as *gros vins* du Midi. There was also some Moroccan red and some Spanish red Rioja. They were all cheap

wines, but honest and sound, providing fair value, as long as no special claims were made for them.

But, then, according to the published British reports, there was some very fancy juggling of these wines in a series of blendings, bottlings, and labelings. One mixture, after bottling, suddenly became a "Médoc-claret-type." A second combination of these same wines, after bottling, was labeled as "Vieux Papes," a "Châteauneuf-du-Pape-type." When some of this was blended with one of the lighter wines, the result was bottled and defined as a "Burgundy-type." After the addition of still more of the lighter wine, the result was bottled and defined as a "Beaujolais-type," then, for the British market, given a colorfully decorated label, designed to impress naïve English wine buffs, who adore fancy labels with scrolls, printed seals, coats-of-arms, and obscure, mystical assurances of magical and marvelous quality in the wine. The alleged "Beaujolais" was given one of these labels, with the words "Vin de l'Année—Cuvée Speciale du Château de Corcelle—Mis en bouteilles dans nos caves"—and there was a handsome picture of the imaginary château. A mixture of the Moroccan and Spanish reds was bottled and defined, for the British market, as having the character of a 1961 Bordeaux-type and was labeled as "Les Grands Vins des Châteaux—Wines straight from the Château for your table." Another blend of the reds was labeled "Château Vin Rouge" and a blended bulk rosé was eventually labeled as "Château Pipi d'Ange." In London, when one of my British friends tells me that he has found "an unbelievable little wine at an unbelievably bargain price," I tell him that he is surely right—he did indeed get a bargain that is not to be believed!

But the problem of deliberate misrepresentation is, in the general run of the millions of bottles of wine produced every year, extremely rare. Even after you have learned how to spot a phony, there are other, larger, and more complicated considerations when buying inexpensive wines. One result of the American "wine explosion" is that the American producers, struggling to cope with the enormous demand, are planting thousands of acres of new vines and speeding up production in every direction. Another result is that the foreign wine industries, helped and supported by their governments, are flooding the United States with mass-produced, mass-marketed, mass-publicized, so-called bistro, or country, or *ordinaire* wines, with the glamorous promotion that these are the types of wine you would find in small country restaurants if you were touring in that part of the world. The publicity story, as always, involves a slightly rosy interpretation of the facts. Make no mistake about it, some of these wines represent excellent values. They are nowhere near as rough and sharp as the wines that, again and again, have been drawn for me from the barrel standing in the corner of the dining room in some European country inn. And yet the European mass wines that arrive here under the generalized, national labels, although they are more carefully aged and more smoothly vinified, have lost some of their character because they have been mass-blended to achieve millions of gallons of production. Let us take a specific example.

Until quite recently, few Americans had ever heard of a small French wine called Corbières. It takes its name from a large district of vine-covered, rolling hills in south-central France, the part of the country called Le Midi, the home ground of *vins ordinaires*. The Corbières reds are certainly above the average, especially those from some of the slightly higher-grade subdistricts, Corbières Supérieure, or Corbières Roussillon, or Haute Corbières, or, best of all, from the smaller subdistrict of Fitou. I remember joyous days of touring across that lovely country, from the ancient walled city of Carcassonne to the honey capital of Narbonne and on to the slopes of the Pyrénées Orientales, tasting the firm, full-bodied, sturdy reds in dozens of small vineyards, where each wine was a little bit different, according to the ideas and skills of each owner. Now the wines of hundreds of vineyards have been put together into a mass flow for mass promotion in the United States, and the Corbières in New York has a good deal less character than the Corbières in Narbonne.

The point I am trying to make is that, if we have only, say, $2.50 to spend on a bottle, it is not necessarily true, in the world of wine, that mass production can offer the best value. At this price, just as much as at higher levels, there are hundreds of small, individually owned vineyards, making wines of individual character from which to choose, taste, and judge. A small, individual wine can often be a far better value than an averaged-out mass product. At any price level, I enjoy the fun of exploring, and in the following pages I propose to offer some practical pointers. Let us begin with the wines that, everywhere in this country, are the easiest to find and to understand—the *vins de pays* of America.

Quite a few of the California varietal wines, discussed in the previous chapter, are now selling at prices that bring them down within the inexpensive range. (I recently tasted a fine white Chenin Blanc priced at substantially under two dollars and a superior red Zinfandel at between two and three dollars.) But the majority of

inexpensive Californians are still labeled from one or the other of two
different points of view. Instead of naming the wine for its variety of
grape, it may be named, quite frankly, as an attempted reproduction of
a famous European wine type from one of the great viticultural regions
of France or Germany. It may be labeled "California Burgundy," or
"California Chablis," or "California Johannisberg"—or any other
European place name.

Some of these wines are extremely good, but this kind of "generic"
labeling has the disadvantage of a built-in backlash. If you have visited
some of the French wine regions, for example, and have drunk, say,
Chablis on its home ground, you are likely to say, "Well, this
California Chablis is good, but it isn't anything like the *real* French
Chablis." For this reason, I believe the use of these foreign names on
American labels is gradually fading out, but Almadén, the Christian
Brothers, Heitz, Krug, and Martini are still offering their "Chablis,"
Concannon its white "Moselle," and Gallo its "Hearty Burgundy."
Wines of this type are our homegrown *vins de carafe,* and are almost
always far better than the unbottled, unlabeled European *vin ordi-
naire,* served by the carafe or the glass.

The second approach to the labeling of a California wine is to call it
not by a foreign place name but by an invented "proprietary," or
brand name, which the maker copyrights so that it remains his
exclusive property. Under this label the producer then blends a wine to
meet his idea of the broadest possible public taste, using several
different varieties of grapes and the harvest of several different years.
The label then does not include a grape name or a vintage year. Once
you have found one of these wines that pleases your taste, you can
order it again and again, year after year, knowing that it will always
taste pretty well the same. The routine is, frankly, just about as easy
(and as repetitious) as buying your favorite brand of cola or root beer.
The Paul Masson vineyard is, perhaps, the leader in this category,
with its red Baroque, its red Rubion, and its white Emerald Dry.
Other examples are the Christian Brothers' golden-sweet Château La
Salle. And the Villa Armando white Orobianco.

I have already said that my interest and pleasure in wine lies in
exploring everything. One cannot claim to know American wines if
one knows only the Californians. Millions of Americans drink millions
of bottles from New York State, Maryland, Ohio, and other corners of
the country, where I have found good wines in unexpected places. I
picked up one interesting statistic the other day. Apparently more
bottles of sparkling wines, under the general label of "New York State

Champagne," are made by the five companies in the Finger Lakes region than all the bottles combined of the famous French Champagnes imported into the United States. My wine library is seldom without a few bottles of New York Finger Lake wines—or of "Lake Country" wines, the new appellation that indicates that the demand is now so great that all the grapes can no longer be grown immediately around the Finger Lakes, but come also from new vineyards in other, neighboring parts of New York. The majority of these wines are made from native American grapes, and some of the labels are varietal, with such charming and historic grape names as Aurora, Catawba, Concord, Delaware, Elvira, Isabella, Moore's Diamond, and Niagara. I feel that these wines are like charming, rosy-cheeked country girls, bubbling with gaiety, dancing and disporting themselves among the country flowers and fruit trees. They do not claim to have the smooth sophistication of their aristocratic sisters. But if one is a lover of wine (or women), variety is the key to the maximum pleasure of life.

Guided by this basic philosophy, I taste the local wines wherever I go and then, if they are good, try to find out if I can get them nearer to my home. I have tasted worthy wines from the Boordy vineyards in Maryland, from the vineyards of Isle St. George in Lake Erie, from the Tarula Farms district in southern Ohio. In Chicago I tasted a delightfully dry "Illinois Champagne," made from locally grown grapes, and in Wisconsin I regularly drink a charming, honest, unexpectedly dry and fruity "Cherry Wine," made from the superb cherries of Door County more or less as a hobby by a local country doctor.

Whether it be a doctor with his cherries in Wisconsin, or the owner of a small château in a relatively unknown district of Bordeaux, the basic principle holds true: the "little wine," lovingly made by an individual vintner, is the best value even at the least expensive level. Even if we assume that all the wines of the most famous villages of the best known Bordeaux districts are already (or soon will be) priced above the inexpensive range, there remain thousands of other excellent château vineyards to be explored by tasting. From the upper area of the Médoc, for example, near the village of Saint-Estèphe, I have found delightful wines from Château Greysac, Château Loudenne, and Château de Pez. Also an excellent red from the commune of Listrac. From the district across the river, known as the Côtes de Bourg, there are, for example, the Château des Arras and the Château Giraud Cheval Blanc and from the "Côtes-Canon-Fronsac," I have enjoyed the deeply colored, rich, robust, but soft wines from, among others, Château Canon and Château Bodet. From the large Bordeaux district of Entre-Deux-Mers there are very pleasant, honest wines, with strong individual character, from, among others, Château Bonnet and Château Jonqueyres. I could fill the rest of this chapter with the names of château, commune, village, and district wines.

The opportunities are almost as wide in Burgundy, among the less well-known names of domaine, commune, and village wines. Now the two famous regional *vins de pays* of Burgundy—the wines that Burgundians themselves drink on everyday, informal occasions—are being imported into the United States. The very agreeable white is the Bourgogne-Aligoté, made from the hardy Aligoté grape, which is planted on all the more exposed hillsides disdained by the nobler vines, and the Sauvignon de St. Bris, an unusual, almost smoky-flavored commune wine made in the district near Chablis. The red is the Bourgogne Passe-tout-grains, made from a two-to-one blend of the Gamay grapes that grow on the valley floors and the noble Pinot Noir. It is a powerful, robust wine—its name is sometimes translated as "pass-out-again"—but the better versions from the best Burgundy shippers are well worth tasting. From the Burgundian districts a few miles to the south, instead of buying an ultracheap Beaujolais, I would prefer a Mâcon Rouge, preferably with the name of a good shipper. But if you insist on Beaujolais, pay around $3.50 per bottle for the best. Beaujolais Supérieure of one of the major shippers, such as, for example, Drouhin, Jadot, or Latour.

The producers and shippers are equally important in Alsace, which is sending us clean, fruity and lovely white wines, still being offered at prices that make them among the best values in the wine world. The labeling is varietal and the wines labeled as being made from the Sylvaner grape are marvelously refreshing and thirst-quenching, especially the best products of such well-known makers as Dopff, Hugel, Jux, Klipfel, Lorentz, Trimbach, and Willm. Each of these firms also makes wines from the Riesling grape which are more luscious, richer, and slightly more expensive, but still for their quality, representing outstanding values.

A relatively new French import into the United States is one of the most ancient and historic wines of France, the deep red Cahors, named for the town on the River Lot, north of Toulouse. It is among the finest of red wines of France but so little known here that it is still selling at prices that make it, at least for the time being, an extraordinary value. One has to search for it, but the effort is eminently worthwhile.

From the old province of Touraine, on the Loire, the charming light red wines of the two historic villages of Bourgueil and Chinon are now being imported—wines that I have long loved on their home grounds, but which were so little known in the United States that they were rarely imported. They are as fruity and refreshing as Beaujolais and can be drunk slightly chilled. Among the refreshing white wines of the Loire, in the inexpensive range, there are the blended, dry Vouvray, the Chenin Blanc of Anjou, and the Sauvignon Blanc of Touraine.

But the main output of these two ancient provinces continues to be their rosés—veritable rivers of pink wine in an almost dangerously wide range of qualities. My "secret trick" with the labels is to insist on seeing the name of a grape variety associated with the name of the wine. The words Rosé d'Anjou or Rosé de Touraine offer almost no quality guarantee, but the moment you see Rosé de Cabernet d'Anjou, (or de Touraine) the wine must legally be made of 100 percent Cabernet Sauvignon grapes, and this is a substantial guarantee of quality.

Finally, from the mouth of the Loire, near the city of Nantes in southern Brittany, comes the ubiquitous Muscadet, one of the most refreshing little wines for slaking a thirst on a blazing-hot day. It has a lean and hungry feel about it and, because it tastes almost as if it has a squeeze of lemon juice, it is the ideal accompaniment to any ice-cold plate of clams, oysters, or shellfish. There is a very large production of fairly nondescript Muscadet, some of which, in my opinion, is not quite worth drinking, but there are excellent types, usually labeled as coming from the Sèvre-et-Maine district, and naturally the best of these are made by individual vineyard owners on their own estates. This fact is always clearly indicated on the label, according to *appellation contrôlée* or V.D.Q.S. regulations.

Some of my favorite inexpensive Rhône wines come from the immediate area around the great Hermitage hill—not, usually, from the hill itself: those wines are almost always above the inexpensive range. But I regularly enjoy the red, or white, Les Meysonnières from Crozes-Hermitage, also the reds or whites from the village of Saint-Joseph, across the river. These are all from specific vineyards. The more general, blended wines of the Rhône Valley are always legally required to be labeled "A.C. Côtes du Rhône." Among these the wines may be labeled with the name of a blender, such as, for example, the excellent and outstandingly inexpensive Domaine de l'Enclos from the village of Courthézon or the Beaume-de-Venise—or they may be labeled with the name of a local vineyard such as, for example, the Château Malijay in Jonquières. Finally, from the Rhône Valley, there

can be some extraordinary values from among the estate-bottled pink
Tavels, which are surely the finest and strongest in character of all
rosés.

Before leaving the wines of France, I would certainly not forget the
charming, refreshing dry mountain wines of the High Alps of the
Savoy. They include a quite lovely sparkling wine, which takes its
name from a Savoyard village near the Swiss border, the Seyssel Blanc
de Blancs. There are also the joyous little white wines of Apremont,
Crépy, and Roussette, with the fragrantly light red, called by the name
of its grape, Gamay de Savoie.

For the efficient exploration of the inexpensive wines of Germany,
you have to know the basic rules about the labels with what the
Germans call *freie-Fantasie-Namen,* "free fantasy names"—officially
recognized, openly fictional titles of vineyards that do not exist. The
best known of these names are Liebfraumilch, "Holy Mother's Milk,"
and Moselblümchen, "Little Flower of the Moselle." Any wine with
these names should, in my opinion, be treated with the gravest
suspicion. Liebfraumilch was, originally, the slightly irreverent local
name for the wine from the vineyard of the Liebfrauenkirche, the Holy
Mother's Church, in the Rhine town of Worms (and that particular
wine is still very fine), but the name had such powerful sales value that
its use was loosely extended to virtually any kind of blended wine from
any vineyard in this general area. It can be very good. It can also be
terrible. The same warning applies to Moselblümchen, or any of the
other fantasy names.

You might think, for example, that Niersteiner Domthal would be a
wine from an estate in Nierstein. Not at all. Any of the one-hundred-
odd minor vineyards of Nierstein may legally sell its wine under the
copyrighted, registered village appellation of Niersteiner Domthal,
which has no more solid existence than a registration certificate in the
files of the town council. The same pattern is repeated for the
"fantasy" vineyards of other villages, including Bernkasteler Brownes,
Oppenheimer Goldberg, Piesporter Michelsberg, Wiltinger Schloss-
berg, and Zeller Schwarze Katz, among others. None of these names
offers a guarantee of quality, unless you get to know (by tasting
experience) the reliability of the various producers and shippers.

Italy produces at least three charming, light, inexpensive wines: the
Bardolino and Valpolicella reds, from the district between the city of
Verona and the village of Bardolino on Lake Garda, and, from the
nearby mountain village, the white Soave. Some Bardolinos are so
light in color that they are halfway to rosé and can be served slightly

chilled. The sometimes almost steely-dry Soave comes from the foothills of the Alps and seems to carry within itself some of the cold cleanness of the high mountains. Again, since the quality varies greatly from label to label, you must learn to judge the reliability of the shippers.

Spain is a happy hunting ground for inexpensive wines, especially among the light reds of the high mountain districts of the Rioja below the city of Bilbao. Some of these wines are meticulously aged and have an elegance of taste and velvety smoothness far above their price status. If the label calls the red a *clarete,* the wine is of the fruity, light, vaguely Bordeaux type; but if the label shows it as *viña real,* it is darker and heavier, vaguely of the Burgundy type. There are also some delightfully dry whites and sunny reds from the Panades wine district of Catalonia, on the slopes between Barcelona and Tarragona. One of the top producers here is the Barbier family, from their vineyards surrounding their medieval château, San Sadurni de Noya.

Perhaps least well known of all wines imported into the United States are those of the Grand Duchy of Luxembourg, the miniature country sandwiched triangularly between Belgium, France, and Germany. Few people seem to know that the Moselle River, before it reaches its noble wine valley in Germany, rises in France and then for twenty-three miles skirts Luxembourg, where the local vintners seize the opportunity and grow more than two thousand acres of vines along the river's valley slopes. The white wines that come to the United States have varietal labels. The Rivaner, hardly unexpectedly, is a cross between a Riesling and a Sylvaner; the other grape, the Auxerrois, took its name originally from the French town of Auxerre and now, in its new home, makes a light, dryly fruity, refreshingly tart little wine.

One final, unavoidable question remains. My young friends ask it almost every day. What about the "pop wines"? Well. What can a dedicated wine lover say? Perhaps the mistake is to apply to them the word *wine.* Eliminate the idea of wines and you are left with the word *pop.* Should it stand for "popular"—or "pop goes the cork"—or "soda pop"? Yes. That's it! Alcoholic soda pop—flavored confections that might best be served (if only the law would allow) across the marble top of a drugstore soda fountain.

Let no one accuse me of being a rock-ribbed, ultraconservative snob. I have tasted one after another with a deep, religious fervor. Before handing down my judgment, let me point out that these drinks do not involve any such simple process as natural fermentation. They are manufactured manipulations of fruit juices and flavorings with varying degrees of alcohol. I found most of the fun in the names. Zapple—you guessed it—is flavored with apple. Sum-Plum—do I have to tell you? Boone's Farm Strawberry Hill is fruity with a country feeling. Key Largo is "orange citrus." Bali Hai is "tropical fruit." Spañada is a slightly sweetened takeoff on Spanish Sangriá. Ocean Spray could hardly avoid being cranberry juice. Ripple comes in a ripple bottle, in various colors, including "Pagan Pink."

The bottle shapes and labels come by the dozen. So do the new and sweeter versions of Cold Duck, although here there is less manipulation, more of a classical blending of naturally fermented wines. But it, too, makes its basic appeal to young people raised on soft soda drinks.

None of these "pop wines" is in any way suitable as an accompaniment to food. They are too sweet. They are for midafternoon on the beach, ice-cold out of a cooler, splashed around over ice cubes. Some of them now come in twelve-ounce bottles. That puts them right into the family. Alcoholic soda pop.

CHAPTER 22

THE RIGHT WINE FOR THE RIGHT PERSON WITH THE RIGHT FOOD

Three Makes the Perfect Marriage

The most fundamental reason, of course, for having one's own wine library is that any successful dinner requires at least one proper wine, and more often two, three, or even four. The fact that more and more Americans are agreeing with this point of view is proved by the "wine explosion." In the last fifteen years our consumption of wine has doubled, and every year for the last five years we have increased our buying of table wines by an average of 15 million gallons a year. The current estimates are that we are now drinking about 275 million gallons a year. I sometimes idly wonder how many of those gallons were enjoyed in the proper setting, at the proper time, with the proper food.

I am always being asked questions about the "perfect marriage" of food and wine. But is "marriage" the right word? Does not it still imply complete fidelity—the same two partners always together, their relationship controlled by fixed and immutable rules? The partnerships of food and wine are not like that at all. They can change almost every night. They involve wildly undisciplined romance—a trial love affair joyously started one evening and abandoned as a total failure the next. There is almost unlimited fickleness, infidelity, and variation of mood. It may be the spice of variety. It is not the continuity of marriage.

Some people try to enforce a shotgun marriage of food and wine with a straitjacket of fixed rules. White wine, they say, with white chicken and white fish. Red wine with red meat. Pink wine with pink lamb. This is the lunatic fringe of menu planning. It can lead to dinner-table disaster. Try serving a great white Steinberger from the Rhine with a delicately poached fillet of sole. The fish will taste like blotting paper. Or try matching a rare venison steak, covered with Marchand de Vin Sauce, to a beautiful young, bright raspberry-colored Beaujolais of last year's harvest. The charming wine (perfectly delightful with the right dish) will taste like watery red ink.

To find the perfect wine partner for your planned menu, you must think of more than color. First, I believe there should be the element of romance. How often does the lilting name of a wine add to the moment when a beautifully decorated dish is presented at table. A bottle of Valpolicella di Verona seems to exude the ambience of the city where Romeo and Juliet fell in love. The wine can help you establish the mood of your party: informal and simple, or luxuriously spendthrift. But the most important factor of all is the character and personality of the wine.

The marvel of wine is that almost every vineyard is in some way different from every other and produces a slightly different wine every year. Yet there are strong and continuing family resemblances between wines of the same district in the same region. Whether they be red or white, dry or sweet, still or sparkling, some wines are gentle, light, modest, uncomplicated in bouquet and taste; others are dominant, subtle, and complicated on the tongue. Foods, also, can be delicate and gentle or powerful and spicy. The secret menu-planning trick is never to allow a too-dominant wine to overpower a gentle dish (as the Steinberger did to the sole), or a too-dominant dish to overpower a gentle wine (as the venison did to the Beaujolais).

I have incorporated these vital principles into my "Basic Wine and Food Affinities" chart at the end of this chapter. It is probably the most flexible reference chart you have ever seen. It is not a set of rules, but an invitation to experiment. Once you know *why* you are putting wine X with food Y, you can make up your own rules as you go along and break them whenever you are struck with an idea for an interesting experiment. In fact, in the right-hand column of the chart I suggest for each of the wine types a few of these unusual, offbeat combinations. They are marvelous stimulants of conversation at the dinner table. One friend said to me the other day, "I don't believe anyone can call himself a true gourmet until he has tried red wine with fish." Perhaps he is right.

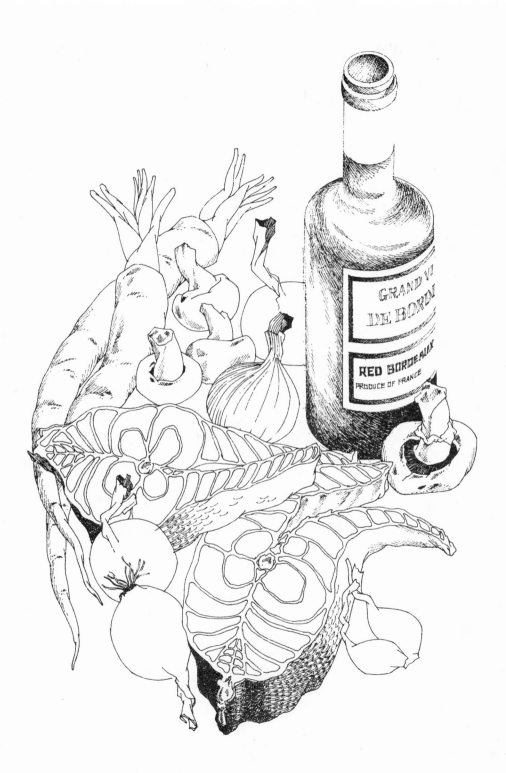

A few notes of explanation of the chart. It begins (left-hand column) with the three major types of white wine, because these are the most universally available, have the widest range of uses, and are, in general, the best with which to start experimenting. Then follow the two major types of red wine, the rosés, and the two sharply different types of sweet wine. Naturally, within each of these broad definitions, there is an infinity of variations among districts, regions, and countries. I try to indicate this enormous variety by listing (in the second column) some of the labels to look for. The countries are in alphabetical order; within each country, I list the wines approximately in order of their importance. I have, of course, tasted charming wines in many other places besides those listed (for example, in Algeria, Australia, Austria, Chile, Greece, Hungary, South Africa, and Yugoslavia), but these wines are not yet sufficiently widely distributed to be included here. In the third column, I try to define the character of the wine to help you plan your experiments with the foods suggested in columns four and five.

Certainly, for me, experimentation has been the key to my education in wine. I remember a beach picnic on the Mediterranean coast of France, a few miles from Marseille, when I had my first truly authentic Bouillabaisse, the world's most wonderful fish stew. First we went out with the fisherman in his boat and caught about a dozen different kinds of fish. Meanwhile, at the edge of the beach, the fisherman's wife started a fire and hung over it a huge witch's cauldron of a black iron pot, half-filled with wine, aromatic vegetables, and fresh herbs. As our boat headed back to the shore, we cleaned and scraped the fish, so that they were dead only a few minutes before being plopped into the bubbling liquid over the fire. At least a dozen bottles of dry, light white wines were cooling in a small stream under the trees.

That day I learned a primary lesson: how good it is, before a fine meal, to drink, as an apéritif, a bottle of bone-dry, ice-cold white wine. We began with an Alsatian Sylvaner, which both slaked the thirst and, with its faint touch of acidity, stimulated the appetite. It was accompanied by small canapé slices of goat cheese, ripe black olives, and unsalted nuts.

Now the Bouillabaisse was ready, a superb gastronomic experience, which taught me how to recognize the subtle combinations of different types of fish with various wines. We opened several bottles at a time and then, taking a single mouthful of each fish in turn, noticed how an added sip of one wine would bring out a certain taste quality, while a sip of another wine would produce a different effect. Chablis and Muscadet are, of course, the classic wines with fish, but there are at least a dozen other dry whites worth trying, from every wine-producing country.

I have continued my research at fish cookouts in the High Alps, with the crackling Crépy and the dryly sparkling wines from Seyssel; in Germany, with light young Moselles from Piesport, Graach, Zeltingen, or Erden; in Italy, with the almost metallically dry Soave, from the hills to the northwest of Venice; in Switzerland, with the Aigle, from the terraced slopes at the headwaters of Lake Geneva; and on joyously gourmand days in San Francisco, I have combined the various versions of the Fisherman's Wharf specialty, Crab Cioppino, with the subtle variations of the dry California whites made from the White Riesling grape or the Pinot Blanc, or the excellently dry "American Champagnes" of the Napa Valley.

On my chart these dry types (the workhorses of the wine world) are followed, further along the power scale, by mellower wines with stronger personalities (which can stand up to the richer and spicier foods) and, at the end of the scale, the dominant and powerful whites. The greatest of these can provide surprises—sometimes even shocks. My first discovery of the impact of the aggressively strong whites came at a dinner at the three-star country restaurant of Paul Bocuse, a few miles outside Lyon, the city that rules the gastronomic heartland of France. Chef Paul served me some of the fishy riches of the Saône and Rhône rivers (including the marvelous local crayfish) prepared with incredibly rich sauces and served with a range of white wines from his cellar. He showed me the elegance and power of the Alsatian Riesling and Gewürztraminer wines; the beauty of the Bordeaux whites, led by such great châteaux names as Carbonnieux, Domaine de Chevalier, Laville Haut Brion and Olivier; the dominant grace of the fine whites from Meursault in Burgundy, from Vouvray on the Loire, and from the famous Hermitage hill on the Rhône. Finally, we opened a bottle of the white wine I consider to be one of the most powerful in the world, Le Montrachet from the Côte d'Or in southern Burgundy, from the 1964 vintage. I found it so dominant that I asked Chef Bocuse whether it would not go well with red meat. His eyes twinkled and, as a shocking experiment, he served it with the main course of our dinner, a rare and red Tournedos aux Champignons, a beef steak with a creamy-rich brown sauce, garnished with wild cèpe mushrooms. I took my first bite of the meat, then lifted my glass of the great white wine, while Chef Bocuse watched with a wicked grin. Red meat and white wine was a near-perfect partnership!

Other medium or strong whites that deserve to be tried in various combinations with food are the wines of the Moselle and Rhine, White Chianti from Tuscany, Orvieto from the hills northeast of Rome (it comes in two quite distinct types: the *secco* means dry, the *abboccato* means rich and fairly sweet), the Spanish white with the lovely name Alella from the Catalan slopes north of Barcelona, Swiss Dézaley (almost certainly the strongest and best of that country's whites), the California medium-dry Sauvignon Blanc and, for a dominant white, the grape that I believe produces the best American white wine, Pinot Chardonnay.

When it comes to red wines, the idea of a beautifully colored château-bottled Bordeaux with red beef is so basic that it needs not a word of discussion. The problem in menu-planning is how to differentiate between the light reds and the big, powerful wines. Recently I stayed as the guest of the owners at one of the greatest vineyards of the world, Château Latour, in the Médoc district of Bordeaux. I spent most of my time with its Wine Master, Jean-Paul Gardère, whose discussions and demonstrations were a revelation. He planned the food every day with the cook of the château, Madame Jeanne Verger, to prove the perfect partnership of the Bordeaux wines with a wide range of simple to complicated dishes. The first major point he proved was the importance to the wine quality, of soil and weather. Each château vineyard, because of its soil, has a certain basic similarity of character in all its wines. Therefore, if you taste the wines of various châteaux, you will soon begin to know which labels strike the best balance between your taste and your pocketbook. But then you should also remember that, depending on the amount of sunshine and rain each summer, the wines of each château will be lighter or heavier, gentler or stronger. So, with practice, you must learn to buy both by château name and by vintage year.

In cold, dry, and sunless years, even such normally great wines as Châteaux Lafite or Latour, can be relatively gentle and light. They can be bought and used, in those years, as if they belonged to the "light reds" on my chart. For example, at Château Latour, we drank the light 1951 vintage with Poulet à la Bordelaise, and the almost equally light 1963 vintage with a delicately creamy preparation of veal sweetbreads.

As to the powerful Bordeaux reds of the great years, the buying problem is largely a matter of knowing the major châteaux names, and these are discussed in the preceding wine chapters. There are, of course, dozens of other names in the near-top class and literally hundreds of fine and noble vineyards. Gradually exploring them and making one's own favorite list is a joyous adventure.

My education in the reds of Burgundy has come partly from my friends the two great Burgundian-born chefs, the brothers Jean and Pierre Troisgros, of the three-star Troisgros Restaurant in the small town of Roanne, also near Lyon. Although they now live and work quite far from Burgundy they have kept their contacts and family friendships with the Burgundian growers and they seem to get hold of the best wines before anyone else has heard about them!

They showed me, with a series of sips from their tasting glasses, that many of the lightest and softest Burgundy reds come from Beaune (labeled Beaune, or Côte de Beaune, or Côte de Beaune-Villages) or from Volnay, a few miles to the south. They also proved how fine a young Beaujolais can be when it is carefully produced and bottled by a single vineyard.

When I arrived for a visit with the Troisgros last October, at the start of the hunting season, Chef Pierre had spent the weekend in the forests of the Garenne and had brought back a *marcassin* (a young wild boar), wild duck, large hares, rabbits, and partridge. For the next few days, we tasted these prizes, superbly prepared and perfectly matched to some of the big Burgundy reds that come, with only a few exceptions, from the villages to the north of Beaune. Our biggest dinner involved the three-day preparation of one of the greatest of all Burgundian game dishes, a Civet de Lièvre à la Royale, hares marinated in brandy and red wine, then filled with an aromatic stuffing and slowly simmered for twenty-four hours. When the magnificently decorated platter came to table, the meat, with its garnishes and sauce, proved to be too dominant in flavor for a 1964 Grands Echezeaux, a moderately light vintage. The wine seemed sharp and thin. Chef Pierre instantly replaced it with a much bigger Burgundy, a 1966 Pommard, Hospices de Beaune Dames de la Charité. This, a more dominant wine, stood up to the power of the food.

For dinner on my last evening, the Troisgros brothers, with slightly devilish smiles, served me a shocker—an offbeat combination to prove that even fairly strong red wine *can*, in a properly planned way, be matched with fish. They prepared a Burgundian Meurette, a stew of local lake and river fish marinated with Burgundian *marc* brandy and simmered in red wine. It was served with a red 1967 Bonnes Mares from the Burgundian village of Chambolle-Musigny. I have since proven, in my New York kitchen, that it is possible to prepare a satisfactory Meurette here at home, using a mixture of fresh- and saltwater fish and shellfish.

Few wines from other regions of the world can equal the power of the great Burgundies, but some come fairly close. There are the big reds of the Rhône, the fine years in Italy, the charming, fairly light Doles from Switzerland, and, from California, the better vintages of wines made from the grapes called Barbera, Cabernet Sauvignon, and Pinot Noir.

I found another surprising but successful partnership of red wine with fish at a small mountain inn among the High Alps, near the Swiss border: the Auberge of the Flowering Hearth, above the village of St.-Pierre-de-Chartreuse. The excellent cook, Mademoiselle Ray Girard, had a large, pink-fleshed salmon-trout, caught that morning in Lake Paladru. Mademoiselle Ray decided to prepare it *à la Genevoise,* which means, on any menu in any country, "as they do it in Geneva," that is, in red wine. The whole fish was gently poached in the locally produced, light red Gamay de Savoie, which was sharp enough to cut the oiliness of the fish. Then it was served with a red sauce and a soft red wine from the Côtes Rôties of the Rhône. Since both these light red wines are now imported into the United States, I have been able to prove in my New York kitchen that the dish tastes equally good on our side of the Atlantic.

At this point, some readers may be thinking, "Why bother with a chart? Just serve rosé wine. It goes with anything!" This is nonsense. Most inexpensive *vin rosé* has so little character that it does not add anything to anything at any time. You might as well drink a glass of colored water. The making of a good rosé is a delicate process. It is more or less like making a fine red wine, from red grapes, with a well-developed character, but stopping the production process before the red color has deepened. This delicate process is bypassed in the making of the poor rosés. They are simply a characterless mixture of red and white wines.

How can one find the best rosés? They are made in specific places, from specific grapes, and the producers are legally required to put the names on the labels.

Is there a place for a good rosé in menu-planning? Indeed there is. It can help to unite several different styles of dishes on a cold buffet table. It can stress the informality of a picnic. It will not be killed by the peppery sauces of a Texas-style barbecue, a Mexican dinner, or an Indian curry.

During the 1970 harvest in Bordeaux I was invited to a memorable lunch by Monsieur and Madame Henri Woltner at their great Château La Mission Haut Brion in the Graves district, just outside the city. Their menu taught me a Bordelais trick of planning food with wine. After the main meat course, a superb roast of veal, there was served, of all things, a rich pâté de foie gras and, with it, believe it or not, a lightly sweet Sauternes wine. I winced in advance as I tasted the two together. The wine cut the richness of the goose livers, while magnifying their flavor. The pâté almost eliminated the sweetness of the wine. It was pure magic!

When I asked Madame Woltner why the foie gras, normally an opening course, was served *after* the meat, she laughed gaily and said, "Because people will eat less of the expensive stuff at this point!" She was, of course, putting me on. She went on to explain that her husband and other Bordeaux producers, when planning a menu, always decide first on the wines they want to show off, then choose the foods that will best go with them. Apart from the famous wines there are many only lightly sweet, yellow rather than golden in color, the products of smaller vineyards and less sunny years, which have all kinds of special uses in menu-planning. They can be served as a buffer between the meat and the dessert, or equally well at the start of a meal. I have used this magic trick many times at my own dinner table with a lightly sweet wine as a cutting edge against some rich, unctuous dish (see the chart).

There are many types of lightly sweet wines: the regional Sauternes (those labels which do not carry the name of a château) of Bordeaux, the wines made from the Gewürztraminer and Riesling grapes in exceptionally sunny years in Alsace, gently sweet types from Anjou along the Loire (usually labeled Côteaux du Layon), and, from California, the wines named for the Malvasia, Muscatel, or Sémillon grapes.

All these are very different, of course, from the great vintages of Château d'Yquem and the other world-famous Sauternes châteaux. Their wines can be almost as sweet and thick as honey, but with a marvelously spicy character. Their classic use is with desserts that are not too sweet, so that the aromatic sugar of the wine is not overpowered. You should never serve them with ice cream, which slightly freezes your taste buds so that you cannot fully appreciate the wine. Nor should they ever accompany any dish containing chocolate, which, as you chew it, also clogs your taste buds. I think the finest of the sweet wines, including the great sweet wines of Germany, are best drunk in place of a liqueur after dinner, either by themselves or with candies, unsalted nuts, or those fine, jumbo-size muscat raisins that come in bunches from Australia.

A final note on cheese with wine. It is invariably a fine partnership. Professional wine shippers always say, "Let me sell wine with cheese, but buy it with apples." They know that cheese brings out the best from any wine, but that the sourness of an apple shows up the worst qualities and provides the buyer with ammunition to cut down the price. Even with cheeses, the rules about domination and strength still apply. Bland and simple cheeses should be matched with less powerful whites, medium-strong cheeses with lighter reds. Only the extremely powerful blues and "stinky" goat cheeses, (as well as such "loud" items as Liederkranz or Limburger) are strong enough to do battle with the most powerful reds. My chart gives a few of the names and will help you to choose your cheeses to match your wines.

I hope I have said enough to persuade you that menu-planning with wine is one of the most fascinating of hobbies, just because there is such an infinity of possibilities. I have never found any hobby that is worthwhile unless it presents a certain challenge to one's ingenuity and skill.

The Basic Wine and Food Affinities

Type of Wine	Specific Wines	General Character	Traditionally Served With	Unusual (But Very Good) Served With
Dry whites Dry Champagnes and other sparkling wines (Serve chilled)	Chablis or Pouilly-Fuissé from Burgundy. Muscadet or Pouilly-Fumé from the Loire. Sylvaner from Alsace. Crépy or Seyssel from the French Alps. Light Moselle from Germany. Soave from Italy. White Rioja from Spain. Johannisberg Riesling or Pinot Blanc from California.	Dry and refreshing, almost lemony. Thirst-quenching.	Canapés before a meal. Clams and oysters. Non-oily fish, grilled or poached. Cold chicken or turkey. Or with all dishes in a simple meal.	Canapés made with soft goat cheese. Olives and unsalted nuts as appetizers.
Medium dry whites Softer Champagnes (Serve chilled)	White Graves from Bordeaux. Corton-Charlemagne or Meursault from Burgundy. Light Vouvray from the Loire. Light Hermitage from the Rhône. Niersteiner, Forster, Bernkasteler, or Wehlener from Germany. White Chianti or Orvieto Secco from Italy. Alella from Spain. Sauvignon Blanc from California.	Gentler and softer; fruity, less sharp. Grapy, rather than lemony.	Smoked salmon. Bisques or cream soups. Fish with cream sauces and fried fish. Hot chicken or turkey with gravy. Cold lamb or veal. Roast pork. Sweetbreads or kidneys.	Main dishes with cheese, such as Veal Cordon Bleu, Veal Parmigiana macaroni and cheese, spaghetti with meat balls and cheese sauce, cheese omelet with herbs or mushrooms. Nutty cheeses such as French Tomme de Savoi or Swiss Gruyère.

295

Type of Wine	Specific Wines	General Character	Traditionally Served With	Unusual (But Very Good) Served With
Rich, powerful whites Sweet Champagnes (Serve ice-cold)	Montrachet from Burgundy. Gewürztraminer from Alsace. Rich Vouvray from the Loire. Johannisberger, Steinberger, or Vollrads from Germany's Rheingau. Orvieto Abboccato from Italy. Pinot Chardonnay from California.	Very dominant. Aromatic and spicy, sometimes faintly sweet. Rich and velvety on the tongue.	Rich preparations of crab and lobster. Roast pheasant. Baked or boiled ham. Simple grills, roasts, or stews of lamb, pork, or veal.	Turtle soup. Red meats such as beefsteak with natural gravy. Simple cheeses such as Dutch Edam or English Cheddar.
Light, young, relatively uncomplicated reds (Serve at room temperature)	Médoc, Red Graves, or Saint-Emilion from Bordeaux (simple recent vintages). Beaune, Volnay or Beaujolais from Burgundy (soft recent vintages). Côte Rôtie from the Rhône. Gamay de Savoie from the French Alps. Bardolino or Valpolicella from Italy. Rioja Clarete from Spain. Cabernet Sauvignon or Barbera from California.	Fruity and gay, a bit feminine. Lovely in color, straightforward in personality.	Simple preparation of red meat, such as steaks with natural gravy or red-wine sauce. Oven or pot roasts. Simple stews or casseroles. Lamb or veal with rich, creamy garnishes or wine sauces. Roast duck. Richly prepared capon, goose, guinea hen, pheasant, squab, or turkey. Medium-strong cheeses, such as Alsatian	Rich, oily fish such as salmon or Salmon-trout à la Genevoise.

Wine category	Wines	Characteristics	Foods
Powerful, dominant reds (Serve at room temperature)	Médoc, Graves, Pomerol, or Saint-Emilion from Bordeaux. Chambertin, Clos Vougeot, Musigny, Pommard, or Vosne-Romanée from Burgundy. Châteauneuf-du-Pape or Hermitage from the Rhône. Barolo or Chianti Classico from Italy. Rioja Clarete from Spain. Pinot Noir from California. (All fine old vintages.)	Dominant and strong, with a very powerful personality. Smooth and velvety, almost heavy on the tongue.	Meurette, the Burgundy fish stew. Muenster, Normandy Camembert, Parisian Brie, or Savoy Reblochon. Red meat with rich sauces, such as Beef in Burgundy and other winy casseroles. All kinds of game birds, such as wild duck, wild pheasant, or wild turkey. Richly stuffed goose. Strong goat cheeses such as Alpine St. Marcellin goat, Loire Chabichou or Ste.-Maure, or Valençay goat, or very strong blue cheeses such as English Stilton, French Roquefort, or Italian Gorgonzola.
Authentic rosés (Serve ice-cold)	Tavel from the Rhône. Pinot Rosé from Alsace. Light young Beaujolais from Burgundy. Rosé de Cabernet from Anjou or Touraine in the Loire. Grenache, Gamay, or, in lesser quantity, Cabernet and Pink Zinfandel from California.	Light, refreshing, and uncomplicated. (But they do *not* go with everything.)	Cold buffet. Barbecued foods. Picnic foods. Rich, oily fish (as above). Buttery cheeses such as Dutch Gouda or Italian Fontina.

Type of Wine	Specific Wines	General Character	Traditionally Served With	Unusual (But Very Good) Served With
Lightly sweet, yellow wines (Serve chilled)	Young regional Sauternes from Bordeaux. Gewürztraminer or Riesling from Alsace. Light sweet Anjou or Vouvray from the Loire. Light sweet Moselle or Rhine from Germany. Light sweet Muscatel or Sémillon from California.	Rich but not cloying. Refreshingly light on the tongue.	Light desserts.	Pâté de foie gras. Rich pâtés and terrines of game meats. Very rich soups. Rich and creamy preparations of lobster.
Honeyed, golden wines (Serve almost freezing)	Sauternes from Bordeaux. Gewürztraminer from Alsace. Sweet Anjou or Vouvray from the Loire. Sweet Moselle or Rhine from Germany. Muscatel or sweet Sémillon from California. (Only the great old vintages achieve this status.)	Magnificently aromatic, heavily honeyed.	Rich desserts. Fruit- or nut-filled soufflés. (But *never* ice cream or any dish with chocolate.)	Candies, nuts, and raisins as a liqueur after dinner.

PART V
The Host at His Home Bar

CHAPTER 23

THE BLESSING CAN
BE MIXED OR UNMIXED

Setting Up and Stocking the Home Bar

From the earliest recorded history of man, an important part of hospitality has been the offering of liquid refreshment. In our sophisticated times it is offered in a variety of ways. It may be the apéritif or cocktail, to lift the spirit and sharpen the appetite. The hot and thirsty guest may be offered a tall, fruit-flavored cooler. When the fur-coated visitor steps in with a flurry of snow, the welcome offering might be a steaming-hot toddy. In the middle of an active morning or a busy afternoon the drink may be a nutritional pickup in the form of an egg beaten into a snowy pink fizz or a creamy yellow flip. Hospitality may be expressed with a vintage wine at dinner or a bright, Green Chartreuse with the coffee. In Scotland there is the tradition of the *doch-an-dorris* (the "dash at the door," sometimes called the stirrup cup), a quick drink served in the hallway to speed and warm the departing guest. Finally, for the house guest, a midnight soother, or nightcap, on the way to bed.

All these drinks can be supplied with relative ease from a surprisingly small number of bottles, provided that there is careful planning and wise buying, and also that you regard your bar as only one leg of a three-legged home system for storing and dispensing liquid hospitality. The bar is where you keep the equipment, the tools, and

301

those bottles of brandies, fortified wines, sweet liqueurs, and spirits that are to be stored standing up and at room temperature. The second leg is your wine library. The third leg is a section of the refrigerator, (either a permanent arrangement if you have the space or organized just for a party) with at least one bottle of dry white wine for mixing, perhaps two or three bottles of basic spirits, a couple of fruit liqueurs for flavoring, plus a choice of sweetening syrups. Also, of course, the refrigerator must supply fresh lemons and limes and an occasional egg or two. The bartender will also raid the kitchen for aromatic bitters, spices, superfine sugar, and boiling water for the hot drinks. Assuming that these are available, the first step is to plan stocking the bar.

An Average-Size Bar

Some choices, of course, depend strictly on personal taste, but my first demand from such a bar would be to supply a substantial number of the best-known and best-liked mixed drinks suitable for the various hours and occasions of the day. It must also supply the dry Sherries or dry Madeiras for the beginning, plus the Ports, the sweet liqueurs, and the brandies and whiskeys for the ending of a lunch or dinner party.

Such a reasonably efficient bar might consist of twelve to fifteen bottles, and the cost would vary according to location. When I priced it at a liquor store in a residential neighborhood of Manhattan, the cost varied, according to choice of labels, between seventy-five and ninety-five dollars. Within this range, I would order:

FORTIFIED WINES
Tawny Port from Oporto
Dry Spanish *fino* Sherry
Italian Campari bitter vermouth
French dry vermouth
Italian sweet vermouth

REGIONAL FLAVORED SPIRITS
Medium-priced French Cognac
Golden Jamaica rum
Straight Kentucky bourbon
Highland single-malt Scotch
Blended Lowland Scotch

FLAVORLESS MIXING SPIRITS
Domestic or imported London-type
dry gin
Vodka

SWEET LIQUEURS
Crème de Cassis
Green Chartreuse
Orange Curaçao

To these "spirituous" bottles one must add three more of multipurpose sweetening syrups, available almost everywhere. Falernum (a generic name, used by several producers) is a highly aromatic sugar syrup imported from the West Indies, flavored with almond oil and ginger. Grenadine is the sweetened juice of the pomegranate and gives its rich red color to any drink that contains even a few drops. My favorite, is orgeat (another generic name, from the French *orge,* meaning barley), a thickened sugar syrup delicately flavored with almonds, orange blossoms, and rose petals. Also, many of the sweet liqueurs can make interesting variations, including maraschino, banana, orange Curaçao, and so forth.

I believe that a strong drink just before dinner dulls the appetite and is an insult to a fine cook. So my first concern in choosing these bottles has been to provide good ingredients for the European-type, light-in-alcohol apéritifs—especially those with a dry and ascetic quality to clean the mouth, sharpen the taste buds, and accent hunger.

A Small-Budget Bar

The fifteen bottles listed above are by no means a minimum. A substantial number of drinks, including many favorites, can still be provided from about half that number. Since good-quality dry gins and vodkas should be entirely colorless, flavorless, and odorless, I consider them virtually interchangeable, especially in highly aromatic mixed drinks. A small bar, therefore, does not have to have separate bottles of dry gin and vodka. So here is my personal list for an eight-bottle bar that, priced at a typical Manhattan neighborhood store, might cost somewhere between forty and fifty dollars.

FORTIFIED WINES
French dry vermouth
Italian sweet vermouth

REGIONAL FLAVORED SPIRITS
Medium-priced French Cognac
Golden Jamaica rum
Straight Kentucky bourbon
Highland single-malt Scotch

FLAVORLESS MIXING SPIRIT
Domestic or imported London-type
dry gin

SWEET LIQUEUR
Crème de Cassis

A Magnificent and Opulent Bar

If the bar could hold them and the cost were no consideration, I would choose about thirty bottles. This is a reasonable number, with every useful and valid ingredient included, but omitting the overpriced, fanciful, fantastic labels. Virtually every drink in the book is possible from this bar, with an infinity of complicated and subtle variations. Again, I have priced the list at a typical Manhattan liquor store, and the cost would lie somewhere between $175 and $200. The full list:

FORTIFIED WINES
Dry Rainwater or Sercial Madeira
Ruby Port—American or imported
Vintage Port from Oporto
Medium-dry Spanish *amontillado* Sherry
Dry Spanish *fino* Sherry
Italian Campari bitter vermouth
Italian Punt e Mes bitter vermouth
French dry vermouth
Italian sweet vermouth

REGIONAL FLAVORED SPIRITS
Apple brandy (either American
Applejack or French Calvados)
Medium-priced French Cognac
Dutch Old Genever
Pernod anis
Dark Demerara rum
Golden Jamaica rum

Light Puerto Rican rum
Straight Kentucky bourbon
Canadian blended whiskey
Corn whiskey
Irish blended whiskey
Blended rye whiskey
Highland Glenlivet single-malt Scotch
Highland Islay single-malt Scotch
Blended Lowland Scotch
Tennessee sour mash whiskey

FLAVORLESS MIXING SPIRITS
Domestic or imported London-type
dry gin
Mexican Tequila
Vodka

SWEET LIQUEURS
Apricot
Crème de Banane
Crème de Cacao
Crème de Cassis
Green Chartreuse
Yellow Chartreuse
Maraschino Cherry
Orange Curaçao
Prunelle (from sloe berries)
Coffee liqueur

CHAPTER 24

THE GREAT FORTIFIED WINES OF THE WORLD

A. Portugal: From Madeira to Port

Portugal is one of the important wine-producing countries of the world, although it is neither the largest nor the best known in terms of glamorous châteaux or household-word labels. Yet the Portuguese have, over the last two hundred and fifty years, created two great and unique wines: Madeira and Port—brilliantly colored, fragrant, and rich.

The story of Portuguese wine begins at least five hundred years before the birth of Christ. The great ships of the Phoenicians sailed the length of the Mediterranean, bringing grape vines from the East and planting them along the shores of lands that would later become France, Spain, and Portugal. Once the vines were established along the coast, farmers took cuttings inland and experimented to find the places and the soils where they would grow best. In northern Portugal there is a great river called the Douro, flowing from east to west into the Atlantic and carving a beautiful sun-baked valley into the hills. Here the grapes grew, if not quite perfectly, at least fiercely and abundantly. When the Romans came, they found the vineyards already well established in a tradition that continued for centuries.

The Beginning of Port

The grapes were crushed by barefoot men, in stone troughs called *lagares*. The new wine was fermented on hundreds of *quintas,* the small estates of individual growers, then poured into long casks called pipes. After a few months of aging, the pipes were carried down the precipitous slopes on the backs of mules to the river bank, and transported on flat-bottomed barges down the foaming rapids of the Douro to the waiting seagoing ships at its mouth. There the pipes were tipped into the water and pushed by strong swimmers to the dangling ropes of the ships, which would carry the wines to thirsty drinkers in towns up and down the coast. Inevitably a thriving harbor city developed at the mouth of the Douro, a city that gave its name to the wine: Oporto.

By the middle of the fourteenth century, Portuguese ships were carrying the wines northward to England and bringing back cargoes of salt cod and woolen cloth. Thus began the historic Anglo-Portuguese partnership that proved to be so important in the development of the wine. Early in the fifteenth century, some of the more intrepid Portuguese sea captains dared to sail out into the Atlantic and discovered a group of islands about five hundred miles offshore, uninhabited and completely covered by forests. The sailors called them Ilhas da Madeira, "Isles of Wood." Rumors about these lovely and fertile islands spread across Europe and soon a small international band of adventurers took a precarious foothold just inland from the snowy-white beaches, where the forests came down to the sea. Besides the Portuguese, there were Germans, Poles, Frenchmen, even a Scotsman.

The Fires of Madeira

The settlers cleared the land by setting fire to the forests. The Isles of Madeira, it was said, burned continuously for seven years. No doubt the richness of the soil and the marvelous yield from the grapes are partly due to the wood ash mixed into the rich earth. The settlers brought sugar cane and grape vines, so the making of wine was soon flourishing on Madeira. The techniques were copied exactly from those of the Douro Valley, and the pipes were floated out to the waiting British and Portuguese ships in the tiny port of Funchal.

By the seventeenth century, so many thirsty Englishmen had developed a taste for the wines of Portugal that British wine merchants began establishing their own trading offices in Funchal and Oporto. At first they just bought the pipes of wine at the docks. Then they began investing in the producing firms and even entering into partnerships with the vineyard owners. This is why, even today, many of the famous names on the labels of Madeiras and Ports are British: Blandy Brothers, Cockburn-Smithes, Cossart-Gordon, Croft, Harvey, Hooper, Leacock, Robertson, Sandeman, Williams & Humbert, and so on.

Until the eighteenth century, the wines of Madeira and Oporto were fairly ordinary *consumo* or table wines. They were being shipped in large quantities across the Atlantic and were great favorites among Virginia planters and Boston businessmen. But now the much better French wines were beginning to compete, and something had to be done about improving the Portuguese wines if they were to hold their own. It was one of the British merchants who conceived the idea that revolutionized Madeira and Port and made them world-famous. His English customers liked their wines strong, but Madeiras and Ports were relatively gentle. The simple trick that changed everything was documented by the year 1720: the addition of three gallons of fine distilled brandy to each pipe of Portuguese wine. This was the beginning of what we know today as "fortified wines."

At first the fortified Madeiras were very harsh. It was said that the brandy lion and the grape lamb would not lie down together. The producers discovered two strange things. If the filled pipes were left for a few days out in the sun to get warm, the wine was softened. Also, it was found that the fortified wine improved greatly in the pipe during a long sea voyage. Apparently the combination of the heat in the ship's hold and the continuous swaying caused by the sea swell made the wine velvety. After that, for almost a century, all the most expensive Madeiras were labeled "East India," which meant that they had been carried to Java and back, through tropic heat, before being sold.

Cooking the Wines

Finally, in the early 1800s, the Madeira producers conceived the fantastic system of "cooking" their wines. The system is called *estufado,* which means, literally, "stoving." The casks are placed in heated stone buildings and kept at a steady temperature between 100° and 140° F. The better wines are heated very gently and kept hot, sometimes for as long as six months. The cheaper wines are heated more fiercely and sold within two or three months. Madeira is the only great wine in the world that is "cooked" before it is bottled.

Meanwhile, on the Portuguese mainland, the red wines of the Douro Valley were also being fortified. But here the technique was unsuccessful. The wines remained fiercely harsh and neither heating nor swaying seemed to do them the slightest good. The lion and the lamb would *not* lie down together, and it soon became obvious to the producers that what was really needed was a period of slow aging for the wine, perhaps over a number of years, "to rub off its sharp corners." But this was impossible in the primitive wooden pipes then in use. The porous walls let in the air and bacteria, so that long before the wine was properly aged it was converted to vinegar. Obviously, the wine needed to be hermetically sealed. Out of this necessity came the cork-sealed, straight-sided wine bottle, a Portuguese discovery that revolutionized the wine industry.

This is the bottle that has made possible all the great vintage wines of the nineteenth and twentieth centuries, sealed in their glass cells, slowly aging for decades in the cool, dark cellars of the great châteaux. Without that bottle, none of us would ever have tasted any great vintage wine. Nor would it ever have been possible to produce any of the greatest Portuguese Ports, many of them aged in the immense and silent "lodges" of Oporto for as long as half a century.

The Differences

These are the basic differences between the various Madeiras and Ports. Madeiras can be either dry or sweet, and the dry types may be used as apéritifs before meals, or (in the same way as dry Sherry) as a light cocktail at any suitable hour of the day. Ports, on the other hand, are all sweet and, like sweet Madeiras, are best served either with the dessert or as an after-dinner liqueur.

The second essential point is to understand precisely what the names on the labels mean. Madeira, with its *estufado* production system, has never been imitated with true authenticity anywhere else. Port, however, has been imitated all over the world and, let us say frankly, with only moderate success. In true Port from Portugal there is a subtle character in the wine that comes from the earth and the climate of the Douro Valley, plus the damp, fog-laden, slightly salty air of Oporto, which simply cannot be reproduced elsewhere.

To try to prevent misunderstandings, the Portuguese wine-makers have now adopted the name Porto for their wine, and since this new name has been registered as a trademark, it cannot be used by anyone outside Portugal. Thus, if you see a bottle on your dealer's shelf marked "Porto," it must have come from Portugal.

The Madeira Types

The best Madeiras (and the safest to buy) are those that list the Portuguese names of the grapes from which they are made. There are four main ones. The driest is Sercial, from grapes grown on the highest ground. This is one of the best for use as a before-dinner apéritif. It is a light amber in color, with a mellow, nutty flavor. Slightly sweeter, but still dry enough for apéritif use, is the Verdelho (now becoming rather hard to find), with a superb golden color and an aromatic, seductive flavor. In Portugal, Verdelho is the all-purpose wine, served before, during, and after meals. (There is a subsidiary type of dry Madeira called Rainwater, a name that is not that of a grape, but refers to the fact that the wine was made on a part of the island where the grapes depend for their moisture on natural rainwater. This is a very pleasant Madeira, dry and light as a simple cocktail, but it seems to lack the strong individuality of the others.)

Of the two sweet dessert or after-dinner Madeiras, the lighter one, Bual, is delicate and very fragrant, ideal with desserts. Finally there is the most luscious, richest, and sweetest of all Madeiras, the Malmsey (a distortion of the name of the malvoisie grape) with a deep-brown color and an ever so faintly bitter quality of caramelized sugar.

Within these four types, there are dozens of different labels at various ranges of quality and price. As with other wines, the finest Madeiras are the "vintage," made from grapes harvested within a single year, the year being marked on the label. Other Madeiras are commercially blended from the wines of several years, and each producer tries to maintain the uniformity of his blend from year to year.

The Range of Ports

As to Port, there are three main types, each with its special character and particular purpose. In years when the weather along the Douro River is nearly perfect—something that happens, on an average, about once every five years—the producers "declare" a vintage year. This is their guarantee that, during this year, they will make wines only from the grapes of the current harvest, with no blending from previous years. These vintage wines are kept in separate storage in the Oporto lodges. After two years of aging in wooden casks the rich purple wine is bottled and left alone until it is completely matured, which may take anywhere from ten to fifty years. Thus vintage Port, whenever it is available, is always of the finest quality.

In years when the weather is less good, the producers have to blend the wines to achieve the best possible balance and character. One wine, for example, may not be sweet enough, while another is too sweet. These blended Ports are generally left in the casks considerably longer than the vintage types. This speeds up the aging process, but the wine then loses its color, gradually turning from the rich ruby to a reddish brown. This second main Port type is known as Tawny. A good bottle of Tawny Port may represent the best possible value, since it usually sells at less than half the price of a vintage label.

The third type is a compromise between the first two. The Port is not left long enough in the cask to grow tawny, nor is it considered good enough to be left to mature for many years in the bottle. After, perhaps, seven or eight years in the cask, it is bottled and sold at once as Ruby Port. It is generally less strong in character and is usually the least expensive type, but good for everyday drinking and cooking.

Serving the Madeiras

Madeiras are best served in the same fairly small, clear glasses normally used for Sherry. The Sercials, Verdelhos, and Rainwaters can, if you wish, be slightly chilled. Old and sweet Madeiras should be at room temperature.

Madeiras have strong affinities for certain foods. A dry Sercial is almost perfect with a terrapin stew, is excellent with turtle soup, and fine with any of the light clear meat consommés. Sercial is also excellent for cooking, since its aromatic flavor does not evaporate and lends character to the dish in which it is used. It blends well with game birds, mushrooms, and chestnuts. In classic French cooking, one of the most basic of all sauces is Sauce Madère. The lightly sweet Bual Madeira goes well with sweet desserts and is outstanding in eggnogs. As to a very sweet old Malmsey, it usually has such a powerful personality that it should be sipped slowly all by itself, after the coffee is finished, perhaps with freshly shelled walnuts.

Port and Foods

A great vintage Port goes marvelously with a great sharp cheese. For the maximum bouquet and flavor, the bottle should be uncorked and left open to the air for about an hour before serving. Then it should be poured into a reasonably large, clear tulip-shaped glass, never filled more than half to allow the bouquet to develop on the surface of the wine. Port is also extremely useful in the kitchen. It might moisten the stuffing for a guinea hen. A fine ham can be boiled in a Port-flavored bouillon. Various meats, including rare roast beef, tongue, veal, or venison are highlighted by a Port wine sauce. A few drops of the wine can be sprinkled onto sliced peaches.

Can one serve Madeira and Port at the same meal? By all means. Begin with a slightly chilled dry Madeira. A Portuguese proverb calls this the wine to lighten the hearts and loosen the tongues, so that the guests become friends around the table. Then at the end of the meal, serve a great vintage Port, which, according to the proverb, is the wine for deep thoughts and serious discussion of life.

But that is not quite the end. The words *Madeira* (the name of the island, given to the wine) and *Port* (the name of the city, given to the wine) have become so intimately known everywhere that the world has made them its public property. Anyone on earth, anywhere, can decide to make a brown or golden wine and then will be free to call it Madeira—or make a sweet red wine and be free to call it Port.

In the early 1900s, when most of these problems developed, no one thought of copyrighting a place name. In fact, there is a United States law stating that if a foreign name or word has been "regularly used in commerce" for a minimum period of years, it is to be regarded as part of our language and may not be protected or restricted. On the other hand, the British government has passed laws ruling that no sparkling wine may be sold in Britain labeled "Champagne" unless it comes from the Champagne district of France, nor any red wine labeled "Port" unless it comes from Portugal. The Swiss government—faced by the hard fact that the word *Swiss* has now legally become part of the American language, so that a piece of American cheese may be labeled "Swiss cheese"—now calls its cheeses "Switzerland Swiss" and has copyrighted that phrase so that it may be used only for cheese imported from Switzerland. A few years ago, when a group of American whiskey distillers tried to change the name of a certain Kentucky village to "Scotch," so that they could set up their distilleries there and label their product "Scotch whiskey," the British government filed a formal protest with our State Department and the project was quietly dropped. The United Nations has set up a commission, called the "Codex Alimentarius," to try to clarify the international problems of "borrowed" names. It will probably take them a hundred years to sort out the mess.

Personally I don't give a damn about the commercial interests involved. What worries me is that if my children grow up tasting only the imitations of Champagne, of Cheddar, of Port, they will never know the glory of the original and real thing. Each of these foods and drinks became world-famous just because it had something unique about it, something rare and wonderful, something close to perfection, something that the imitations can never achieve. I know that imitation is supposed to be the sincerest form of flattery, but I want to hold on to the original perfection.

Madeira has not suffered very much from this problem. It is so difficult to produce—because of the complicated techniques of "cooking" and the unique qualities of the islands' climate and soil—that almost no one has ever tried to make and sell an imitation. I have to say "almost," because an American wine-maker, the Paul Masson Vineyards, has recently placed on the market a "California Madeira." Does it achieve that extraordinary combination of burnt sugar and subtle smoke? Does it succeed in being, at the same time, faintly sweet and vaguely sharp? A hint of honey and a touch of lemon? A delicate balance between luxury and austerity? It does not. But it is a very pleasant and satisfactory apéritif wine for normal everyday consumption.

With Port, however, it is a very different story. Floods of port, whole rivers of port, have been flowing, for almost a hundred years, from virtually every wine region of the world. There is American Port, Argentinian Port, Australian Port, California Port, New York State

Port, Ohio Port, South African Port, and who knows how many more. They all seem to have one quality in common. They seem to concentrate, almost entirely, on sweetness and strength. They seem to be less concerned with bouquet or flavor. They are all for sugar and fire. If that is the sort of port you want to find in a storm, then these imitations are fine. Almost all of them are efficiently made, have a reasonably good color, are filled into safely sterilized bottles, well-corked and handsomely labeled. The makers have solved every manufacturing and marketing problem, except one. They have not succeeded in producing Port. If they would just call their wines by some other name, everything would be easy. They would not invite the impossible comparison. One would be able to say, with confidence and self-assurance, that these are excellent products, obviously satisfying the needs of millions of customers. One would not be compelled to make comparisons as to their delicacy, or as to the feeling on the tongue of sugared raisins—a feeling that is entirely absent in real Ports.

All the same, there are a number of American ports that I regularly enjoy and of which I often keep a bottle or two in my wine library. They include the New York State Great Western Solera, the California Masson Souzão (made from transplanted Portuguese vines of that varietal name), and the two Tawny types from California of Almadén and Martini.

This whole question of using place names on the labels of wines that do not come from that particular place is sharply focused by the extraordinary success, with their sweet red wines, of one California family of remarkable vintners. In 1940 Walter Ficklin decided to plant a small vineyard in the Central Valley, near Fresno, with the five principal Portuguese grape varieties and concentrate on making sweet red wines. Today the Ficklin vineyard and cellars are run by his two sons, David and Walter, Jr. The first, hand-harvested vintage was in 1948. That wine still rests, harmoniously and superbly, in the bottles in the cellars. I recently tasted the 1953 vintage. It was a great wine—the best non-Portuguese sweet red wine I have ever tasted. The crucial point was that the wine was not specially identified as "Port," but was simply called by the name of the grape, which had originally come from the island of Madeira and been transplanted, first to Portugal and then to California: Tinta Madeira—Estate Bottled. That wine proved that the search for perfection depends neither on names nor on places. It is universal.

2015

Too much food!

No hero for
next year - 2016

Just soup &
Veltre's appetizers

McCarthy's Delicatessen
82 Roslyn Avenue
Sea Cliff, NY 11579
(516) 759-9501

3 lbs Ham - (Slice Thin) 11.85

4 lbs. Turkey   26.00

3 lbs Swiss Cheese   14.40

Bill Bill   52.25

Sun AM 10

Jan 1991

too much food

WHERE FOLKS MEET TO EAT
SINCE 1949

B. Spain: From Montilla to Sherry

Sherry is a world unto itself. A world in which the names are all-important. Amontillado. Jerez de la Frontera. Tinaja. Bodega. Oloroso. Palomino. Pedro Jiménez. Solera. These words tell you the first thing about Sherry—it is Spanish. As Spanish as Gazpacho, or an enormous platter of lobster-studded Paella à la Valenciana. As Spanish as a crowd of a hundred thousand people jumping to its feet and yelling, as one, *"¡Olé!"* As Spanish as a portrait by Velázquez, or a love poem by Federico García Lorca. As Spanish as the brown-red Spanish earth.

If your experience of Sherry has so far been limited to trying to figure out the labels of the bottles on the supermarket shelves—"Cocktail Sherry," "Cream Sherry," "Dry Sherry," "Sweet Sherry," "Extra-Dry Sherry," "After-Dinner Sherry," "Bone-Dry Sherry"—you had better begin preparing yourself at once for an entirely new and different exploration. The great Sherries of Spain are something quite extraordinary—and with so much variety that you could buy a new bottle every day for a year and never once repeat the same combination of bouquets, colors, and flavors. They can be appreciated before dinner, during dinner, or after dinner. Sherry can be as light as the stroked strings of a guitar, or as domineering as a charging bull. It can be hungrily dry, or lusciously sweet. To use Spanish Sherry effectively as a tool of your entertaining, as an ingredient of your memorable menus, you should understand a few of its complications. First, the words:

Amontillado. The word made famous, perhaps, by Edgar Allan Poe's horror story, "The Cask of Amontillado." It is the key to the character of Sherry. The city of Córdoba, in the southwest, is said to be the hottest place in Spain. South of the city the land breaks up into rocky hills and valleys, the earth intensely white with chalk, reflecting back the blazing hot rays of the relentless sun. The slopes are planted with one of the hardiest grape vines in the world, the Pedro Jiménez. Ripening in this heat, the grapes develop so much sugar that, when their juice is fermented and aged in huge Ali Baba-type earthenware jars, called *tinajas,* each shaped like a Roman amphora, the wine reaches almost 16 percent of alcohol (just about the strongest of all natural wines) and is as bone-dry as the dusty chalk. The wine took its name from the tiny local town, Montilla. When other growers in other valleys tried to imitate the Montilla, they claimed that their wine was "in the style of Montilla" or, in Spanish, *amontillado*.

Montilla was the first "Sherry"—long before the word was ever used. There is archaeological evidence that it was shipped in earthenware amphorae to Rome for the delectation of the Caesars. When the larger Sherry industry began, Montilla was an important part of it, but not now. So independent are the vintners of Montilla and so famous is their wine that, about thirty years ago, the Spanish government granted Montilla its own separate appellation. Small quantities of this strange and wonderful wine are now being imported into the United States, under its own label, Montilla. It remains, as always, a memorable tasting experience. I consider it the best of all wines to serve with clams and oysters.

Jerez de la Frontera. The name of the town is the name of the wine and the key to its history. When the Sherry industry expanded from Montilla, it moved about a hundred miles southward, partly to find larger vineyard slopes, partly to be near the seaport of Cadiz through which the wine could be shipped to other countries. From the first, export was the key to success. The vineyards were in a triangle of land, barely larger than Manhattan, centered around the small town, called by the Romans Ceret, and later, by the invading Moors, Scheris. When the barrels began arriving in England, the English called it "Scheris wine" and later shortened and simplified the name to Sherry. Meanwhile, the Castilians from the north of Spain were at war with the Moors in the South, and Scheris was on the frontier between the two armies. After the Moors were expelled, the town was renamed, in honor of its role during the war, Jerez de la Frontera, Jerez on the frontier. It was a frontier, also, in another sense. Sherry was being exported in ever larger quantities. The British, demanding more and more of it, brought their money to Jerez and helped expand the business. Some of the greatest producing and shipping firms, although now owned by Spaniards, still keep their original British names. As Sherry "caught on" in almost every country of the world, it was made in dozens of different ways, to please every taste. You must try them all and make your own decision.

Try the Manzanilla—a delicate, pale-gold, nutty-dry type made in the nearby fishing village of Sanlucar de Barrameda, in huge *bodegas* (the stone cellar sheds where the wines are fermented and aged), where, it is thought, the salt air helps to develop a particular taste—subtly fruity, faintly tart. Manzanilla goes superbly with all kinds of canapés and hors d'oeuvres of anchovies, cheese, ham, olives, and shrimp. But even within this Manzanilla style, there are strong character differences between, say, "La Guita" and "La Gitana."

Now begins the joyous (and, happily, lengthy—the job can last for years) exploration of the three main styles of Sherry, each with its infinity of subtle variations. The first, the dry and sharp Sherries, the apéritifs par excellence, are called *fino*. The second, slightly richer and softer, for guests who do not like extreme dryness, and for sipping with a few special dishes at dinner, are called *amontillado*. The third, aromatically and luxuriously sweet for sipping with not-too-rich desserts, or with nuts and raisins after the coffee, are called *oloroso*. Each of the great producing and shipping companies makes at least one Sherry in each style and tries to maintain the chosen character, under each label, year after year by the most brilliantly complicated system of blending in the entire world of wine. Dozens of barrels are linked together in what are called *soleras,* and comparatively small amounts of Sherry are allowed to flow from one to the other—no single barrel ever being allowed to become completely empty—until each barrel of the tens of thousands held in reserve becomes filled with literally hundreds of small doses of different Sherries, from different vintage years, of differing personalities and at different stages of development. It is like painting a portrait by Goya, not on a canvas with hundreds of pigments, but on the taste buds with thousands of flavoring oils. No wonder that some Sherries are among the most complicated of all wines.

But the complications can, with practice, be unraveled and analyzed. When tasting the *finos,* note especially the cleanness and delicacy of flavor, the beautifully balanced brightness and freshness, the strength (too dominant for most table dishes), the elusive and subtle complexities of the scents. At the start of a party dinner, drink a glass of *fino* with a serving of smoked salmon. Each brings out the best qualities of the other. The *finos* that have given me continuing pleasure in dining and tasting during the past few years are included in the second column of the chart that follows. Naturally, there may be some marvelous ones that I have missed.

The *amontillados* are almost always older than the *finos.* A *fino* might be ready to drink in three years. An *amontillado* might take thirteen. Now you should be tasting for the extraordinary depth of flavor, the aromatic pungence, the rich softness, the overwhelming power of the bouquet. An *amontillado* is the thing to serve with turtle soup, or with any rich, clear meat consommé, or with jugged hare, or kidneys in a mustard sauce—any dish, in fact, that is aromatic enough to stand up to the Sherry. The list of *amontillados* that have added to my dining pleasure are in the third column of the following chart.

A sweet *oloroso* has no part to play before or during a meal. It comes with the dessert or at the end. Notice, as you sip it, first, its luscious solidity. It can feel almost heavy and thick on the tongue. It also has a marvelous range of flavors, from flower-scented honey to the spices of the Indies, with an added hint of chestnuts roasting on a winter fire. In fact, after a brisk walk with my dog on a frosty day, I would rather come back to a glass of a great *oloroso* and would find more warmth in it than in the strongest and most aromatic of spirits. One can serve a sweet *oloroso* with a limited number of desserts, preferably not too rich, and not oversweet—such as for example, an English Trifle, with an egg custard and nuts. My list of the *olorosos* is in column four of the chart.

The Favorite Sherries of an Aficionado

NAME OF SHIPPING FIRM	FINO DRY	AMONTILLADO MED/DRY	OLOROSO SWEET
Bobadilla	Victoria	Extra	Cream
Duff Gordon	Pinta	Amontillado	
Garvey	San Patricio		
Gonzalez, Byass	Tio Pepe	Tulita	Nectar
Harvey	Bristol Dry	Amontillado	Bristol Cream
Ruiz Matteos	Los Angeles		
Wisdom & Warter	Pale Fino	Amontillado	Silvercup Cream
Williams & Humbert	Pando	Dry Sack	Canasta
Sanchez Romate	Marismeño		
Croft		Don Federico	
Pedro Domecq		La Ina	Celebration

Although *Sherry* is one of the most Spanish of words, it is not copyrighted or protected anywhere outside Spain. Anyone, in any country, can make a wine of any type and call it Sherry. My complaints, on the previous pages, about non-Portuguese Madeiras and Ports apply with even greater force to all the attempts to make Sherry in the United States, Australia, South Africa, or anywhere else. Far from being a great wine in the United States, "Sherry" was considered, for many years, as something obnoxious. When one spoke of "a sherry drinker" one imagined a ragged, swaying bum, drinking strong wine from a nondescript bottle wrapped in a brown paper bag. Or a drunken hobo, keeping himself warm by upending the bottle to his lips, while he rode the rails under a freight car. Depravity and drunkenness were associated with a bad wine, too sweet, too strong in alcohol, slightly "cooked" to give it a burnt flavor—a travesty of a pure Spanish Sherry.

American sherry has come a long way forward from that bad beginning. There must now be dozens of labels, from "bone-dry" to "cream"—the latter word supposedly implying something very rich, smooth, and sweet. The sweet American sherries are certainly acceptable in some ways, but the "bone-dry" from here, or any other country, simply invite impossible comparisons. The producers do not have the Spanish earth. Nor the Spanish sun. Nor the Spanish natural yeasts, floating in the air of the *bodegas* of Jerez. Nor do they have the millions of gallons of old wine in storage for *solera* blending. Nor—and perhaps this is the most important point of all—do they, as yet, have the Spanish experience. If they did not try to call themselves "Sherry," many of them would be quite excellent apéritif wines. As it is, they invite a comparison that just cannot be sustained.

Yet I regularly drink and enjoy a number of these dry American apéritif wines for the pleasures of their tastes and textures on the tongue and not for any descriptions on their labels. The best of these, in my opinion, is the California Masson Flor, followed by the three cocktail types from Taylor and Widmer in New York and the Christian Brothers in California.

It is less difficult to produce a sweet wine, and many of the American types, from California to New York, with Ohio in between, are efficiently made and of good, all-round quality. They cannot, of course, claim to compare with the great *olorosos* of Spain, but they are lusciously sweet and very satisfactory dessert wines, including, among those I have recently enjoyed, the two cream-types from California of Martini and Masson, with the Golden Solera from Widmer in New York State.

CHAPTER 25

THE GREAT SPIRITS
OF STRONG
AND TRUE CHARACTER

A. Cognacs, Armagnacs,
and Other Brandies

The principal ingredient of Cognac, unlike other spirits, is not alcohol or the mash of grape or grain. It is antiquity. It is experience. It is patience. It is tradition. It is craftsmanship that depends on a complete disregard of time. Everywhere in the Cognac region are the ruins of ancient castles. The vintners move their barrels over roads that were laid in the days of Imperial Rome. The famous firms that bottle the Cognac carry on their ledgers *active* accounts that are older than the United States. And the very specific and legally defined 138,863 acres upon which Cognac grapes may be grown are held, for the most part, by the descendants of the same farmers who first planted the Cognac grape.

You can savor the antiquity in the air as you walk through the narrow streets of Cognac, the small town from which the brandy takes its name. A large amount of Cognac evaporates daily from the casks within the town's warehouses, and the vapor hangs as a mellow and just slightly intoxicating pall over the entire region and all its good people and their activity; everything becomes heady and easy and effortless and ethereal. This way of life, this philosophy, has resulted in the most successful of all alcoholic distillations: a product that is more stable in its market value than the currency of many of the nations to which it is exported from France.

Cognac, like penicillin, had a rather curious and quite accidental beginning. In the Middle Ages the original wines of the Cognac region, being not very good, remained unappreciated in France and were largely sold to sailors who carried barrels of the wine from the banks of the Charente River to the ports of Rochefort and La Rochelle and aboard their ships to their homes in England, Holland, and Norway. When the wars came and taxes were levied both by importer and exporter on each gallon of liquid, the Cognac producers began to distill the wine in pot stills over wood fires and thus decreased both its volume and its taxation; it was intended that the importer would add water. The result was *eau de vie* ("water of life"). In Holland, in the seventeenth century, this concentrate was called *Brandtewijn* ("burnt wine"). In Scandinavia—which, next to Britain and the United States, is the world's leading Cognac consumer—the distillate was sold as *Brandtvin*. In England it was called "brand wine" and, later, "brandy." During the years when local wars prohibited export of this spirit, the farmers stored it in barrels of oak from the nearby forests of Limousin. When the wars were over and the first of these storage barrels were reopened, the Cognac was found to have been marvelously mellowed by time and colored a deep amber by the tannin of the wood.

The process of Cognac manufacture today follows precisely—almost religiously—the same line as this eighteenth-century accident. Cognac is still barreled only in staves of oak from the forests of Limousin. Other woods have been tried; all have proved unsatisfactory. The barrels are still meticulously constructed by hand by master coopers, so slowly and expensively that a barrel must be used forty years by a distiller before its cost is completely amortized. The barrels are often given as dowries in marriages of the region.

All Cognac is brandy, but not all brandy is Cognac. Any country that makes wine can, and does, make some kind of brandy—from very good to simply horrible. But in France, Cognac is the brandy distilled in that strictly delimited area within the *départements* of Charente and Charente-Maritime, from wine *made* in that area from grapes *grown* in that area—and, moreover, only of the *types* of grape permitted for making Cognac. The region thus honored and jealously protected lies

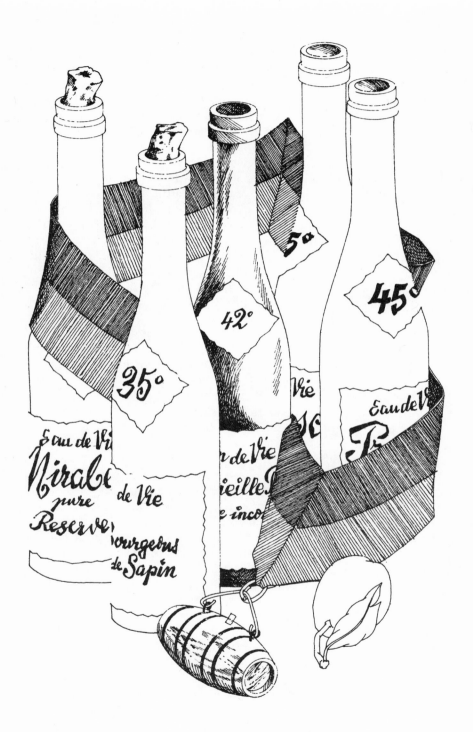

in the west of France, stretching southeastward from La Rochelle, with the little country towns of Cognac, Jarnac, and Segonzac at its heart.

Other parts of France make brandy: a small amount of quite good brandy called *fine de la Marne* comes from the Champagne district around Rheims, and the truly distinguished product of the district of Armagnac, sold under that name, is also legally protected. But only the brandy of Cognac is *Cognac,* the most luxurious, famous, and—in its noblest manifestations—expensive brandy in the world.

The legally delimited area of Cognac is divided (also by the force of law) into six parts, which, in descending order of the excellence of the brandies they produce are: Grande Champagne, Petite Champagne, Borderies, Fins Bois, Bons Bois, and Bois Ordinaires. They lie, very approximately, in concentric circles, with Grande Champagne at the center. (The two Champagne districts have nothing to do with the sparkling wine of that name. The word is derived from the Latin *campania,* meaning "open country," whereas the Bois brandies—*fins, bons,* and *ordinaires*—come from country that was once thickly wooded.)

The brandies of the Grande Champagne, where the soil is thin and chalky, are the most delicate of all in scent and in subtlety of taste; those of the Petite Champagne are perhaps a shade less elegant, fuller in flavor, because the soil is richer. The region of the Borderies has more clay, and its brandies have a somewhat richer quality of their own. They also age more quickly. The three districts of the Bois produce very good brandies, but they lack the finesse of those grown in the innermost regions: they age faster and have more body.

Brandies produced from any one, or any combination, of these six districts are entitled to the name of Cognac, and this in itself is a patent of nobility. But the finest Cognacs of all are those that come solely from the innermost Grande Champagne district or are a blend of not less than 50 percent Grande Champagne with Petite Champagne.

Once the wine has been distilled, the cask takes over. The Limousin oak comes from the Troncais forest (and only from the edge of the forest, at that). English, Russian, and American oak have been tried and found unsuitable—as has oak even from other parts of France. One type makes the maturing Cognac too bitter, another too musty, another too astringent. It is from the oak that the brandy, colorless to begin with, takes its golden hue, a touch of sweetness, and the tannin to increase its staying power. It is in the oak that the fiery young spirit ages into its mellow maturity. There is a mysterious affinity between the wood from Limousin and the Troncais and the brandy from the nearby region of Cognac. Brandy, like wine, matures in wood; unlike wine, it does not mature in bottle: once a Cognac has been bottled, it stays as it is. A 1900 Cognac bottled in 1950 is still a fifty-year-old Cognac today. If it was a good Cognac in 1950 it is a good Cognac now (unless the cork has deteriorated, or the bottle has been badly stored); if it was poor then, the twenty-odd years in the bottle will have done nothing to improve it.

It is impossible to obtain commercially a completely "single," or unblended Cognac, of one year and from one vineyard—though such things exist, of course, in the distillers' stocks. Nor would it necessarily be a memorable experience to taste one. The small growers of the Charentais sell their wines to the big commercial distillers, whose art is to blend vintages, vineyards, and regions so as to produce a perfectly harmonious and balanced Cognac. There are still single *vintage* years to be had, not of a single vineyard—the vineyards of the region are too small—but of a single district. They are found especially in the great Paris restaurants, such as Lasserre, where I once tasted a 1906 Grande Fine Champagne. But such vintaged Cognacs are becoming fewer and will eventually disappear, because in 1962 the French government announced that it would no longer officially certify the age of any brandy beyond five years—and what is not officially certified may not, in France, appear on a label. Brandy in cask evaporates, up to 4 percent a year, so a cask has to be "refreshed" or topped up. It is virtually impossible to prove that any one cask has been topped up only from another cask of the same age, and the government nowadays will permit a vintage label only if the Cognac can be *proved* to be one hundred percent of that vintage.

What, then, of "Napoleon" brandy? There can be no such thing as a drinkable Cognac now in cask that is one hundred percent of the first Napoleon's time, and even one from the third Napoleon's is more than unlikely. A pre-1815—even a pre-1870—Cognac *in bottle* will certainly be expensive, but may or may not be good. So much for dates. As for the name Napoleon, one particular firm, Courvoisier, has always advertised its Cognac as "the brandy of Napoleon," and it has become the custom of certain other firms to use names with similar historical overtones, such as Aigle Impérial or Louis Philippe, to signify one of their finer blends. In much the same way, in fact, Möet et Chandon style their finest Champagne Dom Pérignon, without meaning to convey that what is in the bottle has been maturing since the days of that worthy seventeenth-century monk.

Does the label on a bottle of Cognac, then, give us any indication of its age? Virtually all brandies now easily obtainable are standard brands from well-known firms; and there is much to be said for such brands. The rare old vintage brandies are hard to find and may or may not be worth their very high price. That strangely-shaped bottle with a "private label," which the waiter pours for you at your favorite Paris bistro may or may not be there next year. But the bottles of the world-famous firms, rich and old enough to hold vast and varied stocks (Hennessy, for instance, founded in 1765, has a hundred thousand casks, and Martell, dating from 1715, has four and a half million gallons) contain blended Cognacs of a very high quality that will remain consistent wherever and whenever drunk.

The basic grade of Cognac from the good houses is three-star and is usually simply known as such, along with its house name. It is a sound, workaday Cognac, not usually offered as a liqueur in a restaurant of any pretensions, and intended chiefly as a mixer or, in a French café, with water as a *fine à l'eau.* One step above three-star is the lowest grade of liqueur Cognac suitable for drinking neat after dinner—V.S.O.P., which originally stood for Very Superior Old Pale (in English, because it was specially labeled for the British market, though some French wags have interpreted it as *Versez Sans Oublier Personne,* or "Pour Without Forgetting Anyone"). Some firms simply use their own names followed by the initials, as for example, Prince Hubert de Polignac V.S.O.P. Others (especially in France) use a trade name; Martell Medallion, for instance, or Delamain R.D. Price is the key; in most spirit shops virtually all three-stars are in one price range and all V.S.O.P.'s are in another higher.

It is above the V.S.O.P. level that you find the truly great liqueur Cognacs. It is impossible to classify them, for at each level of distinction (which usually means of price) the top Cognacs of the best firms will differ not in quality but in style. Tastes differ. When I recently visited Cognac for a few days and tasted several labels of Hennessy with two of the firm's directors, they both said that they slightly preferred their Hennessy X.O., which has an average age of fifty years, to their Hennessy Extra, which has an average age of seventy years and costs very nearly twice as much as the X.O. Why? They both said that just as there are those who prefer their clarets youngish and with a slight "edge" to them, so they think that the Extra, magnificent as it is, is almost *too* bland—lacking a little in the liveliness shown by the X.O., which in turn is rounder in flavor and fragrance than the V.S.O.P. (X.O. is loosely equivalent to other firms'

Extra Vieille, or "old"). Frankly, I prefer the Hennessy Extra, but both it and the X.O. are superb.

Even more expensive than the Hennessy Extra is the similarly splendid Martell Extra, which is also an average of seventy years old. Only just below it in price is the distinguished Martell Cordon Agent, averaging sixty years.

Martell and Hennessy are the two "big boys" of Cognac, but I have heard their directors speak warmly of some smaller firms and their Cognacs, notably of Augier V.S.O.P. and Delamain Pale and Dry, so called because it is certainly paler and drier than some other liqueur Cognacs: both are Grande Fine Champagne. The two top grades of Hine are Family reserve, which is a Fine Champagne about twenty-five years old, and Triomphe, which is slightly younger but superbly smooth.

Other firms that produce an outstanding top quality along with their more workaday Cognacs are Bisquit Dubouche with their Extra; and Rémy Martin with their Louis XIII. All these great Cognacs are ideal for a reflective evening over a rare and delicate liqueur.

If your experience of brandies is limited to Cognac, you owe it to yourself to taste the other great name brandy of France, from the district of Armagnac, in the ancient southwestern province of Gascony. It is accepted as the "second great brandy" of France (permitted its own legal *appellation contrôlée)*—Armagnac. It is easy to find on the store shelves. For centuries it has been bottled in a potbellied, Spanish-style, squat flagon, which has remained unchanged in design and shape for centuries and is called (perhaps in honor of the proximity of the Spanish border) the *Basquaise.* Reflecting the climate of this remote, wild and mountainous, almost Spanish land, Armagnac is as powerful and warm as the Southern sun. On the labels, you will find three Armagnac districts; the best is Bas Armagnac; the second-best is Ténarèze; and the third, Haute Armagnac. Somehow, the *Basquaise* flagon seems to match the gaiety and joviality of Armagnac. Cognac may be an elegant aristocrat, but Armagnac is a handsome, dominating country cousin. The Armagnacs that I have enjoyed in the past few years include Larressingle and the Marquis de Caussade.

There are a few California brandies that prove the point that, with devotion to quality, technical skill, plus, of course, the requisite number of years of wood aging, it is possible to produce a brandy that ably competes with some of the excellent European types. I particularly admire the eight-year-old Christian Brothers X.O. Reserve, the ten-year-old Conti Royal and the eight-year-old Setrakian. Some other

American brandies, however, seem to me to be too much sweetened with Muscat sugar, too heavy in body, and somewhat lacking in finesse and mellow smoothness.

After wine grapes have been crushed and pressed, so that the juice can be run off into the fermenting vats, the "jam" or "mash" that is left behind on the floor of the press, consisting of skins, pits, little stalks, and other mushy gunk, is called, in English, the "pomace" and, in French, the *marc* (note, when pronouncing the word, that it is "mahr," with the *c* silent). It still contains about 80 percent liquid and is by no means a waste product. It is scraped out and carried to a nearby distillery, where the spirit that is made from it is also called *marc,* or *eau de vie de marc.* Some of these local brandies are very rough and are strictly for local consumption. A few are quite fine—very fruity and grapey. The *marcs* of Burgundy are generally considered to be the best, and the outstanding two (hardly unexpectedly, both in quality and high price) are the Marc de l'Hospice de Beaune and the Marc du Domaine de la Romanée Conti. There are also excellent versions from the wine villages of Chambertin, Meursault, Montrachet, and Musigny. Those I have tasted recently include the Marc à la Cloche de Bourgogne, the Marc de Marc from the Rhône, and the Romanée Conti.

What is called *marc* in France is called *grappa* in Italy. It is generally rather rough and always very strong. It is fun to drink, but, I must confess, hardly a supreme gastronomic experience. A few are imported, but for the real fire and frolic you have to do your exploring in the country districts of Italy. In village trattorias in the back country behind Venice, I have drunk yellow *grappa,* white *grappa,* and some with branches of fresh herbs resting gracefully inside the bottle. Perhaps the best I have ever drunk was in the Ligurian hills south of Genoa.

There are at least two good brandies from Spain, both considerably sweeter than Cognac and substantially heavier in body. They are distilled out as part of the process of making Sherry, and both labels carry the names of famous Sherry-making companies: the Fundador of Pedro Domecq and the Lepanto of Gonzalez Byass.

One rather famous and good brandy comes from Germany, Asbach-Uralt, with several more from Greece, of which, perhaps, the best known is Metaxa. It does qualify as a brandy, although it is darker, slightly sweeter, and a tiny bit thicker on the tongue than most other brandies. It is distilled in Piraeus, the port city of Athens. One supposes that it is a favorite of the local sailors.

B. The Dry Fruit Brandies of Alsace, Germany, Switzerland, and Other Places

We have now explored all the brandies made from grapes. But the distiller need not stop there. He can produce a spirit from virtually every living plant by converting its natural sugar into alcohol. Vodka came, traditionally, from potatoes. The Scandinavian aquavit starts as wood pulp. Also, of course, the apple is involved in such universally known distillations as American Applejack and the marvelous Calvados of Normandy. In my experience, however, the most delightful of the distilling games is played with the less universal cultivated and wild fruits. These are not sweet liqueurs. They are bone-dry brandies. The fruit is crushed and fermented, so that all the sugar disappears, but the natural oils, which give each fruit its characteristic taste, are held in suspension in the spirits. So what you finally get in your mouth is a concentration, a magnified essence, of the personality of the fruit. The color completely disappears. The liquid is as clear as water. Its name once again, is *eau de vie*, water of life.

There are so many of these different fruit brandies that it is hard to remember them all. I have tasted rare ones in roadside inns in the Black Forest of Germany, in mountain châlets in Switzerland, and in unexpected places in many parts of the world, but by far the largest number and variety of these fruit brandies are made and consumed in Alsace. In that lovely corner of France, the making of fruit spirit from everything that grows seems to be a national sport. If, therefore, these impressions of mine seem to be slightly weighted in favor of Alsace, it is not for lack of appreciation of the beautiful products of Germany, Switzerland, and other countries, but because I have had so many more dramatic experiences with Alsatian friends in the country auberges of their lovely land. More and more of these brandies, incidentally, from Alsace, Germany, Switzerland, and elsewhere are now being widely distributed. They are eminently worth exploring as a *digestif* after dinner, or in place of grape brandy at any time.

Once, in the almost miniature dining room of one of those small inns on the high slopes of the Vosges Mountains in Alsace, I saw twenty-two tasting glasses lined up before one guest, each with a different fruit brandy. The old and whiskered Alsatian gourmet then proceeded to down the twenty-two glasses one after the other and was enraged when, as he rose, slightly unsteadily, from his chair, the waiter offered to help him down the stairs. Among those twenty-two varieties there were spirits from fruits grown in the cultivated fields and orchards along the banks of the Rhine: pear, cherry, apple, the superb Queen Claude greengage plum, apricot, prune, medlar, as well as the *quetsch* purple plum and the *mirabelle* golden plum, both unique to Alsace. And that only starts the list. From the woods and hedges of the mountain slopes come the wilder spirits from the wild berries: blueberry, elderberry, blackberry, the miniature woodland strawberry *fraise des bois,* wild raspberry, the *alizier* service berry, the sloe berry, and even a spirit from the bright red holly berry. Also, as if that were not enough, there are spirits from the bright yellow root of the gentian flower, from cumin seed, from the buds of pine trees, and one, a personal blend of each producer, called simply Tutti Frutti. From Germany, the principal fruit spirits are the Himbeergeist from the wild raspberry of the Black Forest, the Johanisbeer from the black-currant, Heidelbeer from the huckleberry, and Preiselbeer from the cranberry, in addition to the standard fruits. From Hungary comes the marvelous Barack Pálinka made from the especially large and luscious apricots of that most fertile land. From Yugoslavia there is the fiery Slivovitz from the black plum. From Switzerland there are two special glories: the Zuger Kirschwasser, the cherry brandy from the canton of Zug, and the Williamine from the brown Williams pear—the latter being, in my opinion, perhaps the most perfect translation of the character of a fresh fruit into the spirit of a brandy. It is like drinking an essence of pears fresh from the trees.

An Alsatian host, immediately after you have drunk your hot after-dinner coffee, will pour a *rasade,* an ounce or so of his fruit brandy, into your still-hot cup. The warmth will instantly make the bouquet leap up to envelop you with its multiplicity of savors and scents. This is the secret of enjoying the fruit brandies. They should never be drunk ice-cold. Even at room temperature, in a tiny snifter, you should cup one in your hands for a little extra warmth. It is always to be sipped and tasted, rather than drunk.

One of the noblest of the fruit brandies is the Marc de Gewürztraminer, distilled from the famous Alsatian wine grape by, among others, the Trimbach family in the lovely village of Ribeauvillé. Whenever I sip it, I remember a story once told me by my Alsatian friend Xavier Dumoulin. His mother once owned a small inn in the Vosges Mountains. Every morning, precisely at eleven o'clock, a little old lady would come in, sit at the table by the window in the bar, and order a triple glass of *marc.* Then she would bring out of the huge pocket of her skirt a pipe, a tin of tobacco, and a *weck,* a small loaf of bread, which she had baked that morning and which was still warm. Smoking her pipe, she carefully dunked pieces of the bread in the brandy and consumed it with sucking noises you could hear across the room. At last, when she had wiped the glass dry with the last piece of bread, she called out to Xavier's mother, "Pauline, my bread has drunk my brandy. Now give *me* a glass." This ceremony was precisely repeated at exactly the same time every morning for uncounted years. Finally, at the age of ninety-five, the old lady died—no, not what you think—of being knocked down by a runaway horse.

The Kirsch cherry brandy of Switzerland, Germany, and Alsace is made from small black cherries by such famous family firms as Dopff, Etter, Jacobert, Mampe, Mercedes, Riemerschmid, and Schladerer. The brandy called Quetsch takes its name from the Alsatian purple plum. After the Williams pear of Switzerland, I think the *Mirabelle* translates most perfectly into spirit and the one I have especially enjoyed is distilled by the Blanck family in the village of Kintzheim. My third choice is the world-famous Framboise Sauvage, wild raspberry.

There are classic rules in Alsace for tasting these fruit brandies so as to draw from each the full depth of its flavor and savor. I have already said that you warm the glass with your hands; then, of course, you must swirl the glass and let your nose absorb the bouquet. Next, press the glass to your mouth, but take only just enough to wet your lips. Lightly pass the tip of your tongue across your lips. Now take a larger sip. Roll it around your tongue. Hold it in your mouth a full second. Swallow it. Concentrate your judgment on the aftertaste. Now take a full sip and try to analyze, one by one, the complexities of your sensations. What will you find? Each taster's impressions are personal. I can only give you mine.

The blackberry has less scent and is, perhaps, a slightly less satisfactory translation of the fruit. I prefer the elderberry. The blueberry has relatively little bouquet, but if you sip it extremely slowly you get an impressionistic essence of blueberries, not cultivated, as we know them, but in their original, wild state, with all the flowery scents of the fields and the woods. The service berry has an attractive, distant bitterness, but with the bouquet of mountain flowers, somehow combined with the light scent of those little marzipan men we hang on Christmas trees. The spirit made from the buds of pine trees is one of the rarest, the most difficult to distill, and the most extraordinary. The sharpness of the resin is gone, but the ambience of pine remains. It is almost a liquid cough drop. There is a spirit made from the eglantine rose, which, because of the damage done to the pickers by its thorns, is officially called (and the words are printed on the label) *gratte cul* ("scratch arse"). The brandy of the hawthorn berry is seldom found outside private homes in Alsace. It is gentle, subtle, with the distant scent of honeysuckle.

The *baies de houx* is entirely unique to Alsace. The red holly berries are picked in the mountains a few weeks before Christmas, when the frost is heavy on the trees and the labor of picking the berries from among the thorny leaves in sufficient quantity for a single distillation is a heavy task. The gentle, slow distillation is usually over the Christmas holidays. This brandy is, of all of them, the most difficult to understand and like, until you know it well. At first it has a sharpness and bitterness that are almost repellent. But, if you persist and make it your friend, you will find in it the perfume of a mountain forest after a heavy storm of summer rain, with the almost indefinable sense of wet earth, of flowers, of leaves, of roots, of mosses, of mushrooms.

The dry fruit brandies are consoling soothers against the speed and tension of the modern world. They disclose their pleasures slowly, subtly. They offer a moment of contemplative peace, when guests gather within the circle of hospitality and friendship.

C. The Highly Aromatic Genever or Holland Gins

I admit that I am a conservative revolutionary. I would like to revolutionize the drinking of alcohol and go back to something that was, truly, much better at an earlier time. I am not interested in alcohol simply as medicine—simply for the "lift" it is supposed to give me, without any of the pleasures of bouquet, color, or taste. Everybody knows that alcohol, in its absolutely purest state, is as colorless, smell-less, and tasteless as water. My chief interest is in all the exciting, extraordinary, gorgeous, joyous, lovely, marvelous, perhaps partly poisonous, probably unsanitary, wonderful "impurities" that, in the forms of oils and finely suspended powders, become mixed up with the alcohol to make all the greatest drinks in the world. What would there be of Cognac, rum, whisky, wine, if there were no impurities? They would all be one and the same product—vodka. And vodka, as we all know, is required by law to be colorless, smell-less, tasteless. I say, *Vive* the impurities!

Yet the trend everywhere seems to be toward drinks that have less and less taste. People seem to want to absorb their alcohol without knowing that it is going down. Gin is getting drier and drier—tastelesser and tastelesser. More and more drinkers are switching to vodka. Rum is being made lighter and lighter. Now comes the latest "improvement"—lighter, less tasty whiskeys.

In navigating a ship, you can never find out where you are unless you know where you have come from. In navigating among the modern drinks, you cannot understand how far we have come, unless you can taste things as they once were.

Gin was discovered at the University of Leyden in Holland, by Franciscus Sylvius, who used juniper berries to flavor the spirit because, he thought, alcohol alone would taste raw and nasty.

The Dutch, of course, have "modernized" their distilling and now make many "dry" and more or less tasteless gins. But they also stick to the old types, which we call "Holland" and they call "Genever." That name, which means juniper, is the root source of our word *gin*. The mark of the modern *"Genever"* is that, instead of taking the taste away from it, the Dutch distillers grind the juniper berries and other aromatic herbs into their malted barley mash, so that the final spirit is much higher in flavoring oils, has a bouquet of strong character, and tastes of a delectable, fruity, and subtle sweetness. Make no mistake about it, it is a drink of personality and strength. It is not a good mixer in wishy-washy cocktails. A little of it is the essential "secret ingredient" of my Perfect Martini, described in chapter 3. Under the Bols label, it comes from Holland in stone crocks, which should be stored for use in the coldest part of the refrigerator. There is one other, very famous, Genever gin, which is extremely hard to find, but which I consider to be among the very greatest, the most unusual, and the nearest to perfection of all spirits. It is distilled in Holland's northerly and coldest province, Friesland, where it is filled into square, squat bottles. For this reason, it is known all over Holland as "the Old Square from Friesland." This Rolls-Royce of Genever gin is made by a small, family-owned company, headed by an obstinate idealist named Pieter Bokma, who doesn't seem to care very much whether or not he sends his gin overseas. Sometimes it arrives. More often it does not.

Whenever I pass through the Schiphol Amsterdam airport, I pick up a few bottles of Bokma in the duty-free store. The price works out at around two dollars a quart. I keep one of these square bottles in my freezer, where the Bokma Genever becomes slightly thick, like super-dry honey. A small tasting glass of this on a cold winter morning is my idea of nectar.

D. The Range of Rums

Ernest Hemingway once said that rum (which is the alcoholic essence of sugar—the name comes from *saccharum*, Latin for "sugar") has a greater variety of colors and characters, of flavors and bouquets, of strengths and textures than any other distilled spirit. Whiskeys and gins are made from almost every sort of grain. Brandies come not only from grapes, but from a whole range of fruits. Yet all these vary much less than do the rums. One rum may be as colorless and very nearly as tasteless as water, while another may have the color of distilled gold, with a rich and smooth taste to match. Still others are dark mahogany and among the most powerful of all spirits, with more than 75 percent alcohol.

So it's hardly surprising that, say, three carefully chosen bottles of different rums in the home bar can provide such a dramatic array of mixed drinks. Rum may come an hour before lunch as a "fizz" of fluffy white velvet. Or in midafternoon as a tall, fruit-decked punch. Or a frosty daiquiri before dinner. Or in a brandy snifter after dinner. Or in a party punch bowl at any degree of convivial strength. And since good rum has a special affinity for the refreshing citrus juices, with enough character not to become tasteless when served close to freezing, it is my special favorite for almost any kind of icy cooler. Yet no rum drink can be dramatically successful without the "secret factor," which is the right degree of "rumminess."

This is the problem. Few people seem to know how to choose the right rum for the right purpose. Going to the corner liquor store and asking for "a bottle of rum" is about as useless as going to the butcher and asking for "a piece of meat." The late Harold J. Grossman, an authority on the subject, once said that the rums with the greatest character do not speak Spanish, but have the lilting accents of the British Caribbean colonies, coupled with the foggy Cockney of London. What he meant was that some of the finest rums have, for more than two hundred years, been shipped from the West Indies to England to be aged in casks (sometimes for fifteen years or more) in the cold damp atmosphere of the bonded warehouses of the London docks before being blended, bottled, and shipped all over the world. This luxurious operation has been seriously undermined—in fact the whole rum industry has been turned topsy-turvy—by three upheavals in the last thirty years.

First, for almost six years the German submarine warfare in the Atlantic during World War II cut off the shipments of Caribbean rums to London and started the trend toward aging and bottling on their own side of the ocean. The same German submarines also prevented Scotch whisky from reaching the United States, creating an enormous demand for rum—a demand partially met by the virtual "explosion" of mass-production rum industries in Puerto Rico and the Virgin Islands. (These American rums, not subject to the U.S. alcohol import tax, have a considerable price advantage over their imported competitors.) Also, large quantities of light rums were imported from Cuba, the land where the daiquiri was invented.

Second, the coming of Castro eliminated Cuban rum from the U.S. market and gave another enormous boost to the Puerto Rican and Virgin Islands industries.

Third, the granting of independence to the British Caribbean colonies (especially Jamaica, Guyana, and Barbados, in terms of rum) has led to the breaking of centuries-old commercial ties, to the disappearance of famous rum names, and to the taking over of the old estates by new owners with new ideas as to the making and selling of rum. So the search for good rum is bound to involve some knowledge as to how it has developed and how it is made.

Political upheavals are nothing new in the more than two-thousand-year history of sugar cane and rum. The very tall grass with a sweet sap was probably discovered for the Western world by Alexander the Great in the fourth century B.C. during his overland march to India, when he reported finding a sweet-tasting wild plant. Almost a thousand years later Moorish sea captains brought it to the Mediterranean, carried it with them when they invaded Spain, and planted it in the Canary Islands. In 1493 Christopher Columbus called there on his second voyage to the New World and took the first sugar-cane cuttings to the West Indies. Here the tall grass found its ideal combination of soil, water, and weather and has flourished as nowhere else in the world. Very soon the workers in the fields discovered that the juice could easily be fermented in the hot climate and roughly distilled in an earthenware pot. The result was a potent drink, described in a seventeenth-century report on life in Barbados as "kill-devil...a hot, hellish and terrible liquor."

Soon commercial distilleries were set up in various countries and kept supplied with thick sugar molasses brought by ship from the West Indies. One of the first rum distilleries on the American continent was set up by the British on Staten Island in 1664, when they kicked the Dutch out of Nieu Amsterdam and renamed it New York. The industry then moved northward and became colonial New England's largest, most profitable, and most unsavory business. The profits from rum were almost entirely used in a vicious triangle to finance the slave trade. More and more ships were outfitted to bring slaves from Africa to the West Indies, to grow more sugar cane, to ship more molasses to Boston, to make more rum, to amass more profits, to bring more slaves.... At the peak of this cycle, the average consumption of rum in New England was four gallons per year for every man, woman, and child. Finally the American rum industry was undermined and virtually destroyed by the discovery of a far cheaper form of spirits invented by a Baptist clergyman in Bourbon County, Virginia. Today there are still two or three good New England rums (and a couple or so in Florida), but there are sound reasons why the best rums are made in the tropical lands where the sugar cane grows.

Experts say that there are three main factors in the making of a great rum. First is the mineral content of the soil, which affects the sap of the growing cane. Second is the live yeast that must trigger the fermentation of the mash. In certain areas (notably Barbados, Haiti, Jamaica, and Martinique), spores of live yeast are actually floating in the air and settle naturally on the surface of the rum-to-be in the open vats. In other areas, the yeast has to be cultivated in a laboratory and injected into the mash. Third is the natural quality of the water used for the refining. When there is an affinity and unity between local soil, a local strain of yeast, and pure local water, the result is generally a great rum.

But many steps precede the greatness. The historic method of production was to press all the juice out of the cane, using the entire crop for rum. This luxurious and wasteful method is now used by less than half a dozen producers in the entire world. Among the best known of these luxury rums is Plantation Saint James from Martinique, Barbancourt from Haiti, and Eldorado from Puerto Rico. These have too much subtlety for mixed drinks. They are best sipped after dinner from a brandy snifter.

The more efficient method, probably covering 99 percent of all rums, is to make them as an afterproduct of the manufacture of sugar. The cane juice is boiled down until the sugar crystallizes out. The remaining molasses is fermented, refined, and distilled. This may be done slowly, over as long as twelve days in a "pot still," or very quickly, in as little as twelve hours in a mass-production "column still." The first way keeps the natural character of the rum. The second "purifies" the rum until it has neither color nor taste. The final smoothness comes from years of aging in oak casks and highly skilled blending. Each producer tries to keep the same character in his brand year after year. But among the hundreds of different labels, no two rums in the world are exactly alike.

Choosing the Right Rum

One man's rum is another man's poison. The decision is a matter of personal preference, but there are a few basic rules:

1. There is a certain family resemblance among the rums from a particular area. Get to know which of these families you prefer. Taste the aged golden rums for which Jamaica is famous. Try the dark Demeraras grown and distilled in Guyana, but aged and blended in London. (Demerara, incidentally, is the name of a river, a town, and a valley.) Test the light rums from Barbados and Puerto Rico. And these are only a beginning.

2. Within each area, there are usually two or three famous family names that are a reliable guarantee of quality. Start with their products as a standard of comparison. My personal list of the best-known names in alphabetical order: from Barbados, Mount Gay; from Guyana, Lemon Hart; from Hawaii, Leilani; from Jamaica, Appleton and Wray & Nephew; from Puerto Rico, Bacardi, Anejo, and Don Q.

3. Remember that each of the large firms bottles a range of rums for different purposes.
White rums: The lightest, least "rummy," and often least satisfactory. Some are deliberately made colorless and tasteless, so as to be inexpensive competitors of the dry gins and vodkas. The better white rums, in my experience, come from Barbados and Jamaica. They are fine for light daiquiris and other short cocktails, but less suitable for tall drinks and punches.

Golden rums: The all-purpose mixers, varying in a wide sweep from the lightest and palest to the rich and full-bodied, which are a specialty of the great rum estates of Jamaica.

Dark Demerara rums: The most aromatic and powerful, with a velvet smoothness that comes from years of barrel aging. They are too dominant for cocktails, but fine for superpunches with a super punch!

Luxury rums: For sipping straight or on the rocks. The label should specify how many years of aging. Eight years is a good average. Fifteen years makes them soft and silky. Apart from those already mentioned, my favorites include: Lemon Hart's "15-year Golden Jamaica" and Puerto Rican "Ron del Barrilito."

Mixing Rum Drinks

The Calypso entertainers of Barbados often sing the basic recipe for a rum drink with a strong downbeat:

> *One of sour*
> *Two of sweet*
> *Three of strong*
> *And four of weak.*

The *sour* is almost always freshly squeezed lime juice, which has an extraordinary affinity for rum. A very few recipes require lemon, or grapefruit, or other citrus juices.

The *sweet* can always be superfine white sugar, but the secret of "wowing" one's guests is learning to improvise with the various sweetening syrups described in Chaper 23 or liqueurs, which are discussed in Chapter 27.

The *strong* may be straight rum or a mixture of spirits.

The *weak* is usually the crushed ice, but may also be club soda or mineral water.

A note on nibbling: A perfectly made rum drink is so aromatic that it overpowers normal canapés like cheeses, nuts, and olives. Instead, concentrate on bland things with interesting textures: crackly biscuits, Italian Amaretti macaroons, or French Petits Beurre. Perhaps the best hors d'oeuvre with rum is the one always placed before Ernest Hemingway when he sat down on one of the high stools at the La Floridita bar in Havana: a heaping dish of spiced boiled shrimp.

E. Whiskies, Single Malt and Blended

"There are two things in this world I like naked," said the bearded and kilted Highlander in the small Scottish inn, touching to his lips the glass of amber liquid, "and one of them is loud whisky." I hardly knew what he meant. I was eleven years old.

I have since learned some of the truth of his philosophy—especially of that word *loud,* which is the essence of a vigorous point of view about Scotch. The historic enmity between the gently rolling southern Lowlands of Scotland and her wildly mountainous northern Highlands is hardly news. The same sharp division, if not the enmity, persists in the world of whisky.

Just about half of Scotland's *uisge* (one of its original Gaelic names) is produced in the Lowlands, in no more than a dozen enormous, mass-production factories equipped with automatic column stills, which can keep running continuously, day and night, if necessary. An endless supply of grain is fed in at one end and an endless stream of the basic spirit spurts out at the other. Then, in the mile-long blending sheds stacked to the roof with casks of aged essences, the various combinations are mixed (often as many as thirty or forty different essences go into one blend) to create the amber liquids for bottles with shapes and labels recognized around the world.

This is a big, push-button, computerized business, controlled by giant corporations with worldwide connections. Yet to my old Highland philosopher these Lowland blends are "silent" whiskies, with no romance about them, no regional character. "Silent," he said, "because, when I sip them, they don't talk to me as they go down."

The other half of the Scotch whiskies are made in roughly a hundred small, separate distilleries dotted among the romantic glens, sea lochs, and offshore islands in some of the world's most beautiful mountain scenery. Each distillery is no bigger than a group of barns around the yard of a one-family farm. Instead of dry, lifeless grain, the base ingredient is now living malted barley. There is nothing continuous about the operation. It is a batch process in pot stills, which have to be cleaned out after each cycle.

The spirit is produced laboriously, temperamentally, even mysteriously. No one knows the exact combination of mountain spring water, salt air from the sea, and smoky peat fire that makes the product of one distillery different from the next, even two miles down the road. No one dreams of blending one whisky with another. The words of honor on each label are "unblended single malt." These are the "vintage" whiskies, the whiskies my old Highland friend said "go down the throat singing hymns."

It would be perfectly fair to ask what I was doing, at the tender age of eleven, learning about whisky from a Highland philosopher of obviously low moral character. My involvement with the alcoholic aspects of the Highlands was set on the day of my baptism, when I was named Roy in honor of the somewhat minuscule Scottish side of our family, as represented by a maiden aunt, Ethel Roy Pattison McFarquhar. From that moment on, whenever she came from her Highland home to visit us in London she always filled me with delight by treating me as if I were five years older than I really was. As soon as she considered me mature enough, she took me north with her and began to make a Scotsman of me. It was the summer following my tenth birthday. Aunt Ethel had a theory that a boy became a man when he had two digits to his age—and manhood involved the priceless privilege of knowing whisky. I soon discovered that she had either a family or a financial interest in a number of Highland distilleries. She believed in keeping an eye on them. She was a prodigious hiker and knew every shortcut up the glens, across the moors, or over the mountain trails. Her plan was always to sneak up to the back door of the distillery and check the operations before going around to the front door for the social visit and inevitable tasting. What my aunt taught me on these trips made me a lifelong devotee of Highland malt whisky, and I consider her the greatest connoisseur I have known. I can still see every detail of our progress together.

As we came down the mountain in the morning mist, I remember the square blockhouse of the malt kiln below us, with its pagodalike copper roof (through which the peat smoke escaped) glinting in the sunlight with an almost oriental air. Above the distillery there was always a stream running brown with peat as it tumbled over the rocks. This water, which runs just as brown from the faucets of the surrounding houses, my aunt explained, is the major secret of Highland whisky. If chemists knew how to duplicate it artificially, they would have done so long ago. But the mystery remains. After an old pot still is repaired with a new piece, the stillman will always first boil some mountain water in it to "sweeten the new metal."

My aunt began her tour of inspection in the storage barn, stacked to the rafters with sacks of dry barley. She loudly sniffed the air, making sure it was sweet, with no trace of the souring mustiness that warns of dampness and moldering. Next, she went to the malthouse, which always seemed to me like an enormous ballroom, with men performing a slow and complicated dance. The dry barley had now been steeped in the magic brown water and was spread out on the smooth wooden floor. Men moved across it, sliding their feet so as not to crush the pellets, stirring and turning them with long wooden shovels. Soon nature brought each pellet to life, sprouting a tiny green shoot and converting the starch (the basic food for the seed) into sugar. After a week or more of this growth, the barley is said to be "green malted."

In the drying kiln, the growth is abruptly arrested by roasting the malted barley over a smoky fire. The pellets are spread on a fine wire mesh above glowing peat, and the whole atmosphere is charged with the aromatic smoke that will give the special character to the whisky from this distillery. In the next building, the brittle barley, having now been crushed, is soaked with hot water in huge, vatlike mash tuns, where the sugar dissolves into a nonalcoholic liquid called wort. This is strained, the yeasts are added, and the boiling, frothing fermentation begins.

I once tried to lean over the much bruised wooden lip of one of the huge larchwood vats, and the rising carbon dioxide knocked me back as if I had been punched in the face. Perhaps this fermentation is the central mystery of Scotch. Apart from the chemical yeasts, the process is magnified by all kinds of wild and unclassified spores and bacteria settling on the surface of the wort. Some float down from the roof beams, others breed in the unpainted corners of the walls. The fear of disturbing the wild yeasts is the root of many famous stories.

The Old Rope Trick

At one distillery, for instance, there was an old rope conveyor linking the various buildings. One day the rope broke and a sack of coal fell on a man and killed him. The matter was taken to court, and the judge insisted that the old and dilapidated rope must be replaced by a steel chain. "Nah, nah! I canna permit that," said the distillery manager. "It might change the character of my whisky!" The rope, he explained, was a breeding ground for wild yeast spores. The judge, a lover of good whisky, compromised. The chain was installed, but the rope was left in place and was shaken every hour on the hour while fermentation was in progress.

The last building my aunt and I entered was the stillhouse. At first I found it a little frightening; it was rather dark, lit only by the licking flames, and the eerie shapes of the glinting copper pot stills were like the retorts of some giant alchemist. There was a strange and ghostly sound, a distant rumbling felt as a vibration, as if some sleeping monster were slowly stirring in the cellar (actually the sound of a large copper chain being dragged around inside the still to agitate the boiling brew). Suddenly there was a great clang as the stillman took hold of a large wooden ball, suspended by a wire from the ceiling, and crashed it against the side of the pot. By listening to the reverberations, he could tell how hard his brew was boiling. The alcohol vapor rose and entered a narrowing and downward-bending pipe, which led to the water-cooled "worm," where the alcohol was condensed into clear spirit. Finally, after being checked for quality and measured for taxes by the government excise man, it was run off into old Sherry casks, to give it color as it aged and softened over years of waiting in the cool warehouse.

The Scotch Symphony

Aunt Ethel divided the Scotch world into three parts and compared them to sections of a symphony orchestra. She felt that no house was ready for entertaining without at least one bottle of each type. First, there should be one of the fine blended whiskies for everyday use; she likened these to the double basses that give volume and richness to the Scotch orchestra. Second, there should be one of the smoky whiskies from the offshore islands of Islay, Orkney, or Skye; these are the cellos, the essence of all the flavors of all Scotches. The concentrated flavor is not to everyone's taste. Some say it is too "peaty." I do not agree. I think everyone with a serious interest in Scotch should taste at least once, say, an Islay unblended single malt like Laphroaig. Third come the grandest whiskies of all, the lordly Glenlivets and their far-northern cousins, the soaring violins with their extraordinary delicacy and finesse, to be drunk from snifters like the finest of Cognacs. The aged Glenlivets have, *par excellence,* the fruity ambience that Scottish connoisseurs regard as the mark of greatness.

Who invented whisky? The Irish, hardly unexpectedly, say it was Saint Patrick. The Scots stoutly disagree. The oldest official reference is in the files of the Scottish Treasury, an entry dated 1494 of "Eight bolls of malt to Friar John Corr wherewith to make aqua vitae." The Latin name for the "water of life" was then translated into Gaelic among several dialectical variations as *uisge beatha,* then shortened to *uiskie.* Meanwhile, the government had set a tax "on every pynt of aquavytie or strong watters," and this set off the two-hundred-year Whisky War between the revenue agents and the illicit mountain distillers. In 1618 there was an account of the funeral of a Scottish laird when all the mourners were arrested at the wake for drinking bootleg whisky. In fact, in those stirring days, *uiskie* seems to have been strongly connected with funerals.

In the mountain village of Glenlivet, the famous pioneer was George Smith, who, before he "went legal" and took out the first license for the Glenlivet Distillery, spent years as a bootlegger. One Saturday night at the local inn, after he had had a dram too many, he boasted to a friend that he would be sending a firkin of whisky on the North Road to Inverness on Monday. His boast was overheard by a revenue agent, who promptly organized a posse of twenty revenuers and policemen and set up a roadblock. On Monday everything on wheels was stopped and searched, but nothing was found. By midafternoon the line of waiting wagons stretched almost a mile. Then someone called, "Make way for the funeral procession!" The drivers pulled their horses to the side of the road and even the revenue agents stood at attention and lifted their caps. At sundown the fruitless search was abandoned.

Next morning the revenue agent visited George Smith at his farm. Apart from the necessities of the Whisky War, the two men were good friends. "Do you realize, George," said the revenue man, "the money that was wasted on that search? You've always been a man of your word. Why did you make that false statement on Saturday night?"

Smith bristled. "It was not false, Jock. We took the whisky through. It was sold in Inverness last night."

"You did!" said the agent, jumping to his feet. "Can you prove it? Have you a witness?"

"Aye," said Smith, "there's yerself. Man, ye took off yer hat to it."

Every year more and more whisky was made in the Highlands, but so great was the local demand, and so slow was pot-still production, that whisky was virtually unknown outside Scotland, until the invention of the machine that changed everything.

Mass Production Strikes Again

At the Dock Distillery in Dublin an engineer named Aeneas Coffey invented a new kind of still, known today around the world as the

"Coffey continuous-operation column still." In principle, it is a vertical tube with superheated steam blowing up from the bottom and the alcoholic wash dropping down from the top. The two streams meet halfway, and the alcohol is instantly volatilized and drawn off down a side tube. Supremely efficient. Continuous operation. Enormous production. Only one problem: the impurities are so completely removed that the spirit comes out as clear, colorless, odorless, and tasteless as water. You can age it for fifty years in a Sherry cask without the slightest improvement. It is the impurities passed through by the inefficient pot still that give the Highland whisky its character.

Yet the profit-making possibilities of the new Coffey still were so obvious as to make it irresistible. In 1832 a group of Lowland industrialists brought it to Glasgow. Since there wasn't enough barley available to feed into the continuously hungry mouth of the new machine, the operators turned to other grain, mostly corn. The resultant alcoholic liquid is generally known today as "grain neutral spirits." The accent should be heavily on the "neutral." I am very fond of it—for rubbing my back. Try as they would, the early Glasgow industrialists could not sell the stuff as whisky; so they shipped most of it to England, where it was flavored with juniper and sold as gin.

The salvation of the Lowland industrialists and the ultimate international triumph of Scotch were due to an act of desperation by a whisky wholesaler in Edinburgh named Andrew Usher. He was selling good malt whisky brought down from the Highlands, and there was never enough to go around. He was also beginning to dabble in grain neutral spirits, and there was always as much as you wanted of that. Usher conceived the revolutionary idea of blending them. Could he make a little of the Highland essence go an infinitely long way with the grain? He could—and if ever there was a billion-dollar idea in the history of the world, this was it.

The Intoxication of Success

Total cooperation between Highlands and Lowlands did not come easily or immediately. For the next fifty years the Highlanders fought against what they considered to be the deadly and fearful competition of the Lowlanders. This struggle culminated in the famous "What Is Whisky" lawsuit, in which the Highlanders tried to stop the Lowlanders from using the word *whisky* in labeling the blended grain spirits. After four years of legal wrangling, a Royal Commission ruled that spirits distilled from barley or from other grain, in pot still or column still, provided they were produced by Scottish manpower on Scottish soil, could all be labeled "Scotch."

Cooperation having thus been established by force, there followed a half century of unbelievably rich progress. Before 1900 hardly a soul outside Scotland had ever heard of Scotch. By 1950 the entire world was clamoring for it. Demand was always ahead of supply. Colorful leaders arose within the industry and enshrined their names on the bottle labels: John Dewar, John Walker, James Buchanan, John Haig, among others. These men founded companies that have been fantastically successful.

For example, the whisky that sells more than any other around the world is Johnnie Walker Red Label, which is marketed worldwide with eight hundred different labels and bottle shapes. Apparently the package is more important than the goods. A top Walker executive said recently, "It's really amazing how people drink with their eyes. If only they would learn to drink with their tongues, we could sell them better-quality whisky at a lower price."

But the labels remain of paramount importance. They are part of the romance of Scotland, dramatized by the pictures of Highland bagpipers, Highland sword dancers, Highland castles, Highland glens, and Highland mountains, working their charm especially on Lowland labels!

And there is nothing much wrong with the image of Scotch so long as there are new stories about its energizing force. The latest concerns the rumor (obviously started by Scotsmen) that the salmon are not running quite so well these days up the River Shannon, so that wealthy Irishmen have to come to Scotland's River Spey. An Irishman was fishing one of the great pools with no luck when a Scottish lad came along and called out, "How is it?"

"Not a bite all morning,"

"What are you using?"

"Sandworms."

"I have an idea. Cast your hook over to me." The Scottish lad caught the line, took from his sporran a small flask filled with an amber liquid, and carefully lowered the worm on the hook into it. Then he swung it back to the fisherman. At the next cast, the line snapped tight, the reel howled, the rod bent almost double.

"Did the fish take it already?" yelled the Scots lad.

"Begorra no! The worm has a six-foot salmon by the throat."

As to the second of the great whiskeys, Bourbon, in spite of the tall stories, the romance, all the Kentucky colonels, all the frosted Mint Juleps, all the Kentucky Derby Day palaver, the Kentucky charm, and the Kentucky drawl, it is a bit of a shock to discover that Bourbon whiskey was invented in Virginia. In 1789, when it all began, Bourbon County was a part of Virginia. Later it was transferred to Kentucky. Now the law says that anyone can make Bourbon whiskey anywhere, in any county of any state, but, in my humble opinion, the best still comes from Kentucky. Whether I am picking up a bottle to take home, or sitting at a bar in any major city anywhere in the world, I ask for one of the classic Bourbons—Jim Beam, J. W. Dant, Early Times, Glenmore, I. W. Harper, Heaven Hill, Kentucky Tavern, Mattingly and Moore, Henry McKenna, Old Crow, Old Fitzgerald, Old Forester, Old Grand Dad, Old Hickory, Old Taylor, James E. Pepper, Walker's, Wild Turkey, to name only a few—to make sure that I get a prime, true, veritable Bourbon aged for at least two years in a charred white-oak barrel. If you are doubtful about the quality of an unknown brand, hold the bottle up to the light. The color should be a deep red. Then shake the bottle. Small beads will form around the neck. There should be plenty of them and they should hold, to show a good body. Open the bottle. The aroma should be pungent and sweet. Pour about half an ounce into the cupped palm of your left hand. Rub both palms together and, at once, cup them around your nose. The scent should be as clean as country air. If there is anything acrid or harsh about it, don't bother to drink the whiskey. Incidentally, the phrase on the label "Bottled in bond" is no special guarantee of quality, beyond the fact that this particular Bourbon has been aged for at least four years.

I hate to think that it may get harder and harder to find "old-fashioned Premium" whiskeys. My much-loved, authentic rye is already virtually extinct. Only the determined aficionados of Maryland and Pennsylvania seem to be holding out for it. It has that slight variation of taste from the fact that it uses rye mash instead of corn. The only labels I can still find regularly are Old Overholt, Rittenhouse, and Wild Turkey. I refuse to look down my nose at corn whiskey. In fact, I like the stuff when it is properly aged. But there is only one label I can find consistently: Southern Pride.

Which brings us to the slightly less glamorous world of the blended whiskeys, where a little whiskey—usually about one-third—is made to go a long way further by being "enlarged" with two-thirds of colorless, smell-less, tasteless, neutral spirits. But now there is something new—"light whiskey." The trend toward less taste has caught up with American whiskey. These newer, blander types are labeled, among others, Crow Light, J. W. Dant Light, Four Roses Light, Galaxy, Honey Go Light, Red Satin, Royal American Light, and White Balloon, making them sound as if they ought to be called "pop whiskeys."

Canadian whiskey is also blended, but without the neutral spirits. It is a mistake to think of it as rye. The predominant grain mash in Canadian distilling is corn. Canadian law requires that it all be made in Canada and that the minimum age be two years.

It is an exaggeration to think that all Irish whiskey is used up in making Irish coffee. It is also untrue that it is "immensely strong and dangerously heady." It is not a whit stronger than Bourbon or Scotch. Its grain mash is mainly Irish barley, distilled, as in Scotland, with soft, peat-bog water in an old-fashioned pot still. Oh, yes. Something else that isn't true. No potatoes in the mash.

I guess nothing can stop progress. The other day I tasted a "Scotch-type" whisky that had been distilled in Poland. It was called Polmo Starka. It was quite a good drink. Did it taste like Scotch? I would rather not make up my mind. And now there is whiskey from Japan. It is called, I am told, Suntory, properly distilled in a pot still, from Japanese barley and Japanese water, matured in "Sherry casks," all done without mirrors in the "Vale of Yamazaki" near the holy City of Kyoto. In Japan, they say, time is the heart of life. This whiskey is at least ten years old.

Although there are hundreds of different whiskeys—all fiercely competing with each other in the market—they all belong, in reality, to different branches of the same family. They all start with cereal grains, with water and yeasts, with sugar and fire.... They develop their differences by holding within themselves (in different but infinitesimal quantities) their "impurities"—chemical elements with strange names: aldehydes, congeners, furfurels, fusel oils, and so on, drawn from the natural grain, the local water, and the wood of the aging barrels. The possible combinations of these elements are, of course, infinite. Small wonder that there are so many magnificent variations in the tastes of the whiskeys.

CHAPTER 26

THE SPIRITS THAT
LEAVE YOU TASTELESS

A. The "Dry" Gins

We have been discussing in the previous chapter mainly those distilled spirits which have a special character born of the particular place where they were made. This unique quality may be the result of a combination of mineral elements in the soil and yeasts floating in the warm air, resulting in the creation of certain flavoring essences in the fruits, grains, leaves, or stalks from which the spirit is distilled. Often the key factor is the influence of the local water—soft, sometimes faintly salty, filtering through the earth of a nearby hillside. Or the refinement of a particular spirit may depend on a local tradition of fine human judgment and technical skill, passed along from generation to generation of family involvement in small distilleries, where the workers are still masters of the machines.

But now we come to something entirely different. When you buy that quart bottle of clear-as-water, odorless and tasteless "neutral spirit," which you will mix into your drinks, you are dealing with a product that may be the purest thing you have ever known, but certainly has no true connection with any particular place on earth. If you could persuade the Eskimos to work for you, you could set up a gin

351

distillery on the icecaps of Greenland and, provided that you installed the right automated, push-button machinery and brought in the right quantities of raw materials, you could turn out precisely the same gin as you would in a similar plant in the hottest spot on the equator. Among the neutral spirits, the differences between labels are not differences in location or variations in skill, but involve different "recipes"—deliberately different combinations of herbs and spices, each formula being the closely guarded secret (worth millions of dollars) of each particular manufacturer. The fundamental point is that each recipe is not designed to make a drink to stand alone—to be sipped for its own character and complexity—but to play the subservient role of being a relatively tasteless mixer with other, flavorful ingredients.

Let us begin with gin. After the good Doctor Sylvius accidentally invented gin at the University of Leyden in Holland in the seventeenth century, English soldiers (who were then campaigning in the Lowlands) took the Dutch formula back to Britain, where this new, juniper-flavored "Genever," or "Gen," or "Gin," almost instantly became the national sport. Drinkers made it at home. It was estimated that every fourth house in London was a gin mill. Employers provided gin as part of the pay of their workers. Gin was the first spirit to be distilled in the New World, in a plant on Staten Island set up by the Dutch in 1640, in the days before Nieu Amsterdam became New York.

As the British industry expanded, it divided and became more or less concentrated in two centers making two different types of gin. In and around London the distilleries turned out "London Dry Gin," and the original flavoring with Dutch juniper berries was expanded to include Indonesian bitter almonds, German angelica root, Indian cardamom pods, Sumatran cassia buds and cinnamon bark, Moroccan coriander seed, Spanish dried lemon and orange peel, English anise licorice, Italian orris root, and so on. Then, in Plymouth, a local gin drinker named Old Tom discovered the additional pleasure of adding a bit of sugar to the gin, and this led to the large-scale manufacture of "Old Tom," or "Plymouth" gin, from which you get the name of the drink "Tom Collins," originally made with Old Tom gin.

Vast quantities of both types were shipped to the United States, but no one thought about copyrighting the names. So after the usual few dozen years, the U.S. authorities decided that the phrase "London Dry Gin" was now a regular part of the language and could be freely used

by anyone, as a "generic definition" of a style of gin, with no geographic implication. Today, if you see the words "London Dry Gin" on a label, you have no guarantee that the gin was actually made in London. But if you see the words "London Distilled Dry Gin," then it must have been actually distilled in London. The same rule applies to gin distilled in Holland, to the French Old Ladies' Dry, to the German Genever Schnapps, to the Irish distillation, and to any other from any other place. There are also straw-colored gins (the pigment is caramel), and some are flavored with such things as lemon juice or mint, but these seem to break the basic law that dry gin must not provide any very definite flavor of its own.

Since all gins are "distilled out" in continuous-operation, automated column stills with such a degree of efficiency that absolutely nothing remains of the original flavoring oils, it hardly matters from what raw material the neutral spirit is made. The usual formula is about 75 percent corn, 15 percent malted barley, and 10 percent of other grains. The natural starches are converted to sugar and then the yeasts complete the work of transforming the sugar into alcohol. Some English distillers use more barley, claiming that it adds to the smoothness. English distilled gins are widely thought to have exceptional qualities of body and character and a more complete absence of the metallic, raw taste of pure alcohol.

B. The International Family of "Russian" Vodkas

In Russian, "water" is *voda*—"little water" is *vodka*. It's all as simple as that! To the average Russian, for the past few centuries, a shot of vodka has been as essential and normal as a drink of water. No need to sharpen one's nose or train one's tastebuds about it. No need to spend even a second of time in comparing or judging it. Swallow it, stinging cold, in a single gulp and it will keep you warm in the most murderous winter weather. Even in Czarist times it was a relatively democratic drink—equally tasteless, equally a part of daily living, equally appreciated by nobles and peasants alike. Originally it may have been distilled from a mash of potatoes, but even before the Revolution almost all of it was being made by exactly the same process as gin, from a balanced mixture of corn, rye, and wheat. Since there was no regional or Russian secret about it, it was inevitable and natural that the process should be exported—first to the neighboring countries of Poland and Czechoslovakia, then to Western Europe, and finally to the United States.

Today there is just one principal difference between dry gin and dry vodka. While gin may be (and often is) flavored with herbs and spices, any neutral spirit distilled in the United States labeled and sold as vodka must be, in the precise language of the U.S. law, "without any distinctive character, completely without aroma, entirely colorless and tasteless." By repeated filtering through columns of activated charcoal, by being bubbled through with absorbent nitrogen gas, vodka finally emerges as absolutely tasteless as technology can make it. The law does not apply equally, for example, to the classic vodkas imported from Poland. Some of these are colored and flavored in various ways. The *jarzebiak* is slightly colored and flavored with the juice of rowan berries. The classic *zubrówka* is colored a light yellowish green and flavored with a sprig of wild buffalo grass. The *wiśniówka* is made fruity and red with wild cherry juice.

But these are the rare exceptions. As to all the American or other vodkas that are as clear, odorless, and tasteless as water, David Embury, in his book *The Fine Art of Mixing Drinks*, sums it up: "Vodka is really nothin' but 'cawn likker' distilled out ... so as to get rid of all the taste.... If you need some rubbing alcohol to rub your back and the corner drugstore is closed, it will be perfectly all right to use vodka. Of course, it is half distilled water, but that won't harm your back."

C. The Other Tasteless Spirits

The three dry spirits of Scandinavia may all have similar-sounding names and may all be as odorless and tasteless as water, but there are noticeable differences between them. There is only one label from each country, since all alcoholic production is a government monopoly and no competing brands are permitted. The Danish Aalborg Akvavit is certainly the driest and generally considered the best. It is distilled, partly from grains, potatoes, and mashed wood pulp, with a light flavoring of caraway seed. It, too, is gulped down exceedingly cold—often from a bottle dramatically frozen into a block of ice. The normal, safe measure is one ounce, which leaves you enough breath for the customary Scandinavian toast, *"Skål."* Your health! My health! The health of every pretty girl!

The Swedish version is the Gothenburg Aquavit and is noticeably softer. The Norwegian version, the Loiten Aquavit, distilled in Oslo, is just about halfway in softness between the other two.

CHAPTER 27

SWEET FRUIT
AND HERB LIQUEURS

"Drink this, my friend, and you will never forget it!"
Then, drop by drop, with the minute care of a lapidary
counting pearls, the priest ... poured into the glass a
green liqueur, gilded, warm, scintillating, exquisite. The
first sip bathed my stomach in sunshine. "It is the elixir
of Père Gaucher ... " he said, triumphantly. "They
make it at the monastery of the Prémontrés. ..."

Thus the great French writer Alphonse Daudet begins his famous short story that tells how a poverty-stricken small monastery in the south of France quickly achieved wealth and world fame after one of its young monks had succeeded in re-creating from an old family recipe an alcoholic cordial distilled from the aromatic herbs growing on the local hillsides. Daudet's details are obviously fictional, but the underlying theme is true. Some of the greatest liqueurs were invented by monks and are still made from secret recipes in distilleries controlled by church organizations. These herb and spice cordials and the fruit liqueurs are among the strongest and sweetest, the most luxurious and velvety, the most colorful and complex of spiritous drinks.

Is there a difference between a "cordial" and a "liqueur"? Some experts say that the word *cordial* properly belongs to the ancient herbal drinks, originally made not for pleasure drinking, but as

357

medicines and pick-me-ups for ailing monks. The Oxford dictionary
defines *cordial* as "a medicine ... or beverage which invigorates the
heart and stimulates the circulation." Later, when commercial producers began concocting fantastic essences of fruits and flowers, more
for the pleasure than the health of the drinker, these were called
"liqueurs."

There are right and wrong times and ways to serve cordials and
liqueurs. A sweet drink should obviously not be served immediately
before a main meal. Even after dinner, if served too soon a very sweet
liqueur can bring an uncomfortable feeling of oversaturation. Better,
at that point, to serve a brandy. This general rule, of course, is flexible,
since some liqueurs are drier and lighter than others.

One ideal use, I think, is for the guest who drops in (or is invited in)
for a short visit. "Cordial and cake" is ideal for midafternoon. Another
charming invitational variation is to say, "Come in tonight at nine for
coffee and cordials." After a formal dinner, the strategic moment at
which to bring out the liqueurs is often an hour or two after the meal,
when the guests are showing the first signs of being "talked out." The
liqueurs can respark the party. A cordial is fine to speed the parting
guest and keep him warm on his winter way home (but it is not, of
course, for the driver). Thus cordials and liqueurs are useful tools for
the sensitive host—an essential part of the hospitality of the home.

There are several problems about finding one's way in the wide
world of cordials and liqueurs. First, there are so many of them.
Second, one must learn to distinguish between the proprietary names
of the liqueurs made by only one producer and the generic names of
basic flavor mixtures made by many producers. It also helps to know
the names of the great companies, how they developed their products,
and how they make them today.

Apart from the efforts of the monks in their monasteries dating back
to the twelfth century, the commercial development of liqueurs is
inextricably intertwined with the family names of pioneer chemists and
merchants. In 1575 an Amsterdam trader with the East Indies, Erven
Lucas Bols, decided to use some of the spices that he imported to make
a flavored gin and thus founded the House of Bols, which is today the
largest liqueur producer in the world. Another Amsterdam merchant,
Wynand Fockink, started his small distillery in 1679 and founded the
second-oldest of the great Dutch firms. In 1695 a cooper in Rotterdam,
Jan de Kuyper, decided to make some of his own gin to go into his own
barrels; today his is the third-oldest of the famous Dutch names.

In France in 1755 Marie Brizard, daughter of a carpenter, made an

anisette cordial that was enjoyed by King Louis XV, and with her profits from the court she founded the company that still uses her name. Another of the great liqueur families is that of Cusenier, first in Ornans in the Jura Mountains, then in Paris. Some other historic French family names in liqueurs are Bardinet, Cointreau, Dolfi, and Garnier. In Italy the family associated with liqueurs is that of Lionello Stock, who started his distillery in Trieste. In Germany the important family names are Gilka, Mampe, and Riemerschmid.

After repeal of prohibition here and the start of superhigh taxation of imported alcohol, there was a major new development in the liqueur business. If the liquid inside the bottle can be made within the United States, then the bottle can be sold for about three dollars less than the imported version. This hard fact has led some of the great European names to take out, so to speak, American citizenship. They have set up their own manufacturing here, and today the names of Bols or de Kuyper do not necessarily mean a Dutch import. The names of Cointreau and Garnier no longer always mean a French product. These names compete with purely American labels like Hiram Walker. How to choose? A difficult question, because so much depends on personal preference. Let us begin by classifying cordials and liqueurs into six fairly broad groups.

1. The Ancient, Secret-Formula, Mixed-Aromatic Cordials

The name familiar to connoisseurs everywhere, and always the powerful contender for first place among all cordials, is Green Chartreuse, owned by the Carthusian monks and made by them in only two places, at Voiron, near Grenoble in south central France, some miles from their monastery of La Grande Chartreuse, and at their monastery in Tarragona, Spain. The secret formula, said to contain about 130 aromatic herbs, was developed in the sixteenth century and the cordial has been made for sale by the monks since 1735. About a hundred years later they developed Yellow Chartreuse, a lighter and sweeter version said to be "for the ladies," but there is a saying in France that all Yellow Chartreuse would rather be green if it could.

The other great name is, of course, Bénédictine, developed by the monks at the Abbey of Fécamp on the coast of Normandy. There is a record of the drink having been served to François I when he visited the Abbey in 1534. After the French Revolution, when the abbey was pillaged, the secret formula was lost for almost a hundred years. Then it was rediscovered, and for the last hundred years Bénédictine has been made by a commercial firm, but still in the cellars of the old abbey at Fécamp. About thirty years ago, noting that many people like to mix their Bénédictine with brandy, the company developed B & B, a delicious half-and-half mixture of the two drinks.

The famous Basque cordial of Spain, Green Izarra, is actually distilled across the border in France, but its aromatic herbs are picked on the Spanish slopes of the Pyrenees. There is also a lighter and sweeter Yellow Izarra.

Other proprietary herb-flavored cordials worth investigating include, from Italy, the bright yellow Galliano and the slightly citric, highly aromatic Strega; from Spain, the brown-gold Cuarenta y Tres ("Forty-three"); and from the Bordeaux district of France, Vieille Cure (green or yellow).

2. The Cordials with a Single, Dominant Aromatic Spice

The most well-known aromatic cordial is, of course, Crème de Menthe, a generic name used by dozens of producers. When it comes from the distillation it is crystal clear, and I firmly believe (although many will disagree) that the taste is slightly better in this natural state, called "white" on some labels. Most brands, however, are colored green, some rose-pink, or even gold. There is also a lighter, always clear version produced by several makers, called Peppermint Schnapps.

The second most famous spice cordial is Anise or Anisette, generic words used by all major producers. An unusual version comes from Badalona, Spain, under the name Anis del Mono. Another spice cordial, famous in Central Europe for hundreds of years, takes its name from the fact that it is flavored with cumin seed, and is called Kümmel, but it also has the added flavors of caraway and coriander.

3. The Fruit Liqueurs

These are the true liqueurs in the classic meaning of the word. Different fruits react differently to infusion with alcohol, but above all the orange produces the outstanding and accepted liqueur. The word most often linked with orange liqueurs is Curaçao, the name of a Dutch West Indian island. Soon after the Dutch took control of it in 1634, they discovered that a small, sour wild orange there had such an abundance of flavor oils in its greenish skin that it could be distilled into a marvelous liqueur. There was soon such an international demand for Orange Curaçao that seeds of the orange were planted in other tropical countries, and their cultivation has become an international industry. There is a double-strength version called Curaçao Double, and a triple-strength, much drier orange brandy called Triple Sec. All these names are generic. Though there is still one distillery on the original island (its product is imported under the name Senior's Curaçao of Curaçao), magnificent Orange Curaçaos are sent to us from France to add to our excellent domestic types.

Not every make, however, uses Curaçao oranges. Some use Valencias, and the label then reads simply Orange Liqueur. Two world-famous proprietary orange liqueurs use neither the word "orange" nor "Curaçao" but are known simply by the names of their makers—Cointreau and Grand Marnier. Another variation of the orange liqueur uses the tangerine, and the liqueur is always labeled in French as Crème de Mandarine.

The sweet cherry takes second place to the orange in popularity as the informing flavor of a liqueur. The cracked pits are generally included in the infusion to add a slight but dramatic bitterness in the aftertaste. Again, the liquid as it comes from the distillation is clear, and the Swiss versions are sold without added coloring as Kirsch (the German word for cherry). Without question, the most popular cherry liqueur is a proprietary brand from Denmark, Cherry Heering, the second word being the name of the family who founded and has run the Copenhagen company for more than a hundred and fifty years. Other competing producers have launched proprietary names, such as Cherry Kijafa, Cherry Marnier, and Cherristock.

As to other fruit flavors, all the names are, of course, generic and almost all the producers make them. Apricot is sometimes called Abricotine or Apry, and the Hungarian version, Hungaria Baracklikőr, is superb. The blackberry's flavor comes through brilliantly in a liqueur, as does that of the black currant. The peach makes a gentle and subtle drink. The less familiar sloe berry, generally imported from England, is usually labeled Prunelle or Crème de Prunellia in France. Raspberry is generally labeled either Crème de Framboises (in French) or Himbeer Liqueur (in German). Strawberry is almost always Crème de Fraises.

4. Liqueurs from the Essences of Flowers

It can be an extremely interesting experience to taste a bouquet that one has known all one's life only as a scent. There is a Crème de Rose, a Crème de Violette, and a combination of flower essences with a name at which cynics scoff: Parfait Amour. It is imported from both France and Germany and there is also a domestic variety.

5. A Miscellany of Other Flavors

This category begins with a group that includes Drambuie, based on Scotch whisky flavored with heather honey. When the base is Irish whisky, the liqueur is Irish Mist. When the base is American Bourbon and the secret flavorings seem, to at least one regular drinker, to be a combination of Southern peach and honeysuckle, the name is Southern Comfort.

In the second most popular group are the liqueurs flavored with coffee, made in romantic places and known by poetic names. The long list of favorites includes Tía María from Jamaica, Kahlua from Mexico, Espresso Coffee (with even a caffeine-free version) from Italy, Pasha Turkish Coffee from Istanbul, and others with the added flavors of chocolate and mint. Pure chocolate liqueurs are traditionally called Crème de Cacao, and almost every producer has his own version.

6. Conversation-Piece Oddities

There are some famous offbeat liqueurs that achieve such a dramatic appearance that as a surprise factor for the entertainment of party guests they have a value greater than their taste. The first is one of the oldest of all liqueurs. In 1549 King Zygmunt of Poland is said to have visited an ancient monastery in Danzig where the monks offered him a magnificent clear liqueur that he liked so much that he christened it Zwota Woda ("gold water"). That gave the monks the idea of garnishing the water with floating flakes of gold leaf. About fifty years later, one of the old harbor houses used for curing salmon was converted into a distillery for making and selling the first commercial Goldwasser, called Der Lachs ("salmon brand"). There is no longer any copyright on the word *Goldwasser,* but only one type, now made in Germany, may still call itself Danzig (Der Lachs) Goldwasser and still has a salmon on the label. Danzig is now Polish, and its government exports a cordial known as Polmos Zwota Woda.

There is a liqueur from Italy called Fior d'Alpe (because it is said to be flavored with aromatic Alpine flowers) that used to carry inside every bottle a small green branch from a living tree. Nowadays, sadly, the little branch is a plastic imitation.

There is a chocolate liqueur called Marmot Chocolate Suisse, which has, floating in it, literally hundreds of neatly rounded chips of Swiss chocolate. I once poured a two-ounce jigger onto a dinner plate and counted. There were sixty-five "niblets" of chocolate. It's hard to decide whether one is having a drink or eating a snack.

Finally, there is a Swiss liqueur made from the Williams pear, which is bottled with pure magic. Suspended in the liquid inside the bottle is a full-size pear, obviously ten times too large to get through the narrow neck of the bottle. The pears are actually grown inside the bottles. Late in May, when the petals fall off the flowers and tiny pears appear at the tips of the stems, the men slide the empty bottles over the pears and up the stems and tie the bottles to the branches. Sometimes as many as thirty bottles are suspended from each tree. Each pear grows rapidly inside its private little hothouse. Usually about mid-August, when each pear is fully grown, it is carefully snipped from its stalk and allowed to slide gently down to the bottom of the bottle. The same day, the bottles are delivered to the distillery to be filled with the pear liqueur, which preserves the color and freshness of the living fruit almost indefinitely.

The unique drink of the liqueur world is the Pousse-Café, in which several flavors are put together in a glass, yet do not mix. My recipe came many years ago from one of the oldest bars on Bourbon Street in New Orleans, where the drink originated. There are now dozens of variations but this is the original, from the Old Absinthe House, New Orleans.

Pousse-Café

Each drink is made individually. You need a tall Pousse-Café glass, about five inches high, three-quarters of an inch across at the bottom, and expanding to about one and a half inches in diameter at the top. Into this glass you must pour seven liqueurs in an exact order, so that the heaviest remains on the bottom, the next lighter rests on top of it, and each in turn is lighter still. The final result is a gently swaying vertical rainbow of colors.

You have to pour each so gently on top of the previous one that there will be no blurring of the demarcations between the layers of color. There are various ways of pouring: 1. Slide the measured amount of liqueur down the side of the slightly tilted glass. 2. Pour them onto the back of a spoon inserted inside the glass. 3. Pour them down the blade of a knife. 4. Use a large-size eyedropper, a bulb-controlled measuring pipette (from a chemical supply store). I would practice at least once before trying it out at a party.

The other important point is to know the weight of the various liqueurs. This is generally controlled by the alcohol and sugar: the less alcohol and the more sugar, the greater the weight of the liquid. However, various makes of the same flavor may vary in sugar content, so you must experiment before you launch out into your own variations. Here is a specific formula that works (use these exact brands, ice-cold, in this order):

2 teaspoons Marie Brizard Crème de Cacao—brown, the heaviest
2 teaspoons Bols Crème de Banane—yellow
2 teaspoons Cusenier Freezomint—green
2 teaspoons Bosch Anis del Mono—clear
2 teaspoons Cherry Heering—red
2 teaspoons Galliano—bright yellow
2 teaspoons Cointreau—clear, the lightest
1 teaspoon heavy cream

Gently pour the liqueurs into the Pousse-Café glass in exactly the order listed above. Top with the cream. Drink the Pousse-Café without shaking it, so that you taste the various flavors separately.

CHAPTER 28

MATHEMATICS AND MEASURES FOR THE MIXOLOGIST

Equipping and Operating the Home Bar

There was a famous story about President Franklin D. Roosevelt at the White House, where he regularly complained to his friends about his inability to find the perfect measurements for his dream of a "perfect Martini." When there were guests at cocktail time, a dignified tall serving man would slowly wheel in a handsome, very large, bar trolley and the President would move his wheelchair forward and sit behind the trolley, as if it were his laboratory desk. And "laboratory" was exactly the word. The top of the trolley was set up with a complicated, interconnected labyrinth of every kind of professional chemical glass measuring equipment—beakers, flasks, pipettes, graduated tubes, and so on—all linked together by curls and swirls of glass tubing. The setup might have been inspired by the opening scenes of the Alec Guinness movie *The Man in the White Suit*. At any moment one might have expected it all to start going glug-glug, glug-glug.

Once the President was sure that this little scene had riveted everyone's attention, he began the most elaborate improvisation. He carefully took one bottle after another and meticulously poured small amounts into various funnels and measuring flasks. He put on an act of total concentration. He turned tiny faucets on and off. He held measuring glasses up to the light, before pouring the contents from one to the other. He carefully used various multicolored eyedroppers. He built up the tension until the silence in the White House drawing room was palpable. Then, with crashing suddenness, he broke the spell and gave away that it was all a gigantic spoof. With an agonized cry of "Oh, the hell with it!" he slammed everything down, seized a quart bottle of gin, and began wildly pouring it, almost without looking, into the cocktail glasses. As the guests roared, Roosevelt turned to the serving man: "Here, Henry, you take over." Henry, who knew the game and had been watching with a perfectly straight face, then brought out a new set of cold glasses and mixed excellent Martinis in a perfectly normal way.

President Roosevelt's point about the ridiculousness of overelaborate bar equipment is as valid as ever. Gold-plated, overexpensive, and ultrafancy gadgets do not ensure good drinks. Once, on a day when I was moving from one home to another and wanted to celebrate with friends who had rallied to help me, I used a screw-top glass orange-juice bottle as a shaker and a rinsed-out milk carton as a martini jug. Lemons and limes were squeezed by hand, with the juice strained through a clean handkerchief. Lumps of sugar were muddled with a screwdriver. Ice cubes were crushed in a paper bag with the heel of a shoe. There were paper cups instead of glasses—but to all of us tired and thirsty workers, the drinks never tasted better. One guest said, "You couldn't do better with Baccarat glass and Tiffany silver spoons!"

So when choosing bar equipment, let us make efficiency and practicality our first concern. One of the best and simplest liquid measures is a one-ounce medicine glass, available, I believe, from virtually any drugstore at about twenty-five cents. Mine is graduated in divisions of one ounce, in tablespoons, in teaspoons, and in metric milliliters. Then there is a stainless-steel jigger with very clearly visible rings at one-half ounce, one ounce, one and a half ounces, and two ounces. Then my local druggist provided me with two professional glass measuring flasks, narrow at the bottom, wide at the top, with deeply pinched, nondrip pouring spouts—one graduated in ounces and milliliters up to four ounces, the other, in the same way, up to eight ounces.

The practical reasons for different kinds of shakers and jugs are discussed in the following chapter. I have one stainless-steel shaker, fully enclosed, with a tight, screw-on top, for heavy and long shaking of, say, the fizzes and flips. Then one of those standard, two-part

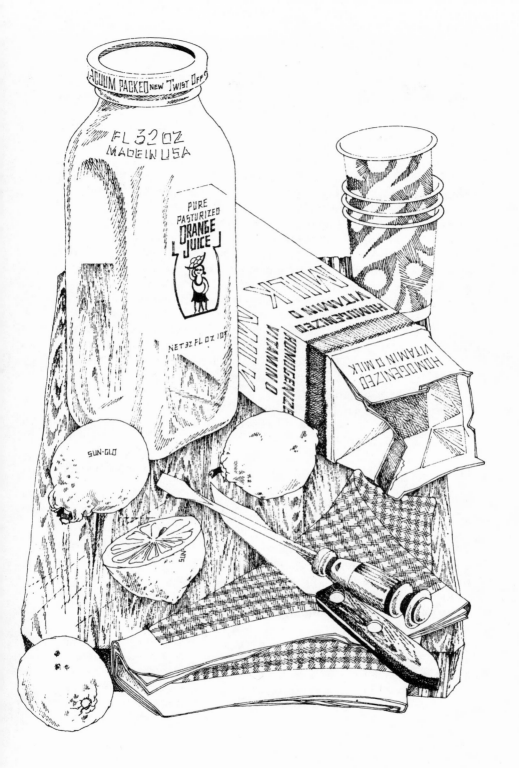

shakers with a big mixing glass, either sixteen or twenty ounces, as the bottom half, and as the top half, a stainless-steel, tightly fitting pourer-shaker, with a fitted strainer. Also, of course, a tall Martini jug with a lip to hold back the ice and a long glass spoon.

As to the other tools, you probably already have most of them. I gave you the profile of a first-class corkscrew in the chapter on dining-room equipment. Also, perhaps, an air-pressure cork remover for old and difficult corks. A good, heavy, and large crown cork opener. Various bottle stoppers for "plugging in" after you have taken off the crown corks. A good solid can opener. A small, strong, and stubby knife for getting off bottle seals. A small, sharp paring and slicing knife with a blade about three inches long and a four-inch handle, with a small cutting board, for slicing lemons and limes. A little French lemon "zester"—a miniature scraper, with teeth, which gets more lemon oil out of the skin with one stroke than half a dozen "twists." Also a small-size "fine-meshed" strainer. A professional, stainless-steel half-lemon squeezer, with strainer attached. A small hand nutmeg grater—to avoid the blandness of preground nutmeg out of a shaker can. A standard set of measuring spoons. An eyedropper. A one-at-a-time cherry or olive pitter.

You can have ice tongs. I use my fingers. As to cracking or crushing the ice, it can be done in a cloth bag with one of those excellent spring-handled ice hammers. But I consider it worthwhile to have an electric crushing attachment to my meat grinder—a rotary chopper with ten different positions for different grades of ice. Then there is a vacuum ice bucket.

At my parties I enjoy the efficiency of two other electrical machines that, although their first cost was relatively high, have, in my opinion, well repaid their capitalization. One is a high-speed fruit and vegetable juicer, which turns at about 3,600 revolutions per minute and, by centrifugal force, will suck the juice out of absolutely anything, from a carrot to a pomegranate. This has enabled me to invent some pretty exotic drinks. But also, in more mundane terms, it provides, for large parties, unlimited quantities of fresh lemon and lime juice with almost unbelievable speed.

My second electrical toy is an advanced design of a stainless-steel electric blender. Its special feature is that it entirely eliminates the bugbear of blades sticking on ice cubes, by the fact that the motor is instantly reversible. From turning at top speed in one direction, it can, in a quarter of a second, flash itself to top speed in the opposite direction. So it can mix drinks, break up ice cubes, churn and froth flips, and generally do almost any job except the slower business of shaking air into a Gin Fizz. This last always involves handwork.

As to glasses and other things for serving, they are discussed in detail in the next chapter. Some of the bits and pieces hardly need a checklist. Stirring rods and swizzle sticks of various lengths. Napkins and coasters for keeping wetness off hands and tables.

Thus armed, we are ready for our first class in the mathematics of mixing. Let us begin by defining our terms:

Dash: Be careful about dashing the liquid straight out from a bottle of, say, Angostura Bitters or Tabasco. Different bottles have different-sized openings. If you want to test first, a proper dash is 1/8 of a teaspoon—a 1/4-teaspoon measuring spoon half-filled.

Drop: 1/10 of a dash; 20 drops make a 1/4 teaspoon.

Teaspoon: 1/3 of a tablespoon—1/6 of an ounce.

Tablespoon: Half an ounce.

Jigger: Depending on the largesse of your hospitality, the capacity of the drinker, and the strength of the liquor being measured, something between a minimum of 1 1/2 ounces and a maximum of 2 ounces.

Half-Jigger: According to the above rule, between 3/4 of an ounce and 1 ounce.

Pony: Always 1 ounce—the maximum safe dose for such potentially dangerous, stinging-cold, swallow-at-one-gulp offerings as 100-proof vodka, or Danish akvavit.

Wineglassful: I always interpret this vague phrase to mean 4 ounces—half a standard measuring cup.

Split: The smallest bottle of Champagne or sparkling wine, almost always between 6 and 8 ounces. Usually enough for two people. Of course, it is much cheaper (and the quality is better) if you pour your sparklers from larger bottles.

Fifth: The standard size of wine or spirit bottle, which holds exactly 1/5 of a gallon—25 and 3/5 ounces. Be careful. There are some variations. All fifth-size American wine and spirit bottles (and all fifth-size imported spirit bottles) are required by U.S. law to hold exactly that amount. Some imported wine bottles, using the metric system, may hold an ounce or two less. They are legally required, however, to print clearly on the label how much wine they do contain. Watch this when making your advance calculations for a large party. These smaller bottles can mean that you are, in effect, losing one bottle out of every twelve you buy.

How Many Bottles for How Many Guests?

When planning a cocktail party, where there will be canapés and tidbits but no very solid food, my basic rule-of-thumb is to count on my guests consuming an average of two to three drinks per person. The calculation is slightly different for a group of friends assembled before dinner and being offered three-ounce servings of such preprandial apéritifs as Madeira, Sherry, or vermouth, or four-ounce servings of Champagne, white wine, or any other unmixed drink—I expect an average of one to two glasses per person.

Once we all sit down at the table, if it is a fairly simple meal with only one wine served from beginning to end, I usually expect each guest to drink an average of three glasses, each partly filled with four ounces of wine. But if there are to be two wines—almost always a white first, with a red to follow—then the added interest in the wine is likely to lead them to drink an average of four glasses (two of each wine) per person. But if there are three wines, or more, so that the dinner becomes more or less a wine-tasting, then the average consumption may go up to five glasses per person. In my experience, it seldom goes above this, since, if you are tasting many wines, you pour much less (sometimes as little as one ounce) for each serving.

At the close of dinner, with the coffee, the proper single serving of a straight brandy or liqueur is one ounce, and I usually allow for an average of two drinks per person. Later in the evening, when the conversation is stimulated by Highballs or whiskies, I again operate on the assumption that the average number of drinks per person will be between two and three—assuming that everything is going well and that the guests will be tempted to stay quite late. When estimating the requirements of club soda, ginger ale, tonic water, or other non-alcoholic mixers, I usually plan for one one-pint bottle for each guest for the entire evening. If the party is a barbecue, a buffet, or a picnic with beer, I usually plan on three twelve-ounce bottles or cans per person.

All these general rules are translated into specific recommendations in the following four charts.

How Many Bottles for a Cocktail Party?

IF THE NUMBER OF INVITED GUESTS IS:	EXPECT TO SERVE THIS MANY DRINKS:	FOR 1 1/2-OUNCE DRINKS, HAVE AT LEAST THIS MANY FIFTH BOTTLES:	FOR 2-OUNCE DRINKS, HAVE AT LEAST THIS MANY FIFTH BOTTLES:
4	8-12	1	1
6	12-18	2	2
8	16-24	2	2
10	20-30	2	3
12	24-36	3	3
20	40-60	4	5
30	60-90	6	8
40	80-120	8	10

NOTE: When you are buying a number of bottles for a large party, there is a saving on cost if you translate the 25.6-ounce "fifth" bottles into the 32-ounce quart bottles.

How Many Bottles of Apéritifs, Champagne, or Other Wines Before Dinner— or After-Dinner Port, or Sweet Sherry?

IF THE NUMBER OF INVITED GUESTS IS:	EXPECT TO SERVE THIS MANY DRINKS:	FOR APÉRITIFS, PORTS, OR SHERRIES,* HAVE AT LEAST THIS MANY FIFTH BOTTLES:	FOR CHAMPAGNE OR WINE,** HAVE AT LEAST THIS MANY FIFTH BOTTLES:
4	4-8	1	2
6	6-12	2	2
8	8-16	2	3
10	10-20	3	4
12	12-24	3	4
20	20-40	5	7
30	30-60	8	10
40	40-80	10	13

* For 3-ounce serving
** For 4-ounce serving

How Many Bottles of Wine for a Dinner Party?

IF THE NUMBER OF INVITED GUESTS IS:	EXPECT TO SERVE THIS MANY GLASSES:	IF SERVING ONLY ONE WINE, HAVE:	IF SERVING TWO WINES, HAVE:
4	12-16	2	3
6	18-24	3	4
8	24-32	4	6
10	30-40	5	7
12	36-48	6	8
20	60-80	10	13
30	90-120	14	19
40	120-160	19	25

How Many Bottles of Brandy or Liqueur to Serve After Dinner?

IF THE NUMBER OF YOUR INVITED GUESTS IS:	EXPECT TO POUR THIS MANY 1-OUNCE SERVINGS:	YOU SHOULD HAVE AT LEAST THIS MANY "FIFTH" BOTTLES:
4	8	1/2
6	12	1/2
8	16	1
10	20	1
12	24	1
20	40	2
30	60	2
40	80	4

CHAPTER 29

THE TWELVE MOST USEFUL
OF ALL DRINKS

At Every Bar Everywhere in the World

L et me confess, at the beginning, that I am not a devotee of mixed drinks. If I were to be sentenced to live the rest of my life on a reasonably comfortable desert island, I would, of course, choose as my companions two lovely ladies and one other man, who would, naturally, have to be an obstetrician. As to the supply of liquid refreshment, however, I would demand, somewhere on the island, a correctly cool cave for the storage of an unlimited supply of the great wines of the world, of the magnificent fortified wines—the Madeiras, Ports, and Sherries, plus a magically unending supply of the supreme spirits—the Cognacs, Armagnacs, and other fruit brandies, the rums, the Scotch malt whiskies.

If against this obstinate point of view, you argue in praise of the fascinating complexity of a mixed drink, I would reply that there can hardly be anything in a glass quite as complex and subtle, as mysterious in its communications with my mouth and my throat, as a truly great old wine, or an aged spirit carrying the multiplicity of aromas and tastes that belong uniquely to the corner of earth where it was made. A magnificent Highland Scotch, for example, seems to be redolent of all the perfumes and savors of a hundred wild mountain flowers.

After thus firmly stating my position, I concede at once that I am in the vast minority. I even admit that I often enjoy a well-made cocktail, a tall, cooling punch, or any other of the multitudinous varieties that will be listed in the following pages.

For at least ten years, whenever I have been kept waiting at a bar—usually by a lovely lady—I have amused myself by asking the barman which are the twelve drinks that he is most often asked to serve. I have played this game in places near and far, from the King Cole Bar of the St. Regis in Manhattan to the Peninsula in Hong Kong, from the La Floridita in Havana to the old Shepheard's in Cairo, from the Raffles in Singapore to the Gritti Palace in Venice. Generally the barman's answer to my question was immediately followed by a practical test of his choices. The results of this immense flow of liquid research are documented in this chapter.

It is no surprise to find that the most universal of all mixed drinks is America's contribution to the refreshment of the world, the Dry Martini, in all its various forms. My own four favorite versions are discussed in detail elsewhere in this book and therefore the Martini is not included here. As to the other eleven, let us, before setting down the recipes, discuss the basic and essential rules for making memorable mixed drinks of any kind—rules that apply with special force to these finely balanced versions of "the people's choices"—and mine.

First, I do not believe in ever trying to imitate the nonchalant bravado of the professional barman, who calmly pours in a little bit of this and a dash of that, judging everything by the sharpness of his eye and the sureness of his hand in tilting the bottle. A busy barman may mix an average of five hundred drinks during one of his working days or nights. We less experienced amateurs, if we are wise, will measure every single ingredient accurately and carefully, making the fullest use of the equipment described in the previous chapter. I have proved, again and again, that even one-eighth of a teaspoon, more or less, of a flavoring liquid can completely ruin the perfect balance of the finished drink.

Second, one must clearly understand the scientific and technical differences between the various methods of mixing: shaking in the mixing glass of a shaker, stirring in a Martini jug, or blending in the drinking glass. These "systems" (to use the favorite word of the engineers) are not in any way interchangeable. You shake when you want to amalgamate, by force, some solidly heavy or thick emulsion, which otherwise would refuse to mix with its friendly neighboring ingredients. For example: sugar, powdery or syrupy, egg yolks or whites, heavy cream, thickly sweet liqueurs.

If the liquid partners are less standoffishly unfriendly, they can best be stirred with ice (preferably with a long, glass spoon) in a well-designed Martini jug.

My own "trick" is first to put all the ice-cold ingredients into the ice-cold jug and stir, quickly and thoroughly. Next I put in the freshly dry ice cubes (carefully sliding them down the side of the jug, to avoid plopping and splashing) and complete the stirring. This gives me a tight control over the degree of dilution with ice water.

The secondary objective of the shaking or the stirring, of course, is to cool the mixture rapidly. The "secret trick" is to learn to know precisely how long to shake or stir so that the proper cooling and mixing will be accomplished without too much of the ice melting. Almost invariably, if, say, you put a total of four ounces of liquid ingredients into a shaker with the ice, the volume will be doubled to eight ounces with melted ice water by the time you pour. When, instead, you stir in a jug with ice cubes, the same four-ounce starting volume will be increased to only six ounces. These figures represent normally expected dilution and are allowed for in the following recipes. But if you shake or stir too long, or if any of your ingredients or utensils is not ice-cold to start with, then there will be too much watery dilution and the drink will not come out right.

If, on the other hand, the extreme cooling and complete mixing are less important, one simply puts ice cubes into the chilled glass and provides the drinker with a swizzle stick with which to do his own quick stirring. Then, if the first sip be taken at once, there is a minimum of watery dilution. This again is allowed for in the appropriate recipes. So the essential discipline is to follow each recipe exactly.

The third major rule for memorable drinking is to make sure that you know the precise temperature of your ice cubes. What nonsense! I hear you muttering under your breath. Ice is ice. Water freezes at 32° F. Nonsense, I reply. If you have a reasonably efficient freezer, the air inside it will be at 0° F. The ice cubes that you break out from the tray in this freezer—all quite dry and sticky to your fingers—are at 0° F. But the ice cubes drowning, after two hours, in your only moderately well-insulated ice bucket are, as near as dammit, at almost 32° F. Obviously, the colder the cubes, the cleaner and sharper the drink!

If the recipe calls for crushed ice, it should be broken up or chopped just before the mixing begins and, for obvious reasons, the bits should not be too small. When, however, the recipe is for a frappe, involving a base of ice in the serving glass through which the drink is to be sipped with a straw, then the ice should be very finely crushed.

Equally obviously, all the bottles of ingredients, all the fruit juices and sugar syrups should be prechilled in the refrigerator, while all the shakers, stirring jugs and spoons, and measuring and straining equipment, plus all the serving glasses, should come straight from the freezer. Naturally, fresh ice, fresh garnitures, and fresh glasses should be brought out from the freezer and the refrigerator for each new round of drinks.

Fourth, the amounts, in each recipe, are for one person. The short cocktails are designed to fill correctly a 4-ounce stemmed cocktail glass without ice, or "on the rocks" in a 6-ounce Old-Fashioned glass. Obviously, these two methods of serving are entirely interchangeable and a matter of taste. (I prefer a cocktail glass, since its long stem provides a handle that effectively prevents the warmth of my hand heating up the glass.) Longer drinks are designed for 10-ounce, 12-ounce, or 14-ounce tall tumblers, filled up with extra branch or soda water, depending on the degree of the drinker's thirst.

Fifth (and, surely, hardly necessary to be said), all lemons, limes, and other natural fruit juices are to be freshly squeezed from refrigerated fruit. Nothing is worse than a drink in which the planned balance of flavors is masked by the taints of chemical preservatives from bottled or canned juices. Virtually the same spoilage can result from using tap water that has been heavily chlorinated. Much better to use branch or bottled water from a mountain spring—but never mineral water.

Sixth, in drinks using egg white, remember that an average egg white equals more than two tablespoons, so you may have to measure out one tablespoon in drinks for one person. Put the white in a cup, beat up a bit with a fork, and then measure. If you try to divide an egg white without beating first, it will stick to the spoon in globs.

SHORT FINAL NOTES (with apologies if you already know these points): The mixers are obviously interchangeable and are a matter of personal taste: club soda, ginger ale, tonic water, even (shame on you!) a cola or sweet soda. Apart from the dry and sweet vermouths, there are other types, which can sharply change the character of a drink but sometimes make interesting variations: the Italian bitter vermouths such as Campari or Punt e Mes, and some specially flavored French vermouths now labeled "Americano." The different types of whiskies can make an enormous difference to the character of a drink. The heavy, smoky Highland single-malts are so dominant and powerful that it is wise never to use them in mixed drinks. The lighter, less dominant blended whiskey—American, Canadian, Irish, and Scotch—are the ones to choose as partners in mixed drinks. (See, also, the notes on flavoring essences, sugar syrups, and other special ingredients in Chapter 25.)

Finally, do not be deceived into thinking that you can get away with low-priced, inferior-quality spirits because "no one will notice in a mixed drink"—a fine rum or whiskey, for example, adds its own brilliance and glow to every drink into which it is incorporated. Only memorable ingredients can make memorable drinks.

My Four Favorite Dry Martinis (See Chapter 3)

MY FAVORITE DRY MANHATTAN
  2 ounces Bourbon, rye, or blended whiskey
  1/2 ounce dry vermouth
  1 dash Angostura Bitters
  Lemon peel

In a mixing glass, mix whiskey, dry vermouth, and Angostura Bitters. Add ice cubes and stir. Strain into a 4-ounce stemmed cocktail glass. Twist lemon peel over glass to extract the oil essence.
(For a REGULAR MANHATTAN—see page 444.)

MY PERFECT DAIQUIRI
  1 1/2 ounces 86-proof Jamaica white rum
  1/2 ounce fresh lime juice
  2 teaspoons Falernum

Shake vigorously with cracked ice for under 15 seconds. Strain into an ice-cold 4-ounce cocktail glass.

CHAMPAGNE COCKTAIL
  5 ounces Champagne
  1/2 teaspoon superfine sugar
  1 dash Angostura Bitters
  1 small orange peel
  1 small lemon peel

In a 6-ounce stemmed Champagne glass, mix sugar and bitters. Fill glass with Champagne and twist orange and lemon peels over drink to extract oil essence. Drop peels into drink and stir gently.

GIN AND SIN
   1 ounce dry gin
   1 ounce sweet vermouth

Pour dry gin and sweet vermouth over 1 ice cube in a 6-ounce Old-Fashioned glass and stir.

SCOTCH SOUR
   1 1/2 ounces Scotch whisky
   3/4 ounce fresh lemon juice
   1 teaspoon superfine sugar
   Orange slice
   Maraschino cherry

In a mixing glass, dissolve sugar in lemon juice, add Scotch, shake with ice, strain into a 5-ounce chilled sour glass. Garnish with orange slice and cherry.

MARGARITA
   1 1/2 ounces tequila
   1/2 ounce Triple Sec
   1 ounce fresh lime juice
   Coarsely ground sea salt

Prepare a 4-ounce stemmed cocktail glass by goating the rim with lime juice and dipping the glass into coarsely ground sea salt. In a mixing glass, mix tequila, Triple Sec, and lime juice. Shake with shaved ice and strain into the salt-rimmed cocktail glass.

OLD-FASHIONED
   2 ounces Bourbon, rye, or Canadian whiskey
   1 teaspoon superfine sugar
   1 dash Angostura Bitters
   Lemon peel
   Orange slice
   Maraschino cherry

Put sugar in a 6-ounce Old-Fashioned glass. Add bitters and muddle. Add ice cubes and whiskey and stir. Twist lemon peel over drink to extract oil essence. Garnish with orange slice and cherry.

MINT JULEP
 2 ounces Bourbon whiskey
 1 tablespoon sugar syrup
 6 mint leaves
 Dash Angostura Bitters
 Sprig of mint

In a mixing glass, muddle the mint leaves gently with the sugar syrup and Angostura Bitters. Into a chilled 12-ounce Highball glass or silver julep cup, place half of the mint concoction and cover with firmly packed crushed ice until the glass is half full. Add remaining muddled leaves and fill glass with more crushed ice. Insert straws and set the drink in the coldest part of the refrigerator for at least 1 hour. Then, taking care not to touch the glass with your hands (wear gloves or hold a towel), pour in Bourbon to 1/4 inch from the top and leave to chill for another hour. Garnish with mint sprig before serving.

BLOODY MARY
 3 ounces vodka
 3/4 ounce fresh lemon juice
 1/2 teaspoon salt
 Several grinds fresh pepper
 2 dashes Tabasco
 4 dashes Worcestershire sauce
 1 teaspoon onion juice
 1 teaspoon grated horseradish (fresh essential, squeezed to remove
  liquid)
 4 ounces tomato juice (chilled)

In a cold mixing glass, mix lemon juice, vodka, salt, pepper, Tabasco, Worcestershire sauce, onion juice, grated horseradish, and tomato juice. Shake well with shaved ice and strain into an 8-ounce stemmed wine glass.

SCREWDRIVER
 2 ounces vodka
 6 ounces fresh orange juice

Pour vodka over ice cubes in a 10-ounce Highball glass and fill glass with orange juice. Stir gently.

SCOTCH HIGHBALL
    2 ounces Scotch whisky
    Club soda

Pour Scotch over ice cubes in a 10-ounce Highball glass. Fill glass with club soda and stir gently.

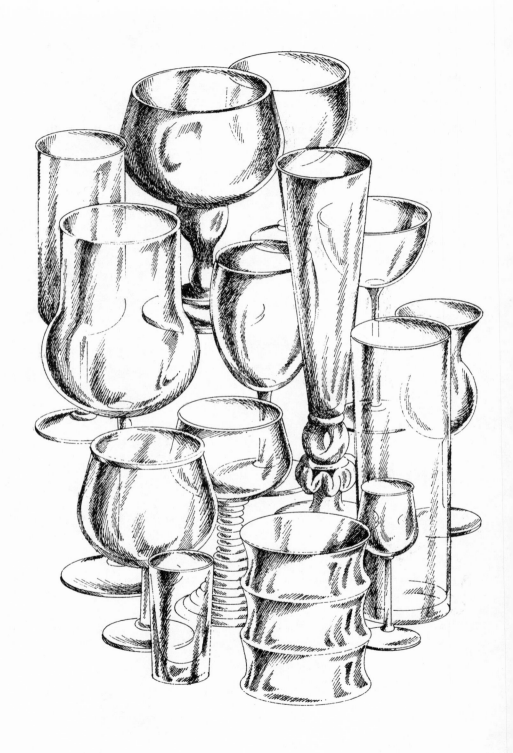

CHAPTER 30

ALL THE MIX THAT'S FIT TO FIX

Or What to Do with That Half-Empty Bottle

During my drinking life I must have read (and, at various times, tried to use) hundreds of "guidebooks" to mixing drinks. I have never found one that did not have severe faults. Some of the less well-organized editions have annoyed the hell out of me! The book may claim to include a thousand recipes, but, when you begin to analyze them closely in terms of trying some of them, they are about as padded as the chest of the umpire behind the batter. I once saw an article in a magazine headed "Different Ways of Mixing a Martini." You drop in a small strawberry instead of the olive and call it a "Bleeding Heartini." An added single drop of Martinique rum makes it a "Martiquini." One drop of Marsala, a "Marsalini." A dash of Scotch and you have a "Highlandini." A drop of orange bitters gives you a "Racket Club Martini." "Racket" is exactly the right word.

It is also a cruel deception in terms of bibulous enjoyment. After all, the ideal balance of flavors in one of the world-famous cocktails is a matter of fine precision of measurement after decades of experimentation by tens of thousands of amateur mixers and professional barmen. There is always only one "best recipe." The variations are inferior compromises to pad out the pages of a book, or confusing attempts by commercial manufacturers to work their particular products into the mixture that everyone is drinking.

Then there is the problem of the inefficient arrangement of these "bar guidebooks." Dozens of different recipes are confusingly assembled under strangely noncommunicating headings. In one book there are thirty recipes for "Puffs." What is a Puff? After laboriously wading through page after page of finely printed liquid ingredients, I find that a Puff is the modernized version of a concoction that originated in Elizabethan England—nothing more than a straight mixture of one liquor or another with milk and soda water. This is not at all what I feel like trying at this particular moment. Then I find lists of "Bucks," "Rickeys," and "Fizzes." My mind goes fuzzy until I am told that they are all more or less the same drink—minuscule variations of the ubiquitous Highball. How complicated. How unnecessarily confusing. In some of these books I have run the tip of my bar spoon up and down the pages so many times that they are stained with streaks of dried-up golden rum! In short, it may take twenty or thirty minutes to find the precisely right idea for a nice new drink for fit your mood or the occasion.

Another special problem that for me has never been solved by any "bar guide" is the matter of the leftover, half-empty bottle of one of the more unusual spiritous or winy, aromatically flavored cordials or mixes. Let's not overcomplicate the problem. We won't expect any book to tell us what to do with Picon, or Suze, or Punt e Mes. Let's pose the question in its simplest terms. An Italian friend who always insists on starting with an apéritif mixed with Campari comes to dinner. I get a bottle. We sip a few "Camparisodas" (as my Italian friend gabbles the name) and then, over the next day or two, I mix some Americanos and a couple of Negronis. The bottle of Campari is now half empty, resting comfortably on the floor of my icebox. What else can I do with it? Not one of my books can tell me.

I am sure that, in practical use, my own assemblage of mixed-drink recipes, which follows below, may be found to have as many unforeseen faults as all the others. But I think I have met the two criticisms defined above. This is not, in any way, a "padded" list. After a lifetime of experimentation, I have gradually reduced my personal repertoire to the mixed drinks included here and in other chapters of this book.

The recipes are organized and cross-indexed mainly by their principal ingredients. If you have a bottle of something or other that is half-empty and in the way, find its generic name among the alphabetically arranged subheads and there you will find suggestions for the various drinks into which it mixes well. For instance, if you have a bottle of the French bitter vermouth Raphaël, look it up under *V* for "Vermouths, bitter." I can't make it much simpler than that, can I?

If, on the other hand, you are not concerned with a particular ingredient, but want to be reminded of the various possibilities within a particular category of drinks, you can also look that up in the same alphabetical way. For example, if it is a hot day and you need ideas for tall coolers, just look up "Tall Coolers." The same for "Apéritifs," or "Punch Bowls," or "Toddies," and so on. Try it. I think you'll like the system.

I promise you that I have not left out of this list a single drink that I consider to be a reasonably pleasurable experience. So—if *your* absolutely favorite concoction is not here, then we must just agree to disagree about its value. Instead of sulking in your corner, try something new. First read the basic instructions, in the previous chapter, for the proper preparation of all memorable drinks—then carefully concoct one of these.

Akvavit, Aquavit
(Danish Aalborg, Norwegian Loiten, or Swedish Anderson)

AKVAVIT SOUR
  2 ounces akvavit
  1/2 ounce fesh lemon juice
  1/2 teaspoon orgeat

In a mixing glass, mix lemon juice and orgeat. Add akvavit and shake with shaved ice. Strain into a 4-ounce stemmed cocktail glass.

HOT SWEDISH GLOGG—page 410.

AMER PICON (See Picon.)

Anis Liqueurs
(French Anisette, Pernod, or Ricard, Greek Ouzo, Louisiana
Herbsaint, Spanish Anis del Mono, Turkish Raki)

BALTIMORE BRACER
   1 1/2 ounces anisette
   1 1/2 ounces brandy
   1 tablespoon egg white

In a mixing glass, mix anisette, brandy, and egg white. Shake with ice
and strain into a 4-ounce cocktail glass.

BLACKTHORN— page 447.

CLOCKWORK ORANGE
   2 ounces Pernod
   2 ounces orange juice

In a 10-ounce chilled Highball glass, put 2 ice cubes. Pour over the
Pernod and orange juice. Stir gently and serve.

KISS ME QUICK— page 419.

OUZO HIGHBALL
   2 ounces ouzo
   Soda water

In a 12-ounce Highball glass, pour ouzo over shaved ice. Fill glass
with soda water and stir gently.

PASTIS MARSEILLAISE
   3 ounces Pernod

In a 6-ounce Old-Fashioned glass, pour the Pernod over 4 ice cubes
and add 3 ounces of ice water—more or less, to taste. Stir gently and
serve.

THE PERFECT POUSSE-CAFE— page 364.

SAZERAC— page 446.

SUISSESSE
    3 ounces Pernod
    1 egg white
    1 1/2 teaspoons superfine sugar

In a mixing glass put the Pernod, egg white, and sugar. Shake furiously with ice until it is the lightest of foams (or, blend at high speed for 10 seconds in 2 ice cubes). Serve in a 6-ounce Old-Fashioned glass.

WHISKEY PERNOD—page 447.

Apéritifs

AMERICANO
    1 1/2 ounces Campari
    1 1/2 ounces sweet vermouth
    Lemon peel
    Club soda

In a 10-ounce Highball glass, pour Campari and vermouth over ice cubes and fill glass with club soda. Twist lemon peel over drink to extract oil essence. Drop peel into drink and stir gently.

BYRRH CASSIS
    1 1/2 ounces Byrrh
    1/2 ounce Crème de Cassis
    Club soda

Pour Byrrh and Crème de Cassis over a single ice cube in an 8-ounce stemmed wineglass. Fill glass with club dosa. Don't stir but serve with a stirring rod.

CAMPARI-CITRON
    2 ounces Campari
    1/4 fresh lemon
    Club soda

Squeeze lemon into a 10-ounce Highball glass and drop lemon shell into glass. Add Campari and ice cubes. Fill glass with soda and stir gently.

CAMPARISODA
 2 ounces Campari
 Club soda

In a 10-ounce Highball glass, pour Campari over ice cubes. Fill glass with club soda and stir gently.

CAMPARI-TONIQUE
 2 ounces Campari
 Tonic (quinine) water
 Wedge of lime

Squeeze lime into a 10-ounce Highball glass to extract juice and drop lime into glass. Add Campari and ice cubes. Fill glass with tonic water and stir gently.

CIN-CIN
 1 1/2 ounces sweet Cinzano vermouth
 1 1/2 ounces dry Cinzano vermouth
 Lemon peel

Pour sweet and dry Cinzano over ice in a 6-ounce Old-Fashioned glass. Stir and twist lemon peel over glass to extract oil essence. Drop peel into glass.

CRANBERRY SPRITZER
 4 1/2 ounces sweet Sauternes wine (chilled)
 1 1/2 ounces Grand Marnier
 3 ounces cranberry juice
 Club soda

In a 12-ounce Highball glass, mix Sauternes, Grand Marnier, cranberry juice. Add ice cubes and stir. Fill glass with soda and stir gently.

DRY VERMOUTH ON THE ROCKS
 3 ounces dry vermouth
 Lemon peel

In a 6-ounce Old-Fashioned glass, pour vermouth over no more than 2 ice cubes. Twist lemon peel over drink to extract the oil essence. Drop peel into glass.

DUBONNET APERITIF—page 403.

KIR
> 6 ounces dry white Chablis wine (chilled)
> 1/2 counce Crème de Cassis
> Lemon peel

In an 8-ounce stemmed wineglass, mix chilled wine and Crème de Cassis. Twist lemon peel over drink to extract oil essence. Stir gently.

KIR WITH SPARKLE
> 6 ounces brut Champagne (chilled)
> 1/2 ounce Crème de Cassis
> Lemon peel

In an 8-ounce stemmed wineglass, mix chilled Champagne and Crème de Cassis. Twist lemon peel over drink to extract oil essence. Stir gently.

LILLET ON THE ROCKS
> 3 ounces Lillet white vermouth
> Orange peel

In a 6-ounce Old-Fashioned glass, pour Lillet vermouth over no more than 2 ice cubes. Twist orange peel over drink to extract oil essence. Drop peel into glass.

MERRY WIDOW— page 404.

MY FOUR FAVORITE MARTINIS— chapter 3, page 19.

PICON VERMOUTH
> 1 1/2 ounces Picon
> 1 1/2 ounces dry vermouth

Pour Picon and dry vermouth over ice cubes in a 6-ounce Old-Fashioned glass. Stir gently.

RASPBERRY CHAMPAGNE
> 6 ounces brut Champagne (chilled)
> 1/2 ounce heavy black raspberry syrup or grenadine
> 3 strawberries, sliced

Pour the black raspberry syrup gently into the bottom of an 8-ounce stemmed wineglass, filled with chilled Champagne and garnish with sliced strawberries. Serve unmixed, unstirred.

SHERRY AND BITTERS
>   3 ounces *fino* Sherry
>   2 dashes Angostura Bitters
>   Lemon peel

In a mixing glass, mix Sherry and Angostura Bitters. Stir with ice cubes and strain into a 4-ounce stemmed cocktail glass. Twist lemon over glass to extract oil essence. Drop peel into glass.

VERMOUTH CASSIS
>   1 ounce Crème de Cassis
>   4 ounces French dry vermouth
>   Club soda

In a 10-ounce Highball glass, pour Crème de Cassis and vermouth over ice cubes, then fill glass with club soda. Stir gently for a few seconds.

Apple Brandy, Applejack, Calvados

APPLE COOLER
>   2 ounces vodka
>   1/2 ounce Calvados
>   Unsweetened apple juice

In a 10-ounce Highball glass, mix vodka and Calvados. Add ice cubes and fill glass with unsweetened apple juice. Stir gently.

PINK LADY
>   1 1/2 ounces dry gin
>   3/4 ounce fresh lemon juice
>   1/2 ounce grenadine
>   2 dashes Calvados
>   1 tablespoon egg white

In a mixing glass, mix lemon juice, grenadine, and Calvados. Add egg white and shake vigorously with shaved ice. When well-combined and creamy, add 3/4 ounce gin and continue shaking. Add the last 3/4 ounce gin, shake again, and strain into 4-ounce stemmed cocktail glass.

Aquavit
(See AKVAVIT.*)*

Bénédictine, Liqueur

BOBBY BURNS—page 449.

DRY ROB ROY—page 449.

FRISCO—page 445.

KNICKEBEIN—page 416.

MONTE CARLO
 1 1/2 ounces Bourbon, rye, or blended whiskey
 1/2 ounce Bénédictine
 2 dashes Angostura Bitters

In a mixing glass, mix whiskey, Bénédictine, and bitters. Shake with shaved ice and strain into 4-ounce stemmed cocktail glass.

Bishops, Hot
(See WASSAIL BOWLS.)

A Bishop, mainly in England, is the same as a Wassail Bowl but without the ale and with roasted oranges in place of baked apples—page 426.

Bitter Vermouth
(See VERMOUTHS, BITTER.)

Brandy—Armagnac, Cognac, German, U.S.

ALEXANDER
 1 1/2 ounces brandy
 1 ounce Crème de Cacao
 1/2 ounce heavy cream

In a mixing glass, mix brandy, Crème de Cacao, and cream. Shake with shaved ice and strain into 4-ounce stemmed cocktail glass.

ALPINE STINGER
 1 1/2 ounces brandy
 1 ounce Fior d'Alpe

In a 6-ounce Old-Fashioned glass, mix brandy and Fior d'Alpe. Add ice cubes and stir.

APPLE COOLER—page 392.

BALTIMORE BRACER—page 388.

BETWEEN THE SHEETS
1/2 ounce golden rum
1/2 ounce Triple Sec
1/2 ounce brandy
1/2 ounce fresh lemon juice

In a mixing glass, mix rum, Triple Sec, brandy, and lemon juice. Shake with shaved ice and strain into 4-ounce stemmed cocktail glass.

BRANDY CHAMPERELLE—page 397.

BRANDY PUFF—page 421.

BRANDY PUNCH (cold for 10)—page 421.

BRANDY SHRUB (cold for 20)—page 436.

BRANDY SOUR
1 1/2 ounces brandy
1/2 ounce fresh lemon juice
1 teaspoon superfine sugar
2 dashes Angostura Bitters

In a mixing glass, dissolve sugar in lemon juice. Add brandy and bitters and shake with shaved ice. Strain into 4-ounce stemmed Sour or wine glass.

BRANDY STINGER
2 ounces brandy
1 ounce white Crème de Menthe

In a mixing glass, mix brandy and Crème de Menthe. Shake with shaved ice and strain into a 4-ounce stemmed cocktail glass.

CAFE CREME DE CACAO HOT—page 413.

CAFE ROYAL HOT
 3/4 teaspoon brandy
 2 ounces hot black coffee
 1 sugar cube

Pour hot black coffee into a demitasse cup. Put sugar cube in teaspoon and balance over the cup while pouring the brandy onto the sugar cube. Flame the sugar cube and slowly lower into the coffee. Stir gently.

CHAMPAGNE PUNCH WITH A PUNCH (cold for 32)—page 421.

CHARTREUSE BRANDY—page 398.

CIDER CUP (cold for 8)—page 422.

FISH HOUSE PUNCH (cold for 24)—page 422.

FRENCH 75—page 397.

GEORGE WASHINGTON'S COLD CHRISTMAS EGGNOG—page 423.

MODIFIED CHARLESTON JOCKEY CLUB PUNCH (cold for 10)—page 423.

MODIFIED U.S. ARTILLERY PUNCH (cold for 10)—page 424.

ORANGE MINT PUNCH (cold for 8)—page 425.

PINK LADY—page 392.

ROCK CANDY PUNCH (cold for 10)—page 424.

SIDECAR
 2 1/2 ounces brandy
 1/3 ounce Triple Sec
 2/3 ounce fresh lemon juice

Shake well brandy, Triple Sec, and lemon juice with shaved ice and strain into an ice-cold 4-ounce stemmed cocktail glass.

ZOOM—page 452.

Brandy, Cherry (Kirschwasser)

DUBONNET FIZZ—page 403.

KNICKEBEIN—page 416.

Brandy, Peach

FISH HOUSE PUNCH (cold for 24)—page 422.

MODIFIED CHARLESTON JOCKEY CLUB PUNCH (cold for 10)—page 423.

SOUTHERN PEACH FRAPPE—page 407.

Bucks
(See HIGHBALLS.)

The original Buck was a Gin Buck—the darling of the Prohibition era. I now consider it simply a variation of the Highball—page 410.

Byrrh, Apéritif Wine

BYRRH CASSIS—page 389.

Calvados
(See APPLE BRANDY.)

Campari
(See VERMOUTHS, BITTER.)

Cassis
(See CREME DE CASSIS.)

Chambéry Vermouth
(See VERMOUTH, CHAMBERY.)

Champagne, Brut

CHAMPAGNE COCKTAIL—page 380.

CHAMPAGNE PUNCH WITH A PUNCH (cold for 32)—page 421.

FRENCH 75
   2 ounces Cognac
   1 teaspoon superfine sugar
   1 ounce fresh lemon juice
   Brut Champagne

In a mixing glass, dissolve sugar in lemon juice. Add Cognac and shake with ice cubes. Strain over ice cubes into a 10-ounce Highball glass and fill glass with Champagne. Stir gently.

KIR WITH SPARKLE—page 391.

MODIFIED CHARLESTON JOCKEY CLUB PUNCH (cold for 10)—page 423.

MODIFIED U.S. ARTILLERY PUNCH (cold for 10)—page 424.

RASPBERRY CHAMPAGNE—page 391.

ROCK CANDY PUNCH (cold for 10)—page 424.

STRAWBERRY CHAMPAGNE PUNCH (cold for 10)—page 425.

Champerelles
(See POUSSE-CAFE.)

A Champerelle is basically a Pousse-Café with the ingredients stirred up so that they mix.

BRANDY CHAMPERELLE
   1/2 ounce brandy
   1/2 ounce Curaçao
   1/2 ounce Yellow Chartreuse
   1/2 ounce anisette

Pour liqueurs into a 6-ounce snifter and stir gently.

Chartreuse Liqueur, Green or Yellow

ALASKA—page 407.

BIJOU
    1 ounce dry gin
    1 ounce Green Chartreuse
    1 ounce sweet vermouth
    Dash orange bitters
    Lemon peel
    Maraschino cherry

In a mixing glass, mix gin, Chartreuse, vermouth, and bitters. Stir with ice cubes and strain into a 4-ounce cocktail glass. Twist lemon over glass to extract oil essence. Garnish with cherry.

BRANDY CHAMPERELLE—page 397.

CHARTREUSE BRANDY
    3/4 ounce Green Chartreuse
    3/4 ounce brandy
    Fresh sprig of mint

Pour Chartreuse and brandy over shaved ice in a 6-ounce Old-Fashioned glass. Stir and garnish with mint.

CHARTREUSE TONIC
    1 ounce Green Chartreuse
    Tonic (quinine) water

Pour Chartreuse over a single ice cube in an 8-ounce wineglass. Fill with tonic water and stir gently.

Cherry Liqueurs, Danish Heering or Kijafa

CHERRY CHOCOLATE
    1 1/2 ounces cherry liqueur
    1 1/2 ounces white Crème de Cacao

In a 6-ounce Old-Fashioned glass, mix cherry liqueur and Crème de Cacao. Add ice cubes and stir.

THE PERFECT POUSSE-CAFE—page 364.

Cobblers
(See HIGHBALLS.)

The Cobbler—although very popular in the late 1800s—is, in fact, simply a Highball-style Cooler filled with crushed ice and decorated with fruit.

Coffee Liqueur
(Espresso Coffee, Kahlua, Pasha Turkish Coffee, Tía María)

L'ESPRESSINA HOTTA
  1 1/2 ounces coffee liqueur
  1 ounce white Crème de Menthe
  Hot coffee
  2 tablespoons whipped cream
  Shaved Dutch chocolate

In an 8-ounce mug, mix coffee liqueur and Crème de Menthe. Pour in hot coffee, stir, and top with whipped cream. Garnish with shaved Dutch chocolate.

BLACK RUSSIAN
  3 ounces vodka
  1/2 ounce coffee liqueur

In a 6-ounce Old-Fashioned glass, pour vodka and coffee liqueur over one ice cube and stir.

Cognac
(See BRANDY.)

Cointreau Liqueur
(See ORANGE LIQUEURS.)

Cold Punch Bowls
(See PUNCH BOWLS, COLD.)

Collins
(See also HIGHBALLS AND TALL COOLERS.)

BUTTERSCOTCH COLLINS
  1 1/2 ounces Scotch whisky
  1/2 ounce Drambuie
  1/2 ounce lemon juice
  1 teaspoon superfine sugar
  Soda water
  Orange slice
  Maraschino cherry

In a 10-ounce Highball glass, dissolve sugar in lemon juice. Add Scotch and Drambuie. Stir and fill glass with shaved ice. Add splash of soda water and garnish with orange slice and cherry.

RUM COLLINS
    2 ounces golden rum
    1/2 teaspoon orgeat
    1 ounce fresh lemon juice
    Club soda

In a mixing glass, mix orgeat and lemon juice. Add rum and shake with shaved ice. Strain over ice cubes into a 10-ounce Highball glass and fill glass with soda. Stir gently.

TEQUILA COLLINS
    1 1/2 ounces tequila
    1/2 ounce fresh lemon juice
    1 teaspoon superfine sugar
    Club soda

In a mixing glass, dissolve sugar in lemon juice and add tequila. Shake with shaved ice and strain into a 10-ounce Highball glass over ice cubes. Fill glass with club soda and stir gently.

TOM COLLINS
    2 ounces aromatic gin
    1/2 teaspoon orgeat
    1 ounce fresh lemon juice
    Club soda
    Orange slice
    Maraschino cherry

In a mixing glass, mix orgeat and lemon juice. Add gin and shake with shaved ice. Strain over ice cubes into a 10-ounce Highball glass and fill glass with soda. Garnish with orange slice and cherry.

WHISKEY COLLINS
    1 1/2 ounces blended whiskey
    1/2 ounce fresh lime juice
    3 dashes Bénédictine
    Club soda

In a 10-ounce Highball glass, pour whiskey, lime juice, and Bénédictine over ice cubes. Stir to blend and fill glass with club soda. Stir gently.

Coolers
(See HIGHBALLS.*)*

Cordials and Sweet Mixes

For a discussion on the various straight cordials, see chapter 27, page 361.

ALEXANDER—page 393.

ALPINE STINGER—page 393.

BRANDY CHAMPERELLE—page 397.

BRANDY STINGER—page 394.

CHARTREUSE BRANDY—page 398.

CHERRY CHOCOLATE—page 398.

GRASSHOPPER
    1 1/2 ounces green Crème de Menthe
    1 ounce white Crème de Cacao
    1/2 ounce heavy cream

In a mixing glass, mix the Crème de Menthe, Crème de Cacao, and heavy cream. Shake with fine ice and strain into a cold Champagne coupe glass.

KNICKEBEIN—page 416.

THE PERFECT POUSSE-CAFE—page 364.

SOUTHERN PEACH FRAPPE—page 407.

ZOOM—page 452.

Crème de Banane, Liqueur

THE PERFECT POUSSE-CAFE—page 364.

Crème de Cacao, Liqueur, Brown or White

ALEXANDER—page 393.

CAFE CREME DE CACAO HOT—page 413.

CHERRY CHOCOLATE—page 398.

GRASSHOPPER—page 401.

THE PERFECT POUSSE-CAFE—page 364.

Crème de Cassis, Liqueur

BYRRH CASSIS—page 389.

KIR—page 391.

KIR WITH SPARKLE—page 391.

VERMOUTH CASSIS—page 392.

Crème de Menthe, Liqueur, Green or White

BRANDY STINGER—page 394.

L'ESPRESSINA HOTTA— page 399.

GRASSHOPPER—page 401.

SCOTCH COOLER—page 451.

Crustas
(See SOURS.)

A Crusta is simply a Sour with the inside of the glass lined with a spiral of lemon or orange peel.

Daisies
(See SOURS.)

The Olde English Daisy is, in fact, a Sour, sipped with a straw through shaved ice.

Drambuie, Scotch Honey Liqueur

BUTTERSCOTCH COLLINS—page 399.

DRY ROB ROY—page 449.

RUSTY NAIL
    1 1/2 ounces Scotch whisky
    1 1/2 ounces Drambuie

In a 6-ounce Old-Fashioned glass, mix Scotch and Drambuie. Add ice cubes and stir.

Dubonnet Blonde or Rouge

DUBONNET APERITIF
    1 1/2 ounces Dubonnet Blonde
    1 1/2 ounces dry gin
    1 tablespoon fresh orange juice
    2 dashes Angostura Bitters
    Orange slice

In a mixing glass, mix Dubonnet, gin, orange juice, and bitters. Shake with shaved ice and strain into a 4-ounce cocktail glass. Garnish with orange slice.

DUBONNET FIZZ
    3 ounces Dubonnet Rouge
    1 teaspoon cherry brandy
    2 tablespoons fresh orange juice
    1 tablespoon fresh lemon juice
    Soda water

In a mixing glass, mix Dubonnet, cherry brandy, and orange and lemon juices. Shake with shaved ice and strain into a 10-ounce Highball glass. Fill glass with soda water.

FRENCH WENCH
    3 ounces Dubonnet Rouge
    6 ounces ginger ale
    Lemon peel

Pour Dubonnet and ginger ale over ice in a 12-ounce Highball glass. Garnish with lemon twist and serve.

GIN ROUGE—page 407.

MERRY WIDOW
  1 1/2 ounces Dubonnet Blonde
  1 1/2 ounces dry vermouth
  Lemon peel

In a mixing glass, mix Dubonnet and dry vermouth. Stir with ice cubes and strain into a 4-ounce stemmed cocktail glass. Twist lemon over glass to extract oil essence. Drop peel into glass.

Egg Nourishers and Pick-Me-Ups

For the Morning-After, Hair-of-the-Dog Pick-Me-Ups, see chapter 31.

AULD MAN'S NOURRISHMENT—page 449.

EGG NOG (hot for 6)—page 426.

EGG SHERRY FLIP
  2 ounces *oloroso* Sherry
  1 whole egg
  1 teaspoon superfine sugar
  Freshly grated nutmeg

In a mixing glass mix the sugar, egg, and Sherry. Add shaved ice and shake vigorously. Strain into a 4-ounce stemmed cocktail glass and grate fresh nutmeg over drink.

GEORGE WASHINGTON'S COLD CHRISTMAS EGG NOG (for 12)—page 423.

INDIVIDUAL EGG NOG—page 417.

KNICKEBEÏN—page 416.

POSSET—page 420.

WASSAIL BOWL—page 426.

Fior d'Alpe, Liqueur

ALPINE STINGER—page 393.

SCOTCH ALPS—page 450.

Fixes
(See SOURS.*)*

A Fix is simply a Sour sipped with a straw through crushed ice.

RUM FIX
   4 ounces dark rum
   1/2 ounce Cointreau
   1/2 ounce lemon juice
   Orange slice

Mix rum, Cointreau, and lemon juice in a 10-ounce Highball glass and stir. Fill glass with shaved ice and garnish with orange slice. Serve with a straw.

Fizzes

BARBADOS PINK FIZZLE
   3 ounces 90-proof Barbados white rum
   1 1/2 teaspoons orgeat
   1 1/2 teaspoons grenadine
   1 ounce fresh lime juice
   2 dashes Angostura Bitters
   1 egg white
   1 ounce heavy cream
   3/4 cup coarsely chipped ice
   Club soda

Mix the rum, orgeat, grenadine, lime juice, bitters, egg white, heavy cream, and ice into an ice-cold blender jug. Blend at highest speed for 10 to 15 seconds, no more. Pour into 8-ounce frosted silver mug or glass. Add a splash or two of club soda.

GIN FIZZ
   1 1/2 ounces dry gin
   1/2 ounce fresh lemon juice
   1 teaspoon grenadine
   Club soda

In a mixing glass, mix gin, lemon juice, and grenadine. Add ice and stir. Strain over ice cubes into a 6-ounce Old-Fashioned glass. Add a splash of club soda. Stir gently.

A NEW ORLEANS GIN FIZZ
    1 1/2 ounces dry gin
    1/2 teaspoon orgeat
    1 ounce fresh lemon juice
    1 tablespoon egg white
    Club soda
    Maraschino cherry

In a mixing glass, combine orgeat and lemon juice. Add egg white.
Shake vigorously with shaved ice until creamy, then add half the gin.
Shake again. Add rest of gin. Strain over ice cubes in a 10-ounce
Highball glass. Fill glass with soda. Garnish with cherry.

SLOE GIN FIZZ
    2 ounces sloe gin
    1 tablespoon superfine sugar
    1 ounce fresh lemon juice
    1/2 ounce fresh lime juice
    Club soda

In a mixing glass, dissolve sugar in lemon and lime juices. Add sloe gin
and shake with crushed ice. Strain over ice cubes into a 10-ounce
Highball glass. Fill glass with soda and stir gently.

Flips
(See EGG NOURISHERS.)

FRAPPES

Remember that any straight cordial can be served on crushed ice
with a short straw, but Crème de Menthe and Pernod are the two most
often used. Here, in addition, are two mixed Frappés.

FROZEN DAIQUIRI
    2 ounces golden rum (chilled)
    1/2 ounce fresh lime juice (chilled)
    1 teaspoon superfine sugar
    4 ounces shaved ice

The success of this rests in starting with all the ingredients well chilled
and the shaved ice frozen hard. Put all ingredients in an electric
blender and blend for 15 seconds until the mixture is the consistency of
snow. Serve unstrained in a shallow Champagne glass with a short
straw.

SOUTHERN PEACH FRAPPE
    1 1/2 ounces Southern Comfort
    1 1/2 ounces peach brandy
    Orange peel
    1 slice fresh peach, peeled

In a mixing glass, mix Southern Comfort and peach brandy. Fill a Champagne glass with shaved ice and pour liqueur over it. Garnish with orange peel and peach slice and serve with short straw.

GIN ROUGE
    1 1/2 ounces gin
    1 1/2 ounces Dubonnet Rouge
    Lemon peel

Pour gin and Dubonnet over ice in a 6-ounce Old-Fashioned glass. Stir, and twist lemon peel over drink to extract oil essence. Drop peel into glass.

MY FOUR FAVORITE MARTINIS—chapter 3, page 19.

Gin, Dry

ALASKA
    1 1/2 ounces dry gin
    1 ounce Yellow Chartreuse
    2 dashes Orange Bitters

In a mixing glass, mix the gin, Chartreuse, and bitters. Stir with ice cubes and strain into a 4-ounce stemmed cocktail glass.

BIJOU—page 398.

BRONX
    2 ounces dry gin
    1/2 ounce sweet vermouth
    1/2 ounce dry vermouth
    3/4 ounce fresh orange juice
    Orange peel

In a mixing glass, mix gin, sweet and dry vermouths, and orange juice. Stir with ice cubes, strain into a 4-ounce stemmed cocktail glass, and add twist of orange peel.

CLOVER CLUB
> 1 1/2 ounces dry gin
> 1/ ounce grenadine
> 1/2 ounce fresh lime juice
> 1 tablespoon egg white

In a mixing glass, mix grenadine, lime juice, and egg white. Shake with shaved ice. Add some of the gin and continue shaking. Add the rest of the gin and shake more. Strain into 4-ounce stemmed cocktail glass.

CRYING REINDEER OF FINLAND—page 443.

DUBONNET APERITIF—page 403.

GIBSON
> 3 ounces dry gin
> 3 dashes dry vermouth
> Pickled pearl onion

In a mixing glass, mix dry gin and vermouth. Stir with ice cubes and strain into a 4-ounce stemmed cocktail glass. Garnish with pearl onion.

GIMLET
> 2 ounces English dry gin
> 1/2 ounce Rose's lime juice

In a mixing glass, mix gin and lime juice. Stir with ice cubes and strain into 4-ounce stemmed cocktail glass. The glass rim may be dipped in sugar.

GIN AND BITTER LEMON
> 2 ounces dry gin
> Bitter lemon soda
> Wedge of lemon

Squeeze lemon into a 10-ounce Highball glass to extract juice and drop lemon into glass. Add gin and ice cubes. Fill glass with bitter lemon soda and stir gently.

GIN AND BITTERS
>   2 ounces dry gin
>   2 dashes Angostura Bitters

Pour gin over ice in a 6-ounce Old-Fashioned glass. Add bitters and stir.

GIN FIZZ—page 405.

GIN RICKEY
>   1 1/2 ounces dry gin
>   1/2 fresh lime
>   Club soda

Squeeze lime into a 10-ounce Highball glass and drop lime shell into glass. Add gin and ice cubes. Fill glass with soda and stir gently.

GIN AND TONIC
>   1 1/2 ounces dry gin
>   Tonic (quinine) water
>   Wedge of lime

Squeeze lime into a 10-ounce Highball glass to extract juice and drop lime into glass. Add gin and ice cubes. Fill glass with tonic water and stir gently.

A NEW ORLEANS GIN FIZZ—page 406.

PINK LADY—page 392.

SIDEWINDER
>   1 1/2 ounces dry gin
>   1 1/2 ounces anisette

Pour gin and anisette over ice cubes in a 6-ounce Old-Fashioned glass and stir.

TOM COLLINS—page 400.

Gin, Holland Genever

BLOODY JENNIFER
2 ounces Genever gin
4 ounces V8 juice
1/2 ounce lemon juice
Dash salt
Dash pepper

In a mixing glass, mix gin, V8 juice, and lemon juice. Stir with ice cubes. Strain into an 8-ounce stemmed wineglass, add salt and pepper, and stir gently.

MY DOWNRIGHT DANGEROUS MARTINI—chapter 3, page 22.

MY INTIMATE MARTINI—chapter 3, page 22.

Gin, Sloe

SLOE TEQUILA—page 438.

SLOE GIN FIZZ—page 406.

Glöggs, Scandinavian
(See also PUNCH BOWLS, HOT.*)*

HOT SWEDISH GLOGG (Serves about 6)
1 quart dry red wine
8 ounces superfine sugar
2 cinnamon sticks
5 cloves
1 twirl orange peel
1/2 cup raisins
1/2 cup almonds
1/4 cup aquavit
Cardamom pods, peeled

Into a large enameled saucepan, mix the wine, sugar, cinnamon sticks, cloves, orange peel, raisins, almonds, and cardamom. Gently heat for 15 minutes. Pour into a punch bowl and flame with heated aquavit.

Highballs and Tall Coolers

ALE SANGAREE—page 432.

Hot Individual Mugs
(See also PUNCH BOWLS, HOT.*)*

CAFE CREME DE CACAO HOT
    1 ounce Crème de Cacao
    1 ounce Cognac
    5 ounces hot black coffee
    1 teaspoon superfine sugar
    Lemon peel

In an 8-ounce mug, dissolve the sugar in the hot black coffee. Add the Crème de Cacao and Cognac. Stir, and twist lemon peel over drink to extract oil essence. Drop peel into mug.

HOT BUTTERED RUM
  1 ounce golden rum
  2 teaspoons dark-brown sugar
  1 teaspoon butter
  4 whole cloves
  Cinnamon stick
  Boiling water (or hot milk)

Place butter and sugar in bottom of a warmed 8-ounce mug. Cream together with bottom of a mixing spoon. Add rum, cloves, and cinnamon stick and fill with hot water (or milk). Stir and serve hot.

HOT NEGUS —page 417.

HOT RUM TODDY
  3 ounces light rum
  1 teaspoon honey
  1/4-inch-thick lemon slice stuck with 3 cloves
  Boiling water
  Cinnamon stick

In an 8-ounce mug, mix the honey and rum. Add boiling water and cinnamon stick and stir. Garnish with lemon slice stuck with cloves.

IRISH COFFEE
  1 1/2 ounces Irish whisky
  5 ounces hot black coffee
  1 teaspoon superfine sugar
  Whipped cream

In an 8-ounce mug, dissolve the sugar in the black coffee. Add Irish whisky. Stir and top with whipped cream.

NEGUS —page 417.

POSSET —page 420.

TOM AND JERRY

　　1 ounce golden rum
　　1 egg, separated
　　1 tablespoon superfine sugar
　　1/4 teaspoon ground allspice
　　1/4 teaspoon ground cloves
　　5 ounces hot milk
　　Freshly grated nutmeg

Beat egg yolk in a small bowl, add sugar, allspice, and cloves, and beat until thoroughly blended. In a separate bowl, beat egg white and add to egg yolk and blend. Spoon into a warmed 8-ounce mug, and add rum and milk, stirring briskly to blend. Grate fresh nutmeg over drink.

VODKA STEAMER PICK-UP

　　2 ounces vodka
　　5 ounces clam juice
　　1/2 ounce tomato sauce
　　1 dash celery salt
　　1 dash Tabasco

Warm the clam juice, tomato sauce, celery salt, and Tabasco, stirring to blend. Pour over vodka in an 8-ounce mug.

Hot Punch Bowls
(See PUNCH BOWLS, HOT.*)*

Juleps

MINT JULEP—page 382.

Kirschwasser
(See BRANDY, CHERRY.*)*

Knickebeins
(See EGG NOURISHERS.*)*

I regard the Knickebein as a kind of bastardized combination of an Egg-Flip and a Pousse-Café, but, in terms of nourishment, leaning toward the former—page 404.

KNICKEBEIN
- 1 ounce Bénédictine
- 1 ounce Curaçao
- 1 ounce Kirschwasser
- 1 egg, separated
- 1 dash Angostura Bitters

In a mixing glass, mix together the Bénédictine, Curaçao, and Kirschwasser. Pour into a Champagne coupe. Separate the egg and drop the yolk gently onto the top of the spirits. In a bowl, beat the egg white until it forms stiff peaks. Carefully mound the whites over the yolk, and add a dash of bitters. This concoction is eaten (or drunk) in three parts. First eat the egg white, then drink the liquid, and, finally, down the egg yolk with the last sip.

Lillet, Gold or Red
(See VERMOUTHS, DRY.*)*

Liqueurs, Mixed
(See CORDIALS AND SWEET MIXES.*)*

(For the discussion of straight cordials, see chapter 27, page 361—for mixed cordials, page 360.)

Mists

A Mist is not truly a mixed drink. It is simply a dose of Scotch or some other spirit poured onto a Frappé base of crushed ice. Therefore, none is included in this department.

Mulls
(See PUNCH BOWLS, HOT.*)*

In the old days in England, Mulled Wine was simply a punch mixture, heated up with a red-hot poker. Nowadays it is easier to "hot it up" on the kitchen stove.

Negus, Hot
(See also HOT INDIVIDUAL MUGS.)

In the days of jolly Good Queen Anne of England, a certain Colonel Francis Negus invented this method of heating up a mug of wine by adding boiling water.

NEGUS
> 4 ounces Port wine
> 1/2 teaspoon superfine sugar
> 1 teaspoon lemon juice
> Boiling water
> Lemon peel
> Cinnamon stick

In a warmed 8-ounce mug, dissolve the superfine sugar in one tablespoon boiling water. Add lemon juice and Port. Fill with boiling water and garnish with lemon peel and cinnamon stick.

Nogs
(See also PUNCH BOWLS, HOT.)

GEORGE WASHINGTON'S COLD CHRISTMAS EGG NOG (for 12) —page 423.

HOT EGG NOG BOWL (for 6) —page 426.

INDIVIDUAL EGG NOG
> 2 ounces Bourbon whiskey
> 1 cup milk
> 1 egg
> 1 teaspoon sugar
> Nutmeg

In a mixing glass, mix the Bourbon, milk, egg, and sugar. Shake with cracked ice and strain into a 12-ounce Highball glass. Grate nutmeg on top before serving.

Orange Liqueur
(Cointreau, Curaçao, Grand Marnier, Triple Sec)

BETWEEN THE SHEETS—page 394.

BRANDY CHAMPERELLE—page 397.

CHAMPAGNE PUNCH WITH A PUNCH—page 421.

CIDER CUP—page 422.

CRANBERRY SPRITZER—page 390.

KISS ME QUICK—page 419.

KNICKEBEIN—page 416.

MARGARITA—page 381.

MILLIONAIRE
    1 1/2 ounces Bourbon or rye whiskey
    1/2 ounce Curaçao
    1 tablespoon egg white
    1 dash grenadine

In a mixing glass, beat egg white, grenadine, and cracked ice until creamy. Add some of the whiskey and Curaçao and shake well, then add remainder of each and shake again. Strain into a 4-ounce stemmed cocktail glass to serve.

THE PERFECT POUSSE-CAFE—page 364.

EL PRESIDENTE—page 431.

RUM FIX—page 405.

SIDECAR—page 395.

Pernod, Anis
(See also ANIS LIQUEURS.)

BRANDY CHAMPERELLE—page 397.

CLOCKWORK ORANGE—page 388.

KISS ME QUICK
 2 ounces Pernod
 1/2 teaspoon Curaçao
 2 dashes Angostura Bitters
 Soda water

In a mixing glass, mix Pernod, Curaçao, and bitters. Shake with crushed ice and strain over ice cubes in a 10-ounce Highball glass. Fill glass with soda water and stir gently.

PASTIS MARSEILLAISE—page 388.

SAZERAC—page 446.

SIDEWINDER—page 409.

SUISSESSE—page 389.

Pick-Me-Ups, Morning-After
(See CHAPTER 31.*)*

Picon
(See VERMOUTHS, BITTER.*)*

FRANCO-AMERICAN HALF AND HALF
 3 ounces Picon
 3 ounces Bourbon whiskey
 Lemon peel

In an 8-ounce Old-Fashioned glass over ice cubes, pour the Picon and Bourbon whiskey. Add a twist of lemon peel, stir gently, and serve.

PICON-CITRON
 2 ounces Picon
 1 ounce lemon juice

In a 6-ounce Old-Fashioned glass over ice, pour the Picon and lemon juice. Stir gently and serve.

PICON DE LEVALLOIS
  2 ounces Picon
  1/2 teaspoon grenadine syrup
  Club soda
  Lemon peel

In a 6-ounce Old-Fashioned glass, over ice, mix the Picon with the grenadine. Add a dash of soda, a twist of lemon peel, stir gently, and serve.

PICON VERMOUTH—page 391.

Possets, Hot
(See also HOT INDIVIDUAL MUGS.*)*

English-style Possets were a mixture of milk, curdled with ale and enriched with eggs—very nourishing and warming on a wintry night.

POSSET (Serves about 4)
  1 cup ale
  2 cups heavy cream
  5 eggs, separated
  1 1/2 teaspoons sugar
  Whole nutmeg
  Ground cinnamon
  Cloves
  Allspice

In an enamel or stainless steel saucepan or top of double boiler, beat together the egg yolks and 3 of the egg whites with the cream and sugar. Mix in the ale, grind nutmeg generously over the top, and add cinnamon, cloves, and allspice, 1/4 teaspoon each. Cook slowly over hot water until concoction thickens, then pour into mugs and serve.

Pousse-Cafés

BRANDY CHAMPERELLE—page 397.

KNICKEBEIN—page 416.

THE PERFECT POUSSE-CAFE—page 364.

Puffs

A cold, long drink of a mixture of milk, sodawater, and spirits.

BRANDY PUFF
 1 1/2 ounces brandy
 1 1/2 ounces milk
 Soda water

In a mixing glass, mix the brandy and milk. Add ice cubes and stir. Strain into a 4-ounce stemmed cocktail glass and add soda water.

Punch Bowls, Cold

BRANDY PUNCH (Serves about 10)
 1 1/2 pints golden rum
 1 1/2 pints brandy
 2 pounds powdered sugar
 2 cups water
 1/2 cup fresh lime juice
 1/2 cup fresh lemon juice
 2 oranges, diced
 1 lemon, diced
 1 pineapple, diced

Dissolve sugar in water. In a punch bowl over a large chunk of ice, mix the rum, brandy, lemon and lime juices, and the dissolved sugar. Stir gently and garnish with diced fruit.

CHAMPAGNE PUNCH WITH A PUNCH (Serves about 32)
 4 quarts brut Champagne (chilled)
 1 quart Cognac
 1 quart dry Sherry
 1/2 pint Curaçao
 4 ounces Maraschino liqueur
 2 quarts club soda

In a punch bowl over a large chunk of ice, mix the Champagne, Cognac, Sherry, Curaçao, Maraschino liqueur, and club soda. Stir gently and serve immediately.

CIDER CUP (Serves about 8)
  1 1/2 quarts cider (chilled)
  7 ounces brandy
  7 ounces dry Sherry
  7 ounces Curaçao
  1/4 cup superfine sugar or to taste
  4 ounces orange juice
  Orange slices
  Thin lemon peels

Dissolve sugar in orange juice. In a punch bowl over a large chunk of ice, mix the cider, brandy, Sherry, Curaçao, and orange juice. Stir and add orange slices and lemon peels.

FISH HOUSE PUNCH (Serves about 24)

The "Fish House" comes from one of three club houses of the "State in Schuylkill," founded in 1732 as a "colony" and claimed to be the oldest men's club in the English-speaking world. The main building is the "State House," where the Club's "governor" has his office and where business is transacted; the second building is "The Castle," where members (limited to thirty and called "citizens") meet and dine formally; the third building is the "Fish House," down by the river bank, where citizens brought the fish they caught in the river to be prepared and eaten informally. On these occasions, the fabled Fish House Punch was served.

Today, the club is just outside the Philadelphia city line. Because of pollution, there is no more fishing, but the club still has its traditional three separate buildings and the punch is still served in the Fish House.

  2 quarts golden rum
  1 quart Cognac
  4 ounces peach brandy
  1 pound dark-brown sugar
  2 quarts water
  1 quart fresh lemon juice

Dissolve brown sugar in water. Add lemon juice and let stand. Elsewhere, mix rum, Cognac, and peach brandy. Pour both mixtures over a large chunk of ice in a punch bowl. Stir and refrigerate to mature for two hours.

GEORGE WASHINGTON'S COLD CHRISTMAS EGG NOG (Serves about 20)
  2 quarts heavy cream
  1 dozen eggs
  1 pound sugar
  1 pint brandy
  1/4 pint rye whiskey
  1/4 pint golden rum
  1/4 pint sweet Sherry
  Nutmeg

Mix the brandy, rye, rum, and Sherry together in a large jar. Add sugar and dissolve. Then separate the eggs and beat the yolks until foamy. Beat in the liquor, very slowly. Beat the cream in a bowl until stiff and add the egg yolk-liquor combination. Then beat egg whites until they form stiff peaks and fold them gently into the egg yolk-cream mixture. Store in a cool place several hours or, preferably, days. Grate nutmeg over the top just before serving.

MODIFIED CHARLESTON JOCKEY CLUB PUNCH (Serves about 10)
  1/2 bottle dry Champagne (chilled)
  1 bottle medium-priced French Cognac
  10 ounces 151-proof dark Demerara rum
  4 ounces dry peach brandy
  2 cups hot not-too-strong tea
  Grated outer rind of 1 lemon
  3/4 cup superfine white sugar
  5 ounces fresh lemon juice

Mix the lemon rind and sugar in a 2-quart mixing bowl. Mash and pound together with pestle or wooden spoon and add the lemon juice, Cognac, rum, peach brandy, and hot tea. Stir thoroughly, cover, and mature in refrigerator for at least 12 hours. Just before serving, pour over a large chunk of ice in a punch bowl and add Champagne. Stir gently and serve.

MODIFIED U.S. ARTILLERY PUNCH (Serves about 10)
  1/2 to 1 bottle dry Champagne (chilled)
  1 bottle 86-proof dark Demerara rum
  1 bottle dry Spanish Sherry
  1/2 cup medium-priced French Cognac
  Grated outer rind of 1 lemon
  3/4 cup superfine white sugar
  2 ounces fresh lemon juice
  4 ounces fresh orange juice
  1 1/4 cups hot not-too-strong tea

Mix the lemon rind and sugar in a 2-quart mixing bowl and mash and pound together with pestle or wooden spoon. Blend in the lemon and orange juices, and tea, and stir thoroughly. Refrigerate to cool, then add rum, Sherry, and Cognac. Stir thoroughly, cover, and mature in refrigerator for at least 6 hours. Just before serving, pour over a large chunk of ice in a punch bowl and add 1/2 to 1 bottle of Champagne to taste. Stir gently and serve.

ROCK CANDY PUNCH (Serves about 10)
  1 bottle brut Champagne (chilled)
  1/2 bottle dry Sherry (chilled)
  1 cup brandy
  1/4 pound rock candy
  1 pint hot tea
  Thin lemon slices

Dissolve the rock candy in the hot tea. Cool and add Champagne, Sherry, brandy, and lemon slices. Stir gently and pour into a punch bowl over a large chunk of ice. Serve immediately.

SANGRIA DE MADRID (Serves about 12)
  2 bottles dry red wine
  1 cup superfine sugar
  6 ounces fresh lemon juice
  4 ounces fresh orange juice
  2 lemons, sliced
  4 oranges, in wedges
  1-2 quarts club soda
  Chunks of seasonal fruits: apples, bananas, pears, pineapple, etc.

In a large punch bowl, combine wine, sugar, lemon and orange juices, lemon slices and orange wedges, 1-2 quarts of club soda to taste, and chunks of fruit. Chill well.

ORANGE MINT PUNCH (Serves about 8)
  1 bottle golden rum
  2 ounces gin
  2 ounces brandy
  6 ounces orgeat
  8 ounces white wine
  6 ounces fresh orange juice
  10 ounces fresh lemon juice
  2 sprigs of mint

In a large pitcher, mix the rum, gin, brandy, orgeat, white wine, orange and lemon juices, and sprigs of mint. Stir and refrigerate to mature for 2 hours. Just before serving, pour into a punch bowl over a large chunk of ice.

STIRRUP CUP (Serves about 8)
  1 pint golden rum
  3 tablespoons dark-brown sugar
  3 tablespoons water
  3 ounces fresh lime juice
  6 ounces pineapple juice
  Lemon peel spirals

Dissolve brown sugar in the water. In a punch bowl over a large chunk of ice, mix rum, fruit juices, and the dissolved sugar. Stir and ladle into 10-ounce Highball glasses over shaved ice. Garnish with lemon peel spirals. Serve with a straw.

STRAWBERRY CHAMPAGNE PUNCH (Serves about 10)
  1 bottle brut Champagne (chilled)
  1 bottle Rhine wine (chilled)
  1 pint club soda (chilled)
  1 quart fresh strawberries
  1/2 ounce fresh lemon juice
  2 tablespoons superfine sugar or to taste

In a small mixing bowl, sprinkle strawberries with sugar and lemon juice. Add 1/2 bottle of Rhine wine, refrigerate, and marinate for 3 hours. Just before serving, mix the strawberries and wine, the remaining Rhine wine, Champagne, and club soda over a large chunk of ice in a punch bowl. Stir gently and serve.

SWEDISH PUNCH (Serves about 10)
  1 quart Rhine wine (chilled)
  6 ounces fresh lemon juice
  3 ounces lime juice
  1/4 cup superfine sugar or to taste
  1 quart club soda (chilled)
  Orange, lime, lemon slices
  Fresh mint sprigs
  Fresh strawberries

Dissolve sugar in fruit juices. In a punch bowl over a large chunk of ice, mix the Rhine wine, fruit juices, and club soda. Stir gently and garnish with lime, orange, and lemon slices, sprigs of mint, and strawberries. Serve immediately.

Punch Bowls, Hot

HOT EGG NOG BOWL (Serves about 6)
  9 ounces Bourbon whiskey
  3 ounces golden rum
  6 egg yolks
  6 egg whites, beaten stiff
  2 tablespoons superfine sugar
  1 pint heavy cream, whipped
  1 pint milk

Beat egg yolks with sugar and spoon into a punch bowl. Add milk, whiskey, and rum, mix well, and fold in whipped cream. Finally, gently fold in beaten egg whites and chill for at least 3 hours.

HOT SWEDISH GLOGG —page 410.

WASSAIL BOWL
  2 quarts ale
  4 ounces superfine sugar
  1/2 pint Scotch whisky
  2 eggs, separated
  1 whole nutmeg, grated

In a saucepan boil 2 quarts of ale with a nutmeg, grated. Add 4 ounces sugar. Pour mix into 2 egg whites and 1 yolk, well beaten; then stir in

1/2 pint of Scotch. Bring almost to a boil again, then pour back and forth between 2 containers until it froths. Pour into a small punch bowl and ladle into punch cups.

Raphaël, Apéritif Wine
(See also VERMOUTHS, BITTER.*)*

RAPHAEL-CITRON
  2 ounces Raphaël
  Lemon twist

In a 6-ounce Old-Fashioned glass, pour the Raphaël over ice cubes and serve with a twist of lemon.

SAINT-BATARD
  4 ounces Raphaël
  2 ounces vodka

In a 10-ounce Highball glass over ice cubes, pour the Raphaël and vodka. Stir gently and serve.

Rickeys
(See HIGHBALLS AND TALL COOLERS.*)*

Rocks

This is not a mixed drink. It is simply a slug of Scotch or some other spirit poured over ice cubes. Therefore it is not included in this department.

Rum, Dark

MARTINIQUE
  2 ounces dark Martinique rum
  1/2 ounce fresh lemon or lime juice
  1/2 teaspoon orgeat
  2 dashes grenadine

In a mixing glass, combine orgeat and lemon juice. Add rum and grenadine and shake with shaved ice. Strain into a 4-ounce stemmed cocktail glass.

MODIFIED CHARLESTON JOCKEY CLUB PUNCH (cold for 10)—page 423.

MODIFIED U.S. ARTILLERY PUNCH (cold for 10)—page 424.

MY BASIC PLANTER'S PUNCH
    2 ounces 86-proof dark Demerara rum
    1/2 ounce Falernum
    1 1/2 ounces fresh lime juice
    1 ounce fresh orange juice
    1 ounce sweet pineapple juice
    2 dashes Angostura Bitters
    Club soda
    Orange slice
    Fresh sprig of mint
    Freshly grated nutmeg

In an ice-cold 12-ounce Highball glass, mix the lime, orange, and pineapple juices, Falernum, rum, and bitters. Add ice cubes and stir vigorously. Fill glass with club soda and stir gently. Garnish with sprig of mint and hang orange slice on edge of glass. Float pinch of nutmeg on top. Serve with long spoon and straw.

MY TIE—page 431.

PINA COLADA—page 431.

RUM FIX—page 405.

TUTTI-FRUTTI, TUTTI-RUM
    2 ounces golden rum
    1 ounce dark Demerara rum
    1/2 ounce Martinique rum
    1 ounce pineapple juice
    1 ounce papaya juice (canned)
    1 ounce fresh lime juice
    1/2 teaspoon orgeat
    Slice of fresh pineapple

In a mixing glass, combine orgeat with pineapple, papaya, and lime juices. Add the 3 rums. Shake with fine ice, and strain into a 14-ounce

Highball glass filled with shaved ice. Garnish with slice of fresh pineapple.

Rum, Golden

BARBADOS PINK FIZZLE—page 405.

BETWEEN THE SHEETS—page 394.

BRANDY PUNCH (cold for 10)—page 421.

EL CONQUISTADOR
    1 1/2 ounces golden rum
    2 ounces fresh orange juice
    2 ounces pineapple juice
    1 ounce lemon juice
    1 ounce coconut milk
    1 1/2 ounces grenadine
    Pineapple chunk

In a mixing glass, pour the rum, orange juice, pineapple juice, lemon juice, coconut milk, and grenadine. Shake with shaved ice and strain over ice cubes in a 12-ounce Highball glass. Garnish with pineapple.

MY PERFECT DAIQUIRI—chapter 29, page 380.

STANDARD DAIQUIRI
    1 1/2 ounces golden rum
    1/2 teaspoon orgeat
    1/2 ounce fresh lime juice

In a mixing glass, mix orgeat and lime juice. Add rum and shake with shaved ice and strain into a 4-ounce stemmed cocktail glass.

FISH HOUSE PUNCH (cold for 24)—page 422.

GEORGE WASHINGTON'S COLD CHRISTMAS EGG NOG (for 20)—page 423.

GROG WITH PASSION
   3 ounces golden rum
   1/2 ounce Falernum
   1 ounce fresh lime juice
   1 ounce fresh orange juice
   1 ounce pineapple juice
   1 ounce passion fruit nectar
   1/2 cup shaved ice
   Fresh sprigs of mint

In a blender, mix the rum, Falernum, lime, orange, and pineapple juices, fruit nectar, and shaved ice. Blend for 15 seconds and pour over shaved ice in a 14-ounce Highball glass. Garnish with sprigs of mint and serve with a straw.

HONEY BEE
   2 ounces golden rum
   3/4 ounce fresh lemon juice
   1/2 ounce honey

In a mixing glass, mix lemon juice and honey. Add rum, and shake with shaved ice. Strain into a 4-ounce stemmed cocktail glass.

HOT BUTTERED RUM—page 414.

HOT EGG NOG BOWL—page 426.

HOT RUM TODDY—page 414.

MOJITO
   3 ounces golden rum
   1 ounce fresh lime juice
   1/2 teaspoon orgeat
   Club soda
   Fresh sprig of mint

In a 10-ounce Highball glass, mix orgeat and lime juice. Remove mint leaves from stem, add to glass, and muddle. Add rum and fill glass with shaved ice. Add a splash of club soda and stir gently.

MY TIE
  1 1/2 ounces dark rum
  1 1/2 ounces golden rum
  1/2 ounce Curaçao
  1/2 ounce orgeat
  1/2 ounce fresh lime juice
  Sprig of mint
  Fresh pineapple stick

In a mixing glass, mix dark rum, golden rum, Curaçao, orgeat, and lime juice. Shake with shaved ice and pour over shaved ice in a 14-ounce Highball glass. Garnish with sprig of mint and pineapple stick. Serve with straw.

ORANGE MINT PUNCH —page 425.

PINA COLADA
  1 1/2 ounces golden rum
  3 ounces unsweetened pineapple juice
  3/4 ounce canned coconut milk
  2 slices fresh pineapple
  2 dashes dark rum

In a blinder, mix golden rum, pineapple juice, coconut milk, 2 slices of pineapple, and the dark rum. Blend at medium speed for 15 seconds. Pour over shaved ice in a 10-ounce Highball glass. Serve with a straw.

EL PRESIDENTE
  1 1/2 ounces golden rum
  1/2 ounce Curaçao
  1/2 ounce dry vermouth
  1 dash grenadine

In a mixing glass, mix rum, Curaçao, vermouth, and grenadine. Add ice cubes and stir. Strain into a 4-ounce stemmed cocktail glass.

RUM COLLINS—page 400.

STIRRUP CUP—page 425.

TOM AND JERRY —page 415.

St. Raphaël
(See RAPHAEL.*)*

Sangarees
(See HIGHBALLS AND TALL COOLERS.*)*

An Anglicized version of the Spanish word sangría (page 424), which, among English planters in tropical countries, came to mean various mixtures of ales, beers, spirits, and red wines with grated nutmeg.

ALE SANGAREE
    8 ounces dark beer (chilled)
    1 teaspoon superfine sugar
    1 teaspoon water
    Freshly grated nutmeg

Put sugar into a 10-ounce Highball glass. Add water and muddle. Add chilled beer and gently stir. Grate fresh nutmeg over drink.

Scandinavian Glöggs
(See GLOGGS, SCANDINAVIAN.*)*

Scotch
(See WHISKY, SCOTCH.*)*

Sherry, Spanish, Dry Fino

CHAMPAGNE PUNCH WITH A PUNCH (cold for 32) —page 421.

CIDER CUP—page 422.

MODIFIED U.S. ARTILLERY PUNCH (cold for 10) —page 424.

ROCK CANDY PUNCH—page 424.

SHERRY AND BITTERS—page 392.

SOVIETSKY NIETSKY—page 443.

Sherry, Spanish, Sweet Oloroso

EGG SHERRY FLIP —page 404.

Short Drinks

AFFINITY—page 448.

AKVAVIT SOUR—page 387.

ALASKA —page 407.

BALTIMORE BRACER —page 388.

BARBADOS PINK FIZZLE—page 405.

BETWEEN THE SHEETS —page 394.

BIJOU —page 398.

BLACK RUSSIAN —page 399.

BLACKTHORN —page 447.

BLOODY MARIA OLE —page 438.

BOBBY BURNS —page 449.

BRONX—page 407.

BYRRH CASSIS —page 389.

CHAMPAGNE COCKTAIL —page 380.

CIN-CIN —page 390.

CLOVER CLUB —page 408.

CRYING REINDEER OF FINLAND—page 443.

Shrubs
(See HIGHBALLS AND TALL COOLERS.)

In England, various mixtures of fruit juices, spirits, and sugar, properly aged, preferably in a stone crock.

BRANDY SHRUB (Serves about 20)
2 quarts brandy
1 cup fresh lemon juice
Peels from 2 full lemons
Half a nutmeg
3 pints white wine
1 pound superfine sugar

Mix brandy, lemon juice, lemon peels, and nutmeg in a large bottle, cover, and let stand for 3 days. Then dissolve sugar in the wine and add to the brandy mixture. Strain through a piece of flannel and cover to mature for several weeks. When ready to serve, pour over ice in 12-ounce Highball glasses.

Slings
(See HIGHBALLS AND TALL COOLERS.*)*

A Sling is, in my opinion, a cold version of a spiced Toddy.

Sloe Gin

SLOE GIN FIZZ—page 406.

SLOE TEQUILA—page 438.

Suze
(See also VERMOUTHS, BITTER.*)*

SUZIE'S GRENADINE
   2 ounces Suze
   1 teaspoon grenadine syrup
   1 teaspoon lemon juice
   Soda water

In a 6-ounce Old-Fashioned glass over ice, mix the Suze, grenadine, and lemon juice. Add a dash of soda, stir gently and serve.

Sweet Mixtures
(See CORDIALS AND SWEET MIXES.*)*

Swizzles
(See HIGHBALLS AND TALL COOLERS.*)*

A Swizzle is simply a form of Highball, violently stirred until it foams.

Tall Coolers
(See HIGHBALLS.*)*

Tequila

BLOODY MARIA OLE

    2 ounces tequila
    2 ounces tomato juice
    1/2 ounce fresh lemon juice
    1 dash Worcestershire sauce

In a mixing glass, mix tequila, tomato juice, lemon juice, and Worcestershire sauce. Shake with shaved ice and strain into a 6-ounce Old-Fashioned glass over ice.

MARGARITA—page 381.

SCREWDRIVER DEL SOL

    2 ounces tequila
    6 ounces fresh orange juice

In a 10-ounce Highball glass, pour tequila and orange juice over ice cubes. Stir well.

SLOE TEQUILA

    1 1/4 ounces tequila
    1/2 ounce sloe gin
    1 ounce fresh lemon juice
    1/2 ounce grenadine
    Pineapple slice
    Maraschino cherry

In a 12-ounce Highball glass, mix tequila, sloe gin, lemon juice, and grenadine. Stir and add shaved ice. Garnish with pineapple slice and cherry. Serve with straw.

TEQUILA COLLINS—page 400.

TEQUILA KAVE

    2 ounces tequila
    2 teaspoons strong coffee
    Bitter lemon soda

In a 6-ounce Old-Fashioned glass, mix tequila with strong coffee. Add ice cubes and fill with bitter lemon soda.

TEQUILA SOUR
   1 1/2 ounces tequila
   1/2 ounce fresh lemon juice
   1 teaspoon superfine sugar
   Lemon slice
   Maraschino cherry

In a mixing glass, dissolve sugar in lemon juice and add tequila. Shake with shaved ice and strain into 5-ounce stemmed sour glass. Garnish with lemon slice and cherry.

TEQUILA STRAIGHT
   1 1/2 ounces tequila
   Lemon wedge
   Pinch of coarse salt

Serve tequila in a shot glass with salt and lemon wedge on the side. The technique is to suck the lemon wedge, take a little salt on the tongue, and then take a swallow of the tequila.

TEQUILA SUNRISE
   2 ounces tequila
   1 ounce fresh lemon juice
   1/2 ounce grenadine
   1 teaspoon egg white

In a mixing glass, mix tequila, lemon juice, and grenadine. Add egg white and shake with shaved ice. Strain into 6-ounce Old-Fashioned glass over ice cubes.

Toddies
(See HOT INDIVIDUAL MUGS.*)*

Triple Sec
(See ORANGE LIQUEURS.*)*

Vermouths, Bitter
(Campari, Picon, Punt e Mes, Raphaël, Suze)

AMERICANO—page 389.

CAMPARI-CITRON—page 389.

CAMPARISODA—page 390.

CAMPARI-TONIQUE —page 390.

FRANCO-AMERICAN HALF AND HALF—page 419.

NEGRONI
   2 ounces gin
   2 ounces sweet vermouth
   2 ounces Campari
   Lemon peel

Pour gin, vermouth, and Campari over ice in a 10-ounce Highball glass. Twist lemon peel over drink to extract oil essence. Drop peel into glass.

PICON-CITRON—page 419.

PICON DE LEVALLOIS—page 420.

PICON VERMOUTH —page 391.

PUNT RETURN
   2 ounces Punt e Mes
   3 ounces pineapple juice
   Lemon peel

Pour Punt e Mes and pineapple juice over ice in a 6-ounce Old-Fashioned glass. Stir and twist lemon peel over glass to extract oil essence. Drop peel into glass.

RAPHAEL-CITRON—page 427.

SAINT-BATARD—page 427.

SUZIE'S GRENADINE—page 437.

Vermouth, Chambéry

MY MOST DANGEROUS MARTINI —page 22.

Vermouths, Dry

Vermouths, Sweet

BOBBY BURNS—page 449.

BRONX—page 407.

CIN-CIN—page 390.

GIN AND SIN— chapter 29,—page 381.

HARRY LAUDER—page 449.

MANHATTAN, REGULAR—page 444.

NEGRONI—page 440.

ROB ROY—page 450.

Vodka

BUGS BUNNY
>   3 ounces vodka
>   4 ounces carrot juice (chilled)
>   1/2 teaspoon grated horseradish
>   2 dashes Worcestershire sauce
>   1/2 ounce fresh lemon juice
>   1 dash Tabasco

In a mixing glass, mix vodka, carrot juice, horseradish, lemon juice, Worcestershire sauce, and Tabasco. Shake with shaved ice and strain into an 8-ounce stemmed wineglass.

BULLSHOT
>   3 ounces vodka
>   5 ounces beef bouillon (chilled)
>   2 dashes Worcestershire sauce
>   Freshly ground pepper

In a 10-ounce Highball glass, pour vodka and bouillon over ice cubes. Add Worcestershire sauce and stir well. Grind fresh pepper lightly over top.

MY DOWNRIGHT DANGEROUS MARTINI—chapter 3, page 22.

CRYING REINDEER OF FINLAND
    1 ounce dry white wine
    1 ounce vodka
    1 ounce dry gin
    Dash of dry vermouth
    2 cranberries

Pour dry white wine, vodka, and gin over ice in a 6-ounce Old-Fashioned glass. Add a splash of dry vermouth and stir well. Garnish with 2 cranberries (these are the tears).

DIRTY DOG
    4 ounces vodka
    4 ounces fresh grapefruit juice

In a 10-ounce Highball glass, pour vodka and grapefruit juice over ice cubes. Stir well.

MOSCOW MULE
    2 ounces vodka
    1/2 ounce fresh lime juice
    6 ounces ginger beer (chilled)
    Slice of lime

In a 10-ounce beer mug (preferably copper), mix vodka and lime juice. Add ice cubes and fill mug with ginger beer. Garnish with slice of lime, slit to hang on side of mug.

SOVIETSKY NIETSKY
    2 ounces vodka
    1 teaspoon dry Sherry
    1 teaspoon dry vermouth

In a 6-ounce Old-Fashioned glass, mix vodka, Sherry, and vermouth. Add ice cubes and stir.

VODKA GIMLET
    2 ounces vodka
    1 ounce Rose's lime juice (sweetened)

In a mixing glass, mix vodka and Rose's lime juice. Add ice and stir well. Strain into 4-ounce stemmed cocktail glass.

VODKA ON THE ROCKS
   3 ounces vodka

In a 6-ounce Old-Fashioned glass, pour vodka over no more than 2 ice cubes.

VODKA SOUR
   2 ounces vodka
   1 ounce fresh lemon juice
   1/2 teaspoon superfine sugar
   1 dash Angostura Bitters

In a mixing glass, dissolve sugar in lemon juice. Add vodka and bitters and shake with shaved ice. Strain into 4-ounce stemmed Sour or wine glass.

VODKA STEAMER —page 415.

Wassail Bowls
(See PUNCH BOWLS, HOT.*)*

Whiskeys—American, Blended, Canadian

MY FAVORITE DRY MANHATTAN —chapter 29, page 380.

MANHATTAN, REGULAR
   1 1/2 ounces Bourbon, rye, or blended whiskey
   3/4 ounce sweet vermouth
   1 dash Angostura Bitters
   Maraschino cherry

In a mixing glass, mix whiskey, sweet vermouth, and Angostura Bitters. Stir with ice cubes. Strain into a 4-ounce stemmed cocktail glass. Garnish with cherry.

MONTE CARLO —page 393.

OLD-FASHIONED —page 381.

WHISKEY COLLINS —page 400.

WHISKEY SOUR
　　2 ounces blended whiskey
　　1/2 teaspoon superfine sugar
　　1 ounce lemon juice
　　Orange slide
　　Maraschino cherry

In a mixing glass, dissolve sugar in lemon juice. Add whiskey and shake with shaved ice. Strain into 4-ounce stemmed sour or wine glass. Garnish with orange slice and cherry.

Whiskey, Bourbon

ARCTIC COOLER
　　2 ounces rye or Bourbon whiskey
　　2 ounces fresh orange juice
　　Ginger ale
　　Orange peel
　　Orange slice

In a mixing glass, mix whiskey and orange juice. Twist orange peel to extract the oil essence. Drop peel into glass and stir with ice cubes. Strain into 10-ounce Highball glass and fill glass with ginger ale. Garnish with orange slice.

BOURBON AND GINGER
　　2 ounces Bourbon whiskey
　　Ginger ale

Pour whiskey over ice cubes in a 10-ounce Highball glass. Fill glass with ginger ale. Stir gently.

FRISCO
　　2 ounces Bourbon whiskey
　　1 ounce Bénédictine

In a mixing glass, mix whiskey and Bénédictine and stir with ice cubes. Strain into 4-ounce stemmed cocktail glass.

HOT EGG NOG BOWL—page 426.

INDIVIDUAL EGG NOG—page 417.

MANHATTAN
  MY FAVORITE DRY —chapter 29, page 380.
  REGULAR —page 444.

MILLIONAIRE —page 418.

MINT JULEP —page 382.

MONTE CARLO —page 393.

NEW YORKER
  1 1/2 ounces rye or Bourbon whiskey
  1/2 ounce fresh lime juice
  1 teaspoon superfine sugar
  2 dashes grenadine
  Orange peel

In a mixing glass, dissolve sugar in lime juice, and add whiskey and
grenadine. Shake with shaved ice and strain into 4-ounce stemmed
cocktail glass. Twist orange peel over drink to extract oil essence. Drop
peel into drink.

OLD-FASHIONED —page 381.

SAZERAC
  2 ounces Bourbon whiskey
  1 dash Peychaud Bitters
  1 dash Angostura Bitters
  1 dash Pernod
  Lemon peel
  1 lump sugar

In a mixing glass, muddle the lump of sugar with 1 teaspoon water
until dissolved. Add the Bourbon and a dash each of Peychaud and
Angostura Bitters. Mix well with cracked ice until chilled. Add a dash
of Pernod to a 4-ounce Old-Fashioned glass, swish it around, and
throw out the excess. (The original recipe called for absinthe, but this
is now legally forbidden in most countries.) Rub the rim of the glass
with lemon peel. Now strain the liquor into this Pernod-lemon-scented
glass, stir, and serve.

WHISKEY COOLER
  2 ounces rye or Bourbon whiskey
  1/2 ounce fresh lemon juice
  1 teaspoon superfine sugar
  Ginger ale

In a 10-ounce Highball glass, dissolve sugar in lemon juice. Add whiskey and ice cubes. Fill glass with ginger ale and stir gently.

WHISKEY ON THE ROCKS
  2 ounces Bourbon whiskey

In a 6-ounce Old-Fashioned glass, pour whiskey over no more than 2 ice cubes.

WHISKEY PERNOD
  3 ounces Bourbon or rye whiskey
  1 teaspoon anisette
  1 teaspoon Pernod
  3 dashes Angostura Bitters

In a mixing glass, mix whiskey, anisette, Pernod, and bitters. Shake with shaved ice and strain into a 4-ounce cocktail glass.

Whiskey, Irish

BLACKTHORN
  1 1/2 ounces Irish whiskey
  1 1/2 ounces dry vermouth
  3 dashes anisette
  3 dashes Angostura Bitters

In a mixing glass, mix whiskey, vermouth, anisette, and bitters. Stir with ice cubes and strain into a 4-ounce cocktail glass.

IRISH COFFEE —page 414.

Whiskey, Rye

ARCTIC COOLER —page 445.

GEORGE WASHINGTON'S COLD CHRISTMAS EGG NOG—page 423.

MANHATTAN
  MY FAVORITE DRY—chapter 29, page 380.
  REGULAR—page 444.

MILLIONAIRE—page 418.

MONTE CARLO—page 393.

NEW YORKER—page 446.

OLD-FASHIONED—page 381.

ROCK AND RYE
  2 ounces rye whiskey
  1 teaspoon fresh lemon juice
  Lump of rock candy

In a 6-ounce Old-Fashioned glass, mix whiskey, lemon juice, and rock candy. Add ice cubes and continue to stir to chill.

WHISKEY COOLER—page 447.

WHISKEY HIGHBALL
  2 ounces rye whiskey
  Club soda or ginger ale

Pour rye whiskey over ice cubes in a 10-ounce Highball glass. Fill glass with club soda or ginger ale. Stir gently.

Whisky, Scotch, Blended

AFFINITY
  1 ounce Scotch whisky
  3/4 ounce sweet vermouth
  3/4 ounce dry vermouth
  2 dashes Angostura Bitters
  Lemon peel

In a mixing glass, mix Scotch, sweet and dry vermouths, and Angostura Bitters. Add ice cubes and stir. Strain into a 4-ounce stemmed cocktail glass. Twist lemon peel over drink to extract oil essence. Drop peel into glass.

AULD MAN'S NOURRISHMENT
  2 ounces Scotch whisky
  7 ounces cream
  1 egg, beaten lightly
  1 teaspoon superfine sugar
  Freshly grated nutmeg

In a mixing glass, mix Scotch and cream. Add beaten egg and sugar. Shake with shaved ice and strain into 12-ounce Highball glass. Sprinkle with freshly grated nutmeg.

BOBBY BURNS
  1 1/2 ounces Scotch whisky
  1/2 ounce sweet vermouth
  1/2 ounce dry vermouth
  2 dashes Bénédictine
  Lemon peel

In a mixing glass, mix Scotch, dry and sweet vermouths, and Bénédictine. Add ice and stir. Strain into a 4-ounce stemmed cocktail glass. Twist lemon peel over drink to extract oil essence. Drop peel into glass.

BUTTERSCOTCH COLLINS—page 399.

DRY ROB ROY
  2 ounces Scotch whisky
  1/2 ounce dry vermouth
  2 dashes Drambuie (or Bénédictine)
  Lemon peel

In a mixing glass, mix Scotch, vermouth, and Drambuie (or Bénédictine). Add ice cubes and stir. Strain into a 4-ounce stemmed cocktail glass. Twist lemon peel over drink to extract oil essence. Drop peel into glass.

HARRY LAUDER
  1 1/2 ounces Scotch whisky
  1 1/2 ounces sweet vermouth
  1 teaspoon water
  1 teaspoon superfine sugar

In a mixing glass, dissolve sugar in water. Add Scotch and vermouth and stir with ice cubes. Strain into 4-ounce stemmed cocktail glass.

HIGHLAND COOLER
  2 ounces Scotch whisky
  1/2 ounce fresh lemon juice
  1 teaspoon superfine sugar
  2 dashes Angostura Bitters
  Club soda

In a mixing glass, dissolve sugar in lemon juice. Add Scotch and Angostura Bitters. Stir and strain over ice cubes into 10-ounce Highball glass. Fill glass with club soda and stir gently.

HIGHLAND FLING
  2 ounces Scotch whisky
  4 ounces milk
  1 teaspoon superfine sugar
  Freshly grated nutmeg

In a mixing glass, dissolve sugar in the milk. Add Scotch and shake with shaved ice. Strain into a 10-ounce Highball glass. Add ice cubes and sprinkle freshly grated nutmeg over top.

ROB ROY
  1 1/2 ounces Scotch whisky
  3/4 ounce sweet vermouth
  2 dashes Angostura Bitters
  Lemon peel

In a mixing glass, mix Scotch, vermouth, and Angostura Bitters. Add ice cubes and stir. Strain into a 4-ounce stemmed cocktail glass. Twist lemon peel over drink to extract oil essence. Drop peel into glass.

RUSTY NAIL—page 403.

SCOTCH ALPS
  1 1/2 ounces Scotch whisky
  1/2 ounce Fior d'Alpe
  Lemon peel

In a mixing glass, mix Scotch and Fior d'Alpe. Add ice cubes and stir. Strain into 4-ounce stemmed cocktail glass. Twist lemon peel over drink to extract oil essence. Drop peel into glass.

SCOTCH COOLER
2 ounces Scotch whisky
1 teaspoon white Crème de Menthe
Club soda

Pour Scotch over ice cubes in a 10-ounce Highball glass. Add Crème de Menthe and fill glass with soda. Stir gently.

SCOTCH HIGHBALL —page 383.

SCOTCH OLD-FASHIONED
2 ounces Scotch whisky
1 teaspoon superfine sugar
2 dashes Angostura Bitters
Lemon peel
Slice of orange

Pur sugar into 6-ounce Old-Fashioned glass. Add Angostura Bitters and muddle to blend. Add ice cubes and Scotch. Stir, and twist lemon peel over drink to extract oil essence. Drop peel into glass and garnish with orange slice.

SCOTCH SOUR —page 381.

WASSAIL BOWL —page 426.

Whisky, Scotch, Highland Single Malt

SCOTCH MIST
2 ounces Scotch malt whisky
Lemon peel

Pour Scotch into a 6-ounce Old-Fashioned glass filled with shaved ice. Twist lemon peel over drink to extract oil essence. Drop peel into glass.

STONE FENCE
2 ounces Scotch malt whisky
7 ounces English hard cider
Thin apple slice

In a 12-ounce Highball glass, mix Scotch and cider. Add ice cubes and stir. Garnish with apple slice.

Wine, Red, Dry

HOT SWEDISH GLOGG —page 410.

SANGRIA —page 424.

Wine, Rhine, White

STRAWBERRY CHAMPAGNE PUNCH —page 425.

SWEDISH PUNCH —page 426.

Wine, Sauternes, Sweet

CRANBERRY SPRITZER —page 390.

Wine, White, Dry

CRYING REINDEER OF FINLAND —page 443.

KIR —page 391.

ORANGE MINT PUNCH —page 425.

Zombies

This ridiculous outcropping of the worst features of the "roaring twenties" should now be eliminated and forgotten. I shall permit no Zombie recipes in this book.

Zooms

Another drink from the wild days just after the end of Prohibition, but this one is worth at least a single recipe by which to remember it.

ZOOM
   3 ounces Cognac
   1 teaspoon honey
   2 teaspoons boiling water
   1 tablespoon heavy cream

Put honey into a mixing glass and add boiling water to dissolve. Add shaved ice, heavy cream, and Cognac. Shake and strain into a 4-ounce stemmed cocktail glass.

CHAPTER 31

THE HAIR OF THE DOG--GLASS-TO-MOUTH RESUSCITATION

Please Don't Drink Your Bathwater

How many people, I wonder, know the background of the expression "the hair of the dog" in describing the unpleasant feelings of mental and physical insecurity when one wakes up on "the morning after"? It was, I believe, an old English medical maxim—at a time when vaccination against rabies was not quite as general as it is today—that, if you were attacked by a wild dog, you must at once, to be sure to recover from your wounds, eat some of the hair of the dog that bit you. We were never given any advice as to how we might expect, first, to catch our dog and, second, to gain its permission to pull out its hairs. Yet, "hair in the mouth" is a pretty apt description of how one feels in the early morning after.

The best definition I have ever read of this seriocomic condition was written by the English social commentator of the Victorian era Nathaniel Gubbins. He described how, one morning at around nine o'clock, a visitor presented himself at the front gate of a British army base and asked to see a certain Captain Brown. The message was sent in and, after a decent pause, the Captain's orderly came out to the visitor at the gate and explained, "I'm sorry, sir, but the Capting won't be ayble to see you this mornin'. You see, 'e ain't feelin' too well. He just got up, drunk 'is bath and 'as gorn back ter bed."

Personally, I have never had to go quite to that extreme, but, often enough, during those first, unholy minutes after waking up at crack of dawn, I admit that my head feels as if it were the Leaning Tower of Pisa and my tongue is a piece of sandpaper stuck in the neck of a glue pot. This sort of condition requires some immediate and soothing lubrication, but water would hardly be close enough to the hair of the dog that bit me the night before. What I need, primarily, is a sharp and tangy waker-upper—either immediately, even before my first cup of coffee, or if I *can* face food, as glass-to-mouth resuscitation with my breakfast. Each of the following recipes is for one serving, and amounts are based on the rough rule-of-thumb that the early morning "dog" can hardly bring himself to swallow more than five ounces in each glass of liquid medicine. Unless otherwise specified, each drink looks and tastes best in one form or another of a tall-stemmed, thoroughly chilled six- to ten-ounce wineglass.

1. When the awakening is not too bad, but I feel I *absolutely must* instantly slake my horrible thirst before taking more than a dozen steps from my warm bed, I head straight for the kitchen refrigerator, where I always keep on hand the ingredients for one or the other of these revivers:

Coup de Taureau—Bullshot à la Française

On a bleak morning, this is the finest of fog-cutters—a far, far better thing than any standard vodka Bullshot. Pour into a chilled glass, 4 ounces of ice-cold, clear, totally fat-free beef bouillon (obviously, not the kind with gelatin, then add 1 1/2 ounces of ice-cold Grande Fine Champagne Cognac and a few drops of fresh lemon juice. Stir thoroughly, then float a paper-thin slice of lemon on top. The main ingredients and the glass must be ice-cold. Otherwise, use 1 or 2 ice cubes. Part of the revivifying effect comes from the beautiful color—an amber shade of topaz.

Fruited Champagne
To Lead You Out of the Black Forest

Champagne is an almost magical medicine from which to absorb a reasonable modicum of early-morning confidence-to-meet-the-day. For just such an emergency, I always keep in my refrigerator at least a couple of those practical small 6-ounce "split" bottles of one or other of the top-label brut Champagnes. The "secret trick" of

adding a small dose of a compatible fruit brandy was taught me by the great French chef Pierre Troisgros, after I had dined not wisely, but too well, in the dining room of the Hôtel des Frères Troisgros in Roanne. I awoke next morning with the sorest of heads and, when I complained at breakfast to Pierre, he said, "I will give you something to cut off your head." He sliced 3 or 4 fresh strawberries into the bottom of a chilled glass. (Whole raspberries, pitted and sliced cherries, fresh orange sections, or other seasonal fruits will do just as well.) He gently blended into the fruit 1 1/2 ounces of German Waldhimbeergeist, the dry brandy made from wild black raspberries in the Black Forest. Then he filled up the glass with iced brut Champagne and I downed it before it had any chance to warm up. The rest of my day was perfect and I was soon hungry for a Troisgros lunch.

2. On some "recovery" mornings, I am less instantly thirsty, but feel the need for solid sustenance in the form of a light, Continental-style breakfast. To work up my hunger, I walk my faithful dog, Ñusta, as far as our local French bakery, where I find hot-from-the-oven brioches and croissants. These are consumed with sweet butter and an array of English or Belgian fruit jams or jellies and bitter Seville orange marmalade. There will also be classic *café au lait,* poured into the cup with two simultaneous streams of hot milk and black coffee. And, to clear my head before the coffee, I will replace the standard orange juice by one or other of these light pick-me-ups:

Early-Morning Peach and Pear Kir

Slide 2 ice cubes into a chilled glass. Stir in, one by one (and all chilled), 1 ounce of Crème de Cassis, 1 ounce of peach nectar, 2 teaspoons of dry pear brandy, 1/2 ounce of grenadine, and 1/4 teaspoon of freshly squeezed lemon juice. Fill up the glass with a very dry, first-class Chablis, or another equally dry white wine (see following recipe). Stir thoroughly, then float on top a paper-thin slice of lemon. Drink very cold.

Muscadet Clam Juice of Nantes

Bear in mind here that the wine is the stand-in for the normal lemon juice. So the chosen wine must be ultradry and quite sharply tangy. A good Muscadet, with its refreshing acidity, is the ideal. The second choice would be a first-class Chablis. Third, an Alsatian Sylvaner of a less-sunny-than-average, bone-dry year. Slide a single ice cube into a chilled glass. Pour in equal parts (both ice-cold) of clam juice and wine. Add a single dash of Worcestershire sauce, stir vigorously, and drink very cold. It clears my head quite marvelously!

3. Sometimes I wake up from a night of celebration absolutely starving. There is nothing I want more in this world than a solid, multi-course English-style breakfast of eggs, fish, and meat. I may begin with Irish oatmeal porridge, laced with cream and maple syrup. Then, perhaps, finnan haddie, or smoked kippers, followed by bacon, ham, hash, or sausage with eggs, or chops, or kidneys, and muffins with marmalade. The head-clearing liquid refreshment will be very carefully chosen. With such a meal, the spiritous drinks of strong character tend to clash and do more harm than good. The answer to the problem, in my opinion, is to use the tasteless alcohols, drawing from them their "water-of-life" qualities of resuscitation, but letting the taste of each drink be dominated by the flavors of fruits or vegetables:

Scandinavian V8

Slide a single ice cube into a glass previously thoroughly frosted in the freezer. Add 3 ounces of V8 juice, 1 1/2 ounces of Danish Akvavit, a single dash of Angostura Bitters, and a single drop (no more) of Tabasco. Stir vigorously, float a sprig of green watercress on top, and drink extremely cold.

Cape Cod Screwdriver

Slide 2 ice cubes into a thoroughly chilled glass. Add 3 1/2 ounces of cranberry juice and 1 1/2 ounces of vodka. Stir vigorously and drink very cold. This is just about the finest fast-waker-upper I know for a morning when one has had only an hour or two of sleep and must still catch a crack-of-dawn plane.

P-and-P, or, for Short, Pi-Pi

This might be called a "dawn dessert" and is best served with, or immediately after, the breakfast coffee. It is slightly rich, definitely sweet, obviously healthy, and usefully laxative. Slide 2 ice cubes into a thoroughly chilled glass. Pour over them 1 1/2 ounces of papaya nectar, 1 1/2 ounces of prune juice, and 1 1/2 ounces of Swiss Cherry Kirschwasser. Stir vigorously, then float on top a teaspoon of heavy cream.

4. For mornings when I have no real desire for food and yet at the same time there is a certain gnawing feeling in my stomach, I have developed and tested my own:

Emergency Menu for a Pick-Me-Up, Hair-of-the-Dog Breakfast

Franco-Swiss Onion Soup without Cheese, with Kirschwasser

Have on hand the finest available canned, dehydrated, or frozen onion soup. (Or, if you happen to have your own supply of homemade, so much the better.) Heat the soup up to boiling. Do not use any cheese or toast. Serve in the classic individual, lidded, small earthenware casserole, thoroughly preheated. Just before you take the first spoonful, stir in 1 1/2 ounces (or more, to taste) of a fine dry Swiss Cherry Kirschwasser. The faint sweetness of the *eau-de-vie* has an extraordinary affinity with the equally faint sweetness of the onions.

My Secret Method for Emergency Anchovy Toast

Let me warn you that you will find this so good, under the right conditions of the early morning, that you may be tempted to think that it would be equally good as an hors d'oeuvre for a dinner party. Do not be mistaken. The secret of its early morning effectiveness is in its extreme saltiness—much too salty for any other time of the day, or for more civilized physical conditions. Set a shallow soup bowl over simmering water to act as a double-boiler. As it heats up, coarsely chop the entire contents of a 2-ounce can of flat fillets of anchovy, then put them into a mortar with their oil and pound to a paste. (Or, if you are despicably lazy and shamefully uncritical, you may use manufactured anchovy paste from a plastic tube!) Put a 1-inch cube of butter to melt in the now-hot bowl. Have ready, at the side, a lightly beaten egg. When the butter is just melted, add the egg and gently work together with a wooden spoon. When the egg shows the first signs of coagulating, work in the anchovy paste and a shake or two of red cayenne pepper. While everything is heating up, toast some thin slices of good white bread. Keep on gently stirring mixture. When it has about the consistency of whipped cream, spread it thickly on the toast and serve instantly on a very hot plate. It should burn your mouth as you bite into it. Accompany it with black coffee. The best morning medicine in the world!

5. Finally, there comes that worst morning of all, when one feels that absolutely nothing, but nothing, can possibly do the slightest good. Clearly, food is out of the question. Obviously, finding the strength to get up and stay up is going to be virtually impossible. What is needed is a shock treatment. Over the years, I have developed and perfected the four shockers that help me most:

The Cold Towel

Put into the jug of an electric blender, 1 whole raw egg, 2 ounces of a fine Armagnac, 1/2 teaspoon of sugar, and 1/3 cup of cold milk. Blend at medium speed for about 5 seconds, until mixture is smooth and frothy. Slide 2 ice cubes into a well-chilled glass. Pour in the mixture from the blender and drink down fast. This one is gentler—slightly less shocking—than the others which follow below.

The Surgeon Major

Use a glass at room temperature. In a small bowl, thoroughly beat an egg. Pour it into the glass and add three grinds of black pepper. Fill up the glass with iced, brut Champagne, then give it one good stir and drink it down as fast as you can.

The Doctor's Eye-Opener

Use an extremely cold glass. Pour in the juice of half a lemon and 1 1/2 ounces of a first-class California brandy. Stir vigorously, then, just before raising it to the lips, dust the top surface with a couple of shakes of red cayenne pepper. Try to down it in a single gulp. Resist the immediate desire to rush to cold water. If you feel dizzy, hold on to the table for a couple of minutes.

The Scorched Earth

Do not use any ice cubes. Using a 10- or 11-ounce chilled wineglass pour in 1 1/2 ounces of a fine Spanish brandy, then half-fill with iced, brut Champagne. Give it one, good stir, then drink it as fast as you can. Lie down at once, before you fall down.

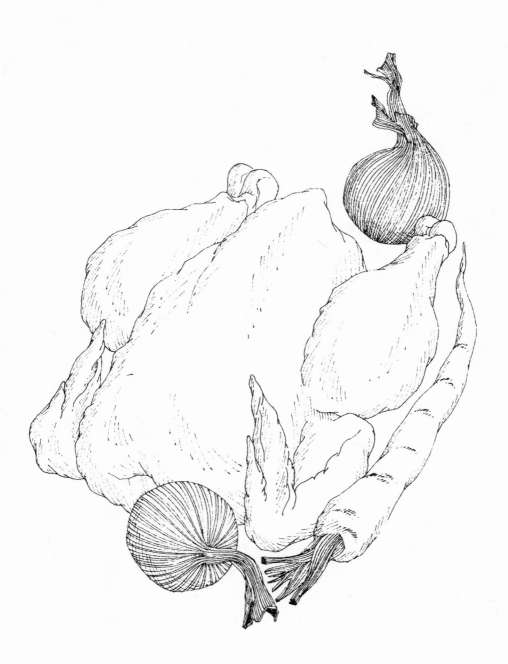

Index

463

About the Author

Roy Andries de Groot is a member of 72 food and wine-tasting societies. He is the president of the International Gourmet Society, Commandeur of Chevaliers du Tastevins and a member of the Grand Conseil de Bordeaux. Besides being the food and wine editor of *Esquire* magazine, Mr. de Groot has contributed to *Gourmet, House Beautiful, McCalls, Ladies' Home Journal* and other magazines. He has appeared regularly as "Gourmet-in-Residence" on NBC's TODAY as well as on shows dealing with food on CBS and NET. Mr. de Groot is also the author of FEAST FOR ALL SEASONS and RECIPES FROM THE AUBERGE OF THE FLOWERING HEARTH.